VEDIC COSMOLOGY
Based on Selected Hymns of
Ṛgveda and Atharvaveda

India's Scientific Heritage

Founder Editor : Late Dr L M Singhvi

General Editor

Dr S N Bhavsar

Guest Editor

Robert W. Boyer

17

VEDIC COSMOLOGY

Based on Selected Hymns of *Ṛgveda* and *Atharvaveda*

PARAMESWARAN MURTHIYEDATH

MOTILAL BANARSIDASS PUBLISHERS
PRIVATE LIMITED • DELHI

First Edition : Delhi, 2018

ISBN : 978-81-208-4167-3

Also available at

MOTILAL BANARSIDASS

41 U.A. Bungalow Road, Jawahar Nagar, Delhi 110 007
1 B, Jyoti Studio Compound, Kennedy Bridge, Nana Chowk, Mumbai 400 007
203 Royapettah High Road, Mylapore, Chennai 600 004
236, 9th Main III Block, Jayanagar, Bengaluru 560 011
8 Camac Street, Kolkata 700 017
Ashok Rajpath, Patna 800 004
Chowk, Varanasi 221 001

MLBD Cataloging-in-Publication Data
Vedic Cosmology
Based on Selected Hymns of Ṛgveda and Atharvaveda
by Parameswaran Murthiyedath
ISBN : 978-81-208-4167-3
Bibliography and Index
I. Hinduism II. Vedas III. Rigveda
IV. Atharvaveda V. Murthiyedath, Parameswaran

Printed in India

by RP Jain at NAB Printing Unit,
A-44, Naraina Industrial Area, Phase I, New Delhi–110028
and published by JP Jain for Motilal Banarsidass Publishers (P) Ltd,
41 U.A. Bungalow Road, Jawahar Nagar, Delhi-110007

Foreword by the General Editor

'Vedic Cosmology' by Parameswaran Murthiyedath, consists of some Ṛgvedic and Atharvavedic hymns with English translation and comments along with many geometrical figures, identified from the *Ṛgveda* texts. Parameswaran with a Vedic family background is an engineer by profession. About seven years back he got attracted to the Vedas through the *Śulba sūtra* of *Baudhāyana*, which deals with the geometry and construction of sacrificial altars for performing the traditional *yajñas*. The book is claimed to be the "Physics and cosmology of the Veda." He resorted to philosophy and etymology for deciphering, the hidden meaning behind the hymns, scientifically (*śāstrīyata*) and he deciphered the hidden meanings behind the hymns, referring to *Vedānta*, *Tantra* and *Vyākaraṇa*, but the main thrust of the contents of the book was derived from the *Śulbasūtra*. Vedas according to him reveals the theories of creation of the universe; a universe which has a 3D spherical shape, which upon 2D convolution, would look flat i.e., geometrically speaking. This is corroborated by the *Śulbasūtra*, especially by that of *Baudhāyana*. The notion as such exhibit similarities especially with modern science along with issues like those of matter, energy, gravity, space-time etc. He says that the Vedic theories, ideas, concepts and the terms appear to be more pregnant and meaningful this way than those rendered by traditional commentaries. In other words, this way it has better clarity and conclusiveness.

This unconventional approach, not attending to conventional norms like those of the *ṛṣi, devatā, chandas, viniyoga, svara* and the thematic rules of grammar, may not satisfy traditional Vedic pundits. Still, the numerical source and the numerical base often exhibited by the Vedas and brought out by him in this work should remain uncontroversial. It is this positive point that is to be emphasized and the author's intention behind it is to cover the past and provide an insight for the future, and explore the other possibilities to enrich the Vedic tradition in different ways.

Prof. S N Bhavsar, PhD
Pune, India

Contents

List of Figures

Foreword by Prof. V P N Nampoothiri

One, looking at the night sky and the diverse biological activities on the planet earth, always wonders and asks questions like what makes the universe as seen, what are the laws which preserve the structure of the universe, how did the universe come into being? etc. etc. First two questions pertain to understanding the universe as it is observed and belong to the branch of science called cosmology. Last question is related to the mechanism by which the universe came into existence and is related to what is referred to as cosmogony. Observation of the structure of the universe using equipments like telescopes and cameras is called the astronomy. Astronomy is the input to cosmology. A thinking mind on reflecting about the universe and its structure will get wonder struck by the symmetries and the dynamics of the universe and would wonder whether it is a part of a grand design by a super intelligence. It is sufficient for one to look inwards to oneself to realise the complex dynamics of life processes on this planet. For, one of the most complex objects of nature is the human brain and we are yet to completely understand the working of the human brain.

In a recent book "The Grand Design" Stephen Hawking ponders upon the cosmogony and the cosmos. He says that for the creation of the universe, one need not bring in the hypothesis of God - a super intelligence sitting up somewhere designing and fabricating the universe. Laws of physics do not forbid the spontaneous creation of particles from vacuum. There is no need of a God to perform this trick. Vacuum fluctuations will cause the creation of the universe. He was talking about the cosmogony as described by institutionalized religion which would describe a personified god as the ultimate cause of the universe. In the Indian context the story is different. The Universe is not created by some super intelligence. It is a manifestation of the already present; that formless extension called the *Parabrahma*. A phase transition from formlessness to form-ness. Indian philosophy is rooted in this concept of cosmogony which was interpreted by many seers in the past.

Indian concpet of the creation of the universe is well presented in the Vedas - especially in the *Ṛgveda*. The present book "Vedic Cosmology" is a unique work in which the author, Mr Parameswaran Murthiyedath tries to dig out this knowledge from the hymns of the *Ṛgveda*. The *Ṛgveda* is an encrypted form of knowledge which is difficult to decode. The author has succeeded in his attempt, to a remarkable extent, to unravel the mystery of the origin of the universe, as told by the *Ṛgveda*.

In this book, Parameswaran re-reads some of the hymns like *Puruṣasūktam* and *Nāsadīyasūktam* of the *Ṛgveda* to mine out valuable knowledge related to the Cosmogony according to ancient India. He also seeks the help of *Gāyatrī* and some other hymns of the *Ṛgveda* to investigate the underlying patterns of a theory of the creation of universe. In fact Parameswaran brings out the theory of the creation of the universe, that occurred as a result of *yajña*. This book is also valuable in another point of view related to the *yajña*s like the *somayāga* and the *Atirātra*, which are still prevalent in Kerala. An important ritual in the *Atirātra* is called the *Pravargya* related to purification of the whole universe. This is explicit in the following *Śāntimantra* which is chanted in the beginning of *Pravargya* offerings.

"Peace on Earth. Peace in Space. Peace in the Heavens. Peace in all Horizons and Directions. Peace in Fire. Peace in the Air. Peace in the Sun. Peace in the Moon. Peace in the Constellations. Peace in the Waters. Peace in the Plants and Herbs. Peace in the Trees. Peace towards Cattle. Peace towards Goats. Peace towards Horses. Peace towards Mankind. Peace in the Absolute (Brahman). May there be Peace. Only Peace. May that Peace be in Me, Peace Alone. Through that Peace may I confirm Peace in myself, And Peace in all bipeds and quadrupeds. May there be Peace in me, Peace alone."

Parameswaran finds close relationships between the *Śulba sūtra* and the *yajña* rituals which leads him to the underlying connection between mathematics and the *Ṛgveda*. Geometry and dynamics of the universe as depicted in the section - "Vedic Cosmos"- is an important subject that is raised in the book by Parameswaran. He also touches upon the numbers principle and the universe.

Relationship between numbers and nature is one of the strange phenomena identified by scientists in various fields of science. Relationship between Fibonacci series and its encounter with natural phenomena are famous. One would be wonder struck to realize the fact that the frequency of light emitted by hydrogen atom can be represented as the difference between the inverse square of positive integers. Parameswaran brings out the significance of numbers in his book, as obtained from the Veda. In short the "Vedic Cosmology" is a unique book and Parameswaran throws good light on the Indian concept of the universe as embedded in the Vedas.

Prof. V P N Nampoothiri
International School of Photonics,
Cochin University of Science and technology,
Cochin 682 022, India

Preface

It is well acknowledged that the *Ṛgveda* contained statements on cosmogony and cosmological matters. This volume is an interpretation of selected hymns of the *Ṛgveda*[1] and the *Atharvaveda*[2] and is to enquire into the principles of cosmology contained in the selected hymns. At the same time it is an also enquiry into the nature of a Supreme Divinity, as defined by the Vedas. This interpretation would largely concern itself on the subject of the physical events that might have taken place in the course of the creation of the universe.

I had earlier scripted my own interpretation of four major *śulbasūtras* and was pleasantly surprised to notice while handling the Vedas that many statements of the *śulbasūtras* and their geometrical content had a strong connection with the geometry, the birth and existence of the universe, as conceived in the Vedas. I might have followed most unorthodox methods of handling the Vedic Sanskrit and I am quite sure that no *paṇḍit* would ever approve of it. However, I am fairly satisfied since the physical events of creation of the universe, as described here, brought out the divine nature of such events equally well. It was straight away conceived that though my interpretation relied more on what I know of physics and the specific geometry, in each case the subject

[1] *Ṛgveda* Sanskrit text from www.mum.edu/vedicreserve as on 18.2.2014

[2] *Atharvaveda* Sanskrit text from www.mum.edu/ vedicreserve as on 18.2.2014

had to become a statement on the Supreme Divinity proper or the other divinities wherever found named. Actually this was not difficult as almost all of the statements had an element of divinity well attached. The Supreme Divinity of *Brahma* was ever relevant. But it was the other nomenclatures such as *Indra, Mitra, Varuṇa* etc., that needed careful handling. In this commentary they got presented more as physical entities and phenomena, in the first instance. But the Vedic text is a very complex subject and this type of prioritizing and conclusions there-of might not be fully justified. The names of divinities in no way got underrated in this narration, even if those were not always specifically stated. What was really avoided in this interpretation was the style of rendering that ended up in common and usual benediction and prayers. The underlying thought behind this approach was that the *Ṛgveda* text with more than 10,000 verses could not come merely as such a set of prayers, but had to come constituted into some well thought of ideas and theories; whatever be their nature.

In the course of interpretations, the meanings of many words got locally formalized along with the other terms in the same verse. A concept that went deep was that no statement should arise which would be in conflict with matters already stated. Besides it was also felt that the content presented here should rely on Veda itself for meanings, clarity and verification and not on the subjects and theories of the later literature. In short, what was insisted upon was an all embracing internal consistency.

A serious impediment in following the subject narrated here would be the ability of the reader to follow the geometry of the universe described, which happens to cover space and time equally. The reader should be able to appropriately conceive the necessary 2-dimensional and 3-dimensional visuals, in the absence of which the entire narration could appear either vague or meaningless. On the other hand, if that difficulty is managed, the subject would appear to be a profound set of consistent statements. We could get astonished to notice such scientific temper and precision thought processing in these ancient texts.

It was indeed felt that the long existence of the Veda as *śruti* and *śabda* had a different divine significance as well. The power of the *śabda* to create, communicate, propagate and inspire was well pronounced by the Vedic texts themselves, and this should have been acting as the fountainhead for all of us, all this while. It was that which flowed to us from the millennium past that produced magical results in shaping us into what we are today. In this progress though the meanings of the Veda appeared before us in many styles, still it was the *śabda* that always guided us and inspired us.

In this book, as a principle and firm approach, no word of any verse had been intentionally omitted from the set of meanings of that verse. Further, many composite terms were split as much as possible into their *dhātu* or phoneme level, to obtain a coherent set of meaning. It was insisted that these set of meanings should not come into conflict with certain central principles of the *Ṛgveda* that were gleaned out of the text, in the course of writing this monograph. "To this day there is no internally consistent and coherent interpretation of the Vedas." - said B.G Sidharth.[3] A continuity of meanings based on the internal consistency is expected to unfold from the interpretations given here. It is true that this is an attempt to redeem what the Veda had to state on matters of science and also that it is an enquiry whether there was anything that came to us from so distant a past in which we could be more happy and proud of. As a search for the universal principles of existence the *Ṛgveda* had very serious matters to state for the present and for the future.

I am thankful to Prof. V P N Nampoothiri, who kindly consented and provided a Foreword for this book. I am equally thankful to Prof. S N Bhavsar, for a detailed review of the manuscript, for his comments and necessary guidance.

[3]The Celestial Key to the Vedas - by B.G Sidharth

I am indeed thankful to Shri R P Jain and others of Mottilal Banarsidas for considering to publish this book, and for very kindly putting up with my frequent anxious enquiries.

Introduction

A set of brief commentaries on selected *Ṛgveda* hymns dealing with cosmology is being presented in this book. It will be found that the Vedic sages conceived the birth of the universe in majestic styles. It demands a basic knowledge of modern cosmology to admire the sophistication of thoughts that was seen to come from the Vedic sages. It is found stated that the *vaidikayajña* had its origin in the basic fear that man felt of the fire and he turned these into a sort of adoration. Many were satisfied with this and similar explanations and looked at the rituals with disdain. Perhaps no concerted effort, to understand more of the concepts that went into these rituals were made so that it would help to understand the Vedas better. The commentary on the hymns furnished here indeed tell altogether a different story. We can see that the Vedic sages conceived complex scientific theories fairly accurately and if so wished these could be compared to modern scientific accomplishments. The rituals that we observe to have run concurrently might have had significances that came complementary to the text and were even capable of enlivening the very text. It is known that the *āṅgika* always accompanied the *vācika* and at times led the way.

By methods obviously quite different from those of our times the sages were able to realise several matters of nature to a great degree of conceptual accuracy. It was possible that the system of *śruti* and the *yajña* rituals were intelligently devised in order to perpetuate such knowledge. The Vedic sages did not entertain any illusion that this knowledge could be properly transferred to the next generation and therefore obviously devised the system of *śruti* to preserve the text. It could be assumed that once, when the chain of interpreters was broken, for some reason or the other, the set of theories that it specifically carried became un-redeemable. It is rather strange that the possibility of understanding the scientific meanings of the Vedic text and reconcile with it would not be much different even today than those times and that original posting was to posterity.

This interpretation of some selected hymns of the Vedic texts would be found to tend to be "physics", as we know now it. The complex definitions and the descriptions of divinity was achieved through the objects and phenomena of earthbound realities. Simple and Capable imagery was collected from the man's precincts, to describe the creation and existence of the complex universe. The terms and objects of obscure nature were avoided as much as possible. The *yajñas* of those times possibly consisted of such precise geometrical patterns and matching dramatic presentations as were required to communicate effectively.

The *Ṛgveda* would appear unique in many ways. It appeared to be poetry, odes to a Supreme Divinity and at the same time, science. There appeared a general lack of of emotions in the descriptions of the text. It did not express fear or extreme reverence. It kept away from happiness, anger and sadness. Even while describing the horrendous occurrences and wolfish behavior it maintained an equanimity. It however admired nature in great measures and contained apparently consoling words to man and declared that it was a universe of all excellence, calm and quietude. In this respect the *Ṛgveda* is much different from the literature on philosophy and rituals of the later times. It described the growth of the universe as from heaven till this earth, not because the earth was the outer limit, but for the reason that the perceiver was stationed at the earth. It was one or the other of a language of the earth that was used for such descriptions. It was one or the other of the phenomena of some clarity that was used for the imagery.

The *Ṛgveda* which consists more than 1000 hymns and more than 10,000 verses could only be based on certain well formed principles and ideas. The right and wrong of the Vedic meanings should surface from the Veda itself, and should be independent of the later literature and *śāstras*. Many of the traditional approaches in the interpretation of the Veda had not often met with great success or in other words many have opined that no meanings have ever come up that would enable declaring that the Veda is a cohesive set of statements. At the same time many have said that the *Ṛgveda* is a flow of divine *śabda*, and it is *apauruṣeya* It was the verse "*saptāsyāsan paridhayastri: sapta* —" of RV10.90[4] and the geometry of the Vedic altars as expounded by *Baudhāyanaśulbasūtra* [5] that provided the strong and unavoidable connection between the two. It confirmed that there could not be any *yajña* without Veda and any Veda without *yajña*. Whatever came as the geometry of the Veda or the *śulbasūtras* was nothing less than the glimpses of the geometry of the universe itself. But more than stipulating the physical geometry of the universe, the Veda relied on geometry for anchoring down the principles of space and time. The theories of creation of the universe became an essential part of an enquiry into that Supreme Divinity and the complex nature of a universal existence.

This interpretation relied on the dictionary of Monier Williams[6] and Apte. It was the basic meanings at the *dhātu* and phoneme level that was selectively taken and used. But these things alone would not suffice to make one glean out a semblance of a meaning for any part of the Veda. Great

[4] *Ṛgveda* 10.90

[5] *Baudhāyanaśulbasūtraṃ* text from www.mum.edu/ vedicreserve as on 18.2.2014

[6] Monier Williams Sanskrit Dictionary- www.sanskrit-lexicon.uni-koeln.de/monier as on 18.2.2014

trust was placed on an approach and at the same time no preconceived notion about the Veda was entertained at any time. Therefore, neither the common interpretations nor the later time literature, *śāstra* texts and ideas had greatly influenced the contents of this book.

Some of the most frequented terms that appeared in the Vedic texts had to be evaluated appropriately. Let us start with the term "*na*" which traditionally would mean "we" or "no". In the interpretation followed here, the said meanings would make no sense at all, since by saying "no, no" no *bhautika* meanings could progress. Here it will be interpreted as "as" or "like that". Similarly the term "*pra*" would invariably mean "to the surroundings", "around" or "forward". The term "*uta*" would mean "woven as a spider's net" or its thematically equivalent "interactive" or "interconnected". Since the Vedic sages had not hesitated to mention the divine names in many places as they appeared, the term "*deva*" was interpreted as "heaven" or "shining" and so on.

Since the names of well known divinities like *Indra, Mitra, Varuṇa* got resolved as their equivalent physical entity or phenomena, it would be only fair not to dwell on those subjects at this juncture. Since the *Ṛgveda* could only be read as a set of *sūtra*s (more or less), based on the ideas gathered from other parts of the *Ṛgveda*, which exact term came as the verb in a verse was not insisted upon. It was firmly believed that the *Ṛgveda* remained a huge text with a central set of meanings. No doubts were ever entertained on the veracity of this structure.

In this interpretation, one particular meaning of a *dhātu* might have been found more acceptable than the others. At the same time the other meanings were not totally neglected. It was often felt that, for a clear set of meanings to come up, a conscious level of perception and inference should accompany these acts. If the Vedas are called *mantra*s, it was felt that along with the rhythm, the pleasant *śabda* and that inexplicable silence that would always appear, those meanings that came out should also have the like qualities. The same *māntrikata* should have come into the expressions and the meanings. However, one can not claim any success in this matter and what more it was difficult to conclude on what exactly the sages and poets really meant to say, that is to say, which would come as the exact proposal made by any particular verse. Perhaps, there was no such thing ever at all.

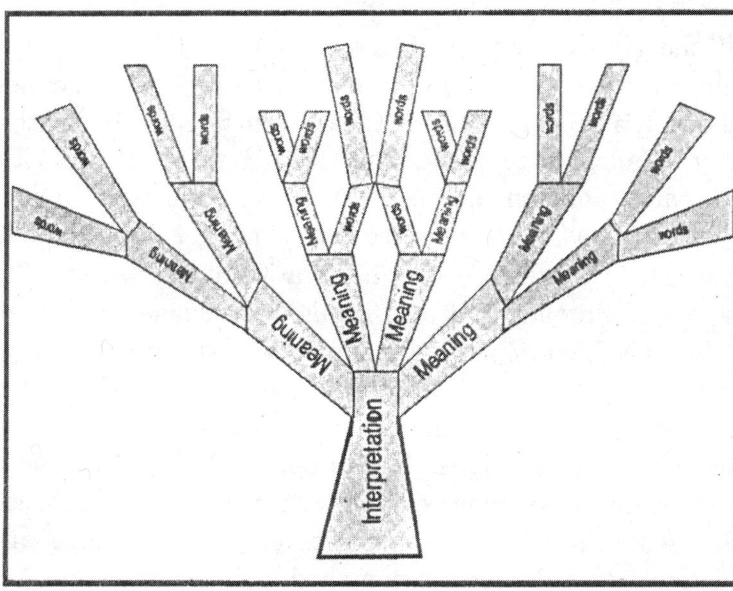

In a way, the verse "*dvā suparṇā sayujā sakhāyā samānaṃ vṛkṣam* –" [RV1.164.20][7] indicated the structure of the meanings of the *Ṛgveda*. A Pipul tree with identical branches to both sides could be compared to the streams of meanings of equal importance which stood in a like fashion. Those very streams of meanings only came from a set of words which often had multiple meanings. The full set of meanings of many a verse would be more or less complete only with the confluence of all streams, remarkably similar to that tree.

[7] *Ṛgveda* 1.164.20

The close identification of words and verses of the *Ṛgveda*, with a semblance of creation all by itself, the attendant inscrutability, the sounds that resonated, the multiple streams of meanings that flowed from it, could be a divine experience all by itself. An enquiry into it could have appeared as a bliss and satisfaction. But it would be almost impossible to collect all such meanings in the course of handling the huge *Ṛgveda* text. For the most demanding and discerning persons, the recourse would be a *yajña* or as of now, a suitably devised platform for discussions.

If the *Ṛgveda* contained descriptions of the creation of the universe and the attendant complex scientific principles, it follows that appropriate technical terms had to be synthesized from a language of that time. His Highness Swami *Cinmayānanda* spoke on the necessity for the formation of such new terms on his Youtube video - "Karma Yoga in Bhagavad Gita (Part A)",[8] which is very illustrative of this aspect. The Vedic sages did that and also brought in geometry to their aid, through the *yajña*s on the one hand and through a set of arbitrary calculations of space and time, on the other. The *yajña*s had not only geometry, but also had facilities built in for detailed discussions. The proof of such arrangements having existed is visible even today, in the very composition of the Vedic altar space. The geometry of the *yūpa* and the *uttaravedi*, a demonstration shed called *havirdhāna*, an assembly by the name of *sadas*, facility for daily routines and rituals by way of *prācīnaśāla* with a kitchen and the *yajamānapatni* etc. could be means of prolonged discussions. The vedic sages could have used the *yajña*s to consolidate the intended meanings. However, a long and dark period that possibly came descended, could have gradually obliterated the once prevalent meanings of the Veda.

The *bhautika* set of meanings of the *Ṛgveda* would not progress without being reasonably correct, because those state-

[8]Youtube video- Karma Yoga in Bhagavad Gita (Part A)-By His Highness Swami *Cinmayānanda*.

ments would have to conform to the vivid physical sequences with clear temporal definitions, accrued internally. The huge body text of the *Ṛgveda*, with more than 10,000 verses would act as a deterrent, as soon as an inconsistency surfaced. Here, the precise geometry that was presented in Chapter-9 of this book could be perhaps taken to ceratin extent, as the proof of correctness or appropriateness of the method of interpretation employed. It is quite clear that the very meanings of *bhautika* nature had to manifest as an array of ideas leading to the realisation of the various aspects of that Supreme Divinity and that universal consciousness. Today we could only remain dumbfounded at the complexities, intricacies and precision nature of those thought processes that the Vedic sages employed, when we observe that many of such ideas outclassed even the modern scientific theories, in its own selected fields and extents.

From the components of descriptions that appeared it would be clear that the thoughts of the venerable sages could not be fully communicated in a language and a text. Language, widely relying on visibilities, on mass and the movement of mass could not be taken as fully capable of communicating that effectively of the complex nature of the creation of the universe or the nature of a Supreme Divinity. Right from the Vedic times or earlier, a system of presentation relying on the 16 principles of communication and the 16 principles of existence could have been widely in use. The *pañcabhūta*, the *pañcendriya*, the 5 *karmendriya* and the mind added to it were the 16 *tattvas*, which the *Praśnopaniṣad* called the *ṣoḍaśakala* were selected by the sages for effective communication. All we learn about modern cosmology, also came from a similar set of words spoken and written on the subject. Beyond that and into the mathematical realms, few could have proper access.

Out of the many later literature and *śāstras*, that appeared after the *Ṛgveda*, it was only the *śulbasūtra* that has been quoted here and that too, quite often. The fact that the *śulbasūtra* dealt with geometry, and since these geometries could not have many different presentations, was indeed a major consideration. Thus the geometry and the theories that it could help to formulate was found ṭo be quite useful.

We would find severe repetitions of many terms and ideas in the *Ṛgveda*. We can not assume that a total freedom existed while selecting and using these terms and even ideas, during the composition of the Vedas. The segments of the *Ṛgveda* presented here brought out the colourful 3-dimensional universe as a cognizable 2-dimensional geometry and a matching description. Certain selected terms, therefore, would be found stacked up in the verses, as standard nomenclature to convey the idea of the 3-dimensionality. It is not claimed here, that the Vedic intentions were strictly to present the physical aspects of creation of the universe and were thus the efforts to bring out and state the science of those days. Nothing less than an enquiry into the nature of the Supreme Divinity could be the central Vedic intent. ⋆⋆⋆

1

Puruṣa Sūkta-The Cosmic Man

This famous and much revered hymn, known as *puruṣasūkta* (RV10.90) brought out the concept of the *Puruṣa*, a divine entity that lay stretched through the universe. It proposed that the universe came into existence by a series of *yajña* of nature. It is a sophisticated hymn with multiple levels of meanings including a geometrical configuration, furnished in Chapter 9.

[(16) षोडशर्चस्यास्य सूक्तस्य नारायण ऋषिः। पुरुषो देवता। प्रथमादिपञ्चदशर्चामनुष्टुप्। षोडश्याश्च त्रिष्टुप् छन्दसि।]

RV10.90.01 सहस्रशीर्षा पुरुषः सहस्राक्षः सहस्रपात्।
स भूमिं विश्वतो वृत्वाऽत्यतिष्ठद्दशाङ्गुलम्॥

[सहस्र - 1000 ◇ शीर्षा - manifested with heads ◇ पुरुष - the *Puruṣa* ◇ सहस्र - 1000 ◇ अक्षः - eye; axis ◇ सहस्र - 1000 ◇ पात् - feet; descended ◇ स भूमिं - with the earth forms; with the volume ◇ विश्वतो - reaching everywhere; as the universe ◇ वृत्वा - circularity that moved ◇ अत्यतिष्ठद् - greatly unstable; moving ◇ दशाङ्गुलम् - watermelon; 10 fingers; 3 digits of the finger]

The *Puruṣa* manifested with 1000 heads (apexes), 1000 axis-es, 1000 declinations, manifested as the earth-forms and a volume that reached everywhere as great circularity's that came moved, remained restless, vibrant and appeared like a huge watermelon.[1]

Alternately; the *Puruṣa* with 1000 heads, 1000 eyes and 1000 feet, got enlarged along with the universe, as circularity's that moved, to become the universe resembling a very large and round watermelon.

Still alternately; 1000 from the head, 120 as the *Puruṣa*, a 1000 configurations came from different centres, with a 1000 descends and as the circularity's and the area (volume) that reached everywhere, reckoned by the 3 digits of the finger, taken twice.(Thus it became a description of a geometry which will be presented in Chapter-9.)

It essentially said that the *Puruṣa* stood with 1000 heads (apexes), 1000 axis-es and 1000 declinations. There were 1000 *Puruṣa* thus positioned around the apex centre of the universe. The *Puruṣa* thus would lie in a spherical space and in multidimensional ways, the heads resting towards the apex. This description closely fitted with the description in the 14th verse commencing "*nābhyā āsīdantarikṣam* - -". The *Puruṣa*, was encompassing the enormous universe being omniscient and omnipotent. The power, control and sagacity of the *Puruṣa* extended to the whole of the universe, and these attributes were achieved by many (1000) centres of intellect, observance and operation. The physical shape of the universe was stated as that of a perennially restless, very large watermelon and at the same time it was implied to have a distended cover. The movement referred here could only be a constant, never ending and minute expansion and contraction of the exterior mantle or of the different levels or altogether a dynamic order and a state of resonance, that extended to all of the universe.

In addition to the above there was a statement that the universe expanded as circularity's along with the *Puruṣa* and

---

[1]Monier Williams - feed word 'dashaa'

with a corresponding increase in volume achieved in stages and yet instantaneously. The comparison to the well visible watermelon was significant in more than one way. The smooth and dark exterior mantle being in a state of inertia did not have the freedom of dissolution or inordinate distensions, well controlled by the state of resonance. The colourfully red interiors could distantly mean presence of *Agni* and the presence of bodies of high temperatures. The imperfectly roundish shape of the watermelon just fitted with the concept of the moving nature of the *jagat*. On reading with the descriptions to follow, the birth of the universe from a central point of origin could naturally have only a shape of a sphere and could yet be only imperfect in shape at any point of time due to its dynamic nature. The dynamic nature could be of pulsations, but with the many centres of influence as already stated, an absolute spherical roundness was anyway not allotted to the universe. The very concept of absolute circularity (for a circle of inherent irrationality and transcendental nature) was not perhaps accepted by the Vedic set, which notion was discernible in the later *śulbasūtra* texts as well.

The term "*daśāṅgulam*" could also be a reference to a spherical shape as if formed by the ten fingers held in front of a dancer to represent the lotus flower. The ten fingers would then represent the paths of creation from the heaven and the gap in between as the darkness that stood on both sides.[2] Of course altogether just like a striped watermelon itself.

RV10.90.02 पुरुष एवेदं सर्वं यद्भूतं यच्च भव्यम्।
उतामृतत्वस्येशानो यदन्नेनातिरोहति॥

[पुरुष - *Puruṣa* ◇ एव - only ◇ इदम् - thus ◇ सर्वं - all; everywhere ◇ यद् - somehow; whatever way ◇ भूतं - those born; occurred ◇ यच्च - whatever ◇ भव्यम् - would occur ◇ उत - well connected ◇ अमृतत्वस्य - with an immortality ◇ ईशानो - divinely ◇ यद् -

[2]This concept will be found presented in RV1.140.08, 1.141.02

somehow, many ways ◇ अन्नेन - on food principle ◇ अतिरोहति - greatly arising]

Thus only the *Puruṣa* reached everywhere, with those that many ways came born, as already occurred and in many ways that would later occur, as a divine manifestation, as an immortality that manifested in many ways and as the food principle that arose in yet more ways.

The universe came to its great enormity, raised intensively on a food principle, and so it existed and so it shall exist. The primordial and infinitesimal manifestation, from which, though this *Puruṣa* came into being, on the "seed and food" principles, it ever since had this multifaceted imperishable and mighty existence and would continue to be so. Though a *bījabhāva* got invested into its original existence, at the very moment of creation, the suggestion here was more of its immediate and spontaneous transformation into this mighty form of an *annabhāva*. This transformation to the *annabhāva* was immediate and the expansion and growth was by the consumption of the self than anything external. The multiplying effect and the exponential growth that ensued were with this *annabhāva*, as a seed would do. With this, the concept of the sublime and original union of the *Puruṣa* and the *Prakṛti* was pronounced, bringing forward the necessary temporal definitions. Thus the very first of creations was of complex nature.

This description approximately fitted with the cosmological concepts on the origin of the universe propounded by the modern physicists. "The Big Bang Theory" would perhaps be found similar in principle. Here, an instantaneous growth was suggested, while the modern theory had an additional super intense temperature as the first manifested form and indeed totally devoid of the *annabhāva*. Though the concept of temperature whether high or low, did not get stated through out this description, it was essentially latent. Here and for the Vedic set, the term "*Agni*" was temperature and energy in all invisible and visible forms, colours and their combinations, which manifested as an agent as well as a witness to every process and in every object of the universe. This being the essential concept, nothing was, therefore, exempt from its presence. Instead of a single Big Bang of the modern theories, the concept here was that its growth into its present enormous form was from several points of origin by simultaneous manifestations and yet occurring instantaneously and in stages. The process and capability that was built into its growth was thus slightly different from the popular modern theory. A quantitative equivalence of all things that happened later was not invested into the beginning of the process.

RV10.90.03 एतावानस्य महिमातो ज्यायांश्च पूरुषः।
पादोऽस्य विश्वा भूतानि त्रिपादस्यामृतं दिवि॥

[एतावानस्य - moving to the proximity ◇ महिमातो - moving greatly ◇ ज्यायांश्च - conquering (as a sector of a circle) ◇ पूरुष - arising as cleansed ◇ पादो - in stages, legs ◇ अस्य - in the manner of ◇ विश्वा - that reached everywhere ◇ भूतानि - objects and properties manifested ◇ त्रिपादस्य - in stages and dimensions of three (as the sides of a triangle) ◇ अमृतं - as immortality ◇ दिवि - shining; from the heaven]

Thus the great, mighty, majestic and enormous *Puruṣa* existed, the objects and properties coming moved to the proximity and arising upon getting purified and cleansed. Upon manifesting from the heaven, those greatly descended and reached everywhere in the universe. The *Puruṣa* came eternal and immortal in nature, coming into existence in all the 3 dimensions and in several stages, till the end.

Alternately; Becoming larger to the proximity like the sector of a circle, arising afresh again, with the 1 ÷ 4th, having born to everywhere, and as a triangular form that came eternally shining.(See Chapter-9 on geometry.)

Thus the universe came into existence as much purified and in majestic stages. While as great, mighty and omniscient with a 1000 power centres it came, there was a central causal point from which such powers flowed. This supported the earlier stated spontaneous moment of creation from a causal point which now got stated to have exerted an eternal control over the many and distributed power centres. The growth of the universe was from the one point of the three that stood in the heaven, expanding as triangular formations, in 3 dimensions and directions in well defined measures. The universe grew along these circularity's which came in huge proportions. Yet only an approximately spherical universe was born. An equivalence of the three co-ordinates, the term shining eternally, and declaring a conceptual sphericity which along with the meaning of *brahmāṇḍa*, as yearning to be spherical, presented the geometric scheme of the universe.

The creation of the universe was thus said to be a systematic progress to its immense size and shape, in spite of being instantaneous. The reference to the three could equally apply to the 3 points of reference as would be explained in the Chapter-9 on geometry, the 3-dimensionality as well as the particular triangular composition of the expansion or the 3 divisions of each of the *vyāhṛti*.

RV10.90.04 त्रिपादूर्ध्व उदैत्पुरुषः पादोऽस्येहाभवत् पुनः।
ततो विष्वङ्व्यक्रामत्साशनानशने अभि॥

[त्रिपादूर्ध्व -upwards as the three steps (triangular)◇ उद - rising ◇ इत् - going ◇ पुरुष - *Puruṣa* ◇ पादो - as stages ◇ अस्य - in such manner ◇ इह - till here ◇ अभवत् - and till nothing further occurred ◇ पुन - then later ◇ ततो - as those that ◇ विष्वङ् - reaching everywhere ◇ व्यक्रामत् - as the divided arrangements ◇ स - with ◇ अशना - consumption ◇ नशने - extinction ◇ अभि - progressing]

The *Puruṣa* arising in three steps (triangular in formation) from the source and getting projected higher (outward) in principle, later spread across the universe as the ones that came from the earlier and as the arrangements that were obtained by divisions, reaching everywhere, progressing to the proximity by consumption and by extinction (or disappearing), till here (the earth) and till the end where nothing further manifested.

Alternately; rising from the three points at the measure of 120, distanced in stages and later those things (triangles) equally reached as spread (revolved) all over, with corresponding gaps. (See the Chapter-9 on geometry.)

The 3 dimensional growth of the *Puruṣa* simultaneous with the growth of the universe was by building upon itself and the progress outward was as if by systematically feeding upon itself. It came into existence as a progress from what earlier existed in all through its several stages. The concept of a point of origin of physical manifestations, different from an epicentre of the powers was necessary and was maintained. In these complex phenomena, the very cause manifested itself as the effect to subsequently become larger causes and then still larger effects and in this process also created such emptiness, only to be later partially got filled up by the similar actions of a 1000 new power centres. The term "*ūrdhva*" was indeed appropriate as in the three dimensional universe no particular sense of horizontality prevailed and all directions could be termed as upward or forward. A growth process defined by "*sāśanānaśane*" was thus central to the very concept of the *puruṣasūkta*. Thus without any plane being specific, the process of growth took place equally in all directions to become this enormous universe along with the *Puruṣa*. A reference to the three points from the middle one of which a triangular formation took off was also made by the term "*tripādūrdhva*".

The union of the *Puruṣa* and the *Prakṛti* was imagined not only as capable of quantitatively and qualitatively multiplying, but also creating and occupying larger spaces and this concept necessitated the term "*sāśanānaśane*". The term "disappearing by consumption", additionally connoted the emptiness left behind and thereby indicating spaces progressively occupied as an essential part of growth. The everlasting cause, along with the sublime union of the *Puruṣa* and the *Prakṛti* from the beginning till now and the *annabhāva* bringing in the birth and dissolution of the effect were of traditional Indian philosophical content. The very reason for the first of such *yajña* or the inspiration behind it was therefore, non-negotiable, being derived from the ever present unseen divine mind and *icchāśakti*.

RV10.90.05 तस्माद्विराळजायत विराजो अधि पूरुषः।
स जातो अत्यरिच्यत पश्चाद्भूमिमथो पुरः॥

[तस्माद् - from that ◇ विराळ - sovereignty ◇ जायत - born and moved ◇ विराजो - as shining brilliance ◇ अधि - from above ◇ पूरुष - arisen as cleansed ◇ स - with ◇ जातो - those born ◇ अत्यरिच्यत - great emptiness ◇ पश्चाद् - and later ◇ भूमिम् - the earth forms; volume ◇ अथो - more and more ◇ पुर - abodes and regions]

From the sovereignty that shined above, as born and moved from the *Puruṣa*, great evacuations and emptiness came into effect by moving. Later it progressed further by increasing in volumes. The universe grew from that which shined above, getting purified and cleansed as risen from the *Puruṣa* and then acquired diverse nature along with the volumes and regions that came grew.

The birth of the later regions and the celestial bodies were firmly and interactively bonded to the hierarchical order of the universe and yet were diverse in nature. Those were envisaged as manifested from the very *Puruṣa*. It resulted in the growth of the universe into an immense volume. The description "interactively bonded and yet diverse in nature", as inferred here, could be a statement on the totally interactive nature of the existence of the universe as well as the galaxies and the celestial bodies individually and collectively, resulting in several hierarchical orders. All the existence and movement of the celestial bodies were thus firmly related to the *Puruṣa* conceived as causal to all. The diverse nature mentioned could only be the properties of the objects that ensued including the temperatures associated with them. This diversity was posited on to all the fields and objects. The term "*paścādbhūmimatho pura:*" could also mean to be 7 *vyāhṛtis* by which the universe was constituted, an essential compositional and geometrical concept of the Veda.

The above 5 verses described the beginning of creation and the subsequent state of the universe, which presented a rational thought and approach which stated that a finite entity was born and yet sufficiently stated its infinite nature as well. Neither the overall physical shape was finite nor the power centres. The process described using the term "*sāśanānaśane*" was a concept which stated the "emptiness" left behind at the point of respective origins, both in the case of the first of origins and the later 1000 power centres. An infinitesimal origin might not be able to pour out such vastness, energy and objects without a concept of a "*sāśanānaśane*" and a self dependent growth in place. The intimately attached, moving and orbital nature of the later regions and bodies, retained the relation to their respective causal points which then was estimated as a physical vacuum, or an emptiness that manifested. There indeed was a difficulty in conceiving a subsequent existence of an object at the very centre since that entity would have a finite form and would erect corresponding physical barriers. It was in this context that the process described by "*sāśanānaśane*" became capable of providing the emptiness at the central zone and at the same time maintaining a relationship in the subsequent growth. The term "*sahasraśīrṣa*" denoted the distributed presence of minds and propounded a theory of omnipresent consciousness extending all over the universe. The process of growth described here was almost similar to the common birth and death while maintaining the concept of *annabhāva* of matter and the concept of the eternal feed-stock.

Though 1000 could be taken to mean as many, since this is equal to 10^3, a suggestion that the growth that took place in all the three directions was conceptually equal in value could be read into it. With the meaning of " *akṣa*" as axis, along with their 1000 extensions and declinations presented concepts of strong sets of "fields", distributed all over the universe. These countless and strong fields could be assumed to spread as a complex network of emptiness created by earlier processes or to strengthen these vacuums to such an extent that this would enable the formation of gigantic forms of energy, vortex and super densities. Or let it be the very basic and hypothetical possibilities. The theory was thus capable of substantiating the growth into an enormous universe, on a self sustaining course. And it was stated that all those things happened spontaneously.

The possible major difference this process described here might have with the modern science would be that, instead of manifestation of a super temperature phenomenally equated to all future values, a self sustaining growth was imagined here. It might contain an argument that if the very initial cause and effect could exist or get born, there could not be anything to prevent multiple generation of the same subsequently and yet instantaneously. The act of growth to enormous masses and systems of diverse nature by feeding upon itself, leaving a possible nothingness behind was thus identified as a statement on the emptiness and field forces that were created around.

RV10.90.06 यत्पुरुषेण हविषा देवा यज्ञमतन्वत।
वसन्तो अस्यासीदाज्यं ग्रीष्म इध्मः शरद्धविः॥

[यत् - progressed ◇ पुरुषेण - from the *Puruṣa* ◇ हविषा - as products of oblations ◇ देवा - from the heavens ◇ यज्ञमतन्वत - as the parts of the body obtained by *yajña* ◇ वस् - stationed ◇ अन्तो - till end ◇ अस्यासीद् - derived as ◇ आज्यं - clarified butter ◇ ग्रीष्म - burning ones ◇ इध्मः - those containing fire ◇ शरद् - the cold ones ◇ धविः - that flowed]

From this *Puruṣa*, the products of oblations, the heavens and the objects in the form of *yajña* derivatives got stationed as moved till the as if clarified butter getting extracted. Those burning, those containing the fire and those cold ones had flowed down. It was from the *Puruṣa* and by the oblations offered as the *yajñas* of the gods, that the derivatives were so obtained, as the ones that remained or moved till the end reaching up to the earth. These became parts of the body of the self and in this manner countless parts got manifested. Those contained *Agni* and these flows of afflictions came from the *Agni*.

The universe got its enormous size by multiple stages of creation effected by the many heavens that came into existence around the first of heavens, from where all, the process of creation progressed in similar manners. As the *yajña* of the *Puruṣa*, and as the afflictions that accompanied, many things were born and they remained wherever they were born to or moved further and this process continued till the earth and till the end of the universe. Some of them merged with others and some of them contained intense heat. There was thus an incessant flow of matter and energy from the very source, which multiplied, agglomerated or perished. The verse also brought forth the meaning of the four seasons of the earth and might carry the suggestion that these contiguous natural conditions also owed their existence to the divine existence above. That way it suggested that these phenomena were nothing but the *yajña* of nature and all along the *Agni* played its part. On the other hand, the reference to the seasons could mean the cyclic occurrences with which the universe steadily progressed to its enormous size. In addition to the above, it also referred to the highly potential beginning and the desolate ends of the universe.

This way the verse could be interpreted, as a statement of diminishing scales of temperatures with which various objects of the universe came into the surroundings. Therefore, objects of Sun-like lustre and temperature, objects with much lesser levels of the same or varied properties, and objects like this earth with hot masses hidden inside as well as totally cold objects were born, as many flows that came distributed to many places. The different objects of the universe came only as *yajña* and as a flow from the afflictions that accompanied. This would imply that the matters of this earth or our solar system were not yet specifically discussed.

RV10.90.07 तं यज्ञं बर्हिषि प्रौक्षन्पुरुषं जातमग्रतः।
तेन देवा अयजन्त साध्या ऋषयश्च ये॥

[तम् - From those ◇ यज्ञम् - as the *yajña* ◇ बर्हिषि - that swirled like a bunch of grass ◇ प्रौक्षन् - and sprinkled around ◇ पुरुषं - the *Puruṣa* ◇ जातम् - born ◇ अग्रतः - till the ends ◇ तेन - by that ◇ देवा - heavens ◇ अयजन्त - till the ends where oblations have ended ◇ साध्या - subdued ◇ ऋषयश्च - as flowed ◇ ये - those]

From the *Puruṣa* and out of the *yajña*, came those swirled and sprinkled around as if from a bunch of grass and those heavens came into existence till the end, till nothing was further born. From those that somehow got stationed, further flows occurred in a subdued manner. These *yajña*s and oblations that came moved quickly and till exhaustion, had sprinkled around and had come from the *Puruṣa*. The universe progressively emaciated towards the end as the flows of those that occurred from the first of heavens and the subsequent heavens.

As if the reeds of grass spread into different directions, as if the objects that got showered from these shafts of growth, from the heaven the paths of creation took off along with the many heavens that came into existence. The universe became mighty and enormous, all as manifested from the *Puruṣa*. As the heavens that stood around the heaven like the spots of the well spread plumes of a peacock and as the paths of creation that flowed from such heavens, the universe grew to mighty proportions. Matter flowed out of those *yajña*s and automatically became the constituents of this immensely large universe. Those were the *yajña*s and oblations that moved instantly from the heaven and which occurred till the very end of the universe, in cyclic repetitions. The process exhausted all by itself by the time it reached the end and ultimately those flows had stopped. The processes emaciated and only objects of lesser intensity got delivered, lesser in temperature and the objects getting flung afar. Thus the density of occupation had gradually reduced. All objects and energy thus came from the *Puruṣa* as a series of sprinklings that occurred to the neighbourhood. That way the universe was filled, for there were a thousand *Puruṣa* that lay in several directions (the heads remaining at the heaven). The invariable presence of *Agni* was realised in all the processes, past, present and future and everything was essentially a *yajña* in character. It was more than to simply suggest the *yajña* as an effort but reiterated the very presence of an all pervasive *Agni* in every objects and processes. Conversely, it was not possible to disassociate this *Agni* from any of the objects and processes.

The universe have geometrically limited ends, in spite of being imeensely vast. The subject brought forward here would be found very much repeated in the *Ṛgveda*. Here it was also stated that while the objects moved as a flow, there were those lesser objects that got sprinkled from the mainstream, those that got positioned to the proximity. Thus many objects got sparsely distributed which bore allegiance to the main stream flow and to the objects that stood above.

RV10.90.08 तस्माद्यज्ञात्सर्वहुतः संभृतं पृषदाज्यम्।
पशूँन्ताँश्चक्रे वायव्यानारण्यान्ग्राम्याश्च ये॥

[तस्माद् - from that ◇ यज्ञात् - as *yajña* that moved ◇ सर्वहुत - by oblation of all ◇ संभृतं - amassed ◇ पृषद् - the spots of ◇ आज्यम् - clarified butter ◇ पशून् - as the visibilities ◇ तां - from those ◇ चक्रे - cyclically ◇ वायव्यान् - (as if) moved by a wind ◇ आरण्यान् - through the spokes (as a forest) ◇ ग्राम्याश्च - like the villages ◇ ये - as those]

From that (from the *Sat*) and from the *yajña* moved all, those products of oblations, the spots that stood amassed, created like curdled butter. Those visible objects came with cyclic progresses and those moved as if divided through the spokes of a wheel. Those stood like forests and those stood like the expanding villages. From that as *yajña*s and total sacrifices extending to all and by a process of evolution, came the animals of the forests, the avian and the village beings, born like butter accrued by churning of curdled milk.

It was from what remained in the heaven that the products of the *yajña* moved outward. It was in the heaven that the visibility occurred first. At the same time many of diverse nature and properties came into existence. Those were the cyclic growths and then the cyclic emaciation that culminated in the sparsely populated ends of the universe. With the geometrical specificity of a *rathacakra*, a progress commenced from the hub of the heaven, proceeding through the spokes as the paths, ending up in the rim, the end limits. That was a progress in many respects comparable to the growth of a village.

The objects and living things of this earth were also born out of a similar *yajña* and by a process of evolution and by birth of characteristically different things and different existences. This process was applicable to all that happened later. The curd and butter paradigm could also be discerned in the very formation of the universe. Though it could be surmised to be born out of an evolutionary process of what existed, nothing was really born without an accompanying *yajña* principle and divine guidance. It was by the invariable association of the *Agni* in every process, applicable, i.e., even to an evolutionary process, that these got classified as *yajña*s.

Many things were born in a camaraderie fashion, got protected, got swelled. Emptiness got formed and cyclic repetition of all the above indeed occurred. From the original oblations, entirely new type of objects were born which coexisted pleasantly. This process continued till the very end of the universe. A mutual exchange and interactive nature between objects of diverse properties existed in spite of the severe churning and agitation that occurred in their making. These creations which remained ever protected, swelled and multiplied several times. The objects that were swallowed by others and the emptiness that was created, came into existence in cyclic repetitions. While the objects transformed in several ways, the emptiness also transformed correspondingly.

RV10.90.09 तस्माद्यज्ञात्सर्वहुत ऋचः सामानि जज्ञिरे।
छन्दांसि जज्ञिरे तस्माद्यजुस्तस्मादजायत॥

[तस्माद् - from that ◇ यज्ञात् - as the *yajña* that moved ◇ सर्वहुत - as all products of oblations ◇ ऋच - according to law ◇ सामानि - as equal sets ◇ जज्ञिरे - as the *yajña* ◇ छन्दांसि - definite movements bound to measures ◇ जज्ञिरे - as the *yajña* ◇ तस्माद् - from that◇ यजुस् - as the *yajña* ◇ तस्माद् - from that ◇ अजा - till nothing born ◇ यत - progressing]

From that (from the *Sat*) moved the *yajña*s and the products of oblations, maintaining the laws of creation, manifested and moved as equal sets that came into all directions and as the *yajña*s that moved bound to definite measures. As the *yajña*s that came from *yajña*s, the universe progressed till nothing was further born.

All were created as *yajña*s and as the products of oblations that commenced from the heaven and from the *Sat*. Those were the *yajña*s that took place equally into all directions and then from ever new positions. Those were the *yajña*s that took place in well defined measures and with divine aspirations and intentions. Those came born and those which stood potently for progressing further as new creations, were flung into similar *yajña*s and this process got cyclically repeated, till the process got exhausted and then nothing was further born. Those were the *yajña*s that came with the divine praises and hymns. Those also brought the sky with the 7 *vyāhṛti*s into existence with the 3 sub-divisions of each.

From a similar *yajña* and oblations, the *ṛk*, the *sāma*, the *chandas* and the *yajus* came born and descended to us. Like the objects and the living things born out of a process of *yajña*, so was the knowledge born. Just because the knowledge was derived as an operation of the mind, divine minds, would not exclude the presence of the ***yajña*** principle. In the physical and mental processes as well, the nature of a *yajña* and the *Agni* should be reckoned as present. The *yajña* principle thus extended to the very infinitesimal phenomenon of the universe covering all that came animate and inanimate.

RV10.90.10 तस्मादश्वा अजायन्त ये के चोभयादतः।
गावो ह जज्ञिरे तस्मात् तस्माज्जाता अजावयः॥

[तस्माद् - from that ◊ अश्वा - moved and spread ◊ अजायन्त - moving till the end where nothing was further born ◊ ये - those ◊ के - somehow ◊ च - and ◊ उभयादत - as those came to both sides ◊ गावो - that progressed ◊ ह - distanced ◊ जज्ञिरे - out of *yajña* ◊ तस्मात् - from that moved ◊ तस्माद् - and from those ◊ जाता - that came born ◊ अजा - till nothing was born ◊ वयः - a body]

From those that came into existence, moving and spreading till the end from that earlier state of unborn, getting delivered to both sides as those that somehow came into existence in whatever form those came about, moved and distanced. Those were the products of *yajña*s and were the ones that moved from those that came born first, until nothing was further born and thus getting culminated in the body of the universe.

From those that came into existence directly from the heaven, the creation further progressed. From those first born ones, the creation progressed, maintaining a balance between opposite sides, as delivered, as born and as distanced. And from those so came born, the creation further progressed in a cyclic repetition of whatever happened earlier, but to modified dimensions and measures. It was a progress of divisions, births and movements that gradually emaciated to the ends. Thus it reached this earth from a state of unborn, many coming born and then ended as nothing further born.

To this earth, it descended as the horses and all others with two rows of teeth like the cow, goat and the sheep. The mammals of a higher evolutionary order were also ordained in a similar way. The birth of many classes of living objects and the evolutionary process continued. Here also the concept of the *yajña* would apply. The diversity that was observed did not exempt from reckoning the relevance of the *yajña* principle and the presence of the *Agni* from any process.

The 9th and 10th verses, said that the instant growth that occurred from the epicentre was by maintaining a left-right balance (equilibrium and symmetry) till the end. In this great voyage of creation both construction and destruction took place. There were objects of excellence and shines, as well as lifeless entities. Things were created as well as destroyed. The concept of a biological manifestation and destruction was maintained by the term "*jajñire*". All those thus created remained regulated, controlled and yet remained interactive to one another.

RV10.90.11 यत् पुरुषं व्यदधुः कतिधा व्यकल्पयन्।
मुखं किमस्य कौ बाहू का ऊरू पादा उच्येते॥

[यत् - progressing from ◇ पुरुषम् - the *Puruṣa* ◇ व्यदधुः - divided and pulsating ◇ कतिधा - how many got delivered ◇ व्यकल्पयन् - so divided till nothing could be imagined ◇ मुखं - as the face ◇ किमस्य - as which ◇ कौ - how many ◇ बाहू - hands ◇ का - how many ◇ ऊरू - thighs ◇ पादा - and feet ◇ उच्येते - it is said]

Having moved from That and from the *Puruṣa*, having issued out through the divided and pulsating *vyāhṛtis*, how many ways got delivered, if when contemplated, considered severally and in differentiating manner as to what manifested as the face, what as the many hands, the many thighs and the many feet, till that end where all imaginations had ended?

It was from the inexhaustible (*avyaya*) *Puruṣa* that everything was created and so would be those to be created. While the *Puruṣa* as a whole was transformed in the hitherto descriptions, where the different parts of the *Puruṣa* such as the intellect, mind or the limbs were not differentiated, now the description turns to such differentiation and use of parts or qualities. Then how was the *Puruṣa* configured in a differentiating manner, as the face, as the hands in the form of trunks and legs attached to it? How did those manifestations progress through the *vyāhṛtis* and their sub-divisions? Here the entity of the *Puruṣa* lay with the heads resting near the epicentre and the legs extending outward and was referred to as a composition that occurred along with the seven *vyāhṛtis*. These matters would be discussed now.

RV10.90.12 ब्राह्मणोऽस्य मुखमासीद्बाहू राजन्यः कृतः।
ऊरू तदस्य यद्वैश्यः पद्भ्यां शूद्रो अजायत॥

[ब्राहणो - from the *Brahma* ◇ अस्य - as ◇ मुखम् - the face ◇ आसीद् - having manifested ◇ बाहू - the hands ◇ राजन्यः - issued out and born ◇ कृत - so created ◇ ऊरू - the thighs ◇ तदस्य - from those ◇ यद् - in many ways ◇ वैश्यः - divided into many ◇ पद्भ्यां - as stages ◇ शूद्रो - that dwindled ◇ अजायत - till nothing was born ◇

The face having manifested from the *Brahma*, and from this face getting issued out, came born, as created from the thighs, many ways coming as the divided stages, steadily getting dwindled and progressing till nothing was further born.

The universe was born from the *Brahma* who provided the first stage from which the strong pathways of growth took shape. From what existed, formed a stage from which the creation commenced taking course to different paths while expanding. These pathways got thinned out while several subways got generated from them. The process continued by which the universe swelled to its enormity till matter and energy came to a state of nothingness and then nothing was further born. Thus all came only from the *Brahma*. That stage which were described as the " *hiraṇyagarbha*" and the "*viśvatomukha*" would be the place of first of manifestations, and from this the universe took shape by distributing matter and energy through well formed pathways, ultimately thinning down to nothingness. This description presented a configuration of the universe similar to what was described in RV10.81.03.

On surface earth, the higher forms of the humans took

classification names within themselves according to the nature of the works done by them and duties enshrined, coming as a progress in the thought process which were not the characteristics of the other living things and this made them to stand apart. The thought was initiated as a part of existence and the early forms that it took were being mentioned. While the names of the derogatory caste system indeed got mentioned here, how could the *Viśvapuruṣa* have anything to do with it? Nothing of this was visible in the *Puruṣa* hitherto described. If at all, the similarity would be to man of this earth and to his deeds and not to the *Viśvapuruṣa*. At the same time the concept of parallelism and similarity of the universe and the *Viśvapuruṣa* at one level and the human body and the human being at another level would be found often implied here and stated in the later literature. But what is more interesting here is that the terms like *rāja* and *kṣatra* derived much more clear meanings, out of association with the physical attributes and occurrences in the process of creation than from the etymological constructions that will be resorted to by the grammarians. It raised pointed questions to the Vedic ambiance and methods of presentation on the one side and the very contribution of the Veda to the development of the Sanskrit language of later periods, on the other. Besides it is clear that the Vedic metaphors belonged altogether to a different class.

RV10.90.13 चन्द्रमा मनसो जाताश्चक्षोः सूर्यो अजायत।
मुखादिन्द्रश्चाग्निश्च प्राणाद्वायुरजायत॥

[चन्द्रमा - from a moon-like composition ◇ मनसो - from the mind ◇ जातश्चक्षो - born from the eye and axis ◇ सूर्यो - Sun like ◇ अजायत - progressed till the state of unborn ◇ मुखाद् - from faces ◇ इन्द्रश्च - and from the *indrata* ◇ अग्निश्च - and the *Agni* ◇ प्राणाद् - to the surrounding; as the *prāṇa* ◇ वायुः - as a wind ◇ अजायत - progressing till nothing further born]

From that which stood with a moon-like composition, from that divine mind (so reckoned), from that eye and axis, came born those that shined like Suns, moving from an earlier state of unborn, along with that face, the *indrata* and the *Agni*, always moving to the surroundings as if by a wind and progressing till the end where nothing was further born.

It was from a state of dullness and unborn, that a state of born first manifested, which then culminated in a state of unborn, in the end. Many things happened in between. The primary matter and form of energy appeared, got much enhanced and enlarged and then got emaciated. It was into the *Soma* that existed in the heaven and the heart near to the epicentre and the axis, a bright spot of matter and energy (*indrata*; a point singularity) manifested and upon the advent of the *Agni* into this, enormous matter and energy flowed out to make the universe. Upon traversing to the very end, it became exhausted of energy, diminished in movements and temperatures. The heaven, where the creations started stood very near to and surrounding the epicentre of the universe known as the *viśvacakṣus*. It was here, in this heaven and into what existed there as the unborn that the bright particle of matter and energy first manifested. Simultaneously the *Agni* entered into it and the process of creation took off to the surroundings.

In describing the birth of the elements of our solar system, it was stated that the moon, the Sun, *Indra*, *Agni* and *Vāyu* (of divine nature) got manifested from different parts of His body. In a parallel analogy, the description compared our body and elements to the celestial bodies; the mind was the moon, the intellect was the Sun, the knowledge and activity being the *Indra*, *Agni* and the *Vāyu* was the breathing.

However, this verse could also be interpreted as to the way in which our Moon (Moon like dark bodies of the universe) was born. A Moon like object could come only from a body of sun-like brilliance and these would traverse up to a point by which the available propagating forces would get exhausted. Even in such instances, the presence of a point singularity (*indrata*) and the presence of the *Agni* in the originating locale would be tantamount.

RV10.90.14 नाभ्या आसीदन्तरिक्षं शीर्ष्णो द्यौः समवर्तत।
पद्भ्यां भूमिर्दिशः श्रोत्रात् तथा लोकाँ अकल्पयन्॥

[नाभ्या - from the hub ◇ आसीद् - came into existence ◇ अन्तरिक्षं - the atmosphere ◇ शीर्ष्णो - as the head ◇ द्यौ - the heavens ◇ समवर्तत - equally placed ◇ पद्भ्यां - as stages; steps ◇ भूमिः - of the earth forms ◇ दिशः - and directions ◇ श्रोत्रात् - coming from the sacred hymns ◇ तथा - coming from those that existed ◇ लोकाँ - to be the universe ◇ अकल्पयन् - till devoid of all imaginations]

From the hub directly manifested the atmosphere, the heaven being the head, in equally placed stages and steps, manifested in all directions till the earth, all coming from the sacred hymns and all moving from those that earlier existed, to become the universe. Then these processes got culminated into the end regions where all (divine) imaginations had ended.

The geometry of the universe is well comparable to the *rathacakra*, having a hub, spokes, rim and a centre of unspecified location. From the hub and navel, from the head and the heaven equally divided to both sides came the atmosphere, in well defined steps, in the direction of this earth as sequential flows. Thus came the universe into existence. These flows were in all directions from the epicentre and the heaven. Here the term "*padbhyāṃ*" indicated the 7 *vyāhṛtis* as the geometrical order of the universe. This statement here closely corresponded with the contents of the first verse commencing "*sahasraśīrṣā*- - -". Instead of the well defined steps stated, if the meaning with the feet reaching up to the earth was substituted, the whole geometrical scheme was not much different. The term "*samavartata*" meant equi-spaced as well as equi-balanced and would be found used quite often in both the meanings. Here in the two different interpretations they took to different meanings.[3] The different parts of the *Puruṣa*

[3]There would appear several words in the Veda that would act as precisely and marvelously conceived technical terms.

were also resolved as the parts of the solar system, particularly the earth and parts of the human body. . While the *Puruṣa* concept was formed, the characteristics of the man got superimposed on Him and later the same was allocated on to the worldly bodies. Thus the superimposition and the reflection suggested were mutual.

RV10.90.15 सप्तास्यासन् परिधयस्त्रिः सप्त समिधः कृताः।
देव यद्यज्ञं तन्वाना अबध्नन् पुरुषं पशुम्॥

[सप्त - seven ◇ अस्य - as ◇ आसन् - having come ◇ परिधय - as the limits ◇ त्रिः - with three ◇ सप्त - and seven ◇ समिधः - positioned equally ◇ कृताः - having created ◇ देव - from the heaven ◇ यद् - somehow ◇ यज्ञं - as *yajña* ◇ तन्वाना - the body parts that moved ◇ अबध्नन् - coming separated ◇ पुरुषं - from the *Puruṣa* ◇ पशुम् - as the visibilities; as protected and swelled]

Seven boundaries came into existence and all these seven divisions got further divided into three of equal values. Many were created from the heaven by several types of *yajña*s, and then got separated from those to become the parts of the universe. They all came separated from the *Puruṣa* to become the visibilities that manifested and thus a protected universe swelled out.

The 7 limits (*paridhi*) that was mentioned would mean the 7 *vyāhṛtis*, conforming to the concepts of the geometry of the universe. Then 3 sizes by divisions were allotted to each of the *vyāhṛti* to become a total of 21 boundaries. Therefore, the first of these would be known simply as heaven and which further took the earlier said names of *hiraṇyagarbha*, *viśvatomukha* etc., in the Vedic texts. These *vyāhṛti*s were formed as plunged and swelled from the heaven to become this very large universe. It was by divine *yajña*s that these became basic circular definitions of the atmosphere. It was the same way the shining objects of the universe got born.

The *vaidikayajña* enacted this occurrence as the *yajña*s in which the *uttaravedi citi*s were made into the 21 sizes in seven groups of three each, as mentioned in the *śulbasūtras*.

The later *vaidikayajña* rites symbolically represented the very *yajña* of the *Puruṣa* and therefore verily was in veneration of those original *yajña* by which the birth of the universe and the processes got enabled. The sizes of the *uttaravedi* progressed in 7 sets of 3 each commencing from the 7.5 to 101 square *puruṣaṃ* in area, according to the *śulbasūtras*.[4] The fact that the 7.5 *puruṣaṃ citi* was termed as *prathama* could be with an additional significance of denoting the space where the very first ever of the *yajña* that took place.

RV10.90.16 यज्ञेन यज्ञमयजन्त देवास्तानि धर्माणि प्रथमान्यासन्।
ते ह नाकं महिमानः सचन्त यत्र पूर्वे साध्याः सन्ति देवः॥

[यज्ञेन - as the *yajña* ◇ यज्ञम् - and *yajña* ◇ अयजन्त - till the end where the *yajña* had ended ◇ देवा - from the heavens ◇ अस्तानि - blown away as the many ◇ धर्माणि - as per the rules ◇ प्रथम - from that came first ◇ अन्य - as the others ◇ आसन् - having taken position ◇ ते - those ◇ ह - distanced ◇ नाकं - as the sky ◇ महिमानः - of great measures ◇ सचन्त - with the benedictions till the end ◇ यत्र - as those ◇ पूर्वे -from the earlier ◇ साध्याः - coming subdued ◇ सन्ति - from the *Sat* ◇ देवः - and the heaven]

The universe came born out of *yajña* after *yajña*, till the end where all *yajña* had ceased. It came born from those that stood as the heavens and were born according to the divine rules. Having come from those that came first, having blown away and much distanced as the great arrangements that came from the heavens and out of the benedictions that got offered, all of these got subdued towards the end and the universe came only by objects getting born from those that came just earlier, though initially manifested from the *Sat* and from the first of heavens.

Perhaps it was not known what existed earlier and also what manifested as the first. But as *yajña* conducted as per divine rules and the repetition of the same, continuous and

[4]However the size of 101 and the naming of the size of 7.5 sq. *puruṣaṃ* as *prathama* is not without some contradictions, according to this author.

great arrangements came into the universe till the very end where all *yajñas* had ended. In this creation of the universe, there was a chain of manifestations from whatever existed earlier, which started in the heaven and the *Sat* and continued till the very end. There were divisions and movements in each instance, just as it occurred from the heaven. That was the manner in which the universe became so enormous and till this earth and beyond. Those were the divine gifts that were delivered as per divine rules. As the principle of the *Puruṣa* and as the *yajñas*, that went on creating, the many shining objects and energy forms of the universe were brought into existence. It was by the cyclic repetitions of the *yajña* and by the formation of the heavens that this immense universe got created.

Thus the *puruṣasūkta*, indirectly stated that the *vaidika yajñas* were in commemoration of those earlier and original ones of nature. The meaning of the *vaidika yajña* was brought out from the above set of statements as one that came about in veneration of the very origin of the universe and the processes that ensued. This vaguely answered two vital questions; one of how the *yajña* rites came about and then the reason for those rites. But perhaps those were not all and the rituals might have been conceived for a better realisation of God by direct acts resembling the process of creation. The first of the *yajña* and many subsequent ones were of nature itself during the birth of the universe. As a result the universe was born. The subsequent many *yajñas* were also by nature. Thus the galaxies and stars were born. Then came this solar system, the earth, the seasons and the living things. Then the mammals and the human beings of a higher evolutionary order, the intellect and the thoughts of classification. These progressive developments were realised by the sages verily as *yajñas* and instituted such *yajñas* in representative fashion and in total veneration of those that originally took place. It was also realised that commencing from those original *yajñas* and extending to the ones that was proposed later, the common agent could be nothing other than the *Agni* being invariably present at all times. Incorporating the *Agni* into the *yajña* canons realising it as the supreme participator and a witness became tantamount.

The *puruṣasūkta* presented one particular view in which the presence of *Agni* or temperature was actually not much stressed or stated. This hymn however, dealt with the origin of the universe in a superbly imaginative fashion and reached conclusions comparable to modern scientific thoughts as far as its very essential statements were concerned. The text was dexterously conceived to mean different and yet co-existing sets of meanings. Without naming the *Agni*, except once, the same was brought in as the very genus of all creations and as the ever sustaining form of energy. It presented the order of the birth and the growth of the universe in a poetic and rhythmic style of rendering. The whole of the hymn was considered very auspicious by many and was used in their daily invocations, for an unknown period of time.

It is not meant here that the *yajña*s were merely the presentations of the physics of the universe. The *Ṛgveda* text would not keep away from the divine aspects for a moment. At the same time the *yajña* culture could not have been existing simply as divine rituals and propitiation of gods alone, when the importance attached to the geometry was taken into account. The *yajña* culture that came to us might also contain important pointers to the history of the Vedic period.

★★★

2

Nāsadīya Sūkta-Matters of Origin

The term *Bhāvavṛttaṃ* connoted cosmogony and in the *Ṛg-veda* 4 hymns came with this title. Of these the *nāsadīyasūkta* is quite well known and well discussed and the hymn RV10.190 is known as the *aghamarṣaṇasūkta*. The other hymns with the same topic are RV10.130 and RV10.154.

RV 10.129 (Nāsadīya Sūkta)

The *nāsadīyasūkta* is a much discussed segment of the *Ṛg-veda*, and presented an universe that started with uncertainty and ended in uncertainty. It brought out the state of initial non-existence and the subsequent existence in vivid details and wondered at the very inexplicable nature of creation.

[(7)सप्तर्चस्यास्य सूक्तस्य परमेष्ठि प्रजापतिऋषि। भाववृत्तं देवता। त्रिष्टुप् छन्दः]

RV10.129.01 नासदासीन्नो सदासीत्तदानीं नासीद्रजो नो व्योमा परो यत्। किमावरिवः कुह कस्य शर्मन्नम्भः किमासीद्गहनं

गभीरम्॥

[न - as ◇ असद् - from a state of non-existence ◇ आसीद् - came ◇ नो - as ◇ सद् - the *Sat* ◇ आसीत् - came ◇ तदानीं - from those ◇ न - that ◇ आसीद् - came as ◇ रजो - a particle of dust ◇ नो - as ◇ व्योमा - the atmosphere ◇ परो - to distances ◇ यत् - progressed ◇ किम् - where ◇ आ - manifested ◇ वरिवः - the wide space; bliss; comfort ◇ कुह - to where distanced ◇ क - what ◇ अस्य - as ◇ शर्मन्नम्भः - the protected celestial waters ◇ किम् - how ◇ आसीद् - came ◇ गहनं - a state of denseness ◇ गभीरम् - and profundity]

Directly came from a state of non-existence into a state of existence, directly came from the *Sat*, to become those that came manifested from a particle that directly came into it, got born from it, distanced and progressed as the protected atmosphere and those circularity's that somehow got formed along with the celestial waters that enveloped the universe. All these came from somewhere and somehow to become a state of super-denseness and profundity.

The universe was born from a state of non-existence to a state of existence. It came from a state of almost nothingness to the next state of a super density. A shining particle of matter manifested into the heaven, somehow from somewhere and from that an atmosphere got formed to encompass all of the universe. This atmosphere stood as circularity's that progressively distanced from the point of origin. Simultaneously, a universal celestial water flowed around, descending and enveloping all that came from the paths of creation, till the very end of the universe. From where all these came and to what extent, measures, densities and a state of profundity it grew was not known. Known it was, that all came from almost nothingness to become the enormous universe.

In the beginning there was nothing at all, not even a speck of anything. Nor was there any space extending anywhere and beyond. Therefore, no answer existed to questions of any limiting factors, boundaries or of any of its contents.

Since nothing whatsoever existed in the beginning of the universe, no restraining forces whatsoever could have been there. Therefore, anything as existing before the original creation was beyond imagination and was totally unknown. Into this total non-existence, what manifested as a particle of matter? For what divine reason that this atmosphere that extended till the very end of the universe came? This atmosphere which acted as a protection and refuge to all the objects that traveled and took position in it. This atmosphere that held the celestial waters, into which everything came born. Then what manifested as the emptiness and as the denseness of the universe? These were really not known.

RV10.129.02 न मृत्युरासीदमृतं न तर्हि न रात्र्या अह्न आसीत्प्रकेतः।
आनीदवातं स्वधया तदेकं तस्माद्धान्यन्न परः किं चनास॥

[न - as ◇ मृत्युः - mortality ◇ आसीद् - came ◇ अमृतं - immortality ◇ न - as ◇ तर्हि - at that time ◇ न - as ◇ रात्र्या - the night manifested ◇ अह्न - the day ◇ आसीत् - that came ◇ प्रकेतः - the shining objects ◇ आनीदवातं - issued and led by wind (emaciated) ◇ स्वधया - all by the self ◇ तद् - that ◇ एकं - one ◇ तस्माद् - from that ◇ ध - got placed ◇ अन्यन्न - unprecedented food principle; as others ◇ परः - distanced ◇ किं - somehow ◇ चनास - as the benevolence]

Mortality and immortality manifested simultaneously as the night and the day that would come one after the other and those bright things were led forward as issued out and moved as if by a wind. All of these came all by themselves from that One and only One, on an unprecedented food principle, got positioned, distanced and got emaciated, to provide the benevolences of the universe.

From that which stood inert and immobile as if dead, an immortality came into existence with the goodness and benevolences of the universe as its contents. It descended as the light that shone and the time that was born. It had the path of creation that stood like the day with the darkness around as the night. Thus visibility descended from the heaven to the proximity. All of these came from that shining particle of matter, and the *Sat* that remained in the heaven and grew on the eternal and unprecedented food principle to become this enormous universe. Those were the repeated and cyclic processes of creation, just like the days and nights that would go on appearing. Those were the paths of creation and the darkness that alternated around the heaven.

Earlier, no death or immortality existed; no night, daylight, time and the sight that got derived out of it. That only existed, which issued out as the self and grew all by itself as the eternal feedstock and without the help of anything external. Mortality and immortality did not exist as nothing was yet born. Neither darkness, light nor time existed. There was nothing to see and notice. And what was then born was born again as the eternal food and thereby grew all by itself without any external help. In the beginning, all the four dimensions with which existence was defined were naught. "That" as the very cause and effect only existed, which then grew to its immense size on the food principle.

RV10.129.03 तम आसीत् तमसा गूळ्हमग्रेऽप्रकेतं सलिलं सर्वमा इदम्। तुच्छ्येनाभ्वपिहितं यदासीत्तपसस्तन्महिनाजायतैकम्॥

[तम - from darkness ◇ आसीत् - came ◇ तमसा - those associated with darkness ◇ गूळ्हमग्रे - till the fathomless ends ◇ अप्रकेतं - where visibility had ended ◇ सलिलं - floating ◇ सर्वम् आ - all manifested ◇ इदम् - till here, thus ◇ तुः - powerfully ◇ श्येन - the falcon ◇ अभ्व - of immense ◇ पिहितं - surreptitiously ◇ यदासीत् - somehow coming ◇ तपसस्तन् - as smote from heat ◇ महिना - became great ◇ जायत - born and progressed ◇ एकम् - from that one]

From darkness came those associated with darkness and those that surreptitiously stood, till the fathomless ends where the visibility had ended. All manifested till here as the many that somehow brought by that powerful and immense falcon and as those that smote from an immense heat. But all these were still those that came from That, the only One, born and progressed to become this great universe.

From the darkness smote a darkness with fathomless ends and until there where the visibility had ended, as an arrangement of everything that came exploding from a particle, floating in the atmosphere, many ways progressing; all manifesting out of a roaring and enormous heat. From a dark existence in the heaven, from that inert state, when a shining particle of matter and energy suddenly manifested and when an intense and roaring heat entered into it, the universe spread and descended to this enormous size. As the paths of creation that descended to the surroundings, along with a darkness that extended till the very end of the universe, objects floated in the atmosphere. The paths of creation progressed many ways till the end. It was as if an immortality was brought down till this earth by that immense falcon that remained in the heaven.

It was that roaring immense heat that created and propagated everything in the universe. The objects floated on the waves of those divine sounds and got carried away to great distances. Thus it was that the shining particle that it once was, became this immense universe. Thus it was out of a darkness, the visibility and an all pervading darkness manifested simultaneously. That was the very beginning of creation. It took place out of a darkness to include an all pervading atmosphere of unknown ends and as the darkness and the bright paths that descended. The darkness mentioned earlier was merely the state of the unperceived and the unknown. Then there was no space and time and it was along with the manifestation of visibility and a darkness that the four dimensions ever came into being. It was only after the sudden appearance of that tiny speck of matter that the entities first mentioned and the properties of anything could ever occur. This tiny matter was instantaneously transformed into that immense size by the induction of a roaring great heat and temperature. The roaring intense heat should be now almost equated to the total of all the values that occurred later. It then exploded into different entities of large diversities along with an immense expansion. The speck of the matter that formed initially was the manifestation of a *bījabhāva* which then acquired the *annabhāva*, to become this immense universe. It started as the *indrata* of unprecedented properties and beyond definition. A speculation as to a lapse of time between the formation of the tiny matter and the great expansion that took place could not be perhaps sustained since almost all the potential of creation was found invested onto an instantaneous upheaval in the very beginning.

This verse, in a way, also stated the gist of some prevalent theories on how the universe came. One as a universe that was brought down from the heaven by a great falcon. One as the immense and roaring heat that created the universe. One as an expansion on the basis of a divine food principle that extended from a point of origin in the heaven till the earth.

RV10.129.04 **कामस्तदग्रे समवर्तताधि मनसो रेतः प्रथमं यदासीत्। सतो बन्धुमसति निरविन्दन् हृदि प्रतिष्या कवयो मनीषा॥**

[**कामस्तद्** - in desired measures ◇ **अग्रे** - till the ends ◇ **समवर्तत** - equitably placed ◇ **अधि** - from above ◇ **मनसो** - from the mind ◇ **रेतः** - as the semen virile; a flow ◇ **प्रथमं** - the first ◇ **यद्** - somehow ◇ **आसीत्** - came ◇ **सतो** - from the *Sat* ◇ **बन्धु** - connected to ◇ **मसति** - in great measures ◇ **निः** - downward ◇ **अविन्दन्** - till nothing gained ◇ **हृदि** - from the hearts ◇ **प्रतिष्या** - coming poured down; got mixed ◇ **कवयो** - reduced ◇ **मनीषा** - intelligently]

Everything manifested in desired dimensions and measures till the end, equitably placed from above and as manifested from a divine mind. Down flowed the semen virile, many ways coming from the *Sat*, and connected to it proceeding greatly downward in a measured way till the end and till nothing further gained. All manifested from the hearts as poured down and getting mixed; all manifested with the intelligence that went on reducing.

Moving equitably from a high position as desired till the

ends, remaining as the first ones, flowing down and getting born repeatedly, proceeded directly in many ways and yet maintained the relation with *Sat*. Manifesting from a divine mind, getting evacuated from the many hearts, getting sprinkled, getting reduced and in such ways everything came intelligently. The creation that commenced from the heaven, brought about a set of first born to the proximity and to below. From these and from their high positions, the creation further progressed equitably into all directions. Those that came born from the first born, and out of those that remained with a potential to produce further, rained down as the objects that came till this earth and beyond. They manifested intelligently, maintaining allegiance to the earlier state and the state of the *Sat*.

In two ways the creation progressed; one as if from a mind and the other as if by processes of evacuation from the hearts. While the creation progressed, two types of objects came into existence; one as those which could generate further and the other which could only become smashed and become smaller. From the first ones which stood with the potential to generate, the shining paths of creation could be seen to take off and these would further have an epicentre of its own, the divine mind. The other, of the broken heart, threw the smaller objects to the surroundings. Both of these acted as centres of interactive influence to the surroundings and these bore different types of voids in their original positions. The evacuated hearts stood as if centres of the force fields, with their influence limited to the objects thrown around. From the hearts of the ones that stood potent for creation, a chain of creation flowed down and thus a larger and extended chain of influences came into existence.

An intense heat was born along with the primary particle of matter that was formed scattering matter outward and expanding. The matter and energy were described as showered out along with this great expansion and by this process created emptiness at the point of origin. The expansion that took place was in equal measure, in all the three dimensions and into all directions. All these happened instantaneously as stated earlier. According to this description, the universe could only have a spherical shape, nearly so or yearning to be so. The point of origin was thus empty of matter and yet controlled everything below. Thus the phenomenon of emptiness should be assumed to have necessarily traveled along with the expansion of the universe. This in turn created thousands of subsidiary centres of power and influence. Therefore, these subsequent and yet immediate thousands of expansions should be imagined to scatter matter and corresponding emptiness and how could we conclude as to what amount and extent of the emptiness earlier made were then filled as well? The process continued till this earth and into other directions.

RV10.129.05 तिरश्चीनो विततो रश्मिरेषामध
स्विदासीदुपरिस्विदासीत्। रेतोधा आसन्महिमान
आसन्त्स्वधा अवस्तात्प्रयतिः परस्तात्॥

[तिरश्चीनो - transverse; across ◇ विततो - blossomed ◇ रश्मिः - as the rays ◇ रेषा - coming with roars ◇ मध - placed by the self ◇ स्विद् - secreted ◇ आसीद् - having come ◇ उपरि - from above ◇ स्विद् - secreted ◇ आसीत् - having come ◇ रेतो - as the semen virile ◇ धा - provided ◇ आसन् - positioned ◇ महिमान - as great arrangements ◇ आसन् - positioned ◇ स्वधा - from inherent strengths ◇ अवस्तात् - moving away and to below ◇ प्रयति - as gifted ◇ परस्तात् - further to distances]

As the roaring rays that blossomed and spread across and as secreted from those, smote and again from those secreted and smote more, losing heat in the process and got positioned accordingly. Those that the semen virile provided became the great arrangements that came flowing, issuing out and from those further issuing out, thus progressing and descending to the surroundings with inherent strengths. Thus objects got positioned far and wide.

From all high positions, just as it happened from the

heaven, the growth of the universe took place along the paths of creation as if the rays that would flash around the Sun and from these the objects getting sprinkled again to the surroundings. The creation of new paths and new objects was repeated ever so many times from all the potential entities to become this very large universe. The objects lost heat during these progresses and while those came to great distances. Eventually, though instantly, whatever earlier stood as potential growth centres became no longer capable of creating further. Thus the great roars had subdued to murmurs.

The earlier formed matter of the universe spread across from the earlier state to a great later state, as the roaring rays smote in all directions which carried the objects that secreted and secreted again from these secretions, eventually burning out. It flowed downward, to the surroundings and outwards from the self that it was. These growths were totally instantaneous. The roaring great original heat smote down and away and as the universe grew started losing temperature. The expansion that took place brought in the great flows of matter to the surroundings. Thus, though it was stated that in the later state the matter was cooled, the description obviously did not dwell on the state of the matter through out the spectrum. It should be all the same inferred that there were several combinations of the hot as well as the cold objects that came up to great distances as well as held nearer, transgressing into the fields of one another to become a complex structure. Thus the second stage of the birth and expansion of the universe got concluded.

RV10.129.06 को अद्धा वेद क इह प्र वोचत् कुत आजाता कुत इयं विसृष्टिः। अर्वाग्देवा अस्य विसर्जनेनाथा को वेद यत आबभूव॥

[को - what all ◇ अद्धा - thus manifested ◇ वेद - as properties ◇ क - which ◇ इह - till here ◇ प्र - to the surroundings ◇ वोचत् - out of words ◇ कुत - from whom ◇ आ - came ◇ जा - born ◇ ता - as those that came ◇ कुत - by whom ◇ इयं - thus ◇ विसृष्टिः - got discharged ◇ अर्वाग् - from a point downwards ◇ देवा - the heavens ◇ अस्य - as ◇ विसर्जनेन - as discharged ◇ अथा - then ◇ को - what all ◇ वेद - properties ◇ यत - got ordained; progressed ◇ आ - manifested ◇ बभूव - and existed in the atmosphere]

What all properties thus issued out reaching till here, out of the words that came to the surroundings, somehow again got issued out, somehow again got born, somehow descended from the heavens, as if discharged to become the many properties that manifested, progressed and got positioned in the atmosphere and thus got ordained?

What was then the property that appeared here, out of the words that came to the surroundings, how became derivatively born and how thus became the many creations that descended as the bright objects, which by evacuation and emission got reconfigured as what all further properties? What all came as the heavens under the heavens, from where the creation still continued? By whom all these were started and by whom these were carried forward? What was the property of that from which the first of manifestation took place? By which divine words that came, brought many creations to the surroundings? Into what properties these objects then got re-configured by loss or by gain as the properties that came to the surroundings? One could not know completely, about what originally existed and into what forms it later got transformed. What was the divine sounds and vibrations that caused the division of the existing into many and their wider distribution to become the immensely large universe and how all it came was not known. It was the sounds that appeared as a roar of sufficient strength to carry out the functions that was earlier identified as cause and effect. But now the sounds became widespread to the surroundings and became of lesser intensity. However, it was known that the properties went on transforming and got into reducing intensities when the process of multiplication continued.

The description of expansion of the universe in which the *Agni* was the prime motive force and motor, came to an end with the subjects that got presented up to and including the

5th verse. What happened later could be explained by the term " *visarjanenā*" which denoted the birth of further matter by a process of birth and dissolution which was termed as evacuation and emission. The description now came to a part where the creation of objects advanced by the common birth and death, as if they carried life. This would include such evolution of objects of characteristically different nature as well, and acquisition of properties by such living and non living objects should also be taken as included. There was no longer those sudden expansions and instantaneous phenomena, stated earlier. Though it was stated that several such objects were thus born, it was not specifically mentioned that these phenomena belonged to earth as such or whether it was meant as something that universally occurred.

RV10.129.07 इयं विसृष्टिर्यताबभूव यदि व दधे यदि व न।
यो अस्याध्यक्षः परमे व्योमन्त्सो अङ्ग वेद यदि वा न वेद॥

[इयं - thus ◇ विसृष्टिः - got discharged ◇ यत् - and progressed ◇ आ - manifested ◇ बभूव - and existed in the atmosphere ◇ यदि - in many ways ◇ व - and besides ◇ दधे - got obtained ◇ यदि - in many ways ◇ व - not only that ◇ न - as ◇ यो - whatever ◇ अस्य - form ◇ अध्यक्षः - as the supreme authority; from the eye and axis above ◇ परमे - supreme, distancing and mutating ◇ व्योमन् - atmosphere ◇ सो - getting destroyed ◇ अङ्ग - as parts ◇ वेद - and properties ◇ यदि - from which ◇ वा - moved ◇ न - as ◇ वेद - property]

Thus, though got discharged, progressed and so got manifested and existed in the atmosphere in many ways, not only that, though got created in many ways, not only that, though came as what so ever, those came only from the eye and axis above and got distanced through the supreme atmosphere as the parts that got destroyed and as those born of new properties and from that moved further as still new ones and still new properties. Thus manifold creations manifested and progressed in many ways and with many properties that went on changing.

From a place and space of unknown properties and unknown whereabouts, came the universe was but well known. However, it was not known what all ways it manifested and what all properties it brought about. It was not known into what all properties these themselves later got modified. But it was well known that all progress took place from a position above to the surroundings and downwards at all times. It was not known, from what entity this original creation had occurred, what its contents were, or what those were not, or who was the overlord of that supreme space that came into existence or of what properties those parts came into existence. It could not be said what was the nature and property of the original matter that underwent all these transformations and growth. It could not be stated what it originally contained or whether it contained anything at all. It could not be said what was the property of the supreme and primordial space or was it of any property at all. The concept of the eternal food was mentioned in the second verse but perhaps there was no matching descriptions to carry the idea forward. The subject of growth was only as a take off from the first speck of matter. However, the idea of the *annabhāva* could be identified to exist subcutaneously to the described main events and processes. In fact it would be found essentially present in some of the processes in spite of the ferocious nature of the processes imagined. The significance of the sound and the cosmic vibrations and its varying intensities were presented both as the cause and effect that got extended substantially till the very end.

The *nāsadīyasūkta* basically put forth a theory which introduced an all powerful *Agni* at the very beginning of the growth of the universe, i.e., For the growth from a tiny speck of matter to its immense size. The value and nature of this *Agni* was equated to the total value of all that happened later and yet instantaneously, both in terms of matter, mass, as well as all the energy forms. The *Agni* presented was of such horrendous values and totally capable of creation in the very beginning and then carry it forward to conclude as the immense later form of the universe. This hymn did not rely on the concepts of *Puruṣa* and *Śakti* or the concept of the eternal food and the *annabhāva*, in a conspicuous manner. Therefore, this also did not resort to the common birth and dissolution concept that was visible in the *puruṣasūkta*. However, as it could be the case with many hymns, the theory did not totally discount other concepts such as the growth on the basis of a food principle etc. For example, it passingly mentioned about the bird *Suparṇa* and its flight from the heaven. The text reflected wonderment, awe and looked at the profound nature of occurrences and at the premises from which these came. It acknowledged the inexplicable nature of some aspects of the birth of this universe and yet went on putting forward a strong theory, the content of which almost got repeated by the modern science, though acquired by their own separate sets of means and conclusions. There was a unique philosophical vein in the text, which had attracted many for a long time.

Though from the beginning of this hymn statements came about a state of non-existence, it is doubtful that such a state was an acceptable notion that appeared in the other segments of the *ṛgveda*. It was always found stated as from a state of existence to other states of existence and the heavens that manifested from the heaven etc. Therefore, it would be more proper to divide the *pada* as " *na - ā - sad - āsīd*" and stick to the theory of the many existences that came from an inexplicable first existence. And yet it was interpreted as non-existence for the reason that the notion went well with the ambiance of the hymn. Therefore, the meaning that should be really got into should be the very inexplicable nature of the primordial matter and nothing more. Also, it should not be taken that the *asadāvastha* simply as non-existence.

RV 10.130

[(7) सप्तर्चस्यास्य सूक्तस्य प्रजापत्यो यज्ञ ऋषि। भाववृत्तं देवता। (1) प्रथमर्चो जगति (2-7) द्वितीयादिषण्णाञ्च त्रिष्टुप् छन्दसी।]

RV10.130.01 यो यज्ञो विश्वतस्तन्तुभिस्तत एकशतं देवकर्मेभिरायतः। इमे वयन्ति पितरो य आययुः प्र वयाप वयेत्यासते तते॥

[यो - By whatever ◇ यज्ञो - *yajñas* ◇ विश्वत - reached everywhere ◇ तन्तुभि - as if a string and ◇ तत - as those from those ◇ एकशतं - from one by a hundred ◇ देव - divine; heaven ◇ कर्मेभि - action and thus ◇ रायत - regally gifted as those ◇ इमे - thus ◇ वयन्ति - moved to the proximity ◇ पितरो - swelled quickly; spokes of wheel ◇ य - and ◇ आय - reached ◇ युः - got separated ◇ प्र - to the surroundings ◇ वय - interwoven ◇ अप - to below; away ◇ वय - as a body ◇ इति - etc. ◇ आ - manifested ◇ सते - from the *Sat* ◇ तते - as those and further from those]

What all manifested to become the body of the universe by the *yajñas* that reached everywhere came manifested from the *Sat*. A string of *yajñas* took place and objects came repeatedly from the earlier ones, as from one by a hundred times of those that came from the many heavens. A regal action of gifting progressed to the proximity, quickly swelling, reaching everywhere, getting separated and yet standing like a woven net.

By whatever *yajña* the universe came, those came well connected to reach everywhere in the universe getting repeated a hundred times from the one that stood earlier. Those entities came to the surrounding and stood as a woven net, repeatedly manifesting as those that came from those, moving to great distances and to below. From a point of origin, in whatever form of *yajña* that the universe came, it came till the end of the universe as descended from the earlier ones. It came as the heavens that came from the heaven as the paths of creation and objects thereof and as those that got issued out of such heavens. Setting off distances to one another and descending to the surroundings and yet woven well together, the universe grew to its enormous size. Out of unknown *yajñas* that took place at the heaven, near the point of origin, matter flowed to the proximity to become the body of the universe, with parts interconnected and loosing lustre as they progressively moved away. It was stated that the universe became less bright and more cold in the outer regions.

The term "*ekaśataṃ*" that appeared in this verse, could cause some confusion for two reasons. One, that the Monier-Williams dictionary returns a meaning of 101. The other is that in the *Baudhāyana* and in the *kātyāyana Śulbasūtraṃs*, the sizing of of the *uttaravedi citi* got stated as 21 sizes commencing from 7.5 sq. *puruṣaṃ* and ending in the size of 101. This matter is not getting brought into the meanings of the verse.[1]

RV10.130.02 पुमाँ एनं तनुत उत्कृणत्ति पुमान् वि तत्ने
अधि नाके अस्मिन्। इमे मयूखा उप सेदुरू सदः
सामानि चक्रुस्तसराण्योतवे॥

[पुमाँ - crushed and moved ◇ एनं - thus ◇ तनुत - reduced to a small size ◇ उत् - sprang out ◇ कृण - created from that which stood at a height ◇ अत्ति - moving constantly as those ◇ पु - purified ◇ मान् - breathed out from the self ◇ वि - divided ◇ तत्ने - from that which stood like a Sun ◇ अधि - above ◇ नाके - as heavens ◇ अस्मिन् - and parts ◇ इमे - thus ◇ मयूखा - as the rays that smote ◇ उप - downward ◇ सेदरू - along with getting broadened ◇ सदः - occupying ◇ सामानि - as those equally ◇ चक्रु - as a wheel; cyclically ◇ तस् - fading away ◇ अरण्य - along the spokes ◇ ओत - interwoven ◇ वे - as a web]

The universe came from a divine knowledge that stood above. From that which remained there, upon getting crushed, made into a small size and purified, the entities sprang out as the parts of the universe that got breathed out of the heav-

---

[1] As the author have acquired a different geometrical concept in connection with the term "*pañcāśata*" (105) found mentioned in more than one place in the *Ṛgveda*.

ens and those constantly moved away. From that which stood like a Sun, the rays smote downward and away. The paths got broadened and also got emaciated while distanced. The universe stood like a wheel with hubs and stood interwoven like a spider's web.

The universe came into existence, from what stood in the high heaven upon minutely minced, divided into small parts and got purified. Many heavens manifested interwoven and maintaining a hierarchical order. The *vyāhṛtis* shot out from the centre as the rays smote downward. The paths of creation flowed down as the thick paths that went on emaciating. From those heaps, everything moved equally and interwoven as if along the spokes of a wheel. The *yajñas* took place using the body of the *Puruṣa* and the heavens came down, the paths of creation got formed and the objects of the universe that came descended spread to the surroundings.

It was only well connected to that place above, the heaven, that the first of *yajña* of the *Puruṣa* ever took place. This occurred in equal measures and in all directions. The accumulation of masses had mountainous nature which extended into all directions. At the same time the paths of flow from the heaven were as if through the spokes of the chariot wheel. The different objects and energies of the universe was thus born out of oblation of the *Puruṣa*, upon getting minutely minced. The comparison to the wheel and spokes imply an equitable distribution into all directions while proceeding away from the centre. Further it suggested reduction in the interplay of forces, while distances were traversed. Above all it also meant that the universe was spherical or nearly so. If the universe was sectioned through the centre, or if any particular expansion is viewed at, it looked like a *rathacakra*. The presentations hitherto described the process of creation of the universe and the phenomena as occurred in three stages. First, the instant origin from a central point near heaven; next the formation of further solid objects and loss of heat; and then those of the creation by evolutionary processes that occurred.

RV10.130.03 कासीत्प्रमा प्रतिमा किं निदानमाज्यं किमासीत् परिधिः क आसीत्। छन्दः किमासीत्प्रौगं किमुक्थं यद्देवा देवमयजन्त विश्वे॥

[कासीत् - from what came into existence ◇ प्रमा - metred out to the surroundings ◇ प्रतिमा - as a symbol ◇ किं - what; how ◇ निदानम् - based on ◇ आज्यं - curdled ◇ किम् - what; how ◇ आसीत् - came into existence ◇ परिधिः - limits ◇ क - from whom; which; what ◇ आसीत् - came into existence ◇ छन्दः - the metrical measures ◇ किम् - from where ◇ आसीत् - came into existence ◇ प्रौगं - as a group that stood around ◇ किम् - which ◇ उक्थं - as the divine words ◇ यद् - somehow ◇ देवा - as the heavens ◇ देवम् - from the heaven ◇ अयजन्त - till the end of all oblations ◇ विश्वे - reaching everywhere]

From what came the universe into existence, as an arrangement that directly got metered out to the surroundings? What as symbol, based on what, with what as it's limits it came into existence? From where and in which precise measures it stood as a group to the surroundings? Which divine words guided this creation and the evolutionary cycles that came into existence as if curdled milk? Which all heavens moved from which all heavens till the ends where all the *yajña* had ended and resulted in the universe that reached everywhere?

Where and based on what the universe stood was not known. It was not known whether a model existed earlier based on which the universe could be built. The size of the universe was also not known other than that it was enormously large. Which were the group configurations in which the objects stood was also not clear. How many heavens came from the earlier heavens, though from each of which separate paths of creation took off, was also not known. It was but known that the universe expanded to such an extent and stood with such limits that there by the end of all, the *yajña* of high orders had totally ended.

From where the *chandas* came, from which the *praugam* came, in which god's veneration, all the *yajña* from the heaven till the end were carried out resulting in those that reached everywhere? What all were the measures that existed, what was the model available and what were the considerations of size before the universe was created? Though the universe was born out of the *yajña* of the gods, from the heaven till the end, to whom should be allotted the very reason that came and of what sense of proportion, stages and triangular nature of expansion (with the apex at points in the heaven) that the universe was conceived, were not known. The reference to the *chandas* was recalling the metrical configuration of $3 \times 7 = 21$ by which the 7 *vyāhṛtis* were reconfigured.

It was these spectacular cosmic events that the later *vaidikayajñas* adopted as specific sets of geometrical configurations. The term "*praugam*" used here would be seen referred to as the triangular forepart of the chariot. According to the *Baudhāyana śulbasūtra*, the *uttaravedi* originally was of similar trapezoidal and triangular shapes, facing east. But more relevantly and to the context, the universe only came into existence methodically and as a divine occurrence.

RV10.130.04 अग्नेर्गायत्र्यभवत् सयुग्वोष्णिहया सविता सं बभूव।
अनुष्टुभा सोम उक्थैर्महस्वान् बृहस्पतेर्बृहती वाचमावत्॥

[अग्नेर्गायत्रि - as the *Agni* and *gāyatri* ◇ अभवत् - till a non - existence ◇ सयुग्व - in companionship ◇ उष्णि - burning ◇ हया - distanced and progressed ◇ सविता - and coming spread ◇ संबभूव - born and assembled in the atmosphere ◇ अनुष्टुभा - manifested with the praises ◇ सोम - the *Soma* ◇ उक्थैर्महस्वान् - as the words of praise that mightily moved ◇ बृहस्पतेः - greatly descended ◇ बृहती - became immense ◇ वाचम् - with words ◇ आवत् - that moved to the proximity]

With the *Agni* and burning along with the *gāyatri*, the creation progressed and distanced till the end where nothing existed, objects spreading and getting assembled in the atmosphere. The divine words of praises originally manifested and the *Soma*, mightily moved and greatly descended to become this immense universe. Thus the universe only came from the divine words that came to the proximity.

What all manifested with the *Agni* and the *gāyatri*, was found led and enjoined with the divine *Savita*, and those were born by the oblations of the *Soma*, and all came along with the divine praises that came to the proximity, descended steeply and became this enormous universe. The questions were that, from where, by whom and how the universe came into existence. It was with the *Savita*, that divine intellect that shined as everywhere, it was with the divine sounds and cosmic vibrations characterised by the *gāyatri*, it was with the divine prayers and hymns and it was with the division of the *Soma* and its flowing down as the paths of creation that the universe came into existence: It came down as the oblations and it grew from a size to a larger size. Those were divine occurrences and at the same time physical phenomena all the way down. And thus the manifestation of the universe could not be said to have occurred from anything singular and in any single way. It manifested as space, time and temperature and it came in several stages. It came from heavens that came from heavens.

The fire that manifested first came from or along with the *gāyatri* and along with it the space and time were also born. Those born out of these and as a consequence of a great disturbance in the *Soma*, proceeded to the proximity and lower spaces and got greatly enlarged to become this immense universe. The very motive forces for the downward journey and expansion of the universe were refreshed and replenished by the sound or the cosmic vibrations of appropriate later values. Thus it was that all were born from the divine words that were uttered.

Perhaps it was explicitly meant here that the *Agni* was born out of the *gāyatri* appearing as the sounds and vibrations that manifested. It should be assumed that the *gāyatri*, in a way, represented the fundamental cosmic vibrations and that such a phenomenon was essential for the creative process to commence. This presupposed that the temperature, space and time were simultaneously born, for which the phenomenal reason was the original cosmic vibrations that manifested as the divine words uttered. This identified the vibrations as existing in the temperature, space and time as inseparable components of a wholesome existence. The plethora of complexities packed into the Vedic verses touched astonishing levels. In the term "*gāyatri*" itself a clear geometry and 3 dimensional space was visible. Thus geometry is well ingrained into the very thoughts and expressions, as this volume would amply demonstrate.

RV10.130.05 विराणिमत्रावरुणयोरभिश्रीरिन्द्रस्य त्रिष्टुबिह भागो अह्नः। विश्वान् देवाञ्जगत्या विवेश तेन चाक्लृप्र ऋषयो मनुष्या॥

[विराणिमत्रा - issued out as minutely divided ◇ वरुण - by *Varuṇa* ◇ यो - somehow ◇ अभिश्रीः - to spread ◇ इन्द्रस्य - from the *indrata* ◇ त्रिष्टुब् - metrically ◇ इह - till here ◇ भागो - as parts ◇ अह्नः - instantly ◇ विश्वान् - breathed out to reach everywhere ◇ देव - from the heaven ◇ अञ्ज - swirling ◇ गति - moved ◇ आ - having come ◇ विवेश - divided, entered and settled ◇ तेन - from there ◇ च - and ◇ अक्लृप् - unspecified ◇ र - issued out ◇ ऋषयो - flowed somehow ◇ मनुष्या - reaching till man]

The universe was brought into manifestation by *Varuṇa* upon minutely mincing whatever existed in the heaven and then everything flowed in many ways till man. Matter moved many ways spread from the *indrata*, as the parts that instantly and metrically reached here and everywhere. Breathed out and swirled out from the heaven, those moved getting much divided, entered into positions, settled there and then issued out in unspecified manners.

By dividing the *Soma* minutely and spreading to the proximity and only upon the appearance of shining particles of matter and energy, that the universe manifested. Along with the sounds and vibrations that came as roars and travelling along the roaring waves, the universe expanded. Cut to parts like *triṣṭubh*, the universe got swirled out and got led from the heaven, as ordained by a Supreme Divinity. Matter was distributed with a roaring sound or in other words with a widespread effect of the same original vibrations which not only moved the objects, but also manifested as temperature in the objects. A process of systematic decimation and division of the division was effected by the same cosmic vibrations. The growth of the universe was by such multiple divisions ending up in its immense later size, and all such efforts were guided by a supreme spirit. The use of the term "*triṣṭubh*"[2] referred to the multiple metrical divisions.

Out of a primordial sound and the cosmic vibrations and with a waveform propagation through the atmosphere that extended till this earth and beyond, the universe took its form and shape. As swirled out of the heavens, and as moved over the roaring waves, the propagation of the products of the *yajña* was possibly not rectilinear in nature. Such terms as direct, only denoted the tendencies that appeared from time to time.

RV10.130.06 चाकॢप्रे तेन ऋषयो मनुष्या यज्ञे जाते पितरो नः पुराणे। पश्यन् मन्ये मनसा चक्षसा तान् य इमं यज्ञमयजन्त पूर्वे॥
[च - and ◇ अकॢप् - as disordered ◇ रे - issued out ◇ तेन - from those ◇ ऋष - flowed ◇ यो - moved many ways ◇ मनुष्या - came till man ◇ यज्ञे - as *yajñas* ◇ जाते - as those born ◇ पितरो - swelling and fording from the paternity's ◇ नः - that ◇ पुराणे - existed earlier ◇ पश्यन् - as the visibilities ◇ मन्ये - considered as ◇ मनसा - from the mind ◇ चक्षस - from the eye ◇ आ - having come ◇ तान् - breathed out from those ◇ य - and ◇ इमं - thus ◇ यज्ञम् - as *yajña* ◇ अयजन्त - till the ends without oblations ◇ पूर्वे - from the earlier]

What came as disordered(in unspecified manner), flowed and issued out in many ways till man. Those manifested out of the *yajñas* as born, forded away and swelled from the

[2]Notice the odd and even numbers of 4 and 11 as well as fractions of 1/3 etc.

paternity's that existed earlier. Those visibilities came in principle from the minds and from the eyes and as breathed out from the earlier. Thus all came out of the *yajñas* till the very end whereby, all the oblations had ceased.

From the heaven that stood near the *Viśvacakṣus*, the creation commenced as *yajñas* which stationed many objects to the surroundings and to below. From what manifested first, by an apparent disorder and upheaval and due to the swirling action, swelled out and new things came born from the earlier ones. These became the visible objects of the universe that came from the *yajña* of the gods. They moved from the epicentres of the corresponding events, which centres acted as the minds and the eyes that saw all and till the very end. Thus all were born only from whatever existed earlier. There were repetitions of the same process to the surroundings and downward as several flows, one of which reached man and this earth. There were several repeated appearances of those centres of power everywhere. There were several *yajñas* that took place and by the time the universe was fully expanded. By the end of it all the *yajñas* had totally ceased.

Our not so ancient forefathers saw, meditated and found that the universe that flowed and culminated in man was originated as *yajñas* commencing from a focal point of an eye, and from a divine mind, just as the *yajñas* that had occurred earlier (possibly referring to an earlier *kalpa*). It was only later that our not so ancient forefathers, realising the significance of that original series of *yajñas* which culminated in the creation of everything till man conceptualized the *yajñas* of their times. These were given a representative character of what earlier happened.

RV10.130.07 सहस्तोमाः सहछन्दस आवृतः सहप्रमा ऋषयः सप्त दैव्याः। पूर्वेषां पन्थामनुदृश्य धीरा अन्वालेभिरे रथ्यो३ न रश्मीन्॥

[सहस्तोमा - with powerful praises manifested ◇ सहछन्दस - in powerful metrical measures ◇ आवृतः - encompassed ◇ सहप्रमा - in mighty dimensions and measures ◇ ऋषय - moved as flowing

◇ सप्त - as the 7 ◇ दैव्याः - divine sets ◇ पूर्व - from the earlier ◇ एषां - moved as if hastening ◇ पन्थाम् - as the paths ◇ अनुदृश्य - associated visibilities ◇ धी - from an intellect ◇ रा - issued out ◇ अन्वालभिरे - taken in hand and moved ◇ रथ्यो - a chariot ◇ न - as ◇ रश्मिन् - and rays that smote]

With the powerful chanting of the hymns, encompassed by the *chandas*, with appropriate and mighty dimensions and measures, the seven divine ones smote like rays. From the earlier ones, the paths of creation flowed along with the associated visibility that manifested, courageously progressing like a chariot and as if taken in hand by many divinities.

With the divine sounds and cosmic vibrations, with the well defined stages of creation and in appropriate dimensions and measures, the seven *vyāhṛtis* took off from the earlier, with the paths of creation flowing and the visible objects getting showered from these paths. The seven divine definitions which were dictated by the *chandas* and the 7 × 3 configuration came into existence. Upon getting broadcast from the focal point, the paths of creation spread. Those had their beginning from the heaven with a locus on the *Viśvacakṣus*. These progressed as a chariot would progress and were cast all around as the rays of the Sun. These formations also looked like a chariot wheel with spokes. Thus, what existed in the heaven near the centre got transformed into the later complex universe, having progressed through defined routes. The comparison to the *rathacakra* was also to impress upon the integrity of the universe as a system and to represent the progress of matter in many directions. It was also stated that the whole of creations were watched from the epicentre or in other words there was a divine order in what came from the initial chaos.

RV 10.154

[(5) पञ्चर्चस्यास्य सूक्तस्य वैवस्वति यमि ऋषिका। भाववृत्तं देवता। अनुष्टुप् छन्दः]

RV10.154.01 सोम एकेभ्यः पवते घृतमेक उपासते।
येभ्यो मधु प्रधावति ताँश्चिदेवापि गच्छतात्॥

[सोम - the *Soma* ◇ एकेभ्यः - from that one only ◇ पवते - those purified ◇ घृतमेक - sprinkled from one ◇ उपासते - as those seated ◇ येभ्य - from which ◇ मधु - sweetness ◇ प्रधावति - greatly rushed out ◇ ताँश्चिद् - reckoned as those that ◇ एव - only ◇ अपि - to the proximity ◇ गच्छतात् - obtained as moved]

Only from the *Soma* and that singular One, those got sprinkled, got seated and a sweetness also greatly gushed out, from which the universe manifested from those went on moving to the proximity; so it was reckoned.

The universe came from the *Soma*, the seed substance and the source of all. It got enlarged as if by a wind, scattering objects to the surroundings and from those issued further to the surroundings. It was a progress that gradually emaciated to the respective proximity until the very end. The *Soma* acted as the seed substance as well as the very intoxicant, sweet as honey for this exciting process of creation. The growth of the universe had the intoxicated mix of abandon and desire in the beginning. What were so obtained were broadcast from the heaven to the surroundings and became a stable existence by instant growths to the respective proximity and to the surroundings.

RV10.154.02 तपसा ये अनाधृष्यास्तपसा ये स्वर्ययुः।
तपो ये चक्रिरे महस्ताँश्चिदेवापि गच्छतात्॥

[तपसा - from a heat ◇ ये - those ◇ अनाधृष्य - invincible ◇ तपसा - hotness ◇ ये - those ◇ स्वर्य - resounding ◇ युः - driven away ◇ तपो - from heat ◇ ये - those ◇ चक्रिरे - cyclically manifested ◇ महस्ताँश्चिद् - from those became great it was reckoned ◇ एव - only ◇ अपि - to the proximity ◇ गच्छतात् - obtained as moved]

Those that came from heat, i.e, out of an invincible hotness, those that came from a roaring, resounding hotness, those that came from the heat that cyclically manifested and from those became great by moving to the proximity; so it was reckoned.

All the objects and energy of the universe came as a consequence of the appearance of a spark of heat into the *Soma*. An invincible hotness had suddenly appeared. Then there were waves and waves of this heat and their cyclic repetitions. This heat later appeared in appropriate measures and gradually emaciated, just as the universe did. Just as stated in the *nāsadīyasūkta*, here also an intensive heat was envisaged which was not only enormous but also roaring, resurgent and repeating. This heat was declared as the energy and motive force behind all creation, enjoining with the *nāsadīyasūkta*. However, certain concepts of the *puruṣasūkta* were also taken in, as it was stated that it re-surged and repeated. Something similar to the term of "*saśanānaśane*" was found necessary which would enable and sustain such growth. At the same time, this could also be a statement of growth and propagation in the wave form. However, several singularities had formed on the periphery of the heaven and several paths had simultaneously taken off. Thus the universe that emerged was of enormous size and of great might.

RV10.154.03 ये युध्यन्ते प्रधनेषु शूरासो ये तनूत्यजः।
ये वा सहस्रदक्षिणास्ताँश्चिदेवापि गच्छतात्॥

[ये - those ◇ युध्यन्ते - struggle, turmoil and restraint ◇ प्रधनेषु - bountiful deliveries to the surroundings ◇ शूरासो - courageously ◇ ये - those ◇ तनू - body parts ◇ त्यजः - abandoned ◇ ये - those ◇ वा - movements ◇ सहस्र - a 1000 ◇ दक्षिण - clever ways ◇ अस्ताँश्चिद् - flung away as emaciated ◇ एव - only ◇ अपि - to the proximity ◇ गच्छतात् - obtained as moved]

Those that came from many struggles and turmoils that occurred till the end, with bountiful deliveries to the surroundings, with several parts of the body coming courageously moved or got abandoned and flung away; though this way the universe came, a thousand clever manifestations took place and all came emaciated while moved to the proximity.

The growth of the universe took place as several sets of different configurations. All were as a result of sequences of turmoil and struggle, that appeared till the very end. In one way, the heat aggregated to a larger forms, then objects also became smaller, as well as objects lost heat. In another way, the intense heat was retained by some. In yet another way, a process of emaciation only took place. Thus there were a 1000 ways in which these transformation took place. Significantly, though the universe came with whatever as its contents, those thinned out, emaciated as it expanded.

RV10.154.04 ये चित्पूर्व ऋतसाप ऋतावान ऋतावृधः।
पितृन्तपस्वतो यम ताँश्चिदेवापि गच्छतात्॥

[ये - those that ◇ चित् - from a heap; mind ◇ पूर्व - from the earlier ◇ ऋतसाप - as per rules came to the proximity ◇ ऋतावान - breathed out downward as per rules ◇ वृधः - enlarged ◇ पित् - swelled ◇ ऋृन् - continued to move inheriting ◇ तपस्वत् - temperature ◇ यम - as per the rules ◇ ताँश्चिद् - emaciated ◇ एव - only ◇ अपि - to the proximity ◇ गच्छतात् - obtained as moved]

Those that came from a heap that existed earlier, descended according to rules, moved to the proximity according to rules, had expanded and enlarged according to the rules. Though progressed inheriting heat and temperature, they all manifested only by emaciating to the successive proximity and manifesting as whatever obtained.

Into whatever that earlier existed as a heap, heat manifested, got afflicted and distressed, got blown up, got enlarged containing brilliant objects had also became those that lost such heat. It was a progress marked by the laws of creation. It was a progress of the offspring that came from a paternity, of those that got generated and this process repeated several times. All came into existence due to the multiple manifestations of the heat and temperature in appropriate measures occurring at appropriate levels. Simultaneously, brightness and darkness issued forth which stood near to one another. So there were objects that were distressed or reduced in essence; there were objects totally unaffected and which did not reconfigure further. Typically these were hot or cold and came promiscuous or not; they had come just as occurred. There were thus destruction, loss or gain of heat and their many configurations. As the bright paths of creation formed, the darkness indeed stood beside.

Referring the term as the "heap" and as the one that tapered upwards like a conic section would also be appropriate with the overall geometry of the universe. For this original heap stood with the apex not gracing the epicentre and the base remaining in the heaven. The limits of the heaven, often referred as the *Viśvatomukha* and the *hiraṇyagarbha* was just a small radial distance wide from the epicentre. Further it would be found stated that it was only by squeezing out the honey from the *Soma* that it flowed down by such terms as - "*tad grāvāṇa: soma sutomayobhuva ..*"[3] - suggesting an original heap. This heap pictured as a triangle would be swept around, not only into a conic section, but also with reference to the very epicentre of the universe to form a complex 3 dimensionality. It was from this, the objects of the universe took off as several flows that came in many directions.

RV10.154.05 सहस्रणीथाः कवयो ये गोपायन्ति सूर्यम्।
ऋषीन् तपस्वतो यम तपोजाँ अपि गच्छतात्॥

[सहस्रणीथा - as positioned in 1000 ◇ कवयो - getting reduced ◇ ये - as those ◇ गोप - protected ◇ अयन्ति - pervading to the proximity ◇ सूर्यम् - as Sun like ◇ ऋषीन् - strong flows ◇ तपस्वतो - with temperature and heat ◇ यम - as per rules ◇ तपोजाँ - as born from heat ◇ अपि - to the proximity ◇ गच्छतात् - obtained as moved]

Positioned in thousands as the ones that went on reduc-

[3]See RV1.89 and chapter 7.

ing, those that somehow pervaded as protected and those that shined to the proximity like a Sun, the ones that flowed with temperature and heat and in this way all got manifested. Those came born and moved according to the rules and those came out of the heats that moved along with creation. Those were obtained as the ones that came to the proximity.

The universe gradually depreciated towards the end in a 1000 ways. Some shined like the Sun and the others lost all heat and brightness. From some the heat flowed out while some others gained heat. All of these obeyed the rules of creation. In spite of the different states into which the objects became, apparently the total of the heat in the system of the universe could be assumed as stated to be a constant; though the theory of the resurgent repetitions could not be set aside. This summary explanation reiterated the 1000 diverse ways in which the transformation and the growth of the universe took place. The very source of energy for this process of creation was a temperature that first manifested in the *Soma* and which grew in a roaring and resurgent fashion to become great upheavals that carried the hot masses far and beyond. All these happened with the help of the divine sounds; the cosmic vibrations that arose as per the divine rules. One aspect that was perhaps unique in this hymn would be that except for the word "protected" no divinity as such was brought into the narrative. The term "protected" could also be more than the divine protection and could mean to be the configuration of regimes of individuality.

RV 10.190

[(3) तृचस्यास्य सूक्तस्य माधुच्छन्दसोऽघमर्षण ऋषिः। भाववृत्तं देवता। अनुष्टुप् छन्दः]

RV10.190.01 ऋतं च सत्यं चाभीद्धात्तपसोऽध्यजायत।
ततो रात्र्यजायत ततः समुद्रो अर्णवः॥

[ऋतं - by the divine laws ◇ च - and ◇ सत्यं - from Truth ◇ च -

and ◇ अभि - forward ◇ इद् - only as ◇ ध - positioned ◇ अत् - moved ◇ तपसो - with temperature ◇ अधि - from above ◇ अज - till nothing born ◇ अयत - progressing ◇ ततो - as those from those ◇ रात्रि - as the night ◇ अज - till nothing born ◇ अयत - progressing ◇ ततः - as those from those ◇ समुद्रो - the ocean ◇ अर्णवः - and the waves of agitation]

Out of divine laws and Truth came the universe. It came only by moving forward and getting positioned by heat and temperature. It was by births and movements from high positions that the universe came manifested. It progressed as those that came from those, till nothing further was born. It progressed as the night (darkness) till the end, where nothing was further born. It came moved along the (cosmic) ocean and the waves of agitation that manifested into it.

The manifestation of the universe was a simultaneous occurrence of many things. From what truly existed in the heaven, from that high and exalted position, upon the manifestation of a heat, the objects of the universe were born and moved. From those that came first, more came to the surroundings and so it repeated till nothing was further born. Along with the paths of creation, a darkness also came till the end. As waves of agitation spread through the atmosphere, the creation progressed to great distances. It was by a divine law that Truth and from Truth everything of the universe manifested. Thus all things came out of *Satya* and from heaven. What was originally *Sat* which along with a divine will and the cause manifested as the universe. From those that were not visible, the very visible existence, the *Satya*, the very first of all *saguṇa* entities, manifested. Only from that, the *Satya*, the growth of the universe could take off. The immense heat came first and it produced the light and darkness spreading across the cosmic ocean and from the great agitations that occurred in it, the entities came moved to distant locations.

The *Agni* as heat and in total equivalence of all that happened later was indeed envisaged here. This verse put forth another important aspect of creation and propagation of matter. The cosmic ocean and the waves in it could be termed as a statement of the fact that such immense motive forces that flung the objects of the universe to great distances could not be invested on to a point or a rectilinear movement. But would require a waveform propagation for several reasons. It would not be possible to strictly effect a directional propagation, unless a waveform was present. The turmoil and distress that was referred to therefore, meant more than a distress but amounted to the generation of appropriate propagation forces of whatever physical forms it would take, to move along a spherical shape. These were described as the waves in the cosmic ocean.

As yet another meaning; by a divine law and from the *Sat*, the Sun above, the light, the darkness, the ocean and its waves manifested progressively. This way the subject presented became matters of this solar system.

RV10.190.02 समुद्रादर्णवादधि संवत्सरो अजायत।
अहोरात्राणि विदधद्विश्वस्य मिषतो वशी॥

[समुद्राद् - in the ocean ◇ अर्णवा - moved as the waves of turmoil ◇ दधि - as curdled; evolved ◇ संवत्सरो - the years ◇ अजा - till nothing born ◇ यत - progressing ◇ अहोरात्राणि - as the days and nights ◇ वि - divided ◇ दधद् - got ◇ विश्वस्य - reaching everywhere ◇ मिष - as opposing ◇ त - ones ◇ वशी - and subsets]

The ocean and the waves of agitation and the turmoil that came into it had moved everything. Those got evolved, like the years that would be and progressed till nothing was further born. Those came as divided into two like the days and the nights. Those were blown away, stood as everywhere and thus became an array of opposites and sub-sets.

The universe came into existence by progressing along the waves that came from agitation, till nothing was further born. The paths of creation took off around the heaven as the days and the night (darkness) that stood side by side.

The process got repeated like the seasons of an year. Those repeated as the year that would come after an year. Those creations moved through the atmosphere in wave forms, akin to the waves of the ocean. It brought in time as a factor that occurred in such a beginning which then had manifestations like the year, day, night etc. These were congenial subsets in some instances and the opposites in other cases. The entire universe had such characteristic divisions as into which it became. The days were the flow of matter and energy and the nights were the darkness that surrounded them and those came in several configurations. The cosmic ocean that took off from the heaven became the media in which the wave form propagation took place.

The placid waters of the sea and its agitations, the days, the nights and several objects and phenomena of this earth and the solar system manifested with opposing as well as identical nature. And from the water were born many and into it dissolved many, being the very carrier media of the *annabhāva*.

RV10.190.03 सूर्यचन्द्रमसौ धाता यथापूर्वमकल्पयत्।
दिवं च पृथिवीं चान्तरीक्षमथो स्वः॥

[सूर्य - as the Sun ◇ चन्द्रमसौ - and like the moons ◇ धाता - manifested as positioned and moved ◇ यथा - appropriately ◇ पूर्वम् - from the earlier ◇ अकल्प - till no imaginations ◇ यत् - progressed. ◇ दिवं - as the heavens ◇ च - and ◇ पृथिवीं - the earths and later ◇ च - as ◇ अन्तरिक्षम् - the atmosphere ◇ अथो - like that ◇ स्वः - from the self]

As the moons that came from the Sun, came indeed those into existence, progressing from the earlier ones to be the later ones, progressing appropriately till the end where all imaginations had ended, manifesting as the heavens, the earths and the atmosphere and it was the very self that manifested as the universe.

As matters of this solar system; extending from the heaven to the earth, the Sun, the moon and the atmosphere and several objects were born without any earlier set definitions.

Dark bodies and objects of lesser heat came from objects that shined like the Sun. Manifestation of the Sun-like and moon-like objects of the universe, occurred only as those that came from the earlier ones to become the many later ones. The universe came as the heavens born from the heavens, as the earths that moved and stationed and as the atmosphere that extended till this earth and beyond. It was from the *Soma* that remained dull in the heaven, that the universe came with such brightness. The primary space from which the creation started is termed as the heaven, and the region till afar as the *antarikṣa* (the atmosphere), at the approximate end regions of which objects like this earth remained. Into this enormous space several Sun-like objects were born automatically and without any earlier set definitions. There was no prepared and made ready atmosphere into which the creations could propagate and the very atmosphere till this earth and beyond was created just along with the objects that traversed.

Perhaps one purpose of this *sūkta* was to differentiate between the concepts of *Sat* and *satya* and to impress upon the fact that the creation as a process would require a clear entity to start with. A further realisation was the necessity for an all prevailing media like Aether into which or along which only the objects could manifest and hence the repeated mentioning of the cosmic ocean and the waves of agitation. In fact the description of the "murmur" and "roar" that were made earlier, could be only be sustained with a media to vibrate. The imagined presence of a cosmic ocean with ethereal qualities prevailing or born along with the paths of creation and the objects, the nature of *Soma* etc. appears to be complex subjects and as far as the *Ṛgveda* is concerned, clarifications could be expected to come up from anywhere in the text. The *Soma* was also compared with the water of this earth as comparable and potential sources of creation.⋆⋆⋆

3

Viśvakarmā-The Architect of the Universe

In Book 10 of the *Ṛgveda*, the 81st and 82nd *sūktas* have the invocation title of "*viśvakarmā devatā*", meaning the architect of the universe and the interpretations below would present more theories on the origin of the universe. It is stated that while this approximately spherical universe indeed came into existence, the position of its axis, the material and source there-of is not really known. And yet the nature and many aspects of the universe will be found well brought out by these two hymns.

RV 10.81

[(7) सप्तर्चस्यास्य सूक्तस्य भौवनो विश्वकर्मा ऋषिः। विश्वकर्मा देवता। (1, 3 - 7) प्रथमर्चस्तृतीयादिपञ्चानाञ्च त्रिष्टुप् (2) द्वितीयायाश्च विराड्रूपा त्रिष्टुप् छन्दसी]

RV10.81.01 य इमा विश्वा भुवनानि जुह्वदृषिर्होता न्यसीदत्पिता

नः। स आशिषा द्रविणमिच्छमानः प्रथमच्छदवराँ आ विवेश॥

[य - and ◇ इमा - thus ◇ विश्वा - as reaching everywhere ◇ भुवनानि - as the universe ◇ जुह्वद् - as enflamed ◇ ऋषिः - that flowed ◇ होता - coming out of the oblations ◇ नि - to below ◇ आसीदत् - directly manifesting and moving ◇ पिता - came swelled ◇ नः - as ◇ स - with ◇ आशिषा - came quickly ◇ द्रविणम् - matter ◇ इच्छमानः - in desired measures ◇ प्रथम - from the first ◇ शद - supreme ◇ वराँ - circularity's moved ◇ आ - came ◇ वि - divided ◇ वेश - and settled down]

The universe manifested directly in an en-flamed state flowing out of the oblations that came descending. All manifested directly, reaching everywhere in the universe, speedily moving forward and swelling in the desired measures. Those circularity's moved and descended from the supreme first one that had manifested and then settled down as divided.

The entire universe was born out of *yajñas* that occurred and out of the accompanying oblations, matter getting hurled out to occupy several places as divinely willed. The oblations that started from a closed space ultimately became the wide expanse of the universe. The matter and energy took to various forms and properties as desired. The paths of creation shot out as flames that came from the oblations. The atmosphere stood in a geometric pattern of concentric circularity's, which later got divided and moved equally forward and backward. The presence of a divine mind, the manifestation of a primary space and many phenomena of extreme severity marked the birth of the universe.

RV10.81.02 किं स्विदासीदधिष्ठानमारम्भणं
कतमत्स्वित कथासीत्। यतो भूमिं जनयन्विश्वकर्मा
वि द्यामौर्णोन्महिना विश्वचक्षाः॥

[किं - from which ◇ स्विदासीद् - indeed came ◇ अधिष्ठानम् - as based upon ◇ आरम्भणं - and held to ◇ कतम् - which ◇ अत् - moved ◇ स्वित - welfare ◇ कथ - how; in what manner ◇ आसीत् - came ◇ यतो - supported; controlled ◇ भूमिं - till this earth ◇ जनयन् - upon getting generated ◇ विश्वकर्म - brought into existence as everywhere ◇ वि - divided ◇ द्याम् - coming from heaven ◇ और्ण - covered with a blanket ◇ उन् - into ◇ महिना - came as a greatness ◇ विश्वचक्षसा - manifesting from the *Viśvaçakṣus*]

Based on which and attached to which indeed it came, as the well being that came progressed? In what all manners it came as the generations that were brought into existence to be everywhere and till this earth? Indeed it is known that the actions of divisions and swelling came moved from the heaven and from an en-wrapped state, as if covered with a blanket, to become a greatness that manifested from the *Viśvacakṣus*.

From which base and pillar it directly manifested, which way it came, how it became the universe, how much it grew, in which all directions it swelled, as the offspring descended from the heaven, oriented to the the *Viśvacakṣus* and thus became this great universe? It was only known that the universe came from an enclosure called heaven, which remained near the *Viśvacakṣus*, the very epicentre of the universe to become this immensely large entity. But it was not known from where it came there and also in what manner and to what size it grew from there and in what all directions that growth took place. Thus it was emphasized that there indeed existed a centre of all events that took place and also that matter and energy flowed from the heaven to become this large universe. Ever since, that epicentre keenly viewed everything below. It was not known what all acted as the pillars to which all the subsequent processes were well tied and from which all processes got repeated to become this enormous universe. It somehow became this universe that reached everywhere.

RV10.81.03 विश्वतश्चक्षुरुत विश्वतोमुखो विश्वतोबाहुरुत
विश्वतस्पात्। सं बाहुभ्यां धमति सं पतत्रैर्द्यावाभूमी
जनयन् देव एकः॥

[विश्वतश्चक्षुः - the *Viśvacakṣus* ◇ उत - connected to ◇ विश्वतोमुखो - as the faces of creation that reached everywhere ◇ विश्वतो -

reaching everywhere ◇ बाहुः - as the hands ◇ उत - interwoven ◇ विश्वतस्पात् - descending to everywhere ◇ सं - together ◇ बाहुभ्यां - progressing as the hands ◇ धमति - greatly blown away ◇ सं - simultaneously ◇ पतत्रै - flew, fell as the protections ◇ द्या - from heavens ◇ वा - moved as ◇ भूमी - the earths ◇ जनयन् - getting generated ◇ देव - from the heaven ◇ एकः - and that only one]

Connected to the *Viśvacakṣus* and the first face of creation having manifested, the subsequent faces of creation came into existence. The interwoven hands (paths) simultaneously reached everywhere, descended everywhere to place the heavens, the earths and a protected 3-dimensionality. Thus all descended simultaneously and all were born or got generated from heaven and from that One and only One.

The universe came into existence from an eye and epicenter, next formed the primary space, with hands and paths of creation extending to the end. The paths of creation flowed simultaneously through all these hands, descending equally from the heaven in 3 dimensions to become the heavens and the earths. It became enormous so as to reach this earth and move beyond, as a divine occurrence. The growth of the universe was thus instantaneous from a space very near to this epicentre, matter flowing through all the routes at the same time and until reaching the end. The term "*viśvatomukha*" would denote the primary space where matter formed for the first time and the subsequent similar faces of creation. This space called heaven came from the eye of the universe. It was from here that matter and energy flowed instantaneously with a left-right equilibrium in all directions. All of these were considered as divine occurrences.

This verse differentiated clearly that it was not at the very epicentre of the universe that matter got formed first, but only at a near location, generally called as heaven and often as the *viśvatomukha*, *hiraṇyagarbha*, that golden ear etc. Further the verse sketched out a picture of the universe having grown through several main trunk routes carrying matter and energy, to be sub-divided into thinner hands until the end of a path. All of these occurred simultaneously and maintained an equilibrium of forces, energy and matter.

While the basic geometry of the universe sketched out by many of these verses would be found identical, there would be subtle variations as per the phenomena described. But they were not different theories but would be descriptions as viewed from different angles.

RV10.81.04 किं स्विद्वनं क उ स वृक्ष आस यतो
द्यावापृथिवी निष्टतक्षुः। मनीषिणो मनसा पृच्छतेदु
तद् यदध्यतिष्ठद्भुवनानि धारयन्॥

[किं - from which ◇ स्विद् - indeed ◇ वनं - as the forest ◇ क - who ◇ उ - ordered ◇ स - as ◇ वृक्ष - the tree ◇ आस - to be fetched ◇ यतो - that supported ◇ द्यावापृथिवी - the heavens and the earths ◇ निष्ट - decided to ◇ तक्षुः - cut it ◇ मनीषिणो - intelligently ◇ मनसा - mindfully ◇ पृच् - mixing ◇ शत - a 100 times ◇ इद् - and so ◇ उ - ordered ◇ तद् - that ◇ यद् - somehow ◇ अधि - from above ◇ अतिष्ठद् - as this unstable ◇ भुवनानि - universe ◇ धारयन् - holding all]

From which forest came the tree, who ordered it to be fetched and used, who decided to shape it intelligently and thoughtfully, and who that stood above ordered everything to be mixed a 100 times to manifest as this unstable (pulsating) universe that held all? From which forest indeed came and which tree was used as the axle for those that came from the heaven to this earth with intelligence and application of a divine mind and only as the divine enquiries to become those that somehow came from above and became the universe?

The universe is comparable to a chariot wheel, seen as a cross section passing through the centre. Being so it was not known where and in which space its axle was established and what supported it. What was the nature of this axle or in other words what constituted matter at this very centre. Who fetched it and who supported the universe was not known. In spite of the well established nature of the universe, what it constituted of, from where it came and upon which it stood were unfathomable subjects. It is but known that everything manifested from what stood above to become the many below. It came as the flows of the paths of creation. Further, it could be noticed that only a supreme intelligence could create the universe and protect it this way for ever. It manifested as a divine enquiry and as a divine accomplishment.

From the above it should not be surmised that the Vedic sages thought that the universe rotated on the axis. It would not be possible to find any such notion anywhere in the *Ṛgveda*. Indeed the geometry of the spherical universe would be found confirmed as obtained by simultaneous rotation and expansion of whatever remained at the heaven. But it would be found, later through these narrations, that according to the Vedic sages, that itself was not a simple rotation about an axis.

RV10.81.05 या ते धामानि परमाणि यावमा या मध्यमा
विश्वकर्मन्नुतेमा। शिक्षा सखिभ्यो हविषि स्वधावः
स्वयं यजस्व तन्वं वृधानः॥

[या - what came ◇ ते - their ◇ धामानि - domain ◇ परमाणि - limits and extent ◇ य - what came ◇ अवमा - as the measure of depth ◇ या - what came ◇ मध्यमा - as the middle ◇ विश्वकर्मन् - accomplished everything ◇ उत - interconnected ◇ इमा - thus came ◇ शिक्षा - cleverly manifested ◇ सखिभ्यो - with companions ◇ हविषि - as oblations ◇ स्वधावः - self regulated ◇ स्वयं - self ◇ यजस्व - as the *yajñas* ◇ तन्वं - moved as body parts ◇ वृधानः - to become enlarged]

What came as the domains, what was their limits and extent, what came as the measure of depth, at which all places were their centres, so that everything got accomplished interconnected and spread as everywhere, cleverly manifested and remained with companions? Having come from oblations that manifested well regulated by the self, as the *yajñas* instituted by the self, the parts of the body came moved and this huge enlargement got accomplished.

In the beginning it was not known what enlargement of size would be achieved in a process of oblation and sacrifice of the self in parts. Into which domain it was born, what was its size and extent and where was its centre were also not known. So it was in the later manifestations as well. All the objects were interconnected as if a woven cloth or web. All were carried out with a clear purpose that was born in a divine mind. In spite of the huge enlargements that took place to whatever size, the objects manifested retained their dependency and relationship with one another and remained interactive to their epicentres. Thus it was a totally interactive universe that was born, in spite of being born from unknown properties and in spite of a later unfathomable existence.

This raised some questions as to the very nature of the epicentre. Was it really a unique point? Was it a collective spacial abstraction which then could supply the same properties to the approximate spheroidal nature till the external mantle of the universe? Did it not then make the very distance to the nearby heaven yet another abstract quantity? Did it not provide the concept of space from the very beginning?

RV10.81.06 विश्वकर्मन् हविषा वावृधानः स्वयं यजस्व पृथिवीमुत द्याम्। मुह्यन्त्वन्ये अभितो जनास इहास्माकं मघवा सूरिरस्तु॥

[विश्वकर्मन् - created everywhere ◇ हविषा - as coming from the oblations ◇ वावृधानः - moved and enlarged ◇ स्वयं - as self instituted ◇ यज - *yajñas* ◇ स्व - of the self ◇ पृथिवीम् - as the earths ◇ उत - interconnected ◇ द्याम् - with the heavens ◇ मुह्यन्त्वन्ये - released and controlled as others ◇ अभितो - to the proximity ◇ जनास - as generated ◇ इह - till here ◇ अस्माकं - all the parts ◇ मघवा - gifted bountifully ◇ सूरिः - as excellence ◇ अस्तु - maintained]

Everything as everywhere came created from the oblations, moving and getting enlarged by the *yajñas* instituted by the self. It resulted in the earths standing interwoven, having moved from the many heavens. Many got released from those that have already come into existence, remained under control and became others getting generated to the proximity and till here. Came all as parts of the universe that were gifted bountifully and as the excellence that came into existence. Thus the universe was getting enlarged by the very deeds of *Viśvakarma*.

Everything indeed was accomplished by the self as an immense enlargement and resurrection from what existed earlier and getting regenerated from what earlier contained. This earth and such other objects of the universe all the time retained the interactive nature with its earlier source of existence, position and state. It was again implied that nothing external was used in such growths and that the universe got filled with many an excellence that was liberally gifted.

RV10.81.07 वाचस्पतिं विश्वकर्माणमूतये मनोजुवं
वाजे अद्या हुवेम। स नो विश्वानि हवनानि
जोषद्विश्वशम्भूरवसे साधुकर्मा॥

[वाचस्पतिं - as the words that descended ◇ विश्वकर्माण - accomplished everything ◇ ऊतये - those interconnected ◇ मनोजुवं - with the mind energised ◇ वाजे - inspired ◇ अद्या - in that manner ◇ हुवेम - as called upon to act ◇ स - with ◇ नो - as ◇ विश्वानि - as those that reached everywhere ◇ हवनानि - by set of oblations ◇ जोषद् - delightfully ◇ विश्व - reaching everywhere ◇ शम्भूः - with welfare and happiness ◇ अवसे - without stopping ◇ साधु - directly ◇ कर्मा - acted]

Divine words descended, accomplishing everything and what were created were kept interwoven. With the mind energised and kept inspired, when called upon to act, brought those many that came out of oblations, the goodness and welfare of the universe kept in mind and the creation delightfully reaching everywhere, acting directly and without stopping;

and this way the universe emerged. So it was praised that everything was accomplished by *Vācaspati*, with his good and powerful words.

With the divine words that dropped into the middle of an occurrence, everything got accomplished with an energised and incited divine mind and by the oblations that happily occurred. The *Vācaspati*, the lord of all *mantras* and the supreme accomplisher energised his mind to a level needed for creation and created the universe by oblations, igniting purposefully. Indeed, He understood what were to be achieved while doing so. A supreme mind that existed which knew the very purpose of the universe, selected such processes of oblation in its creation as required. It was also implied that the process of creation and the very origin of the universe required energy and space and that this came as the first set of cosmic vibrations, i.e, the divine sounds that manifested.

According to this *sūkta*, everything originated from *Vācaspati* with his mind kept energised. It was not known from where matter as such manifested near the point of origin and also in what ways and dimensions that it later grew. It was also not known where the first of epicentres remained. But there indeed was an epicentre of all events from which everything came totally interconnected. That immense creation took place as if in a state of intoxication and there indeed was a substance that provided the very essential matter and the very intoxication required for creation.

RV 10.82

[(6) सप्तर्चस्यास्य सूक्तस्य भौवनो विश्वकर्मा ऋषिः। विश्वकर्मा देवता । त्रिष्टुप् छन्दः]

RV10.82.01 चक्षुषः पिता मनसा हि धीरो धृतमेने आजनन्नम्नमाने।
यदेदन्ता अददृहन्त पूर्व आदिद्यावापृथिवी अप्रथेताम्॥

[चक्षुष - from that eye ◇ पिता - came swollen ◇ मनसा - from

the mind ◇ हि - only ◇ धीरो - courageously ◇ धृत - supported ◇ मेने - from energetic bases ◇ आ - coming ◇ जन् - born upon ◇ अन्नम् - the food ◇ न - as ◇ माने - principle ◇ यद् - somehow ◇ इद् - only ◇ अन्ता - coming till the end ◇ अद् - consuming ◇ अदृह् - vacillating; pulsating ◇ अन्ता - ends ◇ पूर्व - from the earlier ◇ आदिद् - coming soaring up ◇ द्यावापृथिवी - as the heavens and earths ◇ अप्रथ् - spreading ◇ एताम् - to the proximity]

Having arisen from an eye (epicentre) and only as swelled from a mind, those got courageously issued out as the arrangements that resolutely came from energetic bases and born on the food principle, everything somehow manifested till those ends which stood pulsating. Duly bound to the earlier and soaring up by a process of consumption became the heavens and earths that manifested, moved and spread to the proximity.

The enlargement of the universe took place only by movement from the epicentres of each growth, just as it happened originally from the *Viśvacakṣus* and the heaven. The presence of a divine mind, resolve and intellect and a progress with the repeated manifestation of the food principle marked the process of creation. It appeared that the progress was watched by a divine paternity that stood above. Thus came the heavens and the earths to the surroundings, repeatedly manifesting from whatever earlier existed. When the enlargement reached the very end limits of the universe, the food principle that hitherto helped in the instantaneous expansion had waned totally. A divine mind and a divine will were thus ever present in the process of creation. The enlargement and spreading from the heaven happened resolutely and in measured ways and yet did not conform to any particular design. A supreme divine will guided all, till the end.

RV10.82.02 विश्वकर्मा विमना आद्विहाया धाता विधाता
परमोत संदृक्। तेषामिष्टानि समिषा मदन्ति
यत्रा सप्तऋषीन् पर एकमाहुः॥

[विश्वकर्मा - created as everywhere ◇ विमना - manifested as

cast down ◇ आद् - having come ◇ विहाया - moving away leaving behind ◇ धाता - having bestowed ◇ वि - divided ◇ धाता - having bestowed ◇ परम - to most distant ◇ उत - interconnected ◇ संदृक् - seen equally ◇ तेषामिष्टानि - moved from those as the desired ◇ सम् - along with ◇ इषा - the semen virile ◇ मदन्ति - in an intoxicated manner ◇ यत्रा - at the same time ◇ सप्त - as the seven ◇ ऋषीन् - flows ◇ पर - that distanced ◇ एकम् - from one ◇ आहु - as divine invocations]

Created as everywhere, having come cast down and moved away leaving much behind, having bestowed to the most distant places interconnected, maintaining equality, only moved as desired from those had the universe come into existence. The flows of the semen virile came to the proximity and the creation progressed in an intoxicated manner. The seven flows that distanced from that only One, manifested out of a series of divine invocations.

The universe was created as reaching everywhere, energetically accruing those that were issued out and kept interwoven till the distant ends, maintaining equality into all directions, getting mixed as desired and moving to the proximity with intoxication. Thus somehow the 7 *vyāhṛtis* came flowing distancing and always coming from that original one that existed as the heaven. The original one thus became the subsequent many. In the process of creation, many things were left behind, while the progress forward was in a measured way. There was cyclic repetitions of what happened earlier. This progress created and positioned the objects to far off distances and also resulted in the formation of the 7 *vyāhṛtis* and a definite geometry of the universe. Objects and many spheres of influence got mixed into one another. This statement also suggested the formation of wide expanses of nothingness in the process. Many remained as such and many got multiplied and divided. Thus the progress and growth only occurred with extremely violent turmoils. The flow of matter and energy in different routes appeared like the rays of the rising Sun. The growth of the universe always maintained an equilibrium and several equivalences.

RV10.82.03 यो नः पिता जनिता यो विधाता धामानि वेद भुवनानि विश्वा। यो देवानां नामधा एक एव तं सम्प्रश्नं भुवना यन्त्यन्या॥

[यो - whichever ◇ नः - as ◇ पिता - came swelled ◇ जनिता - came as those born ◇ यो - whichever ◇ विधाता - got settled ◇ धामानि - taking positions in many places ◇ वेद - as properties ◇ भुवनानि - in the universe ◇ विस्ह्वा - that reached everywhere ◇ यो - whichever ◇ देवा - from the heavens ◇ न - as ◇ अं - moved ◇ नाम - known as ◇ धा - as bestowed ◇ एक - from one ◇ एव - only ◇ तं - emaciated; as those ◇ सप्रश्नम् - pleated like a basket ◇ भुवना - manifesting as the universe ◇ यन्ति - evolved as ◇ अन्या - the others]

Whichever swelled and manifested as came born, whichever got settled in many places, whichever came as the properties of matter that reached everywhere in the universe, as moved from the many heavens, were all known to have manifested from that only One. All of those progressively emaciated, got bestowed and evolved as others and thus became the universe which stood like a pleated basket.

Born and swelled out from whatever existed earlier, as the many properties that reached everywhere, the universe grew by a process of one becoming the other and the one connected to the other. It manifested as the heavens that somehow came from the earlier heavens and stood interactive to one another. It came as brought out by the divinities differently named. From the heaven and from whatever existed there, bright objects moved at steep angles and as swelled to the surroundings, until a state of nothingness. All the diverse objects of the universe came from the first manifested, though they looked different and extended all over the universe till this earth. All were born totally interconnected, protected and aided by a divine presence, extending till the very end and thus becoming this, one and only, incomparable universe.

RV10.82.04 त आयजन्त द्रविणं समस्मा ऋषयः पूर्वे जरितारो न भूना। असूर्ते सूर्ते रजसि निषत्ते ये भूतानि समकृण्वन्निमानि॥

[त - those ◇ आ - came ◇ यजन्त - as the oblations till the end ◇ द्रविणम् - as matter ◇ सम् - along with ◇ अस्मा - the parts ◇ ऋषयः - flowing down ◇ पूर्वे - from the earlier ones ◇ जरितारो - quickly and emaciated ◇ न - as ◇ भूना - the earth forms manifested ◇ असूर्ते - those not bright ◇ सूर्ते - those bright ◇ रजसि - as dust ◇ निषत्ते - that settled ◇ ये - as those ◇ भूतानि - sets born ◇ सम् - equally and simultaneously ◇ अकृण्वन् - moving from their high positions ◇ नि - downwards ◇ मानि - with a metrical sense]

Those that came out of oblations till the end as matter and as the parts that flowed down quickly from the earlier ones, got progressively emaciated. The earths that came as bright, not bright and in dust forms which had got settled along with those that came born had moved from their high positions and had gained downwards with a metrical sense.

From the earlier ones, essential matter flowed equally and swiftly, derived out of *yajña*s which went on emaciating to the ends. The objects that were created were bright, not bright and dusty as they came. The process appeared to be divinely guided, as regards the property and the distances between them. While some of the objects diminished and got scattered when born, the others gained mass and became larger. This statement should be thought to be valid not only to the beginning of the birth of classes of objects but extended to the later developments, going through the formation of the 7 *vyāhṛti*s and as a distribution that came with a clear metrical sense.

RV10.82.05 परो दिवा पर एना पृथिव्या परो देवेभिरसुरैर्यदस्ति।
कं स्विद्गर्भं प्रथमं दध्र आपो यत्र देवाः समपश्यन्त विश्वे॥

[परो - distanced ◇ दिवा - as the heavens ◇ पर - distanced ◇ एना - coming only as ◇ पृथिव्या - the earths ◇ परो - distanced ◇ देवेभिरसुरैर् - as the brightness that smote from the heavens ◇ यदस्ति - somehow existed as ◇ कं - reduced ◇ स्विद् - sweat ◇ गर्भं - as the wombs ◇ प्रथमं - that came first ◇ दध्र - born ◇ आपो - downwards ◇ यत्र - as the many ◇ देवाः - heavens ◇ सम् - that stood together ◇ अपश्यन् - till the end of all visibilities ◇ त - as those ◇ विश्वे - that reached everywhere]

Distanced as the heavens, distanced as mere earths, distanced as the brightness that smote from the heavens and thus in many ways the universe came into existence. Getting reduced, sweat out, as those that came from the many wombs, as those that came from the first born, as the many heavens that moved downwards, as those that stood together till the end of all visibilities and in such ways those reached everywhere in the universe.

The universe got enlarged as the heavens that manifested to distances and as the earths of different brightness that smote to far off places. It grew as those born from the first born, as the heavens and the visibilities that repeatedly manifested. From the bright heaven above to the surrounding and to far away, till the dark earth much far away, many things were born with varying degrees of brightness and varying levels of descent. Many bright and dark objects were so born in a process of reduction, secretion and containment. The objects and substances thus born were receiving equal divine guidance and attentions. The objects born were hot and cold as they came. The process of secretion stated was by derivation and movement of bodies away from the main stream and which did not possess enough energy to get out of an existing system. This in other words described the branched off directions from the main stream directions in such ways that a 3 dimensional fill was achieved. There was a suggestion that the objects that were not hot and bright remained under the sovereignty of the bright ones above and thus several hierarchies got extended till this earth.

RV10.82.06 तमिद्गर्भं प्रथमं दध्र आपो यत्र देवाः समगच्छन्त विश्वे।
अजस्य नाभावध्येकमर्पितं यस्मिन् विश्वानि भुवनानि तस्थुः॥

[तमिद् - only as emaciated ◇ गर्भं - the wombs ◇ प्रथमं - from the first ones ◇ दध्र - bestowed and positioned ◇ आपो - downwards ◇ यत्र - as the many ◇ देवाः - heavens ◇ सम् - that stood together till ◇ अगच्छन्त - the ends where nothing further gained ◇ विश्वे - reaching everywhere ◇ अजस्य - till nothing born ◇ नाभ - from the hub ◇ अवधि - as led from above ◇ एकम् - from the one ◇ अर्पितं - offered ◇ य - what ◇ अस्मिन् - stood as the parts ◇ विश्वानि - that reached everywhere ◇ भुवनानि - in the universe ◇ तस्थुः - got stationed]

Getting bestowed from the wombs to become the first born, emaciating downwards, standing together till the end, where nothing was further gained, many heavens and those that came from the heavens reached everywhere till nothing was further born. They all came as if from a hub, as led from above, as proffered from the ones that stood above and as emaciated from the self to the proximity, so as to reach and get positioned as everywhere in the universe.

From the womb of darkness came the first born, to descend as the many heavens in an equitable distribution that reached everywhere, till nothing was further born. From the navel got divided and separately swelled and in that manner came till everywhere. Those emaciated to the proximity from wherever they stood. A divine originator guided whatever next happened. Several objects were thus born as an equitable distribution that came from the contents of whatever earlier existed. Those things came as much downwards and as bright as divined. Once again the inevitable bond between the objects was declared. The equality mentioned here was almost akin to indifference or abandon on the one hand but also suggested that objects were scattered away in all directions equitably. It was at the womb of darkness around the epicentre that the unmanifested first manifested as a symbolic form of primary matter and energy. Whatever happened was subsequent to this, though came instantly. It stood like a wheel with its spokes commencing from the hub, the hub standing separated from the epicentre. From the navel of the wheel, the spokes uniformly inclined downwards, the rim being situated at a depth, the volume appeared to be a heap and the view from above appeared like a wheel.

RV10.82.07 न तं विदांथ य इमा जजानाऽन्यद्युष्माकमन्तरं बभूव।
निहारेण प्रावृता जल्प्या चाऽसुतृप उक्थशासश्चरन्ति॥

[न - as ◇ तम् - from darkness ◇ विदाथ - divided, bestowed and stood ◇ य - and ◇ इमा - as those manifested ◇ जजान - as born and born again ◇ अन्य - as others ◇ द्युष् - from heaven ◇ मा - arrangements ◇ कम् - that came as desired ◇ अन्तरम् - from inside ◇ बभूव - born and existed ◇ निहारेण - got excreted ◇ प्र - to the surrounding ◇ अवृता - enveloped ◇ जल्प्या - with murmurs ◇ च - and ◇ आ - came (as murmurs) ◇ असुतृप - gained ◇ उक्थ - as praises ◇ शास - restrained, censured ◇ चरन्ति - moving to the proximity]

Manifesting from a darkness as those that came divided, then as those that got born and born again, as the arrangements of others that came from the heavens as desired, moving from the inside to outside of those that stood enveloped, got born and excreted to the surroundings. All came with murmurs and praises, that repeatedly manifested, moving to the proximity with restraint, to become the universe.

Manifesting from what was thought to be a darkness and from that born and getting born again, all of these came from that which came born from the middle and upon the manifestation of a particle of brightness and heat, got broadcast as the circularity's that distanced. These came only with the murmurs that came from within and moved along as the words of praises that came till the end. The first manifestation took place from what stood as an apparent darkness. Several small spots of bright heat manifested into the heaven and those were capable of emitting, proceeding outward and growing into this very large universe. From whatever came born, many were further born and the process of creation continued. At the same time, it created a very large atmosphere which stood as distinct circularity's much distanced from the heaven. It then covered great distances up to the boundless end of the universe guided by a supreme divine spirit.

From the point of origin several flows took place in equal

measures into all directions. The progress of creation of matter was in a measured way out of a highly turbulent state and yet retained mutual relationship between the objects that came born. The seven *vyāhṛtis* were formed as the circular and invisible rays that got shot out from the centre. The objects that were born were bright, dull or dusty as it occurred. Large distances between these objects were developed. From the womb of darkness manifested a small bright entity which became the very seed entity of the universe. Then the heat manifested into that spot of matter out of the cosmic murmurs to make it shine forth and from that the creation proceeded outward. All such processes received a divine guidance till the end. The murmur and sound caused the beginning of a set of agitations, vibrations and at the same time manifestation of the motive force for the waveform propagation. It was not very specifically stated that the first of manifestations occurred at the epicentre, but only that it came from the womb of darkness. Quite adroitly the concept evaded certainty of the point of origin of the first of manifestations. Since the causative epicentre possibly could not contain matter as such, the statement was as if somewhere in the vicinity, which was somewhere in the first of heavens. It should be noted that though some of the descriptions were about one single line of progress, many bright spots had appeared on the periphery of the heaven, and many paths of creation had come descended.

⋆⋆⋆

4

Soma- The Seed-substance

The *Soma*, an ethereal substance came as an essential subject of the *Ṛgveda* and would get identified as the all providing plenum that descended till the end. Other than all of the hymns of *maṇḍala* 9, there are the hymns of RV 1.91, 8.48 and 8.79 that presented the *Soma* as a subject. An ethereal substance covered all the objects of the universe, from the beginning till the end and it contained the seed matter for all creations. An intellect that guided all was latent in the very *Soma* and therefore, it is more than the Ether of the modern science.

RV 1.91

[(23) त्रयोविंशत्यृचस्यास्य सूक्तस्य राहूगणो गोतम ऋषिः। सोमो देवता। (1-4, 18-23) प्रथमादिचतुर्ऋचामष्टादश्यादिषण्णाञ्च त्रिष्टुप् (5-16) पञ्चम्यादिद्वादशानां गायत्री (17) सप्तदश्याश्चोष्णिक् छन्दांसि]

RV1.91.01 त्वां सोम प्र चिकितो मनीषा त्वं रजिष्ठमनु नेषि पन्थाम्। तव प्रणीती पितरो न इन्दो देवेषु रत्नमभजन्त धीराः॥

[त्वां - moved as thyself ◇ सोम - as the *Soma* ◇ प्र - to the surroundings ◇ चिकितो - as willed ◇ मनीषा - and thoughtfully manifested ◇ त्वं - as thyself ◇ रजिष्ठमनु - honestly, directly and along with ◇ नेषि - well guided ◇ पन्थाम् - paths that came ◇ तव - from thee ◇ प्रणीती - guided ◇ पितरो - swelled swiftly ◇ न - as ◇ इन्दो - the shining particle ◇ देवेषु - from the heavens ◇ रत्नम् - as the diamonds ◇ अभजन्त - not detached till the end ◇ धीराः - gifted from an intellect]

Coming from thyself to the surroundings, moving as the *Soma*, thoughtfully and as willed by thyself, manifested directly (truthfully) in routes led and guided by thyself, swelling out and coming from those as the shining particles and the heavens that came till the end. Gifted by a divine intellect it brought those diamonds that stood on a string.

The self as the *Soma*, upon the manifestation of the appropriate divine hymns as well as upon the manifestation of a tiny shining particle into the heaven, strongly progressed by descending to the surroundings, till the very end, scattering diamond like objects as if held on a string. Into the *Soma* a particle of matter and energy manifested signaling the commencement of creation. The term truthfully might have been presented to suggest the concept of *satya* as manifested at the place where the *Soma* originally existed. It also suggested that the *Soma* remained for a long time potently and expectantly before it manifested as the seed substance of the universe. It then furnished the diamond like objects and the universe got enlarged to the surroundings and downward.[1] Here, the *Soma* was equated to what originally remained in the heaven.

RV1.91.02 त्वं सोम क्रतुभिः सुक्रतुर्भूस्त्वं दक्षैः सुदक्षो विश्ववेदाः।
त्वं वृषा वृषत्वेभिर्महित्वा द्युम्नेभिर्द्युम्न्यभवो नृचक्षाः॥

[त्वं - thyself ◇ सोम - as the *Soma* ◇ क्रतुभि - purposefully ◇ सुक्रतुः - well organised ◇ भूः - as the earths ◇ त्वं - thyself ◇ दक्षैः - cleverly ◇ सुदक्षो - very capably ◇ विश्ववेदाः - as the property

[1]The terms 'surrounding' and 'downward' are standard terms to denote 3-dimensionality.

that reached everywhere ◇ त्वं - thyself ◇ वृषा - as the semen virile ◇ वृषत्वेभिर् - that came from the semen virile ◇ महित्वा - became enormous by moving ◇ द्युम्नेभिः - from the heaven ◇ द्युम्नि - as the heavens ◇ अभवो - till nothing really occurred ◇ नृचक्षाः - coming from an eye that saw up to man]

Thyself as the *Soma*, got well organised to the proximity, cleverly became the earths, thyself very capably, very cleverly reached everywhere as the properties, thyself came as the semen virile that came from the semen virile, got enlarged as the heavens that came from the heavens, till nothing further really occurred and all of these came from that eye that saw up to man.

The *Soma* itself, by its own will, cleverly manifested as the earths, as the many properties that got extended and reached till the end, that end where nothing further was created. Thyself became the semen virile that spread and produced more of the semen virile. Thyself became the heavens that came from the heavens. Everything happened as oriented to that lofty eye that saw up to man and beyond. Realising that the moment had come, *Soma* manifested as objects of excellence that extended up to this earth, resolutely and planning well. Exhibiting an immense power that would carry the self up to this earth, realising that the self was signified for this creation, it showered matter around and progressed to far places bringing in different properties in different strengths. The *Soma* traveled along until the earth and beyond, along with the matter and therefore filled the paths of creation and maintained a close proximity to whatever came created. In this existence of the *Soma* as described, there was both visibility and an ethereal invisibility. There were several heavens that got formed commencing from the first of the heavens and from each of these, the paths of creation containing the semen virile extended away and downwards.

RV1.91.03 राज्ञो नु ते वरुणस्य व्रतानि बृहद् गभीरं तव सोम धाम।
शुचिष्ट्वमसि प्रियो न मित्रो दक्षाय्यो अर्यमेवासि सोम॥

[राज्ञो - issued out from knowledge; from a queenly position ◇ नु - only ◇ ते - as those ◇ वरुणस्य - of *Varuṇa* ◇ व्रतानि - rules ◇ बृहद् - got enlarged ◇ गभीरं - with deep sounds ◇ तव - thyself ◇ सोम - as the *Soma* ◇ धाम - remained; positioned ◇ शुच् - brightly ◇ इष्ट - as desired ◇ अमसि - strongly bound to ◇ प्रियो - endearingly ◇ न - as ◇ मित्रो - with *Mitra*; with friendship ◇ दक्ष - cleverly ◇ अय्यो - somehow moving ◇ अर्यम् - graciously ◇ एव - only ◇ असि - smote ◇ सोम - as the *Soma*]

The *Soma* issued out only knowledgeably to become those that obeyed the rules of *Varuṇa* and got enlarged along with roars, moved with the bright objects that manifested as desired, endeared thyself to all with friendship, cleverly and graciously moved in many ways as thyself and yet remained as the very *Soma*.

With a queenly disposition, along with *Varuṇa*, observing the rules of creation, became immense with the roaring sounds and bringing in corresponding properties. From the *Soma* came the shining flames that smote at will, along with love and friendship, and yet cleverly remained as the same respectable and beloved *Soma* for ever. The term "queenly" signified a strategic central location and the *Soma* was awakened from its original nature upon the advent of the roaring sounds (attributed to the divine chanting of hymns and thus the fundamental cosmic vibrations) and manifested as entities of different kinds. From the heaven, down the line, several queenly positions manifested and the divine sounds came as roars and flames and the paths of creation shot out several times from several positions. The benevolence of the *Soma* manifested as many pleasant qualities in the objects and in their relationships with one another. All through these incidences, the *Soma* remained inexhaustible, respectable and beloved.

RV1.91.04 या ते धामानि दिवि या पृथिव्यां या पर्वतेष्वोषधीष्वप्सु।
तेभिर्नो विश्वैः सुमना अहेळन् राजन्त्सोम प्रति हव्या गृभाय॥

[या - whatever manifested ◇ ते - as those ◇ धामानि - as a set positioned ◇ दिवि - as the heavens ◇ या - whatever manifested ◇ पृथिव्यां - as the earths ◇ या - whatever manifested ◇ पर्वतेषु - as the mountains ◇ ओषधीषु - the plant kingdom ◇ अप्सु - as the water ◇ तेभिर्नो - as those from those ◇ विश्वै - reached everywhere ◇ सुमना - manifested as very charming ◇ अहेळन् - highly praised ◇ रा - issued out ◇ जन् - born ◇ सोम - from the *Soma* ◇ प्रति - in all directions ◇ हव्या - as the products of oblations ◇ गृभाय - as grasped; as seized]

Whatever manifested and got positioned as the heavens and whatever manifested from these as the earths, whatever manifested as the mountains, became the plant kingdom, the water and those that came to the proximity and reached everywhere as excellence, those all got highly praised as the ones born and got issued out of the *Soma*, into all directions coming as the closely held products of oblations.

From the *Soma* came the bulk forms of creation appearing like mountains, flowed the semen virile like water, and the ones produced up to the plant kingdom of the earth. In such earths, the *Soma* proved its worthiness and greatness by providing the seed principle to water, as meant for the plant kingdom and by flowing down from its original exalted position. It spread from the heaven downwards bringing in mountainous forms with its apex at the heaven and other high points of origin. It provided this beautiful and acceptable universe to all, by its very inane nature. It manifested as the heavens that stood around the heaven and as the earths that moved from those heavens. It became this enormous universe repeatedly manifesting from the earlier ones. Here the description of the mountain and the flow of water downward and the birth of the plant kingdom on earth was allegorically presented as the very physical nature by which the *Soma* itself flowed downward and gave birth to life forms. Subsequent to the first set of oblations the flow of the *Soma* and the process of creation was thus of compelling nature.

RV1.91.05 त्वं सोमासि सत्पतिस्त्वं राजोत वृत्रहा।
त्वं भद्रो असि क्रतुः॥

[त्वं - thyself ◇ सोम - as the *Soma* ◇ असि - smote ◇ सत्पतिः - as a mighty lordship ◇ त्वं - thyself ◇ रा - issued out ◇ ज - born ◇ उत - interconnected ◇ वृत्र - the *vṛtrata* ◇ हा - kept aloof ◇ त्वं - thyself ◇ भद्रो - as the excellence ◇ असि - smote down ◇ क्रतुः - as organised and created]

Thyself marched away as the *Soma* with full power and vigour, as if a mighty lordship, thyself manifested as those that got interactively born and delivered, thyself kept the *vṛtrata* aloof and thyself smote down as the one that was excellently organised.

The word '*vṛtra*'[2] was interpreted here as that which existed as the dark parts of the universe. Since by this time in this discussion, the shape of the universe was more or less established as approximately spherical, those regions which were not occupied by mass and matter would be termed as the "*vṛtrata*", a darkness, and would be so meant wherever the term appeared. Therefore, in view of several descriptions about the growth of the universe as mountainous forms that stood with its apex at the epicentre or near about, the rest of the volume was termed essentially as darkness and *vṛtrata* by nature. The *Soma* not only caused the formation of flows as the paths containing the bright objects, it also caused the darkness that stood side by side, but the *Soma* kept this darkness at abeyance successfully. Thus it spread along the chosen paths all through the wide atmosphere and all of the universe thus originated from the *Soma*.[3]

RV1.91.06 त्वं च सोम नो वशो जीवातुं न मरामहे।
प्रियस्तोत्रो वनस्पतिः॥

[त्वं - thyself ◇ च - and ◇ सोम - as the *Soma* ◇ नो - as ◇ वशो - desired ◇ जीवातुं - as medicine providing life ◇ न - as ◇ मरामहे

[2]In this commentary on the phenomena of the origin of the universe, several terms have to be interpreted possibly different to the conventional meanings.

[3]In this discussion and almost always, the term 'atmosphere' would mean the wide expanse of space from heaven to the extreme end of the universe.

- great death ◇ प्रियस्तोत्रो - with beloved hymns ◇ वनस्पतिः - the *Vanaspati*]

Thyself as the *Soma* that provided life as desired acting as a medicine, strongly resisted ultimate death, by chanting beloved hymns in praise of *Vanaspati*. Those paths of creation descended and stood as a forest with many trees and each with many branches.

First it appeared to have descended to a wilderness though it came out of divine prayers and from a divine source. The *Soma* remained in such places, as if praying the *Vanaspati* the god of the plant kingdom in order to attain immortality. The plant kingdom, though was inherited from the very *Soma*, maintained an immortality by going into an evolutionary process based on the *annabhāva*. That very seed matter for the universe also came as the very reason for the existence of the plant kingdom. The ethereal *Soma* hung around and over the streams of matter and things created, as a repository of the seed principle. This invisible ethereal entity was immortal, all by itself. It therefore, appeared that it held the *Vanaspati* in reverence and acted in a like manner.

RV1.91.07 त्वं सोम महे भगं त्वं यून ऋतायते।
दक्षं दधासि जीवसे॥

[त्वं - thyself ◇ सोम - as the *Soma* ◇ महे - became great ◇ भगं - beautiful ◇ त्वं - thyself ◇ यून - as a string ◇ ऋतायते - progressed as per rules ◇ दक्षं - cleverly ◇ दधासि - issuing out and positioned well bound ◇ जी - conquered ◇ वसे - and so remained]

Thyself came as the *Soma*, became great and beautiful; thyself progressed like strings formed according to the rules, cleverly got delivered, got positioned and moved, conquering all.

The universe existed with the paths of creation pervaded with *Soma*, an excellence, which cleverly manifested into various life forms. Though the creation progressed with sequential afflictions, the created remained as sets of excellence. All through these events and for ever the *Soma* enveloped the creations, unseen and not very obvious. The *Soma* remained a benevolent self, in spite of the affliction that it suffered. The *Soma* thus proved its greatness and remained as a huge potency that spread through chosen paths.

RV1.91.08 त्वं नः सोम विश्वतो रक्षा राजन्नघायतः।
न रिष्येत्त्वावतः सखा॥

[त्वं - thyself ◇ नः - as ◇ सोम - the *Soma* ◇ विश्वतो - reached everywhere ◇ रक्षा - providing protecting ◇ राजन् - royally gifting life forms ◇ न - as ◇ धा - bestowing ◇ यतः - and progressing ◇ न - as ◇ रिष्येत् - getting emaciated ◇ त्व - from thyself ◇ अवतः - descended ones ◇ सखा - comrades]

Thyself manifested as the *Soma* that reached everywhere offering protections and royally gifting life forms, greatly bestowing and so progressed, got emaciated and stood steadfast with the comrades that descended from thyself.

Out of the injury and the afflictions suffered by the *Soma*, matter got generated, issued out, got positioned at different places and all of these acted in a camaraderie fashion. The *Soma* provided the necessary protection to all. The *Soma* existed all through the paths of creation to give form to the universe and also assumed the *annabhāva* and thereby maintained immortality. It, therefore, took to such regenerative and evolutionary cycles as suited. But here the terms could also be interpreted as emaciated downwards, since the well established concept was that the universe gradually emaciated to the end.

RV1.91.09 सोम यास्ते मयोभुव ऊतयः सन्ति दाशुषे।
ताभिर्नोऽविता भव॥

[सोम - the *Soma* ◇ यास्ते - from being docile ◇ मयोभुव - became the most pleasant space ◇ ऊतयः - well connected ◇ सन्ति - lovingly with the *Sat* ◇ दाशुषे - as the auspicious risings ◇ त - as those ◇ अभिर्नो - that grouped together ◇ अविता - protected ◇ भव - became]

The *Soma* from a docile state, came to be the most pleasant space well connected to the *Sat* and from it came the auspicious arising of those which were grouped together, the *Soma* offering necessary protections. Thus the *Soma* upon getting agitated became the expansions to the proximity and bestowed many that were born out of the veneration that accompanied.

The *Soma* that remained cold and inactive in the immediate space of *mayobhuva*, upon getting woken up from its deep slumber by the sounds of worship, manifested itself as a series of expansions to the next proximity and by subsequent processes became this immense universe. The *Soma* maintaining a close connection with the *Sat*, flowed out to the successive proximity carrying its creations along, holding those close and thus brought in a well expanded universe, as a magic performed.

RV1.91.10 इमं यज्ञमिदं वचो जुजुषाण उपागहि।
सोम त्वं नो वृधे भव॥

[इमं - thus ◇ यज्ञम् - as *yajñas* ◇ इदं - till here ◇ वचो - as the words ◇ जुजुषाण - and by instant oblations after oblations ◇ उपागहि - progressed downwards ◇ सोम - as the *Soma* ◇ त्वं - thyself ◇ नो - as ◇ वृधे - enlarged ◇ भव - became]

Thus by uttering the words, the verses and out of the oblations that came quickly, as oblations that came after oblations and as the successive *yajñas* that occurred till here, the *Soma* much descended thyself and effected the huge enlargements.

The *Soma* set on a course downwards provided matter that manifested out of a series of *yajñas* which were marked by the chanting of verses. With the advent of a set of sounds and cosmic vibrations, out of afflictions and oblations, it got into such enlargements as to be everywhere and thus became the universe. The specifics of these oblations were defined by the divine words and their power. The movement downward into all directions from the heaven and from the many subsequent heavens brought various objects to great distances.

RV1.91.11 सोम गीर्भिष्ट्वा वयं वर्धयामो वचोविदः।

सुमृळीको न आ विश॥

[सोम - the *Soma* ◇ गीर्भिष्ठा - with the most desirable words that moved ◇ वयं - a body ◇ वर्धयामो - got enlarged by moving ◇ वचो - with words ◇ विदः - and knowledge ◇ सुमृळीको - and the kindness that got extended ◇ न - as ◇ आ - manifested ◇ विश - and settled down]

The *Soma* inspired by the most desirable words, the words matching knowledge and the knowledge that accompanied, got the body of the universe enlarged, became the kindness that manifested and got extended and thus got well settled in the universe.

The enlargement of the universe was accomplished by the divine words, words of appropriate measures which manifested and accompanied the growth at all times. The knowledge and purpose packed into the words, or the quality and strength of the vibrations set the tone of expansion of the universe and the very nature of the afflictions. Thus the words, sounds or vibrations were invested with extreme significance since the associated phenomena only came correspondingly. In other words, there was an incessant association of the sounds and a series of afflictions throughout the process of creation. The words, sounds or vibrations would thus become the very reason, energy and motor of creation.

RV1.91.12 गयस्फानो अमीवहा वसुवित्पुष्टिवर्धनः।
सुमित्रः सोम नो भव॥

[ग - moving ◇ यस् - frothed up ◇ फ - swelling ◇ अनो - breathed out ◇ अमीव - grief and distress ◇ हा - dispelled ◇ वसुवित् - bestowed wealth ◇ पुष्टि - prosperity ◇ वर्धन - increased ◇ सुमित्रः - the camaraderie ◇ सोम - the *Soma* ◇ नो - as ◇ भव - thus stood]

Dispelling the sickness, grief and distress, became a boiling upheaval and the *Soma* bestowed wealth, increased prosperity and co-existed with whatever that came into existence in a camaraderie fashion.

The *Soma* that remained, inactive and sickly for a long

time suddenly underwent a tumultuous upheaval which not only there-by became an excellence but enhanced itself to fill all the paths of creation. Thus the once inactive *Soma* became the active provider and remained so for ever. Yet and in spite of its repeated delivery of matter and energy, the *Soma* did not get depleted in any way. Besides whatever created could not severe the interactive nature with the *Soma* at any point of time.

RV1.91.13 सोम रारन्धि नो हृदि गावो न यवसेष्वा ।
मर्य इव स्व ओक्ये॥

[सोम - the *Soma* ◇ रा - bestowing ◇ रन्धि - from a state of subjugation ◇ नो - as ◇ हृदि - from the heart ◇ गावो - progressed downward ◇ न - as ◇ यवसेषु - as the fodder ◇ आ - that manifested ◇ मर्य - till man and mortality ◇ इव - in that manner ◇ स्व - as the self ◇ ओक्ये - getting suitably located]

From the heart and the heaven, from a state of subjugation, the *Soma* progressed downward and became the fodder that moved till man and got itself suitably placed.

From that space, near to the centre of the spherical entity of the universe, the *Soma* issued out to the extent of our earth. The *Soma* acquired permanence by assuming the *annabhāva* and not only created things but also received those on dissolution, assuming an essential role for existence. Not only objects and energy issued out of the *Soma* but upon dissolution all melted into this ethereal, bright transparency. Thus the *Soma* conquered or controlled all processes of creation.

RV1.91.14 यः सोम सख्ये तव रारणद्देव मर्त्यः।
तं दक्षः सचते कविः॥

[यः - thus ◇ सोम - the *Soma* ◇ सख्ये - in a camaraderie manner ◇ तव - thyself ◇ रारणद् - as the pleasantry bestowed ◇ देव - from the heaven ◇ मर्त्यः - till man ◇ तं - as those ◇ दक्षः - cleverly ◇ सचते - as from worships ◇ कविः - and knowledge]

Thus the *Soma* in a camaraderie fashion issued out pleasantly as thyself from heaven till man, as those that cleverly came from worships and knowledge.

Thus the *Soma* itself came down from the heaven, capable and extending friendship to all. What came forth from the *Soma* were issued out in an amicable fashion, from the heaven to earth. What all created were thus exalted, said the learned. The perpetually shining or god like entities were created, the human beings of this earth were also created; yet all were subject to death and decay. The *Soma* was the source for both the mortal and the immortal entities that came at its pleasure. The *Soma* had efficiently kept at abeyance the darkness that got generated around the flow of creations.

RV1.91.15 उरुष्या णो अभिशस्तेः सोम नि पाह्यंहसः।
सखा सुशेव एधि नः॥

[उरुष्या - securely ◇ णो - with knowledge ◇ अभिशस्तेः - and as the calumny ◇ सोम - the *Soma* ◇ नि - to below ◇ पाहि - as protected; guarded ◇ अंहसः - as the anxiety ◇ सखा - kept as a friendship ◇ सुशेव - acceptable ◇ एधि - spread much; enlarged ◇ नः - as]

From the *Soma* descended those protected entities and those calumnious ones that opposed progress, their relationships anxiously guarded as acceptable friendships and this way it spread and got enlarged.

The benevolent nature of the *Soma* could be realised from the excellent creations, that emanated from the heaven and the opposing forces, as those two in contrast that peacefully co-existed. With a commitment for protection and with good intentions, the *Soma* came downwards as the pleasantries and friendships maintained, making everything favourable, auspicious and happy. The whole of the enlargement of the universe was achieved on this principle and the *Soma* maintained a constant camaraderie between those created, whether good or bad. It remained adequately empowered wherever it existed and maintained an auspicious and happy ambiance.

RV1.91.16 आ प्यायस्व समेतु ते विश्वतः सोम वृष्ण्यम्।
भवा वाजस्य संगथे॥

[आ - manifesting ◇ पि - moving ◇ आय - to the proximity ◇ स्व - from the self ◇ समेतु - assembled; stacked together ◇ ते - those ◇ विश्वतः - reached everywhere ◇ सोम - from the *Soma* ◇ वृष्ण्यम् - showering the semen virile ◇ भवा - and became ◇ वाजस्य - energetically ◇ संगथे - stood together]

Those which manifested to the proximity from the self and found assembled together and thus found to have reached everywhere, came from the *Soma*, as the semen virile showered and as those that energetically came and stood together.

As sprinkled from the *Soma* the universe became a mightily gathered and well stacked existence with many a mighty object. The *Soma* prevailed all over the universe and through the stages of creation and several objects got issued out as sprinkled and got regrouped to become larger entities. The universe was thus found to be a well stacked one (a concept maintained by the *citi* forms) while it got formed till this earth.

RV1.91.17 आ प्यायस्व मदिन्तम सोम विश्वेभिरंशुभिः।
भवा नः सुश्रवस्तमः सखा वृधे॥

[आ - manifested ◇ पि - moving ◇ आय - reaching ◇ स्व - from the self ◇ मदिन्तम - extremely intoxicated ◇ सोम - as the *Soma* ◇ विश्वेभिः - reaching everywhere ◇ अंशुभिः - like a thread; narrowing down ◇ भवा - occurred ◇ न - as ◇ सुश्रवस्तमः - abounding in extreme glory ◇ सखा - along with friends ◇ वृधे - getting enlarged]

Manifested from the self by moving and reaching everywhere, extremely intoxicated by the *Soma* and manifested like a thread, bound to extreme glory and along with the friends that came into existence, the universe got very much enlarged. That which came down as the pleasant things and as darkness, all came from the *Soma* and reached everywhere like threads of great excellence and remained friendly while getting so enlarged.

Though the universe came born with the intoxication provided by the *Soma*, it maintained a steady balance to both sides while getting enlarged. It carried and positioned objects in trajectories, in an equitable fashion. The *yājñika* acquired the necessary exhilaration for the creation tasting the *Soma* and used the same *Soma* as the seed substance for creations. Also it impressed upon the significance of sound or vibrations as the motive force for the division and enlargements.

RV1.91.18 सं ते पयांसि समु यन्तु वाजाः सं वृष्ण्यान्यभिमातिषाहः।
आप्यायमानो अमृताय सोम दिवि श्रवांस्युत्तमानि धिष्व॥

[सं - as stood together ◇ ते - those ◇ पय - as a liquid juice ◇ अंसि - moved and flung away ◇ समु - only equally ◇ यन्तु - guided ◇ वाजाः - coming with vigour ◇ सं - assembled ◇ वृष्ण्या - manifested as the semen virile sprinkled ◇ नि - below ◇ अभि - to the proximity ◇ मा - arrangement ◇ अत् - moved ◇ इषा - strongly ◇ हः - distanced ◇ आप्याय - became full ◇ मानो - it was considered ◇ अमृताय - as the immortality ◇ सोम - the *Soma* ◇ दिवि - from heaven ◇ श्रवांसि - flowing down instantly ◇ उत्तमानि - from the higher ◇ धिष्व - along with knowledge]

Those that got assembled from a liquid juice, those that got moved and flung away equally and in a guided manner, those that got assembled with vigour, the semen virile that moved downwards and to the proximity, the arrangements that got sprinkled from it, they all moved strongly and progressively got distanced. The immortal *Soma* flowed down instantly from the heaven and all were considered of having manifested from the *Soma*. Those that came from those that stood above, came along with knowledge which itself manifested in a like manner.

As the seed substance in conjugation, as a might that came equally guided, as the unending sprinkles, as the immortality that was at hand, the *Soma* came from the heaven as an instant descend, manifesting along with knowledge and destroying enemies. The *Soma* getting widely and equitably distributed, the objects coming sprinkling from it, great descends occurred by moving from where it originally remained. It was considered glorious for the reason that it became an immortality at hand for whatever that got created. In spite of the exhausting phenomena that accompanied the creation, the *Soma* remained inexhaustible and available for birth of new objects. The distribution of the creative process was with equal strength in all directions.

RV1.91.19 या ते धामानि हविषा यजन्ति ता ते विश्वा परिभूरस्तु यज्ञम्। गयस्फानः प्रतरणः सुवीरोऽविरहा प्र चरा सोम दुर्यान्॥

[या - moving ◇ ते - as those ◇ धामानि - taken positions ◇ हविषा - as products of oblations ◇ यज् - out of the oblations ◇ अन्ति - to the proximity ◇ ता - from them came ◇ ते - as those ◇ विश्वा - that reached everywhere ◇ परिभूः - as circularity's ◇ अस्तु - having positioned ◇ यज्ञम् - as *yajña* ◇ ग - progressed ◇ यस् - spewing out ◇ फ - swelling ◇ अनः - breathed out ◇ प्र - to the surroundings ◇ तरण - crossed over ◇ सुवीरो - courageously ◇ अविरहा - manifested without abandoning ◇ प्र - to the surroundings ◇ चरा - moved ◇ सोम - the *Soma* ◇ दुर्यान् - moved and resided]

Those that moved and took position from the earlier ones have come as the products of oblations that reached everywhere. The circularity's that got positioned, those that spewed out of the *yajña* like a boiling upheaval that breathed out to the surroundings, those that crossed over the difficulties and courageously progressed without getting abandoned, all of them had manifested to the surroundings by moving from the *Soma* and took residence or moved further on, as it occurred.

Those that moved from their positions to the proximity upon oblations, the *yajñas* flashed to the surroundings, those that traversed out of boiling upheavals and had provided bold confederations of objects; all of these had come from the *Soma*. Though it had brought a strange set of objects of varying properties, the *Soma* retained its original nature and composure. It moved and cohabited with these objects, comfortably as an invisible entity. The products of oblations spilled out of the *yajñas* and the opposing cowardice (those which tried to retard the progress) were kept aloof by the *Soma*, by descending till the end through the many paths of creation. It provided the protective cover to all that were born by encompassing the paths of creation that extended from the heaven in several branches till the end.

RV1.91.20 सोमो धेनुं सोमो अर्वन्तमाशुं सोमो वीरं कर्मण्यं ददाति। सादन्यं विदथ्यं सभेयं पितृश्रवणं यो ददाशदस्मै॥

[सोमो - as the *Soma* ◇ धेनुं - milked out ◇ सोमो - the *Soma* ◇ अर्वन्तम् - that spread till the end ◇ आशुं - quickly ◇ सोमो - the *Soma* ◇ वीरं - courageously ◇ कर्मण्यं - by acts of creation ◇ दद - bestowed ◇ अति - greatly ◇ साद - moved ◇ अन्यं - as others ◇ विदथ्यं - supported by knowledge ◇ सभेयं - as a good act ◇ पितृश्रवणं - bringing honour to the father ◇ यो - as those that ◇ दद - bestowed as ◇ अश्नद् - incessantly ◇ अस्मै - parts]

The *Soma* spread quickly till the end as if milked out. The courageous acts of creation brought everything from the *Soma*, bestowing many and moving many. All of these came supported by knowledge, as the good acts that brought honour to the father and as the parts bestowed incessantly.

Milked out as the *Soma* that got quickly emitted and as the afflictions that came till the very end, daringly led by the *Soma*, it defined the creative functions, residences and senses of direction. Those became decent entities that brought honour to the father, the *Soma* having furnished all and yet remained the very self for ever. The *Soma* had several responsibilities and it bestowed the necessary energy and it subjected itself to severe afflictions till the very end. And it proved its decency by bringing honours to the creator. It listened to its creator and responded to the vibrations of his words. Yet the *Soma* remained the very self, furnishing its own definitions of creation. The *Soma*, thus was an inexhaustible source for everything. It remained calm and unseen all along. It progressed with courage and never retracted.

RV1.91.21 अषाळ्हं युत्सु पृतनासु पप्रिं स्वर्षामप्सां वृजनस्य गोपाम्। भरेषुजां सुक्षितिं सुश्रवसं जयन्तं त्वामनु मदेम सोम॥

[अषाळ्हं - as invincible ◇ युत्सु - warding off ◇ पृतनासु - competitive; strife ◇ पप्रिं - manifestations ◇ स्वर्षां - by a brilliant intellect ◇ अप्सां - as a liquid ◇ वृजनस्य - as enclosures ◇ गोपाम् - protected ◇ भरेषु - filled ◇ जां - as born ◇ सुक्षितिं - as good earths ◇ सुश्रवसं - coming from the good praises ◇ जयन्तं - winning till the ends ◇ त्वामनु - the lesser ones moved from thyself ◇ मद - exhilaration ◇ इम - as ◇ सोम - the *Soma*]

As an invincible process of warding off the unwanted and as a competitive strife that manifested, as the brilliant intellect that moved along, as the protected enclosures that moved, as the potent liquid that moved, the universe got filled to the brim with the good earths that came into existence and yet all were manifesting from the good praises that went on winning till the ends. All were coming by thy own intellect from thyself along with the lesser ones and with an exhilaration that was accrued from the *Soma*.

The mighty *Soma*, as the repository of the semen virile, as the protection and coverage extended to all that were created, manifested in many ways. It kept the unconquerable darkness at abeyance from the paths of creation. It became the atmosphere and the *vyāhṛtis* that extended till the very end. It rained semen virile and it flowed like water along the paths of creation. It filled the universe with the earth form entities. It became the synonym of co-existence. It manifested along with the divine prayers, the cosmic vibrations and provided the definitions of creation.

Moving differently, quickly and flung up to the earth as the many excellence squeezed out on a war footing, a heavenly and shining liquid flowed down in an exhilarated condition to bring about a universe, protected and defended like a fort, as a good existence that was famous and successful. Yet the *Soma* remained as the very self and a liquid squeezed out and splurged out in different directions reaching up to this earth. The very exhilaration that the *Soma* provided, became the desire for creation. Well defended objects and good existences were so born. Nothing from outside set the dimensions and extent of these developments. The *Soma* was well known to have succeeded in the creation. That which was created were well protected and were fully surrounded by the *Soma* and the *Soma* kept its poise at all times. Later it showed neither any signs of its earlier sickness nor any signs of the initial intoxicated exhilaration.

RV1.91.22 त्वमिमा ओषधीः सोम विश्वास्त्वमपो अंजनयस्त्वं गाः।
त्वमा ततन्थोर्व१न्तरिक्षं त्वं ज्योतिषा वि तमो ववर्थ॥

[त्वम् - thyself ◇ इमा - thus ◇ ओषधीः - as the plant kingdom ◇ सोम - the *Soma* ◇ विश्वाः - reaching everywhere ◇ त्वम् - thyself ◇ अपो - descended ◇ अज - till nothing born ◇ नयः - led by ◇ त्वं - thyself ◇ गा - progressing ◇ त्वम् - as thyself ◇ आ - manifesting ◇ ततन् - as those from those ◇ थ - positioned as ◇ उर्व - broad; extensive ◇ अन्तरिक्षं - atmosphere ◇ त्वं - thyself ◇ ज्योतिषा - shining brilliantly ◇ वि - divided ◇ तमो - as darkness ◇ ववर्थ - and those that stood hiding]

Thus the *Soma* all by thyself became the plant kingdom and yet remained as the *Soma* that reached everywhere. Thyself descended and progressed till nothing was further born. Thyself became the one that manifested from the earlier ones. Thyself became the much enlarged atmosphere. Thyself appeared as the brightness that stood separated from darkness and those that remained hidden in the darkness.

The *Soma* from the unmanifested state became the essence of the universe, expanding through the atmosphere, with own heat and brightness, barricading and resisting the darkness and reaching up to this earth and the plant kingdom. It produced the objects of the high skies and the paths that stood like the trees of a forest. Not only all the objects of the universe were thus born from the *Soma*, it also extended itself up to this earth and caused the formation of the plant kingdom. The creative potency that was seen in the plant kingdom in spite of the nature of its evolutionary character came from the *Soma*. The potential forms of heat and brightness was not limited to the *Soma* in its place of origin. In the process of its downward journey, it held darkness at abeyance. The *Soma* remained as a potent transparent halo over all matter. While it provided the seed substance for all the creations including the evolutionary cycle seen on this earth, it also absorbed the ones that faced dissolution.

RV1.91.23 देवेन नो मनसा देव सोम रायो भागं सहसावन्नभि युध्य। मा त्वा तनदीशिषे वीर्यस्योभयेभ्यः प्र चिकित्सा गविष्टौ॥

[देवेन - from the heavens ◇ नो - as ◇ मनसा - from the mind ◇ देव - from the heaven ◇ सोम - the *Soma* ◇ रायो - royally ◇ भागं - as parts ◇ सहस - powerfully; strongly ◇ अवन्नभि - to the proximity and below ◇ युध्य - fighting ◇ मा - as an arrangement ◇ त्वा - coming from thyself ◇ तन - as offspring ◇ दी - that shined ◇ शिषे - remained ◇ वीरस्य - courageously ◇ उभयेभ्यः - to both side ◇ प्र - to the surroundings ◇ चिकित्सा - along with knowledge ◇ गविष्टौ - as arduous progresses]

From the heaven and from the *Soma*, came a powerful and royal progress, to the proximity and to below, as arrangements that came fighting, as the offspring that shined and those that remained courageously to both sides and to the surroundings; all came arduously progressed with knowledge.

From the heaven and the *Soma* flowed the paths of creation, which brought about the heavens below and to the surroundings. Divine minds stood at the points of origin of many further paths of creations. The *Soma* marched regally to the surroundings, giving and generating. It moved from a higher supremacy to a lower one to bring about a chain of dependencies. The *Soma* royally progressed shining and issuing to the proximity as a result of an upheaval that came on war footing. Thus what came as an arrangement of thyself as if a river flowing to the surroundings and as a flow of the courageous afflictions that occurred, were considered as eagerly manifested from the *Soma*. The *Soma* that remained as a shining excellence at the heart of the universe, got divided and flowed into different directions and out of afflictions came the different entities that filled the space it provided. It became the magic potion of creation. It viewed all that were created as its own children, since all of those came from it. In spite of the afflictions it underwent and the fighting spirit it had to exhibit, it remained only as an excellence and a universal benevolence.

RV 8.48

[(15) पञ्चदशार्चस्यास्य सूक्तस्य घोरः काण्व ऋषिः। सोमो देवता। (1 - 4, 6 - 15) प्रथमादिचतुर्ऋचां षष्ठ्यादिदशानाञ्च त्रिष्टुप् (5) पञ्चम्याश्च जगति छन्दसि]

RV8.48.01 स्वादोरभक्षि वयसः सुमेधाः स्वाध्यो वरिवोवित्तरस्य।
विश्वे यं देवा उत मर्त्यासो मधु ब्रुवन्तो अभि संचरन्ति॥

[स्वादो - the self bestowed as ◇ रभ् - holding firmly to ◇ अक्षि - that eye ◇ वयसः - as a body that ◇ सुमेधाः - intelligently; purposefully ◇ स्वाध्यो - thoughtfully, from own high position ◇ वरिवो - as the wide space ◇ विद् - with knowledge ◇ तरस्य - crossing over; fording ◇ विश्वे - reached everywhere ◇ यं - supported ◇ देवा - by heavens ◇ उत - interconnected ◇ मर्त्यासो - till man ◇ मधु - sweetness ◇ ब्रव - as known ◇ अन्तो - till the end ◇ अभि - towards ◇ संचरन्ति - moved together to the proximity]

Thus the self got bestowed, holding firmly to that eye to become a body that was created intelligently and thoughtfully crossing over the wide spaces and reaching everywhere, supported by the many interconnected heavens to reach man and became known as a sweetness that flowed to the proximity and till the end, along with those that came along.

The self, that remained anxious and with a strong purpose at a high position, i.e., from the heaven, coming down interwoven as a sweetness that descended till man and until the end. A bird that remained, at its own position above consuming nothing, with might and an intention, became an enlargement by moving and reaching everywhere from the heaven, continuously moving forward from heaven to heaven and until man, carrying a sweetness along with it.

The *Soma* flowed down from the high position strongly and purposefully to become the paths of creations and a sweetness descended till man and till that very end where nothing whatsoever manifested. The *Soma* that remained at heaven and near the epicentre, became the universe as a well conceived enlargement holding bright and hot objects. The *Soma* that was the very intoxication and the provider of the desire with which the creation took place, remained as a protective cover to all those objects and energy that were created. It appeared as the *amṛt* that *Suparṇa*, a large bird carried till here. Here the second set of meaning was given for the reason that the universe was also imagined as an enlargement that came as a bird circumnavigating into wider circles, down from the heaven till here and sprinkling all the objects of the universe. That bird *Suparṇa* became the very universe. Later, this bird was brought in as the bird form of the *uttaravedi* of the *vaidikayajña*.

RV8.48.02 अन्तश्च प्रागा अदितिर्भवास्यवयाता हरसो दैव्यस्य।
इन्द्रविन्द्रस्य सख्यं जुषाणः श्रौष्टिव धुरमनु राय ऋध्याः॥

[अन्तश्च - till the very end ◇ प्रागा - coming from the earlier ◇ अदितिर् - as the greatness ◇ भवास्य - existences ◇ वयाता - woven together and from those ◇ हरसो - taken in hand; seized ◇ दैव्यस्य - by a divinity; as from the heavens ◇ इन्द्र - and *indrata* ◇ विन्द् - gaining ◇ रस्य - as a juice; as effected ◇ सख्यं - with friendship ◇ जुषाणः - containing pleasantries ◇ श्रौष्टिव - as if obediently ◇ धुरमनु - as carrying the burden ◇ राय - royally ◇ ऋध् - growing ◇ या - progressed]

Manifesting from the earlier ones till the very ends, a greatness came into existence. As those and those coming from those, attached and woven together as gained from the heavens and from the *indrata*, came all along with a juice that flowed down containing pleasant things. With friendship and obedience what came carried as a burden, became a royal progress and growth.

From a high position and till the very end, it progressed to the surroundings becoming those to constitute a great body, as if taken in hand by a divinity, as if the accomplishments of *Indra*, as the friendship, the obedience, the clear entities, the excellence and the enlargements that would become the universe. The universe became enormous as a progression from a height to below and to the surroundings, setting up many things. Out of a divinity and out of a shining particle of matter, upon dividing whatever that existed, many shining objects were born which remained as a group or objects of individuality, clarity and excellence. A totally interactive universe was thus born with the excellent objects that co-existing or stood alone. Out of the *Soma* and from a shining excellence, came the many subsequent shining excellence.

RV8.48.03 अपाम सोमममृता अभूमागन्म ज्योतिरविदाम देवान्।
किं नूनमस्मान् कृणवदरातिः किमु धूर्तिरमृत मर्त्यस्य॥

[अपाम - as a potent and powerful liquid; as that which came down ◇ सोमम् - the *Soma* ◇ अमृता - as the immortality ◇ अभूम - from an unborn ◇ अगन्म - came forward ◇ ज्योतिर् - as a brightness ◇ अविद - not ceasing ◇ अम - strength ◇ देवान् - as breathed out from the heavens ◇ किं - whatever ◇ नूनम् - at once ◇ अस्मान् - as parts moved ◇ कृण् - from the established high position ◇ अव - descending ◇ दर - breaking loose ◇ अतिः - greatly ◇ किमु - some as ◇ धूर्तिर् - damaged ◇ अमृत - immortality ◇ मर्त्यस्य - till man]

The *Soma*, from a state of unborn flowed down as a powerful liquid, as an immortality that came forward brightly and with unceasing strength and as whatever parts breathed out instantly from the heavens, moving and descending from the established high positions, breaking loose greatly, some damaged, some immortal, reaching till man.

As a potent and powerful liquid that flowed down, the immortality known as *Soma* came forward from an unborn state to become those brightnesses, the heavens and those that suddenly became the parts of the universe. It was from the heaven and from an unborn state that remained there, that paths of creation flowed down and all were known to have come from the *Soma*. It brought forth the shining objects of the universe and the heavens that manifested to below. Out of whatever so came, as the earths and the brightness, some retained the properties and shape and some got destroyed or lost values. Upon getting afflicted, a holocaust descended, out of the *Soma*. Out of a state of unborn and from the heaven, bright objects were born, which immediately took shape moving from the exalted positions and as if moving along the spokes of a wheel to become whatever mortality and immortality, that reached till man. The *Soma* manifested from the un-manifested as an immortality that was installed by the *Agni*. The immortal nature of the *Soma* was extended from the beginning and down to this earth and its habitats. Thus mortality and immortality manifested till the earth.

RV8.48.04 **शं नो भव हृद आ पीत इन्दो पितेव सोम सूनवे सुशेवः।
सखेव सख्य उरुशंस धीरः प्र ण आयुर्जीवसे सोम तारिः॥**

[**शं** - auspicious ◇ **नो** - as ◇ **भव** - occurred ◇ **हृद** - from the heart ◇ **आ** - manifesting ◇ **पीत** - as those swelled, overflowed ◇ **इन्दो** - from a bright spot ◇ **पित्** - swollen ◇ **एव** - only ◇ **सोम** - the *Soma* ◇ **सून** - born ones ◇ **वे** - woven ◇ **सुशेवः** - very dear ◇ **सख** - friends ◇ **एव** - only as ◇ **सख्य** - friendship ◇ **उरुशंस** - praised by many ◇ **धीरः** - as courageous, as delivered by an intellect ◇ **प्र** - to the surroundings ◇ **ण** - from knowledge ◇ **आयुः** - extended ◇ **जीवसे** - and those thrived ◇ **सोम** - the *Soma* ◇ **तारिः** - crossing over]

The auspicious *Soma*, upon the manifestation of a bright spot into its midst, from that heart and that bright spot swelled and overflowed as those born and remained interwoven. Those very dear ones, those friends and the friendship seen, praised by many as a courageous progress, came from an intellect to the surroundings, along with the knowledge that got extended. Those thrived under the protection of the

Soma and thus crossed over the difficulties.

The *Soma* that existed in the heaven upon the manifestation of a drop of energy and matter, came moved downwards and got enlarged, holding on to the beloved children. Those that existed in friendship and extending friendliness around was praised as a courageous existence that came to the surroundings. It was a progress that never looked back and was enabled by the divine persuasions that manifested. It was a progress conceived by a divine knowledge and intellect. A universal affection permeated from the *Soma*. The motive force came from the sound, vibrations and resulted in a wave form propagation which did not look back. The repeated reference to the friendliness was nothing but the ever relevant interactive existence of the universe. But at the same time it indicated a difference to being a relative and those directly connected. Therefore there were objects bound to one another and others that had a slightly distanced existence.

RV8.48.05 इमे मा पिता यशस उरुष्यवो रथं न गावः समनाह पर्वसु। ते मा रक्षन्तु विस्रसश्चरित्रादुत मा स्रामाद्यवयन्त्विन्दवः॥

[इमे - thus ◇ मा - as an arrangement ◇ पिता - manifested swelling ◇ यशस - famous ◇ उरुष्यवो - and securely moving away ◇ रथं - a chariot ◇ न - like ◇ गाव - progressing downward ◇ समना - coming equally ◇ ह - distancing ◇ पर्वसु - with wide steps ◇ ते - as those ◇ मा - arranged ◇ रक्षन्तु - only as protected ◇ विः - divided ◇ रसश्च - as the juice ◇ रित् - that flowed ◇ राद् - effected as ◇ उत - interconnected ◇ मा - as arrangement ◇ स्र - of decreasing ◇ अम - strength ◇ अद्य - in such a way ◇ वयन्त् - moved bound to ◇ वि - divided ◇ इन्दवः - as a drop of brightness]

Thus an arrangement manifested as swelled, famous and secure, moving away like a chariot, progressing and descending, coming equally and distancing with wide steps, to become the arrangements of protections. The divided flows of a juice, the arrangements effected by interconnecting all, but of decreasing strength, moved divided and yet remained bound to that drop of brightness.

Though the universe became a famous and secure place, wholly accredited as the provisions that came into existence from the *Soma*, the very progress was enabled by that singular occurrence of the manifestation of a bright particle into it. It was from that moment that the creation progressed, objects distanced and the multiple arrangements of the universe ever took place. It was then that afflictions got unleashed, protection and equanimity manifested. The universe was well known to have come all the way with an accompanying and matching exhilaration that was born out of the *Soma*. The formation that issued appeared like a well balanced chariot wheel and a strong fortification. The process of creation thus moved like a chariot that would speedily and resolutely move forward.

RV8.48.06 अग्निं न मा मथितं सं दिदीपः प्र चक्षय कृणुहि वस्यसो नः। अथा हि ते मद आ सोम मन्ये रेवाँ इव प्र चरा पुष्टिमच्छ॥

[अग्निं - the *Agni* ◇ न - as ◇ मा - arrangement ◇ मथितं - churned ◇ सं - and collected ◇ दिदीपः - shining protections ◇ प्र - to the surroundings ◇ चक्षय - from that eye ◇ कृणु - loftily set up ◇ हि - only ◇ वस्यसो - more glorious ◇ नः - as ◇ अथा - then coming ◇ हि - only as ◇ ते - those ◇ मद - from the exhilaration ◇ आ - that came ◇ सोम - from the *Soma* ◇ मन्ये - in principle ◇ रेवाँ - jumped and moved ◇ इव - in that manner ◇ प्र - to the surroundings ◇ चरा - moved ◇ पुष्टिम् - as the enhanced ◇ अच्छ - transparencies]

That which came into existence as an arrangement of the *Agni*, by churning out of the *Soma* and getting collected to the surroundings, as the shining protections that came from a lofty eye, were all those that got more glorious and came only in principle out of the exhilaration provided by the *Soma*. These somehow got issued to the surroundings to give forth those objects that moved out of the *Soma*; those transparencies that moved along much enhanced.

Upon the advent of the *Agni* into the *Soma* and out of a

churning upheaval, objects got swirled around the theoretical epicentre, often described as the eye of the universe. The *Soma* was the ethereal substance that, while caused the creation of objects, inexhaustibly encompassed and moved with the objects, to wherever those moved. The epicentre of the universe was clearly described here as devoid of matter and as the centre of the churning action. It was this that necessitated the description of a place of birth or origin and the naming of the *viśvatomukha*, *mayobhuva* etc. which in other words was the first of the 7 *vyāhṛti*s as well. It confirmed that there existed a small distance from the epicentre to the beginning of the first *vyāhṛti* which matched the concept of a clearance between the axle and the wheel. It was also confirmed that though the wheel did not rotate, it remained with the very possibility and was on the brink of an urge; thus as the very genus of an interactive universe. A unique rationality and irrationality was posited on the epicentre and its nature. It was thus that the *rathacakra* was conceived as a supreme symbol capable of representing the geometry and essence of existence of the universe.

RV8.48.07 इषिरेण ते मनसा सुतस्य भक्षीमहि पित्र्यस्येव रायः।
सोम राजन् प्र ण आयूंषि तारीरहानीव सूर्यो वासराणि॥

[इषिरेण - greatly activated ◇ ते - as those ◇ मनसा - from the minds ◇ सुतस्य - squeezed out ◇ भक्षी - consumed ◇ महि - greatly ◇ पित्र्यस्य - as if from a father ◇ एव - only ◇ रायः - royally ◇ सोम - as the *Soma* ◇ राजन् - royally born and issued out ◇ प्र - to the surroundings ◇ ण - from knowledge ◇ आयूंषि - that frothed up and extended ◇ तारी - that forded ◇ रहा - to a loneliness ◇ नि - descended ◇ इव - in such manner ◇ सूर्यो - as the Sun - like ◇ वासराणि - moved in successively diminutive forms]

Those that came from the *Soma*, those that came greatly activated by a mind, those that were squeezed out and greatly consumed, all of these came only from a paternity. All of these got royally issued out and got born to the surroundings, along with the knowledge that frothed up and got extended. Those that forded until a distant loneliness and descended as the Sun-like manifestations had successively moved and had taken to diminutive forms while progressing.

The Sun-like and graceful objects went on getting issued with sizes and properties gradually getting reduced. Issuing out from a highly activated divine mind and as those that were squeezed out of the *Soma*, all got generated and got bestowed to the surroundings, progressing and fording to distant locations. A regal paternity, who kept his mind greatly activated, and who having consumed that which was squeezed out of the *Soma*, caused a series of bright, Sun-like objects to get continuously issued out. The *Soma* moved along with the objects that were thus created, with an invisible enveloping nature. It remained as a readily available regal entity that extended its ever ready benevolence to its subjects. The exhilaration that once was, permeated as the benevolence of the universe that got instituted later.

RV8.48.08 सोम राजन् मृळया नः स्वस्ति तव स्मसि
प्रत्याऽस्तस्य विद्धि। अलर्ति दक्ष उत
मन्युरिन्दो मा नो अर्यो अनुकामं परा दाः॥

[सोम - the *Soma* ◇ राजन् -royally born and issued out ◇ मृळया - compassionately; graciously ◇ नः - as ◇ स्वस्ति - successfully ◇ तव - thy ◇ स्मसि - certainly bound to ◇ प्रति - all directions ◇ आ - manifested ◇ अस्तस्य - flung away ◇ विद्धि - piercing; perforating ◇ अलर्ति - eagerly ◇ दक्ष - efficiently ◇ उत - interconnected ◇ मन्युः - arduously; supposedly ◇ इन्दो - from a bright spot ◇ मा - an arrangement ◇ नो - as ◇ अर्यो - devoted ◇ अनुकामं - most agreeably ◇ परा - manifesting to distant places ◇ दाः - granting; bestowing]

From the *Soma* and from a bright spot that manifested into it, came an arrangement most agreeable and devoted, manifesting after perforating the *Soma*, flowing into all directions and from these came the many objects, graciously, eagerly, successfully and efficiently bestowed, born and flung away interconnected to distant places.

From the *Soma*, upon squeezed out, issued out and generated, a cleverly weaved arrangement of energy and matter, making the self agreeable as issued to the surroundings. From the inert and static conditions in which it existed earlier, the *Soma* assumed a regal posture and got itself squeezed out as extruded to all sides and to the surroundings, simultaneously. While it became the later arrangement of energy and matter closely interconnected and as issued to the distant places, it remained with these, as the most agreeable provider of the seed substance. The term extruded and perforated perhaps required an explanation. The *Soma* that first remained in a secluded and exclusive place penetrated its cover as an extrusion, still containing the matter and energy in its hold all through its journey up to this earth and similar places. It did not flow by breaking the envelope, but flowed as extended arms of creation downward and to far places. The nature of its enveloping the objects was retained all the while. It did not permeate all over the universe but stuck to well defined routes through which creation took place. These extrusions took place to both the sides just as the expansions from the points of origin did, to maintain an equilibrium and symmetry in growth and substance.

RV8.48.09 त्वं हि नस्तन्वः सोम गोपा गात्रेगात्रे निषसत्था नृचक्षाः।
यत् ते वयं प्रमिनाम व्रतानि स नो मृळ सुषखा देव वस्यः॥

[त्वं - thyself ◇ हि - only ◇ नः - as ◇ तन्वः - the body parts ◇ सोम - the *Soma* ◇ गोपा - protecting ◇ गात्रेगात्रे - parts after parts ◇ निषसत् - seated ◇ था - firmly ◇ नृचक्षाः - from the eye that saw up to man ◇ यत्ते - progressed as those ◇ वयं - a body ◇ प्रमि - observing ◇ नाम - specified ◇ व्रतानि - rules ◇ स - with ◇ नो - as ◇ मृळ - kindly; fondly ◇ सुषखा - in good company ◇ देव - from the heaven ◇ वस्य - as the augmented welfare]

The *Soma*, as based on the eye that saw up to man, came from the heaven as the augmented welfare of the universe, by thyself protecting all the parts that came from the earlier parts, got seated firmly and progressed with those to become the body of the universe, manifesting according to the prescribed rules of creation and as those that existed in good and mutually fond company.

The *Soma* that resided near the eye (epicentre) that saw up to man, divided the very self into well protected segments after segments, took appropriate positions, and thus bestowed the parts of the very body of the universe as it came about, as per the well judged rules of creation. Thus a kindness got extended from the heaven to contain those parts that agreeably lived for ever. From its location in the heaven, the *Soma* was made into several parts which got repeatedly divided and which took appropriate positions as it occurred. The term "*pramināma vratāni*" could also be taken as the rules that were earlier declared or as the sounds that manifested at the point of origin. Comparable with the description of the part by part oblation of the *Puruṣa*, the *Soma* was so apportioned in the process of creation. More basic to this process, there manifested the first of cosmic vibrations which came from the well judged and divine rules. It also indicated the very geometry of development of the universe as one that came to the surroundings and as one that bowed down and retreated in reverence. Thus the very statement of reverence and the action thereof, would also become a description of the progress of enlargement and a part of the geometry of the universe.

RV8.48.10 ऋदूदरेण सख्या सचेय यो मा न रिष्येद्धर्यश्व पीतः।
अयं यः सोमो न्यधाय्यस्मे तस्मा इन्द्रं प्रतिरमेम्यायुः॥

[ऋदूदरेण - from the soft interiors ◇ सख्या - with friendship ◇ सचेय - with worships ◇ यो - somehow ◇ मा - the arrangement ◇ न - as ◇ रिष्येद् - afflicted, ruined in many ways ◇ धरि - bearing ◇ अश्व - spread like ◇ पीतः - swelled ◇ अयं - thus ◇ यः - as ◇ सोमो - the *Soma* ◇ नि - descended ◇ अध - then ◇ अय - moved ◇ अस्मे - as parts ◇ तस्मा - as arrangement of fading away ◇ इन्द्रं - from *indrata* ◇ प्रति - in all directions ◇ रम् - stayed ◇ एम - in routes ◇ य - as ◇ आयु - extended]

From the soft interiors of the *Soma* in the heaven, along

with worships, somehow came those arrangements derived out of afflictions, bearing those that many ways spread and thus swelled the universe. The *Soma* itself descended along with the parts that moved to become an arrangement that ultimately faded away. All of these manifested from *indrata*, coming into all directions, in stable and much extended routes.

From a soft interior along with the prayers that came in friendliness, came the arrangements of goodness that manifested from afflictions, which made the *Soma* to swell on and thus it came expanded as several mantles. Yet those that came from the *Sat* and the *indrata*, as the sweet anticipations of the universe. The *Soma* that existed as a soft entity in the beginning and then manifested as the vigorous energy and matter of the universe. From a particle of shining matter and energy, from the *indrata*, the vigorous anticipations of the universe got triggered and moved. Till that moment, the *Soma* had remained inert and inactive. The terms like softness and anticipations created an ambiance of biological progress based on the *annabhāva*.

RV8.48.11 अप त्या अस्थुरनिरा अमीवा निरत्रसन् तमिषीचीरभैषुः।
आ सोमो अस्माँ अरुहद्विहाया अगन्म यत्र प्रतिरन्त आयुः॥

[अप - a liquid form ◇ त्या - as is known, manifested ◇ अस्थुर् - unstable; restless ◇ अनिर - destitute of vigour ◇ अमीवा - sick and sad ◇ निरत्रसन् - not vibrant ◇ त - that ◇ मिष् - by the blinking of the eye ◇ ई - indeed ◇ चीर - as shreds of cloth ◇ भेषु - and beams of light ◇ आ - came from ◇ सोमो - the *Soma* ◇ अस्माँ - as parts that came ◇ अरुहद् - descending ◇ विहाया - expanded and progressed ◇ अगन् - as a mountain ◇ म - the self ◇ यत्र - in many and ◇ प्रतिः - in all directions ◇ अन्त - till the end ◇ आयु - extended]

From that which stood restless, destitute of vigour, sick, sad, not vibrant and known to exist in a liquid form, came to below those that came by the blinking of an eye. Beams of light came flashed like the shredded stripes of cloth hung from a waist. Still the parts that came from the *Soma*, moved, descended, expanded. The self progressed and stood as the mountainous forms that came into many and all directions till the end.

Not only the paths of creations and the excellent shining objects, got issued out of the *Soma*, those forces and entities that opposed all growth, also manifested with equal strength. These destructive forces, weakened or terminated further movements of some, reduced the energy levels of others and even destroyed the created ones. Objects were flung to the wayside making those to be of no consequence or became immobilised. The universe that came from the *Soma* got progressively diluted as it moved outward, as to its contents of matter and energy. The emaciation took place to the size and energy levels of individual objects and groups, as well as to their density of occupation in space. While it so progressed, the objects were re-organised, left stationed behind or got extremely moved. The expansions of the universe took place equally to both sides and in all directions.

RV8.48.12 यो न इन्दुः पितरो हृत्सु पीतोऽमर्त्यो मर्त्याँ आविवेश।
तस्मै सोमाय हविषा विधेम मृळीके अस्य सुमतौ स्याम॥

[यो - from which ◇ न - as ◇ इन्दुः - a spot of brightness ◇ पितरो - moved and forded ◇ हृत्सु - carried and proceeded ◇ पीतो - swelling ◇ अमर्त्यो - as immortal ◇ मर्त्याँ - and mortal; moved till man ◇ आ - manifesting as ◇ वि - divided ◇ वेश - occupants ◇ तस्मै - as those ◇ सोमाय - moved from the *Soma* ◇ हविषा - as the products of oblations ◇ विधेम - in forms moved ◇ मृळीके - favourable ◇ अस्य - in that manner ◇ सुमतौ - like-ably and ◇ स्याम - happily]

That which was a spot of brightness, moved and forded away carrying a burden that got enlarged, swelled and became mortal and immortal manifesting up to man as the divided occupants and those came moved from the *Soma*. The products of oblations moved in favourable forms and became the powers that stood together. Thus several dependents came, which stood happily and pleasantly. All of these came from the *Soma* by the oblations that had occurred.

The creation progressed, born as a spot of brightness into the *Soma*, and getting enlarged from it as this immense universe carrying several types of objects, some of which remained immortal and the others mortal. Many were born till man, as a chain of dependents but all of these were of equitable or appropriate status and became the parts of this pleasant universe. Thus a set of mighty objects came from the *yajñas* and co-existed maintaining good and satisfactory relations to one another.

RV8.48.13 त्वं सोम पितृभिः संविदानोऽनु द्यावापृथिवी आ ततन्थ।
तस्मै त इन्दो हविषा विधेम वयं स्याम पतयो रयीणाम्॥

[त्वं - thyself ◇ सोम - as the *Soma* ◇ पितृभिः - became the progeny ◇ सं - stood together ◇ विदानो - as entities ◇ अनु - and sub-sets ◇ द्यावापृथिवी - from the heaven till earth ◇ आ - manifested ◇ ततन्थ - as those from those stationed ◇ तस्मै - in that manner ◇ त - those ◇ इन्दो - a spot of brightness ◇ हविषा - coming as products of oblations ◇ विधेम - in such forms moved ◇ वयं - as a body ◇ स्याम - with strengths ◇ पतयो - falling and moving forward ◇ रयीणाम् - as the excellence manifested]

Thyself came as the progeny that came from the *Soma* which stood together with the entities and their sub-sets manifested from the heaven till the earth, as those that came from those, taking positions from that spot of brightness. The products of oblations came in such forms as to make the body of the universe to be a descending order of strength and excellence.

Thus from the heaven and from the *Soma*, descended a set of heavens and earths which stood individually or collectively as it came about. In a similar manner, the creation proceeded further from existing states. And yet these were known as manifested out of *yajñas* and born out of the oblations. It was thus that this powerful arrangement of excellent entities much descended from the heaven, coming as an arrangement that sequentially reduced, extending from the heaven to the earth as succeeding entities that got continuously issued from bright spots that continued to appear. The overall structure of the universe consisted of several objects, big and small as manifested from the drops of brightness.

RV8.48.14 त्रातरो देवा अधि वोचता नो मा नो निद्रा ईशत मोत जल्पिः। वयं सोमस्य विश्वह प्रियासः सुवीरासो विदथमा वदेम॥

[त्रातरो - protected and forded ◇ देवा - from the heaven manifesting ◇ अधि - from above ◇ वोचता - by words that came ◇ नो - as ◇ मा - arrangement ◇ नो - as ◇ निद्रा - that remained in sleep ◇ ईशत - a supremacy ◇ मोत - out of; connected ◇ जल्पिः - murmurs ◇ वयं - as a body ◇ सोमस्य - from the *Soma* ◇ विश्व - reaching everywhere ◇ ह - distanced ◇ प्रिय - agreeably ◇ असः - in that manner ◇ सुवीर - courageously ◇ असो - like that ◇ विदथ - knowledge ◇ मा - arrangement ◇ वदेम - from words moved; coursed]

From that which remained as if in sleep in the heaven, upon the words that manifested from above, moved and forded as an arrangement of protection and supremacy, to become the body of the universe. As brought about from the *Soma* to great distances by the murmurs that manifested and which reached everywhere, many arrangements came born courageously and in an agreeable manner. Knowledge and the words had come moved along with this progress.

The *Soma* was awakened from a deep sleep by words that came from above, as if rescued by a divinity from its captivity. This was acknowledged as a courageous act and was stated as came from knowledge. From the *Soma* which remained as if in deep sleep and as if in captivity, a command from knowledge that came as the divine murmurs, set off the process of creation of the universe. It created the heavens that stood around and below and established the three dimensionality of the universe. The universe thus became a courageous existence of many diverse objects with a visible stamp of mutual affection and love. The courageousness referred here was the attribute of unremitting forward progress and the love could be termed as the interactive bond that prevailed all over and for ever.

Many verses of the *Ṛgveda* proclaim the presence of knowledge and the chanting of the hymns in the process of creation. The concept of the essential requirement of fundamental cosmic vibrations that would provide space and energy for the creation appeared to be a well accepted notion which would get stated often. The basic concept here would be that the prayers, words and sounds were addressed to oneself, as addressed to an embryonic entity, which would ultimately become the universe. At a time when the deified forms of worship did not exist, perhaps all prayers would be primarily addressed to oneself. Being part of a whole, i.e, the embryonic state of the universe, the divine prayers were addressed to the self. It was these prayers that acted as the energising forces which triggered the creation of the universe. These were the prayers that later manifested in appropriate measures along with the progress of an expansion. The term "*vocatā*" might, therefore carry a meaning of occurrence of the chanting of the hymns and a set of vibrations of sound that manifested through all stages of creation. The earthly terms of "words" and "sounds" should be taken as the vibrations that manifested in the universal scale and with appropriate dimensions and measures. The very vibrations that set off came from divine knowledge; one of the deep seated Vedic faiths of creation.

RV8.48.15 त्वं नः सोम विश्वतो वयोधास्त्वं स्वर्विदा विशा नृचक्षाः।
त्वं न इन्द्र ऊतिभिः सजोषाः पाहि पश्चातादुत वा पुरस्तात्॥

[त्वं - thyself ◇ नः - as ◇ सोम - the *Soma* ◇ विश्वतो - that reached everywhere ◇ वयोधाः - coming invigoratingly ◇ त्वं - thyself ◇ स्वः - by own ◇ विदा - knowledge coming ◇ विशा - successively manifesting ◇ नृचक्षा - from that eye that saw up to man ◇ त्वं - thyself ◇ न - as ◇ इन्द्र - from that spot of brightness ◇ ऊतिभिः - bound to as well ◇ सजोषाः - enthusiastically ◇ पाहि - protected ◇ पश्चाद् - and later ◇ आद् - coming ◇ उत - interconnected ◇ वा - moved ◇ पुरस्तात् - moved from the earlier]

Oriented to that eye that saw up to man, thyself coming from an invigorated *Soma* that reached everywhere, thyself coming from knowledge that successively manifested, thyself coming enthusiastically, protected and bound to that spot of brightness, and later manifesting as those that came from the earlier, became this immense universe.

Thyself thus came as the very youthfulness that spread everywhere, from that entity of a bright drop, bringing those that remained woven together. Those remained protected and came from the earlier ones to become the later ones. The universe came into existence with the manifestation of a bright spot into the *Soma* and then became the youthful self that got extended until the very end as protected and interconnected entities of bright spots. All of that, that earlier occurred in the heaven near the very epicentre, later reoccurred as extended to far off places and till the very end limits of the universe. There were similarities between the manner in which the very potent *Soma* that existed in heaven and the arrangement of the objects that came later. The youthfulness, protected, interactive nature and the brightness was common to both. The very interactive nature manifested first with the advent of the divine words that were uttered at heaven and which enabled the growth of the immense universe. Thus the universe came into existence only as that which manifested from a former state to that of a later state.

In this *sūkta*, it was impressed that everything came from the *Soma*. The beginning was marked by the appearance of a bright spot and this later grew into the immensely large universe, remaining interconnected. The description in no way changed the geometry of the universe as presented by the *puruṣasūkta* and other hymns. The theoretical point of origin was described as a place from which the entire universe extending up to men was surveyed. The *Soma* prevalent in the adjacent space i.e, the heaven, extended itself as an enveloping entity with the objects that got created contained within. The creation as such only commenced upon the advent of a murmur and the first set of divine and cosmic vibrations intc the bright spot that manifested first. These then were capable of acting as the necessary basic space, time and energy that would become this very large universe.

RV 8.79

[(9) नवर्चस्यास्य सूक्तस्य भार्गवः कृलुर्ऋषिः। सोमो देवता। (1 - 8) प्रथमादार्ष्टर्चां गायत्रि (9) नवम्याश्चनुष्टुप् छन्दसी]

RV8.79.01 अयं कृलुरगृभीतो विश्वजिदुद्भिदित्सोमः।
ऋषिर्विप्रः काव्येन॥

[अयं - thus ◇ कृलुः - skilfully ◇ अगृभीतो - released ◇ विश्वजिद् - as the successes that reached everywhere ◇ उद्भिद् - burst out ◇ इत् - moved ◇ सोमः - the *Soma* ◇ ऋषिः - flowing ◇ वि - divided ◇ प्रः - to the surroundings ◇ काव्येन - intelligently]

Thus the *Soma* flowed divided to the surroundings, intelligently, skilfully, as burst out and released from the heaven and became the successes that moved and reached everywhere.

The sages and the knowledgeable decreed that it was the *Soma* that capably moved from above, sprinkling till the end, bursting off and conquering all and thus reaching everywhere. Thus capably moving and sprinkling till the very end, the *Soma* progressed and conquered the universe as a flow that got divided into the surroundings. The subject of the origin of the universe had received careful attention by many sages and knowledgeable persons. They all agreed that the universe came from the *Soma*.

RV8.79.02 अभ्यूर्णोति यन्नग्नं भिषक्ति विश्वं यत्तुरम्।
प्रेमन्धः ख्यन्निः श्रोणो भूत्॥

[अभि - progressing further ◇ ऊर्ण - blanket ◇ उति - raised ◇ यन् - whatever ◇ अग्नं - as *Agni* ◇ भिषक्ति - cured ◇ विश्वं - came as everywhere ◇ यत् - progressing ◇ तुरम् - instantly ◇ प्रेमन्धः - stood with affection ◇ ख्यन्निः - descending from knowledge ◇

श्रोणो - accumulated as ◇ भूत् - the entities]

After raising the blanket with which it was closely enwrapped and getting cured by whatever way came the *Agni*, manifested as everywhere, instantly came progressed as the entities that stood with affection that got accumulated; all having descended from divine knowledge.

The *Soma* which once remained sick, inert and as if covered by a blanket was suddenly acted upon by a hitherto unknown *Agni* which energized it and made it capable of issuing out as the wide expanse of a sky and its contents. The intensely wrapped up earlier state transformed into a wide sky and the widely distributed objects. Being energised by the *Agni*, the *Soma* got agitated and swirled to the surroundings providing many objects of many properties that eventually matured. It manifested as the interactive nature, love, affection and a universal acceptability. These matters were sufficiently well known.

RV8.79.03 त्वं सोम तनूकृद्भ्यो द्वेषोभ्योऽन्यकृतेभ्यः।
उरु यन्तासि वरूथम्॥

[त्वं - thyself ◇ सोम - as the *Soma* ◇ तनूकृद्भ्यो - made into small segments ◇ द्वेषोभ्यो - as if angrily ◇ अन्यकृतेभ्यः - progressed as made into many others ◇ उरु - broadly expanded ◇ यन्तासि - whatever stood bonded to one another ◇ वरूथम् - as a safe existence]

Thyself came as the *Soma*, upon angrily made into small segments, progressed as made into many others, smote to the proximity, stood bonded together and widely expanded as the universe and a safe existence.

It was as if someone angrily chopping wood that the *Soma* got widely broadcast that the universe came, but it ultimately became a safe existence. It was from those chopped up parts of the *Soma*, that the individual paths of creation flowed. Though the universe was born with such afflictions, anger and violence in the beginning, the later existence showed peace and equanimity.

RV8.79.04 त्वं चित्ति तव दक्षैर्दिव आ पृथिव्या ऋजीषिन्।
यावीरघस्य चिद्द्वेषः॥

[त्वं - thyself ◇ चित्ति - as from a mind; as from a heap ◇ तव - thy ◇ दक्षैर् - cleverness ◇ दिव - as the heaven ◇ आ - manifested ◇ पृथिव्या - as earths that came ◇ ऋजि - directly ◇ इषिन् - and quickly discharged ◇ या - progressed ◇ वि - divided ◇ इर - angrily ◇ घस्य - striking ◇ चिद् - mind ◇ द्वेषः - with dislike]

Thyself, from thy mind and by thy cleverness, became the heaven and the earth forms directly, quickly discharged and progressed, getting divided as if angrily struck by someone, who stood with dislike.

The *Soma*, all by itself, out of its own intentions, powers and cleverness became the many earth forms that stood around and came descended as the heavens and remained in various positions. The *Soma* realised the significance of its existence, made itself into a capable entity, divided itself into parts and got scattered around the universe bringing those shining and bright objects. The *Soma* while it moved along with these objects, it also remained with what were left around and behind. The *Soma* mercilessly divided the self for this purpose. The angry and inimical obstructions that were found to appear as attacking and dividing the created objects, also came from the very *Soma*.

RV8.79.05 अर्थिनो यन्ति चेदर्थं गच्छानिद्ददुषो रातिम्।
ववृज्युस्तृष्यतः कामम्॥

[अर्थिनो - as seeking ◇ यन्ति - in unknown ways ◇ चेदर्थं - whatever purpose ◇ गच्छा - obtained ◇ निः - to below ◇ दद् - well bound ◇ उषो - risen ◇ र - issued out ◇ अतिं - greatly ◇ वव् - wavily ◇ ऋज् - directly ◇ युः - separated ◇ तृष्यतः - progressed longingly ◇ कामम् - and as desired]

Seeking in unknown ways and with whatever purpose, obtained as bestowed to below all bound to one another, again arising from those and issued out greatly, moving directly and in wave forms, got separated and progressed longingly and as desired.

Commencing from the heaven, the *Soma* and the *indrata*, the universe grew in many ways manifesting as the first born and from these born again and thus progressing farther and farther, till the very end. These moved in waveform through the paths, directly coming from what existed earlier and got much separated. These progressed interactive to one another, as if longing for each other.

RV8.79.06 विददात्पूर्व्यं नष्टमुदीमृतायुमीरयत्।
प्रेमायुस्तारीदतीर्णम्॥

[विदद् - from knowledge ◇ यत् - progressed ◇ पूर्व्यं - from earlier moved ◇ नष्टम् - losing ◇ उदीम् - rising again ◇ ऋताय् - moving obeying the extended laws ◇ मि - got established ◇ इरयत् - moving effortlessly ◇ प्रेमा - lovingly ◇ यु: - separated ◇ तारि - crossing over; fording ◇ इद् - only like that ◇ अतीर्णम् - till not spreading]

From knowledge progressed, from the earlier moved, losing, gaining, rising again and getting extended afar, obeying the laws of creation, as effortlessly carried away, lovingly fording away, in separate routes and in such manners it came till the spreading came to an end.

While along with knowledge and as if seeking, the objects came into existence, along with those that stood affectionately or as those which perished or as those that rose again and so those progressed, those came only as the ones that obeyed the laws of creation. All of these came as a progress from an earlier state to a later state and as the new ones that repeatedly manifested. As moved out of the earlier knowledge and intelligence, loosing the blend of what existed, became a sacredly, effortlessly and a lovably bound enlargement. The *Soma* which stood for a purpose and a corresponding significance, intelligently, effortlessly changed the existing composition and became a sacred, lovable and interconnected enlargement. Earlier, what way it remained bound to the heaven, later the same way became effortlessly bound to one another.

RV8.79.07 सुशेवो नो मृळयाकुरदृप्तक्रतुरवातः।
भवा नः सोम शं हृदे॥

[सुशेवो - favourable ◇ नो - and ◇ मृळया - compassionate ◇ कुर् - sounds ◇ अदृप्त - made mild ◇ क्रतुः - created ◇ अव - downward ◇ अतः - as those ◇ भवा - that stood ◇ नः - as ◇ सोम - the *Soma* ◇ शं - auspicious ◇ हृदे - from the hearts]

From what stood as favourable and compassionate, along with the sounds that came into it getting milder, downwards came and stood those that came from the *Soma*, moving from the hearts as the auspicious things that those would become.

At the heart of the universe, at the heaven, the *Soma* had remained and into this came the divine and appropriate sounds, to bring forth the many benevolences. In this process the sounds and vibrations became milder as the universe expanded. Not only excellent objects of the universe came spreading to the surroundings, but also brought forth several heavens which acted as the hearts from which the creation further progressed. Those compassionate nature and acceptability were many time repeated downwards and till the end.

RV8.79.08 मा नः सोम सं वीविजो मा वि बीभिषथा राजन्।
मा नो हार्दि त्विषा वधीः॥

[मा - arrangements ◇ नः - as ◇ सोम - from the *Soma* ◇ सं - and assembled ◇ वीविजो - sped as darts ◇ मा - arrangements ◇ वि - divided ◇ बीभ् - confidently ◇ इषथा - as the semen virile ◇ राजन् - royally born and delivered ◇ मा - arrangements ◇ नो - as ◇ हार्दि - in the hearts ◇ त्विषा - with great turmoil ◇ वधी - and as deaths]

From the *Soma* came those arrangements of those that stood together, those arrangements of the divided movements of the semen virile, and the arrangements of those that got royally born and issued out, in the process of which the hearts got into great turmoils and even got destroyed.

The process of creation initiated from the *Soma*, produced many objects that either stood together or manifested again in different ways. It became an arrangement of the divided. It manifested as the semen virile that spread from the many hearts and from which objects were born and reborn. In such processes the very hearts perished or became devoid of any forms of entity. Here, perhaps we could discern the conceptual differences between the "heaven" and the "heart". From the heaven, the many paths of creation were swung around and so those stood. But from the hearts, the semen virile moved out of the turmoils that happened there, which made these into unidentifiable later existence.[4]

RV8.79.09 अव यत्स्वे सधस्थे देवानां दुर्मतीरीक्षे।
राजन्नप द्विषः सेध मीढ्वो अप स्रिधः सेध॥

[अव - to the proximity ◇ यत् - progressed ◇ स्वे - thyself ◇ सधस्थे - as of equal might ◇ देवानां - as the heavens that came ◇ दुर्मती - the bad intentions ◇ ईक्षे - perceived as ◇ राजन् - royally born and bestowed ◇ अप - downwards; away ◇ द्विषः - with enmity and anger ◇ सेध - that prevented ◇ मीढ्वो - as a competition ◇ अप - downward; away ◇ स्रिधः - evil ◇
सेध - and resisted]

Thyself progressed to the proximity, as those that moved from the heavens, as those that got bestowed and born downwards and along with those came with equal might that which stood with enmity, anger and which prevented creation and again those that resisted these evil ones, as if a competition had descended.

While the *Soma* spread into the surroundings along the chosen paths from the heaven, several such heavens came into existence from which new paths were further born. Along with these developments, those evil things with hostile intentions had also come born of equal might. These bad forces were inimical to the process of creation and wantonly destroyed the ones created. While the value and strength of

[4]All the same, it would not be possible to totally confirm this definition, and the concepts behind the terms like the mind, heart and the heaven needed more clarity.

these opposing forces went on diminishing as the creation progressed, both of these forces presented themselves with equal strength till the very end. The evil entities obviously were those that got issued out from the darkness that stood around the paths of creation, generally sourced to the *vṛtrata*. The *Soma* that remained inert in the heaven, upon the advent of a sparkling particle of matter, rushed down in several paths of creation in several directions around the heaven. As if blown away by a roaring wind, the objects created spread in all directions. From that sleeping entity and upon awakened by a divine intellect, not only many excellent things of the universe were born, but those angry and opposing forces of wanton destruction had also come with equal might.

The three hymns given here emphasized that the *Soma* was the seed substance for the creation not only in the beginning but it also acted as the repository of the seed principle throughout the routes in which the universe grew. It was the very reason and excitement of creation. Its cover of halo extended to all the streams of creation and provided a restraining barrier to an all pervading darkness. It was the unseen bright transparency that spread along the paths of creation. The descriptions here presented subtle variations of the concepts prevalent about the profound subject of how the universe was born, as a sample of the elaborate considerations that went into such subjects during the Vedic times.

★★★

5

Gāyatrī Sūkta-The Supreme Universal Order

Then there is the hymn RV3.62 which contained the famous *gāyatrīmantra* much dear to all of India. The *gāyatri* was found associated with the divinity called *savita*, a brilliant intellect that graced all. The hymn, however, also brought out certain notions of what divinity really meant to be.

[(18) अष्टदशर्चस्यास्य सूक्तस्य गाथिनो विश्वामित्रः (16-18) षोडश्यादितृचस्य च जमदग्निर्वा ऋषिः। (1-3) प्रथमादितृचस्येन्द्रावरुणो (4-6) चतुर्थ्यादितृचस्य बृहस्पतिः (7-9) सप्तम्यादितृचस्य पूषा (10-12) दशम्यादितृचस्य सविता (13-15) त्रयोदश्यादितृचस्य सोमः (16-18) षोडश्यादितृचस्य च मित्रावरुणौ देवताः। (1-3) प्रथमतृचस्य त्रिष्टुप् (4-18) चतुर्थ्यादिपञ्चदशर्चाञ्च गायत्री छन्दसी]

RV3.62.01 इमा उ वां भृमयो मन्यमाना युवावते न तुज्या अभूवन्।
क्व१ त्यदिन्द्रावरुणा यशो वां येन स्मा सिनं भरथः सखिभ्यः॥

[इमा - thus ◇ उ - indeed ◇ वां - propagated ◇ भृमयो - growing happiness ◇ मन्य - reckoned as ◇ मना - having manifested ◇ युव - assembled; youthful ◇ अवते - those as away ◇ न - as ◇ तुज्या - impelled; cast away ◇ अभूवन् - till nothing came into existence

◇ कु - somehow ◇ त्यद् - known as ◇ इन्द्रावरुणा - *Indrāvaruṇa* ◇ यशो - famous ◇ वां - propagated ◇ येन - from whatever those ◇ वां - propagated ◇ येन - from whatever those ◇ स्मा - coming for ever ◇ सिनं - bonded ◇ भरथः - established as filled ◇ सखिभ्यः - with friends]

Thus indeed propagated carrying many a happiness, as regulated arrangements that was reckoned to have come from a divine mind to be an assembly of youthful things. Those came into existence much impelled away till nothing further manifested. These were brought about by the divinity known and famous as *Indrāvaruṇa*. Those became whatever that moved away from whatever that had come earlier, got established interactively bonded to one another and got filled with a friendliness for ever to be.

All those things that manifested in the universe came only regulated by a divine mind and by that exalted divinity called *Indrāvaruṇa*. All happiness seen in the universe, all those objects that stood together as clusters, all those ones that were thrown out to distances, all those that propagated into several directions till nothing was further born, could only be termed as manifested from the deeds of the divinity called the *Indrāvaruṇa*. Upon getting manifested into the heaven and into the *Soma* as a bright particle of matter and energy, everything moved from there along the roaring waves of the atmosphere. All were found to cohabit in friendship and in mutual benevolence. It was the *Indrāvaruṇa* that combination of *saguṇa* divinity who carried out the orders of that *nirguṇa* Supreme Divinity. It was the rare coincidence of the instantaneous manifestation of that shining particle of matter and the auspicious appearance of the divine cosmic sounds and vibrations that set off the process of creation. Those divine forces manifesting separately and at different times could not have set off the process of creation.

RV3.62.02 अयमु वां पुरतमो रयीयञ्छश्वत्तममवसे जोहवीति।
सजोषाविन्द्रावरुणा मरुद्भिर्दिवा पृथिव्या शृणुतं हवं मे॥

[अयम् - indeed thus ◇ वां - propagated ◇ पुरतमो - greatly advanced from the past ◇ रयि - as excellences ◇ इयज्ञ - spread and swirled ◇ शश्वत् - for ever ◇ तमम् - the darkness ◇ अवसे - moved incessantly ◇ जोहवि - whatever products of oblations ◇ इति - and those ◇ सजोष - that unitedly ◇ अव् - impelled by ◇ इन्द्रावरुणा - the *Indrāvaruṇa* ◇ मरुद्भिः - and own sounds ◇ दिवा - as the heavens ◇ पृथिव्या - the earths ◇ शृणुतं - by great prayers; audibility ◇ हवं - and by oblations ◇ मे - evolving]

Thus indeed advanced forward, got propagated the excellences that came from what existed earlier, spreading and swirling to become those ones that stood united. A darkness had manifested along with whatever products of oblations that got impelled. It was by *Indrāvaruṇa* and by the sounds that came from the self that the heavens, the earths and all of the universe manifested. Those came with the great prayers, the audibility and the oblations that manifested and went on evolving further and farther.

Thus propagated, pushed forward, manifested the excellence, a darkness and those that dwell in darkness. Those became the acceptable products of oblations, brought about by *Indrāvaruṇa*. Yet those manifested only out of prayers and the oblations which brought the heavens and earths as if moved by an unseen wind. It was that divine partnership which appeared as the *Indrāvaruṇa* that indeed compulsively propagated the several heavens and earths of the universe to their positions. Those were the products of the oblations of whatever that stood earlier. Those were the excellences that came into existence for ever. It was true that the divine prayers and the cosmic vibrations came as the efforts of creation. It was true that the *Agni* and the *yajña* appeared on each occasion. Yet it was the divine and simultaneous manifestation of that bright particle of matter and the divine sounds and the cosmic vibrations that gave a start to the process of creation.

RV3.62.03 अस्मे तदिन्द्रावरुणा वसु ष्यादस्मे रयिर्मरुतः सर्ववीरः।

अस्मान्वरूत्रीः शरणैरवन्त्वस्मान्होत्रा भारति दक्षिणाभिः ॥

[अस्मे - as the entities ◇ तद् - that ◇ इन्द्रावरुणा - *Indrāvaruṇa* ◇ वसु - positioned only ◇ ष्याद् - mixed ◇ अस्मे - parts ◇ रयिः - of excellences ◇ मरुतः - as from the sounds of the self ◇ सर्ववीरः - with many descendants ◇ अस्मान् - as parts ◇ वरूत्रीः - shelter ◇ शरणैर् - as the refuge ◇ अवन्तु - strongly pushed ◇ अस्मान् - as parts that got breathed out ◇ होत्रा - as issued out of oblations ◇ भार - burden ◇ अति - greatly ◇ दक्षिण - clever ◇ अभि - progressed]

Thus all came into existence as the entities that *Indrā varuṇa* positioned as the mixed parts of excellent nature that manifested from the sounds and as those that came from the self. Many that came descended became the shelter and refuge to many others. Those that got strongly pushed out and strongly breathed out as the burden that came out of the many oblations were found to progress greatly and cleverly.

The entities brought in by the *Indrāvaruṇa*, as the excellence created and as the wonderful deeds executed, became those that were obtained by successive pounding, those that stood daringly together, those clusters of different entities, those issued out of oblations, those shining happiness, those clever manifestations and those refuges of the ones that implored for help. It was with the appearance of that shining particle of matter, with the manifestation of the divine sounds and cosmic vibrations and with the propagation along the roaring waves in the ocean of an atmosphere, that the excellences of the universe ever came into existence. The wonderful deeds of *Indrāvaruṇa* enabled all these. One excellence got divided into several excellences and became several different entities that stood separately or in clusters. It was a daring existence of the visible. Those clever manifestations beamed happiness. Those were the products of *yajña* and accompanying oblations. Each of those existences was a refuge to those that stood under it. The 3-dimensional nature was sufficiently indicated here. It was also implied that the sounds and cosmic vibrations repeatedly manifested till the end.

RV3.62.04 बृहस्पते जुषस्व नो हव्यानि विश्वदेव्य।
रास्व रत्नानि दाशुषे॥

[बृहस्पते - the *Bṛhaspati* ◇ जुषस्व - to his own satisfaction ◇ नो - as ◇ हव्यानि - products of oblations ◇ विश्व - reaching everywhere ◇ देव्य - as the heavens ◇ रास्व - bestowing from the self ◇ रत्नानि - as the diamonds ◇ दाशुषे - and the auspicious risings]

As the satisfaction brought to the surroundings by *Bṛhaspati*, as the products of oblations generated and as the heavens that reached everywhere in the universe, diamond like entities were created by him as the auspicious dawns that arose around.

Auspicious risings occurred as a result of the divine prayers and oblations. The heavens reached everywhere in the universe and entities were generated all around, which twinkled like diamonds. The universe came into existence as the paths of creation that repeatedly issued out of the many heavens that descended from the heaven. Pounded by the roaring sounds, the paths and objects created got widely distributed. Thus all were arrangements brought about by the *Bṛhaspati*, for he decided the extent of the universe.

RV3.62.05 शुचिमर्कैर्बृहस्पतिमध्वरेषु नमस्यत।
अनाम्योज आ चके॥

[शुचिम् - clean and white ◇ अर्के - brilliant like a Sun ◇ बृहस्पतिम् - descended greatly ◇ अधवरेषु - as those that incessantly ◇ नमस्यत - paying homage ◇ अनाम्य - unswerving ◇ ओज - vigour ◇ आ - coming ◇ चके - as the happiness and satisfactions]

From that which stood pure, white and brilliant as if a Sun, descended incessantly and greatly, those ones that paid homage to what stood above, with an unswerving vigour to become the happiness and satisfaction of the universe.

It was *Bṛhaspati* that decided the extents and depth of this universe and it was he who brought those never ending vigours and happiness of the universe to the satisfaction of all. It was he who decided the steepness of the descend and the universe bowed to him in reverence. He decided the extent of the very 3-dimensionality of the universe. Those that descended, came bowing down, bent as well as in straight paths (indicating geometry). Those were the Sun like entities that spread all over the universe.

RV3.62.06 वृषभं चर्षणीनां विश्वरूपमदाभ्यम्।
बृहस्पतिं वरेण्यम्॥

[वृषभं - strong ◇ चर्षणीनां - manifested from that eye ◇ विश्वरूपमद् - a shape that reached everywhere ◇ आ - manifested ◇ अभ्यम् - and advanced ◇ बृहस्पतिं - by *Bṛhaspati* ◇ वरेण्यम् - as the excellence and benevolence]

Moving from that eye and coming with great strength and masculine vigour, manifested the very shape of the universe that reached everywhere with many a happiness taken everywhere as the excellence and benevolence established by the *Bṛhaspati*.

With the excellence, benevolence and happiness brought about by the *Bṛhaspati*, the extent and depth of the universe defined by him, the universe expanded from that lofty eye, to become this much large and enormous. As the paths of creation that flowed from a powerful source and as the several centres of growth spread all over the universe, the creation progressed as per the wishes of *Bṛhaspati*.

These 3 verses described everything as occurred under the directions of *Bṛhaspati*. The sweep and depth of the universe was decided by the *Bṛhaspati*. As anticipated by the *Bṛhaspati*, and out of a Sun like shining entity, many such shining objects were born, got divided and got impelled by the divine sounds and the cosmic vibrations. What all were born remained as excellent entities that came for ever. Thus there indeed was a divinity that decided the very size and extent of the universe.

RV3.62.07 इयं ते पूषन्नाघृणे सुष्टुतिर्देव नव्यसि।
अस्माभिस्तुभ्यं शस्यते॥

[इयं - thus ◇ ते - as those ◇ पूषन् - that *Pūṣan* ◇ आघृणे - sprinkled and glowing with heat ◇ सुष्टुति - with divine prayers ◇ देव - from heaven ◇ नव्यसि - as those that smote new ◇ अस्म - as entities, parts ◇ अभि - advancing ◇ स्तुभ्यं - as a procession that moved shouting ◇ शस्यते - along with regulated praises]

Those that got sprinkled from the heaven glowing with heat, those that smote as the new entities that came along with the divine prayers and advanced as a procession that moved shouting and those that came along suitably regulated by prayers, all of those manifested from the divinity named *Pūṣan*.

Further, as sprinkled by *Pūṣan* and along with the divine prayers those pleasant entities smote from the heaven and progressed. Thus the excellences and benevolences of the universe came riotously advancing. Cleansed and classified by an unseen wind and sprinkled from the heavens and from the paths of creation, a series of pleasant entities came into the surroundings. Those were the creations brought about by the divine sounds and the cosmic vibrations that manifested into the surroundings, when necessary.

**RV3.62.08 तां जुषस्व गिरं मम वाजयन्तीमवा धियम्।
वधूयुरिव योषणाम्॥**

[तां - moved from those ◇ जुषस्व - self satisfaction ◇ गिरं - by words ◇ मम - own ◇ वाज - ardently ◇ यन्ति - held close ◇ इम - like that ◇ वा - moved ◇ धियम् - from an intellect ◇ वधू - as bride ◇ यु - and besides ◇ इव - as ◇ योषणाम् - come with a young woman]

As moved from those with endearing words of own choosing, moved from an existing intellect and moved with a young bride held close and also moved with other young women in the same manner, bringing the ones that came into existence.

With intelligence and own endearing words, an indisposition was converted into a self satisfaction. As if advancing to a young and demure woman with desires and fondly embracing her, led everything as wished. The one which remained in the heaven, indisposed and disenchanted was energised and led as the great satisfaction of the universe. A divine intellect and the appropriate sounds that came into the surroundings converted a disenchantment into a great pleasurable event and a benevolent existence. As if a young woman who longed for procreation went into a divine embrace and as if the long hands flung in ecstasy, the paths of creation flowed around. The universe appears to have come into existence out of divine copulations, that took place one after the other. The objects got sprinkled, carried away and classified by a wind and the universe became a well structured one that was brought about by *Pūṣa*. A suggestion was in the air that the divine nature went on diminishing and in diverse routes, since the process went on with other potential youthful ones and not limited to the bride that was first taken.

RV3.62.09 यो विश्वाभि विपश्यति भुवना सं च पश्यति।
स नः पूषाविता भुवत्॥

[यो - whatever ◇ विश्व - as reached everywhere ◇ अभि - advanced ◇ वि - as divided; diverse ◇ पश्यति - visibilities ◇ भुवना - came into the universe ◇ सं - assembled ◇ च - and ◇ पश्यति - as the visibilities ◇ स - with ◇ नः - as ◇ पूष - *Pūṣan* ◇ आ - brought ◇ विता - and spread ◇ भुवत् - moving in the atmosphere]

Whatever thus got manifested as the greatly diverse objects and visibilities that advanced in the universe, seen to have come as the visibilities that got assembled, moved and spread out in the atmosphere were only so brought by the efforts of *Pūṣan*.

It was the divinity of *Pūṣan* that spread the objects of the universe as divided, as assembled, as reaching from the heaven and as blossomed out into the great atmosphere. It was he who cleansed and classified the universe as if winnowed by a wind, out of the burning and shining single entity into several successive entities of varying brightness, as an extended steady progress through the atmosphere. With words that arose suitable to the occasions, respecting the divine wishes expressed, everything was brought to order that satisfied all. Thus it was the divinity of *Pūṣan* that achieved the healthy order of the universe.

RV3.62.10 तत्सवितुर्वरेण्यं भर्गो देवस्य धीमहि।
धियो यो नः प्रचोदयात्॥

[तत् - from That ◇ सवितुः - broadcast ◇ वरेण्यं - as the excellence ◇ भर्गो - as a great dalliance ◇ देवस्य - from the heaven ◇ धी - with intellect ◇ महि - and greatness ◇ धि - as intellect ◇ यो यो - proportionately ◇ नः - as ◇ प्र - to the surroundings ◇ चोदय - inspired ◇ अत् - and progressed]

As the excellences broadcast from That, as a great dalliance and a great intellect and as the many intellects that got proportionately inspired, the universe progressed to the surroundings.

It was one great dalliance and intellect that provided the intellect to the rest of the universe. There indeed was a divine exchange of intellect among all that existed in the universe. There indeed was an inspiration that went around the universe duly aided by that supreme intellect. This all pervading intellect came from That which stood above all. Alternately; that which existed under the control and magnanimity of the Sun remained inspired with an intellect proportionally derived from the great shining intellect of a magnificent divinity. This segment of a *mantra* remained a great aspiration of all of India for several millennium. A discussion in more details is furnished after presenting this hymn in full.

RV3.62.11 देवस्य सवितुर्वयं वाजयन्तः पुरंध्या।
भगस्य रातिमीमहे॥

[देवस्य - from the heaven ◇ सवितुः - spread, broadcast ◇ वयं - as a body ◇ वाज - energetically ◇ यन्तः - regulated ◇ पुरंधि - bountiful and liberal ◇ आ - coming ◇ भगस्य - beautifully ◇ राति - generously bestowing ◇ मी - established ◇ महे - as great]

The body of the universe spread from the heaven, moving energetically and in a regulated fashion, manifesting as liberal, bountiful, beautiful and as those that got generously bestowed and got established as a greatness.

As a beautiful body with widely broadcast brilliant objects and as those that came from the heaven, as those that moved winning till the very end, as those that consisted of very vigorous entities, the universe was created by the divine *Savita*, that great intellect and dalliance that spread everywhere.

RV3.62.12 देवं नरः सवितारं विप्रा यज्ञैः सुवृक्तिभिः।
नमस्यन्ति धियेषिताः॥

[देवं - from the heaven ◇ नरः - till man ◇ स - with ◇ वितारं - spreading ◇ वि - divided ◇ प्र - to the surroundings ◇ यज्ञै - as the *yajñas* ◇ सुवृक्तिभिः - with excellent prayers ◇ नमस्य - bowing down ◇ अन्ति - to the proximity ◇ धिय - an intellect ◇ इषिताः - as sent out]

Along with the auspicious and excellent prayers, and as the divided *yajñas* to the surroundings, as set out by a divine intellect, from the heaven till man spread those to the successive proximity, as if bowing down in reverence.

As the acceptable things that spread from the heaven till man, as the much divided *yajñas* that came along with the auspicious prayers, as the divine enquiries that came from an intellect, the universe manifested as if repeatedly bowing to the proximity. From the heaven along with the divine prayers, along with the sounds and those primordial cosmic vibrations and with the much divided *yajñas*, the universe was getting steadily enlarged. Steeply descending to the surroundings, the 3-dimensionality was becoming enormous in size. The shining dalliance and intellect in the form of the divine *Savita* was guiding this progress.

These 3 verses extolled the virtues of *Savita*, the divinity that manifested with Sun-like shines and as one that existed omniscient all over the universe. It was from such an omnipotent divinity the directions came for the very creation. The interactive nature of the universe was more trans-commuted vide these distributed shining objects. Perhaps it was meant to establish a dependency chain more operated through these shining chain of matter than the cold objects of the universe.

RV3.62.13 सोमो जिगाति गातुविद्देवानामेति निष्कृतम्।
ऋतस्य योनिमासदम्॥

[सोमो - as the *Soma* ◇ जि - that conquered ◇ ग - moving ◇ अति - greatly ◇ गा - moved ◇ तु - as the strength and power ◇ विद् - as knowledge ◇ देवानाम् - coming from heavens ◇ इति - in such manners ◇ निष्कृतम् - expelled ◇ ऋतस्य - according to the rules ◇ योनिम् - from wombs ◇ आ - manifested ◇ सदम् - for ever]

With the *Soma* greatly moving and conquering, as the strength, power and knowledge that were manifested, came those things from the many heavens, as expelled from many wombs, as born according to the rules and the universe came into existence for ever.

The *Soma* moved from the *hiraṇyagarbha*, the heaven, to be present in the several heavens that stood around and below and the objects born out of the many wombs manifested in a like manner. While the paths of creation was found repeatedly manifested from the heavens, the objects were found repeatedly born from the potential entities. Yet all of these progressed only according to certain divine laws and out of the divine knowledge that accompanied the very progress.

RV3.62.14 सोमो अस्मभ्यं द्विपदे चतुष्पदे च पशवे।
अनमीवा इषस्करत्॥

[सोमो - the *Soma* ◇ अस्म - as the entities ◇ अभ्यं - manifested advancing ◇ द्विपदे - doubled ◇ चतुष्पदे - and quadrupled ◇ च - and ◇ पशवे - the visibilities woven ◇ अनमीवा - setting aside sickness ◇ इषः - as the semen virile ◇ करात् - moved as hands]

Many entities moved and came advanced from the *Soma* which doubled and then quadrupled, as the visibilities that manifested and stood woven together. Upon setting aside its sick state, the *Soma* flowed as the extended hands of the semen virile.

The multi-forked paths of creation flowed with the *Soma*,

the visible objects sped away in twos and fours and thus the universe came into existence as a healthy and calm place for all. It was a progress of the semen virile and the potential objects that procreated. It was a geometrical progress of everything that occurred. The *Soma* always remained as a protective cover to the objects that came created.

RV3.62.15 अस्माकमायुर्वर्धयन्नभिमातीः सहमानः।
सोमः सधस्थमासदत्॥

[अस्माकम् - as entities ◇ आयुः - extended ◇ वर्धयन् - augmented; increased ◇ न - as ◇ अभि - advanced ◇ म - from self ◇ अतीः - only greatly ◇ सहमान - powerfully ◇ सोमः - the *Soma* ◇ सधस्थ - that stood together ◇ मा - as arrangement ◇ सदत् - moved for ever]

The entities got augmented and advanced from the self, the *Soma* all by itself got powerful and a great arrangement of coexistence manifested and moved from the heaven to stand together for ever.

Along with the wide spread distribution of the objects from the heaven that occurred as originated from the heaven and from the *Soma*, the *Soma* itself flowed down, marking a coexistence that manifested for ever. The *Soma* never kept away from the objects created. The many objects that repeatedly got multiplied on the food principle, the clusters of objects that stood together; to those the *Soma* provided the principle of perpetual coexistence. Though seen as the multitude of objects that came from an earlier one and though seen much traversed to distant places, there was that nature of co-existence, which could be taken as an attribute provided by the *Soma*.

The *Soma* that existed in the *hiraṇyagarbha* upon division and propagation, upon the manifestation of the sound and the cosmic vibrations reached up to the very end of the universe. With the routes that went on progressively multiplied, the *Soma* spread and provided the protective cover for the objects wherever they were. The paths of creation progressed in multiple directions and with multiple divisions into increasing distances and in increasing numbers.

RV3.62.16 आ नो मित्रावरुणा घृतैर्गव्यूतिमुक्षतम्।
मध्वा रजांसि सुक्रतू॥

[आ - manifesting ◇ नो - as ◇ मित्रावरुणा - the *Mitrāvaruṇa* ◇ घृतै - sprinkled ◇ गव्यूतिम् - wetting a pasture land ◇ उक्षतम् - scattered greatly ◇ मध्वा - moving intoxicated ◇ रजांसि - pounding to dust ◇ सुक्रतू - only organising intelligently]

Brought into manifestation by *Mitrāvaruṇa*, sprinkling and wetting a pasture land, at the same time pounding to dust and scattering around, moved as intoxicated and yet everything was organized intelligently.

The semen virile got sprinkled down and the multitude of objects got scattered, as the very intoxicated process of creation. With a divinity manifesting as the *Mitrāvaruṇa*, a never ending sprinkle came that was well connected, continuously expanded, fragmented and impelled in intoxication and yet as those which were devised intelligently. Establishing the 3-dimensionality, propagating over the waves that appeared with roars, getting sprinkled incessantly, pounding with intoxication, thrown out in abandon, the universe continuously expanded and yet only as an intelligent existence that came for ever. Thus the intoxication seen did not prevent the intelligence to prevail. The primordial cosmic vibrations established the 3-dimensionality that took off from the heaven and the objects and energy got propagated by the same forces. The divine combination that came to be known as *Mitrāvaruṇa* achieved all these. A touch of pounding cattle and dust raised in search of pasture lands was latent in the description indicating the style in which the universe marched to its enormity.

RV3.62.17 उरुशंसा नमोवृधा मह्ना दक्षस्य राजथः।
द्राघिष्ठाभिः शुचिव्रता॥

[उरुशंसा - with extensive praises ◇ नमोवृधा - increasingly bowed down ◇ मह्ना - became great ◇ दक्षस्य - cleverly ◇ राजथः - born, bestowed and stationed ◇ द्राघिष्ठ - stretched ◇ अभिः - progressively ◇ शुचि - cleanliness; whiteness ◇ व्रता - that came as per rules]

The universe manifested along with the extensive prayers and as if bowing down in reverence, objects getting cleverly bestowed, born and stationed and at the same time the *Soma* getting manifested as a cleanliness that progressively got stretched to the proximity as per the rules.

With the divine prayers that came from the self, as if bowing down in reverence to the divinity above, *Soma* the transparency flowed down at all angles and thus came the objects that got greatly scattered. The universe came swooping down from the heaven, the *Soma* getting progressively extruded to the proximity and emaciated systematically while it progressed. These achievements were attributed to the divinity of *Mitrāvaruṇa*.

RV3.62.18 गृणाना जमदग्निना योनावृतस्य सीदतम्।
पातं सोममृतावृधा॥

[गृणाना - manifested as sprinkled ◇ ज - born ◇ मद् - with exhilaration ◇ अग्निना - from the *Agni* ◇ यो - somehow ◇ न - as ◇ आवृतस्य - enveloped ◇ सीद - directly ◇ तम् - emaciating ◇ पातं - falling ◇ सोमम् - the *Soma* ◇ ऋता - as per rules ◇ वृधा - growing steadily]

Sprinkling down with exhilaration somehow came directly, enveloped by the *Agni*, then moved, descended, emaciated and thus manifested the very *Soma* steadily getting enlarged, as per the rules.

The *Soma* that remained under wrap, flowed down enveloping the objects that it provided till the very end. The *Soma* gradually emaciated as it descended according to the divine rules of creation. The tongues of flame as the paths of creation shot out of the heaven and the heavens below till the very end. It was the intoxicating *Soma* that thus manifested as the paths of creation, with the divine help of *Mitrāvaruṇa* and with the participation of the *Agni*. It was the primordial cosmic vibrations, the waveform propagation and the 3-dimensionality that was instantly established which brought the universe and these were therefore remembered as the acts of *Mitrāvaruṇa.*

This hymn of 18 verses was presented as 6 segments, each devoted to some of the divinities that appeared in the *Ṛgveda.* Thus explanations of what constituted to be named *Indrāvaruṇa, Bṛhaspati, Pūṣan, Soma* and *Mitrāvaruṇa* was presented as the *saguṇa* divinities of sufficient clarity. The divinity of *Savita*, presented in the very middle of the hymn, perhaps could be termed both *saguṇa* and *nirguṇa.* It was a comfort to notice that statements of sufficient connection between the physical objects, the phenomena and the attribution of divine nature to these, appeared as part of the very text of the *Ṛgveda.*[1] What was described here, avoided the term *Agni* as it was something sufficiently clear, and also postponed the details of many, such as the *Aśvin, Vācaspati, Brahmaṇaspati* etc.

In fact, here, two combinations i.e, one of *Indrāvaruṇa* and the other of *Mitrāvaruṇa* was presented. We would also find these terms separately as *Indra, Mitra* and *Varuṇa.* It could be presumed that the divinity got expressed as relevant to the object or the phenomena under discussion. Thus the very manifestation of a particle of shining matter needed the cosmic vibrations and propagation and therefore the divinity was named as *Indrāvaruṇa.* Likewise the establishment of the 3-dimensionality also needed the cosmic vibrations and propagations and therefore the divinity became *Mitrāvaruṇa.* It was thus confirmed that the divinities were to be seen in association with the occurrence of either an object or a phenomena that would repeatedly manifest.

It is necessary to look into the *gāyatrīmantra* in more detail as it was this that remained as the supreme invocation for thousands of years, indeed realising its extreme significance.

---

[1]In other words, it confirmed the correctness of an approach.

The meanings that accrued here is also moderately getting compared with some of the modern concepts of cosmology.

It said in brief, that- "As the excellence broadcast from That, as a great dalliance and a great intellect and as the many intellects that got proportionately inspired, the universe progressed." Or along with the terms "*aum bhūrbhuva sva*" - "this solar system under the control and magnanimity of the Sun, so existed with an intelligence that was duly and proportionately inspired by a greater and magnificent universal intelligence."

The divinity of *Savita* was presented here as the divine dalliance and intellect that accepted the responsibilities of the universe from that Supreme Divinity. That divine *Savita* stood beyond definition and got described neither as *nirguṇa* nor *saguṇa*, but was termed only as a dalliance and intellect that reached everywhere. From the very beginning, from this divinity many responsibilities of creation were accepted by an array of several *saguṇa* divinities. It was some of the important of those divinities that was presented in this hymn. From the beginning of creation, the objects and phenomena that manifested were described as the contributions and functions of these divinities. But, beyond the first of creations and extending into the present existence, that Supreme Divinity and the intellect of the divine *Savita* should be imagined to have stood relevant for ever.

It is true that the earth, its atmosphere and the sky are governed by a set of rules of this solar system. The definitions of their existence, orbital movement and energy levels are indeed basically decided by the Sun. But this defined existence acquired full meaning only upon its own intelligence constantly getting inspired by a greater universal intelligence. That greater intelligence belonged to the integral whole of the universe of which this solar system is a part. That sovereign universal intelligence is the one that provided and sustained the universe for ever. This established an equation between the universe and our solar system in which there is a conspicuous reciprocity and transfer of intelligence and information. Since this relation is not an isolated phenomenon confined to our solar system but remains extended to all of the systems of the universe and all of the individual entities, our solar system could be said to receive just its due share. The great universal intelligence itself, it should be assumed, got reconstituted by the individual intelligences of the sub-systems, of all entities and of all phenomena. This constant exchange of information and influence between one another in appropriate modes and levels defined the very nature of existence of the universe.

While there are many verses in the *Ṛgveda* that described the birth of the universe, which we called the *ādisṛṣṭi*, and that which described the series of those phenomena, looked upon from various angles, this single line statement of "*gāyatri*" could be said as one that pertained to the very existence i.e, *sthiti* of the universe and one and all of its elements, while being equally applicable to the stages of creation. We know it better as a daily invocation of the Sun than anything else, along with the words "*aum bhūrbhuvasva*", possibly added at a later period.

We could also say that it was indeed one of the most profound statements that emanated from the *Ṛgveda*. It would appear that this statement would more or less agree and closely correspond with some of the statements of the Quantum Cosmology and may be other theories as well. It is found that while explaining some of the phenomena of the Zero Point Vacuum (ZPF), statements of comparable descriptive content surfaced. In an introductory note on the book "Science & The Akashic Field" by Erwin Laszlo the following statement was made.

"*Even the stability of our planet in its orbit around the Sun derives from vacuum energy inputs. As the earth pursues its orbital path, it looses its momentum; given a constant loss of momentum of the gravitational field of the Sun - in the absence of an influx energy from the ZPF - would overcome the centrifugal force that pushes the earth around its orbit and the earth would spiral into the Sun. This means that in addition to inertia, gravity and mass, the stability of both atoms and the solar systems is due to interaction with the Zero Point Field of the vacuum."*[2]

It is possible to identify meanings matching to the above from the *gāyatri* and this should not be averred as merely being inventive. For throughout the *Ṛgveda* not only several scientific statements could be identified but many that *inter alia* supported this theory itself. Among them, the following hymns i.e, 1.91, 8.48 and 8.79 that configured in chapter-4, as the descriptions of the *Soma* could be identified particularly significant, here. Not only the specifications and details of the *Soma* closely corresponded with the description of Aether, it was described as the very repository of matter and energy, even if these were extensions of the embryonic forms. The *Soma* that once situated at the centre of the universe later and along with the creation flowed to such distant places as this earth and remained as an invisible cover to all. It was into the *Soma* that matter dissolved upon death and it was from the *Soma* that matter and energy manifested. It was this white transparency that withheld the surrounding darkness effectively.

It is stated here that much more than a camaraderie in existence, the universe and its elements remained interactive and that such intelligence and intellect as required for a sustained and stable universe are getting exchanged every moment. A totally interactive world was repeatedly emphasized by the *Ṛgveda* at several places. It was stated that from that primordial location, often referred as the "*hiraṇyagarbha*" and the "*viśvatomukha*" when matter and energy flowed reaching up to the far end of the universe such as this earth, the *Soma* remained as an unseen shroud over them all. This concise description of the *Soma* would agree with the Cos-

[2]The aquarian Theosophist volume 6,8 of June 17, 2006.

mic Plenum that the modern physicists would put forward. The common refrain among us that the universe is infinite (*ananta*) could not be taken as a Vedic tenet. It was stated that the universe is a finite quantity, though immensely and immeasurably large and upon dividing the spherical universe into the 7 parallel *vyāhṛtis*, in the last of which only we resided. We could quote here what Hartmutt Mueller, a German astrophysicist stated on the subject.

"*The observed dimensions of all entities from the atoms to the galaxies is determined by the interaction with the density - pressure waves propagating in the vacuum. According to the 'Global Scaling Theory', the universe is dimensionally limited; on the lower end of the dimensional horizons, matter density is the greatest and on the upper end it is the lowest. This is due to the vacuum - based pressure waves. Because the universe is finite...*"[3]

It is not inferred here that all the modern scientific statements had been already stated in the Vedas. In fact the Vedic people could be assumed to have had different methods of realising the truths of nature including the origin of the universe and its existence. One could not think of the modern methods of observations, mathematical tools and the corresponding evaluations to have existed at those times. Yet somehow they were able to arrive at precise and pointed inferences about these subjects and formulate unique theories. We find the Vedic minds were kept prepared to process complex ideas, then present it as poetic renderings and in the process evolve words and meanings of truly technical nature.

The extent of meanings that would emanate from the *gāyatri* could be said as unlimited for the reason that it stated a universal law of existence. These could satisfy the seekers of the *ādhibhautikta* meanings and the *ādhyātmika* meanings equally. Stated all, firmly reposed invariably on *daivīkata* proper. The Vedic description that the universe is

---

[3]The aquarian Theosophist volume 6,8 of June 17, 2006.

with highly energised and dense core regions which went on getting diluted in the process of expansion to arrive at a cold and distant exterior could be compared with what Hartmutt Mueller stated, as quoted above. Using a slightly different terminology the Vedic reference to the absolute core and upper regions as well as the lower strata was very specific and had 7 prominent stages. The term "*dhīmahi dhiyo yo na:*" constituted the principal statement of the interactive existence of the universe, of which our solar system was pointed out as a typical example.

To what extent the concept of the *Soma* is relevant here could be speculative. From the segments preseted here, while bringing out the *ādhibhautika* meanings of parts of the *Ṛgveda*, it would be noticed that, in spite of each of the verse being self standing and complete as a presentation of a concept, the overall concepts would be non-contradictory and would appear as presentations of different perceptions of a central set of themes. Thus the universe conceived would be an approximate spherical entity of 3-dimensional specific composition, of an equitable left right balance, that which grew into all directions instantly and remained at a state of resonance. The *Soma* enveloped all matter and energy that got created and traveled to far off regions and restrained the surrounding darkness. All dissolution and manifestation occurred to and from the *Soma*, at all times. That which flowed from the *hiraṇyagarbha* upon extruding the closely wrapped cover, reached up to the far end of the universe including this earth. The invisible, yet bright *bījasatta* went on modifying those objects and living things of this earth as well.

Though the Vedic verse is without the part "*bhūrbhuvasva*" by declaring the sovereignty of the Sun, this part could be taken in a way as stated and included. But the Vedic *gāyatri* not only meant this solar system but all other similar systems of the universe and all that took position till the far ends of the *vyāhṛtis*. Besides the Vedic verse also did not mean this earth, its own atmosphere and its upper skies, but it meant everything up to the Sun and under its sovereignty. Therefore, the inclusion of the term "*bhūrbhuvasva*", in a way imposed limitations into the extent of the meanings. A clear sense of geometry and conceptual accuracy visible in the statements of the Vedic verses would suffer if the *svar*, *bhuva* and the *bhū* was added as this earth and parts above it and the overall set of meanings would be correspondingly shrunk.

But it is yet another aspect that is perhaps more important. It is stated here that though all the planets, objects and systems of energy are under the sovereign control of the Sun, it could not be taken to be totally independent of the rest of the universe and the supreme and the greatly spread intelligence that was named as "*Savita*" was positioned supreme, hierarchically just below to the very Supreme *Brahma*. Moreover, the intelligence of each of the individual existence communicated separately or collectively with that supreme intelligence. It is here that the statement have a striking similarity with what Erwin Laszlo said and quoted earlier. The solar system could not have a supreme sovereignty over every aspect of its existence but have to sub-serve that supreme intelligence of the universe at all times. It is only upon interacting with this supreme intelligence by way of a reciprocated transfer of information and intelligence that this solar system could exist. The counterbalancing and sustaining forces should be expected to avoid such catastrophe as that which Erwin Laszlo visualised. It is this supreme intelligence that existed as the very essential intellect of the universe that ultimately defined the existence of all. It was named as *Savita*, got well defined by the *gāyatri* and was closely held to our hearts for the past several millenniums.

The meaning of the *gāyatrīmantra* as conceived here could easily accommodate the *ādhyātmika* meanings as well. This supreme intellect could be a universal consciousness that prevailed all over the universe. It directed and controlled all the existence of the animate as well as the inanimate. All our actions are guided by this supreme intellect and we pray to this intellect to guide us. We pray to this intellect to distill us into better and better forms of existence. As an equation of existence it presented a structure of entities that stood individually and collectively. It is the supreme intellect that pervaded through the universe as a super consciousness.

In terms of the *ādhibhautika* meanings, the status of the *gāyatri* could be stated as a magnificent one line equation of existence. It did not go into the details of the creation of the universe, and that which occurred as a set of grotesque and horrifying sequences of events and of abstract imponderable nature. It did not remain as a statement on the matters of this earth, or this solar system. But in clear terms, precisely and in concise fashion it stated the very equation of existence. One could see here a statement that is a supreme command. It is the very command which none could transcend. Thus RV3.62 brought out the characteristics of the major 6 divinities that would be encountered in the description of the birth of the universe. Most of them had the *saguṇa* attributes and at the same time were necessary to be identified as divinities as well as physical entities and phenomena. Without the presence and actions of *saguṇa* divinities how could the universe could be brought about at all?

We would now see what else and more would be presented here about that intellect and dalliance that pervaded as everywhere known as *savita*, which stood in between that supreme divinity of *nirguṇa Brahma* and the *saguṇa* divinities such as *Indra, Mitra, Varuṇa* etc.

RV 2.38

[(11) एकादशर्चस्यास्य सूक्तस्य शौनको गृत्समद ऋषिः। सविता देवता। त्रिष्टुप् छन्दः]

RV2.38.01 उदु ष्य देवः सविता सवाय शश्वत्तमं तदपा

वह्निरस्थात्। नूनं देवेभ्यो वि हि धाति रत्नमथाभजद्वीतिहोत्रं स्वस्तौ॥

[उद् - rising ◇ उ - got confirmed ◇ ष्य - mixed ◇ देवः - from the heaven ◇ सविता - came spreading ◇ सवाय - as squeezed out ◇ शश्वत्तमं - endlessly and for ever ◇ तदपा - from that downwards as the offspring ◇ वह्निः - the *Agni* ◇ अस्थात् - positioned and moved ◇ नूनं - immediately ◇ देवेभ्यो - as from the heavens ◇ वि - divided ◇ हि - only ◇ धाति - greatly bestowed ◇ रत्नम् - as the diamonds ◇ अथा - then ◇ भजद् - divided ◇ वीतिहोत्रं - as a feast around a fire ◇ स्वस्तौ - settled down peacefully]

Those that arose from the heaven, took firm positions, got mixed and came from the *Soma* after getting squeezed out and came spreading for ever, issued out as many an offspring that descended instantly, divided and greatly bestowed from the many heavens which shined like diamonds, got further divided and then were found peacefully to settle down, as if a feast around a fire.

Out of the divine brightness in the heaven, as the juices squeezed out and everything set aflame, the paths flowed down and from these paths, several bright objects which shined like diamonds were spread around the heaven. Those were the shining ones that came from the single shining one that stood above. This appeared like a feast around a bone-fire, peacefully consuming and existing. The imagery suggested consumption and the glow of satisfaction that prevailed proportionately and just as the diamonds that would glitter according to the light source and the distance. Not only that, the process was repeated several times from those that first potentially came and stood as the heavens below, to be the many that spread, got mixed and rose again to new positions. There was thus a series of diamond necklaces hung in the high skies and these glowed correspondingly. Here the geometry was also well brought forward. The scene described by the term "*vītihotra*" here could be perhaps seen even today in the north-west parts of India.

RV2.38.02 विश्वस्य हि श्रुष्टये देव ऊर्ध्वः
प्र बाहवा पृथुपाणिः सिसर्ति। आपश्चिदस्य व्रत
आ निमृग्रा अयं चिद्वातो रमते परिज्मन्॥

[विश्वस्य - as the universe ◇ हि - only ◇ श्रुष्टये - obeying ones ◇ देव - from the heaven ◇ ऊर्ध्वः - rising up ◇ प्र - to the surrounding ◇ बाहवा - as hands moved ◇ पृथुपाणिः - and arms extended ◇ सिसर्ति - instantly ◇ आपः - downward ◇ चिदस्य - in principle ◇ व्रत - with rules ◇ आ - coming ◇ निमृग्रा - devotedly ◇ अयं - thus ◇ चिद् - apparently ◇ वातो - by a wind ◇ रमते - pleasantly ◇ परिज्मन् - to the surrounding and everywhere]

The universe came only as the loyal ones rising up from the heaven to the surrounding, with the hands moved and the arms extended, proceeding instantly and in principle descending from the existing ones, with the divine rules devotedly followed, manifesting pleasantly to the surroundings and to everywhere, moved and positioned as if by a wind.

Highly respecting the divinity that stood above and reaching everywhere in the universe, the arms of creation got extended downward as per divine rules. It was known as movements effected by an unseen wind. It was known as the helping hand that got extended till the earth. As the fast descending flows in several directions, as if the arms that shot out from above, the paths of creation spread to the surrounding and to below to reach this earth. Whatever so happened, occurred only with the guidance that came from the divinity of *Savita*. Those were the helping hands extended by *Savita*, that universal dalliance and intellect.

RV2.38.03 आशुभिश्चिद्यान्वि मुचाति नूनमरीरमदतमानं चिदेतोः।
अहार्षूणां चिन्न्ययाँ अविष्यामनु व्रतं सवितुर्मोक्यागात्॥

[आशुभिः - quickly advancing ◇ चिद्यान् - progressed in principle ◇ वि - as divided ◇ मुचाति - totally separated ◇ नूनम् - instantly ◇ अरि - hostile ◇ इर् - silent ◇ अमद - cheerless ◇ तमाणम् - darkness ◇ चिद् - as if ◇ एतोः - approached by ◇ अहार्षूणां - gliding away like a snake ◇ चिन्न्या - as if led by a divine mind ◇ याँ - progressed ◇ अविष्यामनु - a set of ready helps ◇ व्रतं -

as per the rules ◇ सवितुः - spread as the strength ◇ मोक्या - separately ◇ गात् - progressed]

When the universe quickly advanced, progressing as a set of ready helps that were instituted as per the rules and spread as the strengths that manifested out of a divine mind, along with these, instantly and separately came a darkness, hostile and cheerless and which glided along like a snake as something that progressed separate from the paths of creation.

From what stood as a heap in the heaven, upon the manifestation of the sounds and cosmic vibrations, came the bright paths of creation that carried the necessary power, the intelligence and a helping nature, but along with these, a darkness had also spread all over the universe. Upon getting inspired by a divine mind and intellect of that universal dalliance, upon manifesting as the shafts of lightning and its much divided branches, the paths of creation rushed down to the surroundings, bringing a darkness as well to prevail. From that silent darkness moved the evil forces of destruction which roamed like snakes. The universe became immense with the well spread entities remaining bonded for ever and yet standing separated. Those were guided by the divine powers above, in the form of a divine mind and a matching intellect. For, that universal dalliance helped and guided everything.

RV2.38.04 पुनः समव्यद्विततं वयन्ति मध्या कर्तोर्न्यधाच्छक्म धीरः। उत्संहायास्थाद्व्यृ१तूँरदर्धररमतिः सविता देव आगात्॥

[पुनः - then ◇ समव्यद् - equally divided ◇ विततं - and spread ◇ वयन्ति - moving to the proximity ◇ मध्या - with the middle ◇ कर्तोः - a cavity; empty ◇ न्य - by taking off ◇ ध - and placing ◇ अच् - motive ◇ शक्म - power ◇ धीरः - courageously ◇ उत् - arising ◇ संहायास्थाद् - as those which stood with ability to rise ◇ वि - divided ◇ ऋतूँ - as the seasons ◇ रद् - split into ◇ अर्ध - halves ◇ अरम् - suitably ◇ अतिः - greatly ◇ सविता - with spreading ◇ देव - from heaven ◇ आगात् - commuted]

Then moved to the proximity, equally divided and spread, with the middle becoming empty like a cave by vacating and getting placed by an inherent motive power that courageously arose, out of those that stood with an ability to arise. Getting split into halves and spreading suitably and greatly, many came commuted from the many heavens just as those that came from the first of heavens. These divisions and repetitions resembled the seasons of this earth that would repeatedly manifest.

Some of those that stood with a potential to create, acted further as the heavens and provided further paths of creation and the objects moved from such centres, in the process of which these centres became empty. But some others which went into pieces found their own motive power and moved away from their original locations. When the objects moved out from the existing ones, their original position became heavily tortured and became empty and caved in. The objects that moved from there spread re-surging or their strength got halved, as it occurred. The progress was also marked by more of the heavens manifesting from those potential ones and from where the process of creation would continue. Thus the epicentres of creation that first appeared manifested repeatedly. At the same time empty force fields also spread downward several times over. Those were the processes that never turned back and those got repeated like the seasons of the earth. These were the intelligent manifestations effected by the divinity named *Savita*.

RV2.38.05 नानौकांसि दुर्यो विश्वमायुर्वि तिष्ठते प्रभवः
शोको अग्नेः। ज्येष्ठं माता सूनवे
भागमाधादन्वस्य केतमिषितं सवित्रा॥

[ना - came as ◇ नौकांसि - as the boats quickly floated ◇ दुर्यो - docking to ◇ विश्वम् - reaching everywhere ◇ आयुः - extended ◇ वि - divided ◇ तिष्ठते - those established ◇ प्रभवः - as occurred to around ◇ शोको - burnt ◇ अग्नेः - by the *Agni* ◇ ज्येष्ठं - the first born ◇ मा - arrangement ◇ ता - as those that came ◇ सूनवे - sons in succession ◇ भा - shining ◇ ग - progress ◇ मा - arrangement ◇ धाद् - bestowed ◇ अन्वस्य - that followed ◇ केतम्

- in the atmosphere ◇ इषितं - set out ◇ सवित्रा - as the divided three; protection impelled]

The universe came as if the boats that quickly floated down and docked everywhere, as those that got divided, extended and got established to the surroundings by the *Agni*. An arrangement of the first born and of those that came from those, as the sons that came in succession occurred. An arrangement and progress of the shining things followed from those that got bestowed and moved through the atmosphere. A divided 3-dimensionality and protection came moved till the end.

The objects that got created floated down from the heaven and took position like the boats down a river. The much divided paths of creation flowed down as modeled by the *Agni*. From those potential first born, many got successively born. Those were the shining progresses through the atmosphere along with a 3-dimensionality that manifested simultaneously. Reaching everywhere and until this earth, not only the earth forms that were totally burnt out came and were stationed in the atmosphere, but also those potential ones that got surrounded by fire, bestowing many new ones. So came the new ones and from them a further group of new ones, some still capable of procreation. And yet it was the manifestation of a 3-dimensionality all over, including the objects and the very atmosphere that marked the advent of creation. These progresses were attributed to that shining intellect and divinity of *Savita*.

RV2.38.06 समाववर्ति विष्ठितो जिगीषुर्विश्वेषां कामश्चरताममाभूत्।
शश्वाँ अपो विकृतं हित्व्यागादनु व्रतं सवितुर्दैव्यस्य॥

[सम - equally ◇ अव - to distances ◇ वर्ति - remained ◇ विष्ठितो - separated and got positioned ◇ जिगीषुः - with winning words ◇ विश्वेषां - rushing to and reaching everywhere ◇ कामः - as desired ◇ चरताम् - as moved to and fro ◇ अमाभूत् - existing as ◇ शश्वाँ - permanently moving ◇ अपो - downward ◇ विकृतं - disfiguring ◇ हित् - as desired ◇ व्या - hiding ◇ गा - approaching

◇ द - cutting off ◇ नु - indeed ◇ व्रतं - as per the rules ◇ सवितुः - as the might that spread ◇ दैव्यस्य - shining from heaven]

From that which shined in the heaven, moved to distances, as two equal and separate progresses of creation, that came from the winning words that reached everywhere; one as the disfiguring forces that stood hidden, which approached and cut off as desired, shuttling to and fro. The other was that shining might that spread from the heaven. Both moved downward and so existed for ever; indeed all manifesting according to the rules of creation.

Out of the heaven and the divine words, two equal forces descended one evil and dark and the other, the benevolent paths of creation. These came into existence from the same set of laws of creation. While one was the beaming might that spread, the other was darkness and the destruction unleashed. It was that shining intellect that prevailed all over the universe that inspired these progresses and maintained the equitable balance between the good and the evil.

RV2.38.07 त्वया हितमप्यमप्सु भागं धन्वान्वा मृगयसो वि तस्थुः।
वनानि विभ्यो नकिरस्य तानि व्रता देवस्य सवितुर्मिनन्ति॥

[त्वया - thyself manifested ◇ हितम् - and got stationed ◇ अप्यमप्सु - as the liquid form to the proximity ◇ भागं - as parts ◇ ध - positioned ◇ अन्वान्वा - successively expanded ◇ मृगयसो - in a manner of chasing animals ◇ वि - divided ◇ तस्थुः - as those positioned ◇ वनानि - in a forest ◇ विभ्यो - divided; separated ◇ नकिरस्य - as scattered ◇ ता - as those ◇ नि - isolated ◇ व्रता - as per the rules ◇ देवस्य - from the heaven ◇ सवितुः - as the might that spread ◇ मिनन्ति - as set up to the proximity]

Thyself manifested from the heaven as the liquid form that moved to the proximity, as the parts that got positioned and successively expanded, as the might that spread to the proximity as per divine rules and yet along with it came those that divided, separated whatever created, as if the animals that would get isolated and would be hunted down in a forest.

In the process of creation and from the very beginning,

there appeared two opposing forces, one divine and shining and the other that was bad and destructive and yet these came from the same source and as per the same divine rules of creation. While the shining objects of the universe, came successively and mightily shining to the proximity, along with it came the evil forces that roamed as if chasing, isolating, and scattering the animals in a forest. Those evil forces came from the darkness and the *vṛtrata*. There were objects that swam, ran and flew, but those remained within the protection and coverage of the *Soma*. There were the processes of hunting, getting divided and getting isolated, there were those that got pounded and dusted or got elongated like a thread and those were also within the ambit of powers of the *Soma*. Those which spread in the universe and made it immense, always observed the divine rules of creation. Those moved from proximity to proximity under the guidance of that divine brilliance and intellect that prevailed.

RV2.38.08 याद्राध्यं वरुणो योनिमप्यमनिशितं निमिषि जर्भुराणः।
विश्वो मार्ताण्डो व्रजमा पशुर्गात्स्थशो जन्मानि सविता व्याकः॥

[याद्राध्यं - as quickly and as far as possible ◇ वरुणो - by *Varuṇa* ◇ योनिम् - from the wombs ◇ अप्यम - to the proximity ◇ निशितं - that thinned ◇ निमिषि - by the wink of a eye ◇ जर्भुराणः - as a flicker ◇ विश्वो - reached everywhere in the universe ◇ मार्ताण्डो - from *Mārtāṇḍa* ◇ व्रजम् - as a bird that swirled and swooped down ◇ आ - that came out ◇ पशुः - as animals ◇ ग - progressing ◇ अत् - and moving up to ◇ स्थशो - remained in deserving places ◇ जन्मानि - taking such life forms ◇ सविता - came spread ◇ व्याकः - in tortuous and enveloped movements]

From the wombs that appeared, moved to the proximity, as quickly and as far as possible, as an act of *Varuṇa* and by the wink of an eye and a flicker, reached everywhere in routes that thinned. A bird swirled and swooped down coming out of *Mārtāṇḍa* the egg, progressed till becoming the animals and similar life forms, all of which came spreading through those tortuous and enveloped movements.

As the deeds of *Varuṇa*, objects came wandering from above incessantly issuing out of the wombs to the proximity, born and separated from that pillar and epicentre. Quickly and happily moved from that cosmic egg called *Mārtāṇḍa*, manifesting as that bird that reached everywhere. As the cows that would move from their stables, all were born into different places, spreading as the highly tortured swirls. Born incessantly from the wombs to the immediate proximity, wandering and propagated over the roaring waves of an ocean that was the atmosphere and as an act of the sounds and cosmic vibrations, different objects came spreading all over the universe. From the *hiraṇyagarbha* and the cosmic egg called *Mārtāṇaḍa*, that large bird flew off and reached everywhere, and thus the universe came into existence. Many first born ones got divided and some of these moved away unwillingly, as if the cows would go away from a cow-pen. They had an invisible sense of belonging to their earlier residences. An interactive nature was all too visible in the process of creation. It was the divine shine and intellect that stood as everywhere that guided these events.

In a way the bird that flew away from its nest and the cows that departed from their pens were behaving in almost identical manners. There was a hidden longing for their earlier positions and this is the very principle much visible in the existence of the universe.

RV2.38.09 न यस्येन्द्रो वरुणो न मित्रो व्रतमर्यमा न मिनन्ति रुद्रः।
नारातयस्तमिदं स्वस्ति हुवे देवं सवितारं नमोभिः॥

[न - as ◇ यस्य - the efforts ◇ इन्द्रो - of *Indra* ◇ वरुणो - of *Varuṇa* ◇ न - as ◇ मित्रो - of *Mitra* ◇ व्रतम् - as per the rules ◇ अर्यमा - of *Aryama* ◇ न - as ◇ मिनन्ति - from the established to the proximity ◇ रुद्रः - by *Rudra* ◇ नारात - as those till man ◇ यस्तम् - located ◇ इदं - thus ◇ स्वस्ति - as the calm and quietude ◇ हुवे - as a sequence of oblations ◇ देवं - from the heaven ◇ सवितारं - that enabled a beautiful spreading ◇ नमोभिः - be reverentially saluted]

For the efforts of *Indra*, *Varuṇa*, *Mitra*, for the rules of *Aryama* which enabled the expansion to the proximity, for those that got located by *Rudra* till man here and still beyond, for the calm and quietude that came by the oblations from the heavens, let that universally spread dalliance be reverentially saluted.

That which was born as a spot of brightness of matter and energy having got energised by the sounds and the cosmic vibrations that manifested, that which became the 3-dimensionality created obeying the rules of co-existence and co-ordination, was found to expand to the proximity, much augmented by severe sounds and vibrations. That which started as divine oblations, was found to establish objects and energy till this earth. It brought the calm and quietude of the universe, through the many heavens that stood in a hierarchical order. That excellent and divine brightness should be saluted with reverence for the peaceful existence that was so brought about. All those created indeed owed their existence to the divinity named *Savita*. Yet this verse had the purpose of stating that though the universe came as created by the above said *saguṇa* divinities, they only stood subservient to the divinity of *Savita*.

RV2.38.10 भगं धियं वाजयन्तः पुरंधिं नराशंसो ग्नास्पतिर्नो अव्याः।
आये वामस्य संगथे रयीणां प्रिया देवस्य सवितुः स्याम॥

[भगं - beautiful ◇ धियं - intelligent ◇ वाजयन्तः - vigorous till the end ◇ पुरंधिं - fertile and bountiful ◇ नराशंसो - as praised by men ◇ ग्नास्पतिः - a divine female and husband ◇ नो - as ◇ अव्याः - brought out of cover ◇ आये - and reached ◇ वामस्य - as propagated ◇ संगथे - met together and remained ◇ रयीणां - as excellence ◇ प्रिया - dear ◇ देवस्य - as the heaven ◇ सवितुः - mightily spread ◇ स्याम - and strongly]

A divine female along with her husband, brought out of cover and from a shy existence, this beautiful, intelligent, vigorous, fertile and bountiful arrangement till the end, as the dear excellences that got propagated, arrived, met together and remained, all coming from the heavens, mightily spreading till the end.

A divine couple brought a shy existence into a vigorous delivery and a corresponding affluence. The universe was created as beautiful, intelligent, vigorous till end, fertile and bountiful, knowledgeably taken through the atmosphere and got stationed as the pleasant meeting places with properties as wished by that supreme power and divinity of *Savita*; so it was praised by men. The arrangement of a universal order of entities and their properties were pleasantly brought into existence by the divine powers of *Savita*. He[4] knew how to filter the different objects into different orders of existence so that the universe became a beautiful, and bountiful place. It was in fact those very properties which stood above, that got manifested into the elements that stood below, in appropriate dimensions and measures.

RV2.38.11 अस्मभ्यं तद्दिवो अद्भ्यः पृथिव्यास्त्वया दत्तं काम्यं राध आ गात्। शं यत्स्तोतृभ्य आपये भवात्युरुशंसाय सवितर्जरित्रे॥

[अस्मभ्यं - as the parts that advanced ◇ तद् - like that ◇ दिवो - as the heavens ◇ अद्भ्यः - the food principle that progressed ◇ पृथिव्यस्त्वया - a body consisting of earths ◇ दत्तं - obtained ◇ काम्यं - as desired ◇ रा - delivered ◇ ध - placed ◇ आ - came ◇ गात् - and moved constantly away ◇ शं - as the auspicious ◇ यत् - connected with ◇ स्तोतृभ्य - the divine prayers ◇ आपये - that flowed down ◇ भव - became ◇ अति - great ◇ उरुशंसाय - expanded prayers ◇ सवितः - blossomed ◇ जरित्रे - and emaciated as the 3-dimensionality]

As the parts that advanced and as the heavens that advanced in a like manner, as the food principle that came forward and the earth forms obtained, all got delivered and placed as desired, as those things that constantly moved away, connected to the auspicious prayers that flowed down.

[4]Though there was nothing hitherto described which suggested a gender for this divinity.

Those prayers much blossomed out and expanded and a 3-dimensionality manifested and emaciated while distanced, to become the body of the universe.

It was those sounds and the cosmic vibrations which came as the divine praises that brought the universe into existence and it was the divinity of the *Savita* that made this manifestation possible, initially and till the end. The prayers that started in the heaven later became an extensive set of prayers to reach all through the process of creation and all over the universe. It enabled the process of creation to greatly progress. It became the excellences of the universe and established the universe as a great benevolence. It brought the various earth forms into existence. It brought in a 3-dimensionality for ever.

This *sūkta* essentially stated that though the birth of the universe could be described in general, as those brought about by the bird *Suparṇa* that took off from *Mārtāṇḍa* and also as those brought about by the divinities of *Indra, Mitra, Varuṇa* etc., the process of creation contained several physical attributes that could not be fully resolved in such a manner. It could be only stated that the shining excellence and divinity of *Savita* oversaw the evolving of all of the properties and events that led to the formation of the universe with the help of the *saguṇa* divinities mentioned here. The sounds and the cosmic vibrations that manifested, the food principle that was found to prevail and the excellences that were established, were all to be reckoned in principle as brought into effect by that shining intellect that stood as everywhere.

RV 4.53

[(7) सप्तर्चस्यास्य सूक्तस्य गौतमो वामदेव ऋषिः। सविता देवता। जगती छन्दः]

RV4.53.01 तद्देवस्य सवितुर्वार्यं महद्वृणीमहे असुरस्य प्रचेतसः।

छर्दिर्येन दाशुषे यच्छति त्मना तन्नो महाँ उदयान्देवो अक्तुभिः॥

[तद् - then ◇ देवस्य - from the heaven ◇ सवितुः - spread mightily ◇ वार्यं - as excellence ◇ महद् - becoming greatly enormous ◇ वृणीमहे - and a great gratification ◇ असुरस्य - as the divinity ◇ प्रचेतसः - flashed to the surroundings ◇ छर् - pervaded ◇ दिर् - bestowing ◇ येन - powerfully ◇ दाशुषे - as the auspicious arising ◇ यच् - somehow ◇ शति - as hundredfold ◇ त्मना - certainly ◇ तन्नो - as from the *Sat* ◇ महाँ - greatly moved ◇ उदयान् - rose and moved as ◇ देवो - shining things ◇ अक्तुभिः - and as darkness advanced]

Then from the heaven an excellence spread mightily to become great, enormous and a great gratification, as the divinity flashed around, powerfully and energetically bestowing and pervading, which was respected by all and which caused the hundredfold auspicious arising, indeed manifesting from the *Sat* by greatly moving, rising and moving again, thereby swelling along with the shining things that came with darkness.

What all got manifested by the divinity of *Savita* could be termed as great. It was a great shining and penetrating brilliance that came as a great gratification descended. It flashed the bright objects and a darkness came to the surrounding, to great lengths and distances. It also generated those evil ones that came from darkness. Thus that divine dalliance brought in the great satisfaction of this universe. It maintained the brightness and darkness of the universe with equanimity. It enabled the repeated manifestations a hundred times.

RV4.53.02 दिवो धर्ता भुवनस्य प्रजापतिः पिशङ्गं द्रापिं प्रति मुञ्चते कविः। विचक्षणः प्रथयन्नापृणन्नुर्वजीजनत्सविता सुम्नमुक्थ्यम्॥

[दिवो - by heaven; the shining ones ◇ धर्ता - coming as supported ◇ भुवनस्य - of the universe ◇ प्र - to the surrounding ◇ जा - born ◇ पति - descended ◇ पिशङ्ग - as the decorated parts ◇ द्रापिं - rushing to the proximity ◇ प्रति - in all directions ◇ मुञ्चते - as those in twisted paths ◇ कविः - intelligently ◇ वि - divided ◇ चक्षणः - from the eyes ◇ प्रथयन् - segments that spread out

◇ न - as ◇ अपृणन् - those obstructing the gifts ◇ नुः - removed from their place ◇ व - as ◇ जी - conquered ◇ जनत् - born and moved ◇ सविता - spread ◇ सुम्नम् - as excellence ◇ उक्थ्यम् - by the prayers]

The universe and the many shining ones came only supported by many heavens, to hold the picturesque parts that got born to the surroundings and to below, rushing to the successive proximity and in all directions, as the twisted paths of creation that intelligently came divided and as the segments that spread out from that eye and epicentre. Removing those that obstructed the progress, conquering them, all were born as the excellences that manifested and spread along with the divine words and prayers.

Created by *Prajāpati*, who lorded over the universe, supported by the heaven, the entities were maintained well decorated, readied by rushing forward and moving intelligently from that eye and through the twisted paths into many directions. As the food principle that came born, conquered, moved and expanded, the universe manifested as the deeds brought about and spread by that excellence of *Savita*. These objects spread and moved to great distances, taking to intelligent methods devised. It was the food principle that moved through the paths of creation that enabled the birth of some and the destruction of others, as an essential process by which the creation progressed. The paths of these movements were curvilinear and in wave forms corresponding to the spherical shape of the universe. The supremacy of the divinity of *Prajāpati* was well acknowledged by all and praised by all.

RV4.53.03 आप्रा रजांसि दिव्यानि पार्थिवा श्लोकं देवः कृणुते स्वाय धर्मणे। प्र बाहू अस्राक्सविता सवीमनि निवेशयन्प्रसुवन्नक्तुभिर्जगत्॥

[आ - manifested ◇ प्र - to the surroundings ◇ आ - as coming ◇ रजांसि - to minute parts ◇ दिव्यानि - that shined ◇ पार्थिवा - as the earths that moved ◇ श्लोकं - out of hymns of praise ◇ देवः - out of heavens ◇ कृणुते - as those stood connected to that which was loftily set up ◇ स्वाय - by ones' own ◇ धर्मणे - set of rules ◇ प्र - to the surroundings ◇ बाहू - as the arms ◇ अस्राक् - tortuously thrown ◇ सविता - having come spread ◇ सवीमनि - as set in motion ◇ निवेशयन् - as entered ◇ प्र - to the surrounding ◇ सुवन् - as Sun like shines ◇ अक्तुभिः - and darkness ◇ जगत् - that repeated; locomoted]

The universe manifested as the shining parts and the earth forms that came to the surroundings till the minutest, out of the divine hymns and out of the many heavens, and as those that descended, from the one above, coming according to ones' own set of rules. The tortuous arms that were thrown to the surroundings, set in motion and spread to the surroundings the Sun-like shines and a darkness that descended to the surroundings and all of these came much repeated.

All got distributed upon squeezed out and spread to the surroundings to be the parts either as the shining ones that moved or as the earth forms that descended from a high seat. Those came as acts of the self obeyed rules, proclaimed by the self. With the arms tortuously thrown around and taking position as it came about, as continuously squeezed out and as the powerful paths of creation that descended while the universe took shape, a darkness also came prevailing to below and around. For all these occurrences, the divinity of *Savita* was ever praised. A waveform of propagation or the curvilinear nature of the paths got well suggested here by comparing to the movement of a snake and by the terms used in the description.

RV4.53.04 अदाभ्यो भुवनानि प्रचाकशद्व्रतानि देवः सविताभि रक्षते। प्रास्राग्बाहू भुवनस्य प्रजाभ्यो धृतव्रतो महो अज्मस्य राजति॥

[अदाभ्यो - as the food principle advanced ◇ भुवनानि - of the universe ◇ प्र - to the surroundings ◇ च - and ◇ आ - manifested ◇ कशद् - as moving ◇ व्रतानि - with the rules ◇ देवः - from the heaven ◇ सवित - spread ◇ अभि - advanced to the proximity ◇ रक्षते - as those protected ◇ प्र - to the surroundings ◇ आ - came

◇ स्राग् - quickly ◇ बाहू - the arms ◇ भुवनस्य - of the universe ◇ प्र - to the surroundings ◇ ज - born ◇ अभ्यो - advanced ◇ धृतव्रतो - sticking to a set of rules ◇ महो - becoming great ◇ अज्मस्य - marching ◇ रा - bestowing ◇ जति - and getting born etc.]

A food principle reached everywhere in the universe advancing to the surroundings upon getting manifested according to a set of rules. Many came moved from the heaven, advancing to the proximity and spreading as those that stood protected to the surroundings. As the arms that got extended to all of the surroundings, as those born and advanced according to the divine rules, came a royal and great march of gifting and generating.

The paths of creation stood as if the universe was embraced by the arms that quickly got extended from the heavens. A universal food principle spread everywhere not only from the first of the heavens, but also from the many heavens that came descending to the surroundings. Those marches to the surroundings were through the tortuous and twisted paths of creation which had all the protection of the divinity of *Savita* which got extended till this earth. Those were the royal marches of gifting and generating through out.

RV4.53.05 त्रिरन्तरिक्षं सविता महित्वना त्री रजांसि परिभूस्त्रीणि रोचना। तिस्रो दिवः पृथिविस्तिस्र इन्वति त्रिभिर्व्रतैरभि नो रक्षति त्मना॥

[त्रिः - 3 was ◇ अन्तरिक्षं - the atmosphere ◇ सविता - that came spread ◇ महित्वन् - as a greatness ◇ आ - manifested ◇ त्री - 3 was ◇ रजांसि - the minutely divided ones ◇ परिभूः - the enclosures around ◇ त्रीणि - 3 was ◇ रोचना - the shining ones that came ◇ तिस्रो - 3 was ◇ दिवः - the heavens ◇ पृथिविः - the earths ◇ तिस्र - 3 was ◇ इन्वति - the great forces ◇ त्रिभिः - 3 was ◇ व्रतैः - the rules ◇ अभि - that advanced ◇ नो - as ◇ रक्षति - the great protection ◇ त्मना - that came from the self]

There was a principle of 3 in everything that manifested. The atmosphere that manifested, spread and which stood as a greatness was 3-dimensional. The minutely divided objects were 3-dimensional. The circular *vyāhṛti* formations of the atmosphere were 3-dimensional. The shining stars were 3-dimensional. The heavens and the earths that got formed were 3-dimensional. The rules of advancement belonged to that 3-dimensional regime. The great protections (regional formations) were 3-dimensional. The motive forces were 3-dimensional. The universe brought in by thyself was 3-dimensional all the way.

Indeed all these laws of 3-dimensional existence came from the greatly spread divinity of *Savita* and so manifested this well protected universe. The 3-dimensionality was stated as an all pervading essential nature of everything in the universe equally applicable to objects, to space and to the phenomena leading to the formation of such entities. The 3-dimensionality was there in the heaven, this earth and the paths that the creation had taken. The shining stars and other objects were thus extended till the end. The universe could be termed only as an immense 3-dimensional system. The paths of creation, the atmosphere and the several objects that came as the components of creation came as a single manifestation from a single source, though indeed these came with many branches and sub-divisions. From the very moment of starting, a 3-dimensionality came into existence which for ever stood as the inseparable space and time correlation. From that primary space came, from that moment came, the very interactive existence of all.

And yet the verse could be interpreted to read that everything manifested from the three points of origin that appeared on the horizon of the heaven. The supremacy of the three divine entities taken as gods, goddesses or the *satva-raja-tamo guṇas*' always ruled the creation and existence.

RV4.53.06 बृहत्सुम्नः प्रसवीता निवेशनो जगतः स्थातुरुभयस्य यो वशी। स नो देवः सविता शर्म यच्छत्वस्मे क्षयाय त्रिवरूथमंहसः॥

[बृहत् - became great ◇ सुम्नः - as a benevolence ◇ प्र - to the surroundings ◇ सवीता - coming spread ◇ निवेशनो - entering

◇ जगतः - and moving ◇ स्थातुः - as established authority ◇ उभयस्य - to both sides ◇ यो - somehow ◇ वशी - bringing into subjugation ◇ स - thereby ◇ नो - as ◇ देवः - the heaven ◇ सविता - spreading; the *Savita* ◇ शर्म - protected ◇ यच् - somehow ◇ शत्व - well distinguished ◇ अस्मे - parts ◇ क्षयाय - emaciating ◇ त्रि - as the 3-dimensional ◇ वरूथम् - shelter ◇ अंहस - against calamity]

The universe became great with the benevolences that manifested to the surroundings, getting spread by entering and moving to both sides and as the authority that got established which brought many into subjugation. It only spread as the protections that many ways came from the heaven to become the well distinguished parts, which process went on emaciating to the end. A 3-dimensionality manifested with many refuges from calamities duly set up.

The divinity of *Savita*, greatly and benevolently brought forward and established the universe by spreading everything from the heavens equally to both sides and as a 3-dimensional shelter from any calamity that would arise. The universe was created by moving objects both ways from the heaven, with the protected entities as its contents and thus becoming a 3-dimensional fortress that withstood calamities. The paths of creation maintained the state of equilibrium and symmetry in generation and spreading. Then there were those objects several ways hidden which were the ominous ones that came from *vṛtrata* which wandered through the paths of creation. Those were the ones that strove for bringing calamity and misfortune to those that gloriously stood.

RV4.53.07 आगन्देव ऋतुभिर्वर्धतु क्षयं दधातु नः
सविता सुप्रजामिषम्। स नः क्षपाभिरहभिश्च
जिन्वतु प्रजावन्तं रयिमस्मे समिन्वतु॥

[आगन् - attached to ◇ देव - the heaven ◇ ऋतुभिः - as if the seasons ◇ वर्धतु - enlarged ◇ क्षयं - decayed ◇ दधातु - those obtained ◇ नः - as ◇ सविता - spread ◇ सुप्रजामिषम् - streaming out as the good offspring ◇ स - with ◇ नः - as ◇ क्षप - diminishing ◇

अभिरहभिश्च - speeding from proximity to proximity ◇ जिन्वत् - the mights that moved ◇ प्र - to the surrounding ◇ ज - born ◇ अव - to below ◇ अन्तं - till the end ◇ रयिम् - as the excellent ◇ अस्मे - parts ◇ समिन्वत् - as those assembled]

Only as attached to the heaven and as if the seasons of the year the universe came getting enlarged, it also decayed while spreading, bringing many into existence and with many a good offspring streaming out. The speeds got diminished when moved from proximity to proximity. The might of the many that were born to the surroundings got similarly reduced when progressed to below and till the ends and it was thus that the excellent parts of the universe pervaded equally in all directions.

The paths of creation came to the surroundings from the heaven, as if the seasons of an year that would appear on this earth, alternating and repeating. Next to the paths of creation stood the darkness, and next to it, the path of creation, completing a circle. And heavens came after heavens till the end of the universe and the process was thus found repeated several times. These paths sprinkled the bright objects of the universe as everywhere. The very inspiration for creation came from that shining intellect called *Savita* and it was His divine gifts that appeared before us.

It was with a clear 3-dimensionality that the universe was born. This property extended till the end, equally applicable to the space and to the objects. In this 3-dimensional existence, a curvilinear progress was tantamount and whatever rectilinear motion observed should be resolved as such. This property extended not only to the positions of the objects that got stationed to the surroundings of the heaven, but also to the trajectories and movements of objects till the very end. Besides, the first born locations and the later ones became centres of power in spite of the fact that nothing perhaps ultimately existed there. Those appeared as perpetually tortured by hidden forces and these interactive forces pervaded everywhere. The universe came into existence as equitable progresses from the heaven which maintained a left-right balance all the time. It came as the paths swirled around the heaven and so got repeated from the many heavens that stood to below.

RV 5.81

[(5) पञ्चर्चस्यास्य सूक्तस्यात्रेयः श्यवाश्व ऋषिः । सविता देवता । जगती छन्दः]

RV5.81.01 युञ्जते मन उत युञ्जते धियो विप्रा विप्रस्य बृहतो विपश्चितः। वि होत्रा दधे वयुनाविदेक इन्महि देवस्य सवितुः परिष्टुतिः ॥

[युञ्जते - as those suitably connected to ◇ मन - a mind ◇ उत - interwoven ◇ युञ्जते - as those suitably connected to ◇ धियो - an intellect ◇ वि - divided ◇ प्र - to the surroundings ◇ आ - manifested ◇ वि - divided ◇ प्र - to the surroundings ◇ अस्य - that way ◇ बृहतो - became enlarged ◇ विपश्चितः - through several routes ◇ वि - divided ◇ होत्रा - oblations that came ◇ दधे - obtained ◇ वयुनाविद् - well according to the rules ◇ एक - from one ◇ इन् - forcefully ◇ महि - became great ◇ देवस्य - from heaven ◇ सवितु - mightily spreading ◇ परिष्टुतिः - as the prayers]

Those came suitably connected and interwoven to a mind, those came suitably connected to an intellect and those came divided to the surroundings and thus all of them manifested only as divided to the surroundings. Getting enlarged through several routes, those were obtained by the many oblations that occurred according to the rules. Manifesting from one, forcefully became great, spreading mightily from the heaven along with the divine prayers.

Suitably connected to a divine mind and an intellect, divided to the surroundings and again got divided the same way, became very large through several routes that issued out of the many oblations and as moved from the earlier ones.

The knowledgeable ones praised the divinity called *Savita* for this. While the paths of creation got formed from the heaven and deposited many objects and when those objects got repeatedly divided and issued out as further objects, those were divinely guided. When the oblations occurred from locations that stood much divided and when the objects were delivered from what existed earlier, a divine nature was present.

RV5.81.02 विश्वा रूपाणि प्रति मुञ्चते कविः प्रासाविद् भद्रं द्विपदे चतुष्पदे। वि नाकमख्यत्सविता वरेण्योऽनु प्रयाणमुषसो वि राजति॥

[विश्वा - reaching everywhere ◇ रूपाणि - as a shape ◇ प्रति - in all directions ◇ मुञ्चते - as those released ◇ कविः - knowledgeably ◇ प्रासादविद् - as if from a height to the surroundings ◇ भद्रं - as auspicious and protected ◇ द्विपदे - in two steps ◇ चतुष्पदे - four steps ◇ वि - divided ◇ नाक - from heaven ◇ मख्यत् - moving energetically ◇ सविता - coming spreading ◇ वरेण्यो - as excellence ◇ अनु - a set of ◇ प्रयाणम् - journeyed ◇ उषसो - rising ◇ वि - divided ◇ राजति - bestowing and getting generated]

A shape reached everywhere with the knowledge that got released into all directions and the auspicious and protected entities came from a height to the surroundings in steps of two and four. Those moved energetically from the heavens through the divided paths; the excellence's spreading and journeying along with the lesser ones. Those arose again and again, became the divided gifts bestowed and in such ways the universe came into existence.

It was due to the wishes and intelligence of the exalted *Savita* that an incessant flow from the heaven, much divided and casting excellences equally in all directions and getting augmented in steps of twos and fours, occurred. The objects spread and reached everywhere in the universe and later occasioned the arising and journey of many, similarly generated and gifted in plenty. The divinity of *Savita* stood over the process of creation of the universe intelligently at all times. The incessant flows that occurred from the heaven, after dividing whatever existed and the subsequent rise, movement, division and generation, still remained in the domain of the shining divinity of *Savita*. Thus an element of suzerainty was allotted to the existence of *Savita*, in spite of mentioning several divinities in the creation of the universe. And these happened till the very end of creation, which occurred in multiple geometric progressions. In addition, the progress maintained a symmetry and equivalence to both sides at all times.

RV5.81.03 यस्य प्रयाणमन्वन्य इद्ययुर्देवा देवस्य महिमानमोजसा।
यः पार्थिवानि विममे स एतशो रजांसि देवः सविता महित्वना॥

[यस्य - as endeavours ◇ प्रयाणम् - and journeys ◇ अन्वन्य - as one and the next ◇ इद् - indeed ◇ ययुः - swiftly moved ◇ देवा - from the heavens ◇ देवस्य - after heavens ◇ महिमानम् - as arrangements that got greatly enlarged ◇ ओजसा - energetically ◇ यः - and as ◇ पार्थिवानि - the earths ◇ वि - divided ◇ ममे - from the self ◇ स - as ◇ एतशो - shining splendours ◇ रजांसि - in dust forms ◇ देवः - and shining, from the heaven ◇ सविता - coming as spread ◇ महित्वना - manifested as a greatness]

Thus as the endeavours and journeys that came one after the other, indeed swiftly moved from the heavens after heavens, as the arrangements that got greatly and energetically pushed, the universe got enlarged, bringing forth from the self, as the earths and the shining splendours that came in many forms, including the dust forms. Thus a greatness spread from the heaven.

How a journey of chasing swiftly became the heavens that came from the heavens and as the bright ones of great strengths, became the many earth forms that got divided, became the many colours, got pounded to dust forms, stood shining and moved, was the very way the universe spread. It was indeed a unique and swift journey, by which the universe came into existence. Great strides were taken while the earth forms were placed as here and there till this earth. Great strengths were exhibited, many things were pounded to dust and those came in all hues, colours and shines. There were multiple divisions and several mutations had occurred.

RV5.81.04 उत यासि सवितस्त्रीणि रोचनोत सूर्यस्य रश्मिभिः समुच्यसि। उत रात्रिमुभयतः परीयस उत मित्रो भवसि देव धर्मभिः॥

[उत - interwoven ◇ यासि - progressing well bound to ◇ सवितः - spread ◇ त्रीणि - as three ◇ रोचनोत - with a brilliance equal to ◇ सूर्यस्य - a Sun ◇ रश्मिभिः - as the rays advanced ◇ समुच्यसि - from apex points ◇ उत - bound as ◇ रात्रिम् - the nights ◇ उभयतः - on both sides ◇ परीयस - swung around ◇ उत - associated ◇ मित्रो - with a friendliness ◇ भवसि - that came into existence bound to ◇ देव - the heaven ◇ धर्मभि - advanced with well laid out rules]

Progressing well bound to a 3-dimensionality, all interwoven, those rays smote down from an altitude with a Sun-like brilliance and along with these manifested the darkness as the nights, positioned on both sides and as swung around the heaven, exhibiting a bond and friendliness that manifested and advanced from the heaven.

From that which stood shining like a Sun, the rays smote down, a 3-dimensionality cleverly got executed and darkness spread and stood on both sides of the paths of creation. Paths of creation swung to the surroundings with the same 3-dimensionality and with the darkness maintained in the gaps as established according to the divine rules. A unique 3-dimensionality thus came co-born, from the very beginning. It was as if the days and nights that would repeatedly appear that the darkness and brightness alternated to each other through the volume expanse of the universe. All came as per the divine rules and with the blessings of the divinity called *Savita* and as manifested from the heaven.

RV5.81.05 उतेशिषे प्रसवस्य त्वमेक इदुत पूषा भवसि देव यामभिः। उतेदं विश्वं भुवनं वि राजसि श्यावाश्वस्ते सवितः स्तोममानशे॥

[उते - connected to ◇ शिषे - the balance ◇ प्र - to the surroundings ◇ सवस्य - as squeezed out ◇ त्वमेक - from thyself as the one ◇ इद् - only ◇ उत - arose ◇ पूषा - purified and moved as

◇ भवसि - bound to the occurred ◇ देव - heaven ◇ याम् - taken course ◇ अभि: - as advancing ◇ उत - connected ◇ इदं - thus ◇ विश्वं - reached everywhere ◇ भुवनं - as the universe ◇ वि - divided ◇ राजसि - gifted and born bound to ◇ श्यावा - came dark coloured ◇ श्वस्ते - as those blown away ◇ सवित - spreading ◇ स्तोमम् - with prayers ◇ आ - that came ◇ नशे - diminishing]

Connected to what was left over came those to the surroundings as squeezed out, rising only from thyself, getting purified and moved from the heavens that got formed, advancing through the paths which stood as a network and thus reaching everywhere in the universe. Getting divided, gifted and born bound to one another, those got blown away to the extent of the dark coloured ones. All of these occurred along with the widespread prayers that went on diminishing while progressed.

All the arrangements of the universe came at its own will and it was that divine and shining intellect that presented the universe like this. What remained cold and frozen in the beginning was agitated greatly, got extracted and got filtered as the seed substance for creation. This was then distributed in different directions till the very end of the universe. Much were gifted and many were generated in the process. What came to be so deposited in the beginnings, became new centres of creation which process continued till the very end and as much as divinely permitted. Sequentially moving to the proximity this great enlargement became emaciated while progressed. It was the hymns and praises that arose at appropriate levels that enabled this progress. The universe thus became all interwoven and so it was known and praised.

Indeed a great mind and intellect acted behind the creation of this great universe. Dividing what existed, moved as the *yajñas* that came to the surrounding as a progress that always obeyed the divine rules. It geometrically progressed, several times arising from what first took form, till the very end of the universe. As an unusual journey that took place, objects were pounded and thrown out till this earth, greatly spreading all the time, as objects of different temperatures and shines. There was thus a flow of shining paths and objects, surrounding which the darkness stood, till the end. Everything got created out of the self that existed originally in the heaven, duly inspired by the sounds of hymns that came surrounded.

RV 5.82

[(9) नवर्चस्यास्य सूक्तस्यात्रेयः श्यावाश्व ऋषिः । सविता देवता। (1) प्रथमोर्चोऽनुष्टुप् (2 - 9) द्वितीयाद्यष्टानाञ्च गायत्री छन्दसी]

RV5.82.01 तत् सवितुर्वृणीमहे वयं देवस्य भोजनम्।
श्रेष्ठं सर्वधातमं तुरं भगस्य धीमहि॥

[तत् - from That ◇ सवितुः - mightily spread ◇ वृणी - satisfactions ◇ महे - great ◇ वयं - as the body ◇ देवस्य - from the heaven ◇ भोजनं - by consumption ◇ श्रेष्ठं - as the excellence ◇ सर्वधातमं - that came and stood as everywhere ◇ तुरं - instantly ◇ भगस्य - beautifully ◇ धी - with an intellect ◇ महि - great]

From That spread those great satisfactions, as a body that was formed from the heaven by way of consumption containing the excellences that instantly took position as everywhere, to become this beautiful universe as created by a great intellect.

It was the great intellect of *Savita* that brought a great satisfaction by bestowing the beautiful and excellent body of the universe. It came instantly spreading by consumption based on the food principle. The arms of creation spread from the heaven in different directions embracing the objects so created. Though it became an extreme enlargement on a self sustaining course based on the food principle, it was the divine nature of *Savita* that saw to the prompt creation and sustenance of such phenomena. That great intellect that pervaded had overseen every progress.

RV5.82.02 अस्य हि स्वयशस्तरं सवितुः कच्चन प्रियम्।
न मिनन्ति स्वराज्यम्॥

[अस्य - like that ◇ हि - only ◇ स्वय - by own ◇ शस्तरं - prayers ◇ सवितुः - divided might that spread ◇ कः - somehow; many ways ◇ चन - great delight ◇ प्रियम् - much liked ◇ न - as ◇ मिनन्ति - swelled to the proximity ◇ स्वराज्यम् - as issued out and born from the self]

It was only in such ways, by own prayers and the divided might that spread, came those many ways manifested. The great delights, much liked by all swelled to the proximity upon getting issued out and born from the very self and in this manner the universe came progressed.

With the sounds of prayers that came from the self and directed to the self, which came many times divided, dominions were set up swelling with pleasant objects and as those that came to the successive proximity. The universe got swelled to the surroundings and to the proximity by the repeated and penetrating recitals bound to the desired words. It was by gifting from the self and yet bringing under thy control, that many dominions of the universe were set up by that brilliant intellect. It was from this divinity that the sounds and vibrations that arose to the vicinity, manifested. The sounds manifested repeatedly as the appropriate words suitable to the occasion which sufficiently energized the ones that progressed. Thus all of the universe would be reckoned as the domain of the divine *Savita*.

RV5.82.03 स हि रत्नानि दाशुषे सुवाति सविता भगः।
तं भागं चित्रमीमहे॥

[स - that way ◇ हि - only ◇ रत्नानि - a set of diamonds ◇ दाशुषे - auspiciously arose ◇ सु - good ◇ व - existence ◇ अति - great ◇ सवित - spreading ◇ आ - came ◇ भगः - progressing brightly ◇ तं - emaciated ◇ भगं - beautifully ◇ चित्रमीमहे - as a wonderful and great existence]

Likewise only a set of diamonds auspiciously arose, as good existence that greatly spread from those that progressed brightly and then got emaciated and thus became a wonderful and great existence.

It was that way that those things with a diamond like glitter descended, beautifully shining to become the great benevolences that spread. All these got gradually emaciated and became a wonderful and great existence. It was a wonderful picture that was painted by that great divinity by decorating the high skies with the diamond like glittering stars. The sounds of worship prevailed all over, from the heaven till the far end. Yet all remained as the great benevolences and excellences that were created by that shining and divine intellect that came spreading everywhere.

RV5.82.04 अद्या नो देव सवितः प्रजावत्सावीः सौभगम्।
परा दुःष्वप्न्यं सुव॥

[अद्या - like that ◇ नो - as ◇ देव - from the heaven ◇ सवितः - spread ◇ प्र - to the surroundings ◇ ज - born ◇ अव - acceptable ◇ स - with that ◇ आ - came ◇ वीः - and moved ◇ सौभगम् - the auspicious ◇ परा - distanced ◇ दुःष्वप्न्यं - the bad dreams avoided ◇ सुव - great existence]

Like that came from the heaven, spreading to the surroundings, the acceptable things born, those that came into existence and moved to distances, auspicious, great and avoiding their bad dreams.

Is it not that way, the divinity of *Savita* kept the bad dreams away from the beloved and converted those acceptable birth of objects to the surroundings, into good fortunes and excellences? It was that shining intellect that withheld the dark and ominous products of the *vṛtrata*, from attacking the noble and dear objects of the universe. Those bad elements were ever trying to disturb the peace that prevailed in the universe.

As yet another meaning; let the great and divine *Savita* provide and promote the well being of our beloved offspring's and maintain them as beautiful ones, keeping their bad dreams away.

RV5.82.05 विश्वानि देव सवितर्दुरितानि परा सुव।
यद्भद्रम् तन्न आ सुव॥

[विश्वानि - reaching as everywhere ◇ देव - from the heaven ◇ सवितः - spreading ◇ दुरितानि - misfortunes ◇ परा - kept away ◇ सुव - good existence ◇ यद् - somehow; many ways ◇ भद्रम् - protected; ◇ तन्न - from that; *Sat* ◇ आ - coming as a ◇ सुव - good existence; well meant]

Reached everywhere in the universe spreading from the heaven keeping the misfortunes away and making them into good existence with many well meant protections that came from the *Sat*.

The divine *Savita* kept away the misfortunes for ever and created the excellence's and gave them an immeasurable protection. From those created, more were created, to be the many excellences of the universe. The participation by *Savita* in the process of creation was as if overseeing the events and properties of the objects and yet accorded an element of freedom in the very process. The divinity that so stood above saw to it that it's excellent nature was reflected on the objects created.

As yet another meaning; let *Savita* the all pervading divinity of the universe keep away the sufferings and provide us with the prosperity as deserved. Let that intellect and eternal shine protect us for ever.

RV5.82.06 अनागसो अदितये देवस्य सवितुः सवे।
विश्वा वामानि धीमहि॥

[अनागसो - that pure one ◇ अदितये - which gave nothing ◇ देवस्य - from the heaven ◇ सवितुः - mightily spread ◇ सवे - upon squeezed out ◇ विश्वा - reaching everywhere ◇ वामानि - as those propagated ◇ धी - with intellect ◇ महि - great]

That which stood in the heaven as pure and bestowing nothing yet, upon squeezed out, spread mightily, reached everywhere, as those that came from a great intellect.

It was that great intellect that squeezed out of the one

that stood in the heaven, very pure and yet giving nothing till then and brought those things into existence, propagating and spreading everywhere. It was the divine *Savita* that penetrated an immobility and made it to flow down as the paths of creation. It was that shining intellect that squeezed out from the *Soma*, filtered it and made it into a pure seed substance and brought in the food principle.

RV5.82.07 आ विश्वदेवं सत्पतिं सूक्तैरद्या वृणीमहे।
सत्यसवं सवितारम्॥

[आ - manifesting ◇ विश्व - as reaching everywhere ◇ देवं - from the heavens ◇ सत्पतिं - by that supreme authority ◇ सूक्तैः - with prayers ◇ अद्या - like that ◇ आ - came ◇ वृणी - satisfactions ◇ महे - great ◇ सत्यसवं - squeezed out of Truth ◇ सवितारम् - beautifully spreading]

From the heavens and from that supreme authority along with prayers manifested the great satisfactions that reached everywhere, as squeezed out of Truth (the *Satya*), and as that which spread beautifully.

Out of the prayers that came from a supreme authority, came the many heavens that stood as everywhere, and a great satisfaction thus descended, upon getting squeezed out, spread and as forded from the *Satya*. That which remained in the heaven as *Sat*, upon getting energised by the sound and vibrations of the hymns, became the universe in a process of consumption that spread. Not only objects of varying brilliance were created as distributed all over the universe, but the shining intellect of *Savita* prevailed over them for ever.

RV5.82.08 य इमे उभे अहनि पुर एत्यप्रयुच्छन्।
स्वाधिर्देवः सविता॥

[य - wherever ◇ इमे - from there ◇ उभे - to both sides ◇ अहनि - instantly ◇ पुर - advanced ◇ एति - arriving ◇ अप्रयुच्छन् - attended by ◇ स्व - self ◇ अधिः - above ◇ देवः - as heaven ◇ सविता - came spreading]

Wherever came to, from there instantly advanced to both sides, arriving as attended by the self that stood above and as spread from the heaven.

Those objects still capable of creation acted like the heaven and from there the creation proceeded further, attended by the heaven above. It was the much repeated spreading that made the universe so immense and yet those came with a left-right equivalence and symmetry. It was that divine intellect known as *Savita* that oversaw to such progresses.

RV5.82.09 य इमा विश्वा जातान्याश्रावयति श्लोकेन।
प्र च सुवाति सविता॥

[य - those ◇ इमा - thus ◇ विश्वा - reached everywhere ◇ जात - having born ◇ अन्याश्रा - becoming another ◇ वयति - as interwoven ◇ श्लोकेन - along with prayers and chanting of hymns ◇ प्र - to the surrounding ◇ च - and ◇ सुव - as a good existence ◇ अति - greatly ◇ सविता - came spreading]

Those that thus reached everywhere, had come born and had become others that stood interwoven and had come along with prayers and chanting of hymns to the surrounding to become good existences that greatly spread.

It was the divine prayers, the sounds and the cosmic vibrations that first manifested from that shining intellect called *Savita*. Then came those shining objects to many places and from those the further paths of creation. It was thus that the excellences of the universe spread as everywhere. This process was applicable to the first of heavens and were equally applicable to all the subsequent heavens down the line. Nothing external ever assisted this process. It was that all pervading intellect and consciousness that brought about the universe.

What existed in the heaven were very much divided, extruded and extended to become this great universe. It was the sounds and the cosmic vibrations which came as the divine hymns that created several domains of the universe with diamond like objects scattered around which processes ultimately and progressively got emaciated. Those which rose out of the afflictions became the beautiful and excellent off-springs to the surroundings and these moved to great distances. From that which remained raw in the heaven, got squeezed out, got filtered and made to flow downwards, as the paths of creation. Those flows of shining objects spread around to form well protected fortresses or in other words distinct group of entities. Progressive divisions and evacuations created emptiness in many places and all of these happened without the participation of anything external.

RV 6.71

[(6) षड्चस्यास्य सूक्तस्य बार्हस्पत्यो भरद्वाज ऋषिः। सविता देवता। (1 - 3) प्रथमतृचस्य जगति (4 - 6) द्वितीयतृचस्य च त्रिष्टुप् छन्दसि]

RV6.71.01 उदु ष्य देवः सविता हिरण्यया बाहू अयंस्त सवनाय सुक्रतुः। घृतेन पाणी अभि प्रुष्णुते मखो युवा सुदक्षो रजसो विधर्मणि॥

[उदु - surging up ◇ ष्य - getting mixed ◇ देवः - from the heaven ◇ सविता - coming spreading ◇ हिरण्यया - extended golden ◇ बाहू - hands ◇ अयंस्त - that remained thus ◇ सवनाय - as squeezed out ◇ सुक्रतुः - well arranged ◇ घृतेन - sprinkling ◇ पाणी - as hands ◇ अभि - advanced ◇ प्रुष्णुते -sprinkled ◇ मखो - happy ◇ युवा - coupled with; youthful ◇ सुदक्षो - capable ◇ रजसो - dust forms ◇ विधर्मणि - till the circumference]

Surging up from the heaven, spreading across and getting mixed, those golden arms got extended till here. Those manifested as sprinkled and got well arranged upon getting squeezed out by those capable hands and became a happiness and youthfulness that got instituted. Objects got sprinkled, dust forms took shape and this process got extended up to the end circumference.

From the heaven, the first platform of creation, golden hands of creation extended in all directions and from these hands new and capable objects got sprinkled incessantly, till the very end of the universe. Those golden hands came from the *hiraṇyagarbha* and contained the seed matter capable of bringing in the youthfulness of the universe. This process started with the skillful extraction of whatever that existed in the heaven. The process continued till the very end of this enormous universe. Those golden hands got extended from that golden one that existed in the heaven.

RV6.71.02 देवस्य वयं सवितुः सवीमनि श्रेष्ठे स्याम वसुनश्च दावने।
यो विश्वस्य द्विपदो यश्चतुष्पदो निवेशने प्रसवे चासि भूमनः॥

[देवस्य - from the heaven ◇ वयं - a body ◇ सवितुः - mightily spread ◇ सवीमनि - as set in motion, upon squeezed out ◇ श्रेष्ठे - as excellent ◇ स्याम - powers ◇ वसुनश्च - wealthy ◇ दावने - granted ◇ यो - somehow ◇ विश्वस्य - reaching everywhere ◇ द्विपदो - in two steps ◇ य - and ◇ चतुष्पदो - 4 steps ◇ निवेशने - entering ◇ प्र - to the surrounding ◇ सवे - upon squeezed ◇ च - and ◇ असि - cut up ◇ भू - as earths ◇ मनः - in principle]

From the heaven, a body came spreading mightily and as set in motion by excellent and auspicious powers, granting wealth that somehow reached everywhere, entering into the surrounding and progressing in steps of two and four, after getting squeezed out and getting divided, to become the earth forms that came into existence.

The divine body of the universe was made possible by *Savita* and out of sacrifices made upon squeezing, distressing and spreading of what existed in the heaven. It was by movements in a geometric progression that objects got stationed till this earth. What existed in the heaven was segmented and individually extended to the surroundings and downwards as different paths of creation that contained the objects and energy. The process was repeated ever so many times.

RV6.71.03 अदब्धेभिः सवितः पायुभिष्ट्वं शिवेभिरद्य परि पाहि नो गयम्। हिरण्यजिह्वः सुविताय नव्यसे रक्षा माकिर्नो अघशंस ईशत॥

[अदब्धेभिः - from a pure existence ◇ सवितः - spread ◇ पायुभिष्ट्वं - as the protected oblations ◇ शिवेभिः - auspiciously ◇ अद्य - that way ◇ परि - to the surrounding ◇ पाहि - only as protected ◇

नो - as ◇ गयम् - progressed ◇ हिरण्यजिह्वः - the golden tongues ◇ सुविताय - that well spread ◇ नव्यसे - as the new ◇ रक्षा - protections ◇ माकिर्नो - the wandering ones ◇ अघशंस - evil forces resisted ◇ ईशत - supremacy]

Protected oblations spread auspiciously to the surroundings from a pure existence and the protections that manifested had progressed out of the well spread golden tongues. Thus this universe had manifested only with ever new protections provided by a supremacy, offering resistance to the attacks of wandering evil forces.

The process set forth by *Savita* as the protected sacrifices that took place in the heaven were found to move the golden tongues of flame that got extended and shot out from heaven. Within this, the objects remained protected from the evil forces outside. Objects moved freely and safely as if floating boats, till the earth. There were many such paths that started from the heaven and extended in all directions. Thus the protected progresses of creation were overseen by the shining divinity of *Savita*.

RV6.71.04 उदु ष्य देवः सविता दमूना हिरण्यपाणिः प्रतिदोषमस्थात्। अयोहनुर्यजतो मन्द्रजिह्व आ दाशुषे सुवति भूरि वामम्॥

[उदु - surging up only ◇ ष्य - getting mixed ◇ देवः - from the heaven ◇ सविता - coming spread ◇ दमूना - as favoured residences ◇ हिरण्यपाणिः - as the golden arms ◇ प्रति - in all directions ◇ दोषमस्थात् - inconvenient bad ones ◇ अयोहनुः - with iron jawed ◇ यजतो - worships; efforts ◇ मन्द्रजिह्व - pleasant murmurs ◇ आ - manifested ◇ दाशुषे - auspiciously arose ◇ सुवति - good existence ◇ भूरि - abundantly ◇ वामम् - agreeable]

Surging up from the heaven, getting mixed up, those favourite residences came spread and those golden arms came in all directions, restraining those inconvenient bad ones with iron jawed will, prayers and worships. With matching efforts came the pleasant murmurs that manifested and auspiciously arose to become the many and abundantly agreeable good ex-

istences.

It was a divine knowledge that brought forth the golden hands as the paths of creation around the heaven. These hands of flame were accompanied by appropriately subdued sounds and corresponding vibrations that had fought and kept away the inconvenient wickedness. These sounds manifested as the snarling growls that distanced the enemies, but were endearing words to others. Thus a strong will and the divine mind extended all through these golden hands of creation and established a more agreeable ambiance and provided beloved housing for all the groups.

RV6.71.05 उदु अयाँ उपवक्तेव बाहू हिरण्यया सविता सुप्रतीका।
दिवो रोहांस्यरुहत्पृथिव्या अरीरमत्पतयत्कच्चिदभ्वम्॥

[उदु - surging up only indeed ◇ अयाँ - successively moving ◇ उपवक्तेव - according to the words descended ◇ बाहू - with arms ◇ हिरण्यया - moved as golden ◇ सविता - came spread ◇ सुप्रतीका - as a beautiful shape ◇ दिवो - from the heaven ◇ रोहांसि - sprouting as distributed ◇ अरुहत् - moving and descending ◇ पृथिव्या - as the many earth forms ◇ अरि - jealous and ◇ इरमत् - hostile powers ◇ पतयत् - descending and moving ◇ कच् - bound ◇ चिद् - to a heap; mind; in principle ◇ अभ्वम् - monstrous]

Indeed only surging up and successively moving along with the words that descended came the golden arms extended, spreading as a beautiful shape, as sprouted and distributed from the heaven and as the earth forms that moved and descended; but along with these moved and descended those jealous and hostile powers of immense monstrosity, bound to the same heap, mind and principle.

While those fondly embracing golden arms got extended from the heaven as the paths of creation that spread all over the beautiful body of the universe and marked the arising of the shining things, manifestation of the earth forms, along came and descended those extremely powerful and monstrous things that would strike the enemy down. Interactively bonded to the epicentre, several golden arms got extended quickly and steadily from the heaven, till this earth holding many things bright. It was like a set of golden hands fondly embraced the body of the universe. There were indeed repetitions of what occurred from the heaven and several new epicentres were born and several divided paths of creation took place. But along with these paths of creation, came the powerful forces, which tried to annihilate those that came into existence. It was the help extended by the golden arms that came from the heaven that protected those benevolent existences at all times.

RV6.71.06 वाममद्य सवितर्वाममु श्वो दिवेदिवे वाममस्मभ्यं सावीः। वामस्य हि क्षयस्य देव भूरेरया धिया वामभाजः स्याम॥

[वामम् - moved agreeable ◇ अद्य - manners ◇ सवितः - spread ◇ वाममु - moved agreeable indeed ◇ श्वो.- as breathed out ◇ दिवेदिवे - heavens after heavens ◇ वामम् - moved agreeable ◇ अस्मभ्यं - parts that advanced ◇ स - as ◇ अव् - impelled ◇ ई - continuously ◇ वामस्य - moved agreeable ◇ हि - only ◇ क्षयस्य - emaciated ◇ देव - from the heaven ◇ भूरे - abundantly ◇ रया - royally ◇ धिय - from an intellect ◇ वामभाजः - as partner at the left ◇ स्याम - empowered]

Moving in the most agreeable manners, moving and spreading agreeably indeed, as breathed out from the heavens after the heavens, moving as the agreeable parts that advanced and those that continuously got impelled as the most agreeable ones and it was then that whatever abundantly came got emaciated. Those ones that royally came from the heaven, came from an intellect and as empowered by the partner at the left.

Manifesting as the acceptable ones, moving out and spreading as established relationships, the heavens came breathed out from the heavens and many parts got squeezed out of the flows that came propagated. Later, the brightness of the many earth forms that issued out got emaciated. Though the universe came in such different ways, yet it only came as if holding the most pleasant partner on the left in a warm embrace. The universe came in a complex manner and as a net result of multiple phenomena that manifested. The universe got enlarged with the paths of creation positioned from the heavens. The brightness of the parts that got created came in several levels, with the earth and dust forms moved by an unseen propagating wind. Thus the interactive nature and its fading levels, the divine inspirations and above all that divine intellect that oversaw all were the essential components of creation. Yet it was only as if lovingly brought into existence by a divine couple.

The eagerness and anxiety of the self that remained at the heaven became the splendid objects extending from the heaven till earth strongly bonded to the self. From the very beginning a left-right balance was maintained. Thus it was the shining intellect of *Savita* that caused the creation of the shining objects from the heaven. It was as if the body of the universe was held closely embraced by that divine brightness. The well set Indian traditions of the wife positioned at the left of the man, the Goddess positioned at the left of God, was presented here by the terms used. In fact, no particular definition of gender for the divine *Savita* was presented, till the 5th and 6th of this hymn. Now, it could be deduced that the concept of the divinity of *Savita* and the very physical universe stood in parallel to the concept of the *Puruṣa*. All the same the overall descriptions firmly rested on the very singular existence of the divinity of *Savita*; that excellent and bright intellect that pervaded everywhere.

From the heaven and from what remained a youthful potency, golden hands carrying the seed substance and the semen virile spread to the surroundings and to below. The contents of the heaven were squeezed, extracted, filtered and extruded downwards as different paths of creation. A 3-dimensional and instant expansion of the universe took place. Born out of the protected oblations, these flows provided the protection to the objects which floated down as if wandering boats. While snarling growls kept away the unwanted, appropriate greetings were provided to the deserving. It was as if embraced with the golden hands of that divine brightness that the universe came born and existed for ever. It was as if that brilliant intellect closely held this universe to the left, those golden hands wrapped around and extending till this earth. The very common, adorable and favourite visual of God and Goddess in India.

RV 7.45

(4) चतुर्ऋचस्यास्य सूक्तस्य मैत्रावरुणिर्वसिष्ठ ऋषिः। सविता देवता। त्रिष्टुप् छन्दः]

RV7.45.01 आ देवो यातु सविता सुरत्नोऽन्तरिक्षप्रा वहमानो अश्वैः। हस्ते दधानो नर्या पुरूणि निवेशयञ्च प्रसुवञ्च भूम॥

[आ - manifesting ◇ देवो - from the heavens ◇ यातु - as progressed and confirmed ◇ सविता - and came spread ◇ सुरत्नो - beautiful diamonds ◇ अन्तरिक्ष - atmosphere ◇ प्र - to the surroundings ◇ वहमानो - as arrangements that carried ◇ अश्व् - spread ◇ वैः - only as ◇ हस्ते - as the arms ◇ दधानो - that issued ◇ नर्या - till man ◇ पुरूणि - abundantly ◇ निवेशयञ्च - entering into the swirls ◇ प्रसुवञ्च - as the good things squeezed out of the swirls ◇ भूम - earth forms]

Manifesting as progressed and spread from the heavens, the beautiful diamonds came firmed up to the surroundings along with and into the atmosphere. The arrangements got carried and spread by the arms of creation that abundantly issued till man. Those created entered into swirls, the earth forms got squeezed out of such swirls and the universe got enormous.

The many stars and shining objects that spread out of the heaven appeared like diamonds and arrangements of several objects that came to the surrounding atmosphere. Those were the highly swirling paths of creation extended downward carrying those till man. It is clear that the hands that arose from the heaven were curvilinear in nature, befitting the spherical universe. The creations also came as several vortex motions that deposited the earth forms in scattered places and these were extended till the far end of the universe. These descriptions of movements, made the geometry of the universe very clear.

RV7.45.02 **उदस्य बाहू शिथिरा बृहन्ता हिरण्यया दिवो अन्ताँ अनष्टाम्। नूनं सो अस्य महिमा पनिष्ट सूरश्चिदस्मा अनु दादपस्याम्॥**

[**उदस्य** - that came up ◇ **बाहू** - the arms ◇ **शिथिरा** - twisted and askew ◇ **बृहन्ता** - coming till the enormous ends ◇ **हिरण्यया** - progressed as golden ◇ **दिवो** - from the heavens ◇ **अन्ताँ** - extended till the end ◇ **अनष्टाम्** - with out loss or harms ◇ **नूनं** - instantly ◇ **सो** - along with ◇ **अस्य** - as ◇ **महिमा** - manifesting greatly ◇ **पनिष्ट** - the praises ◇ **सूरश्चिद्** - with Sun like ◇ **अस्मा** - parts ◇ **अनु** - and similar ◇ **दादपस्याम्** - repeatedly issued out and moved to distances]

The golden and twisted arms arose from the heavens and progressed till the enormous ends and objects instantly manifested from the heavens till the end without loss or harm. Great praises moved along with the creations and Sun-like objects manifested as issued out from whatever earlier got issued out. Thus the universe became much enlarged.

From the heaven, those golden arms surged up to the enormous ends of the universe, as if flung out suddenly, carrying the arrangements that came from the divine praises. The Sun-like parts manifested along with many visibilities. The arms that were excitedly flung downward from the heaven were entwined while being golden and the objects within their fold moved as impelled till the end. So large and praiseworthy were these arrangements in which the self happened to contain Sun-like objects and objects with lesser of the same properties. The sequence was not only applicable to the heaven and the surroundings but extended far and below. Those arms of creation were curvilinear and multi-headed till the very end.

RV7.45.03 स घा नो देवः सविता सहावा ऽऽसाविषद्वसुपतिर्वसूनि।
विश्रयमाणो अमतिमुरूचीं मर्तभोजनमध रासते नः॥

[स - with that ◇ घा - came striking ◇ नों - as ◇ देवः - from the heaven ◇ सविता - coming spread ◇ सह - powerfully ◇ अवा - moving away and to below ◇ आस - seated ◇ आविषद् - as clear entities ◇ वसु - of excellence ◇ पतिः - descended ◇ वसूनि - after excellence ◇ विश्रयमाणो - as the arrangements of shelter ◇ अमतिम् - to unimaginable ◇ उरूचीं - and far reaching distances ◇ मर्त - till man; getting destroyed or diminished ◇ भोजनम् - as the food principle ◇ अध - and besides as ◇ रासते - the juice of the semen virile ◇ नः - as]

Then, the strokes of lightning descended and spread powerfully from the heaven and from those clear entities got stationed. Thus came many an excellence and more of such excellence, descending to become the arrangements of shelter that came to unimaginably far off distances. Those got into diminishing strengths or got destroyed, while reaching up to man and beyond. At the same time, the juice of the semen virile spread as everywhere.

The divine shafts of lightning came spreading from the heaven, as a flow of brightness that manifested. Those were the excellences that came from the lord of excellences. A hierarchical order and corresponding arrangements came elongated to unimaginable distances, overtaking man and the food principle of this earth and these were indeed issued out from the heaven and the *Sat*. It was *Savita*, the lord of good things that brought forth this excellent universe which commenced as a dalliance and spread as several dalliances. The objects while remained within the paths of creation or moved far until the earth and its surroundings were arrangements of many chains of dependencies. The hands of creation were found extended way beyond the living creatures of this earth and acquired immortality through *annabhāva* that manifested.

RV7.45.04 इमा गिरः सवितारं सुजिह्वं पूर्णगभस्तिमीळते सुपाणिम्।
चित्रं वयो बृहदस्मे दधातु यूयं पात स्वस्तिभिः सदा नः॥

[इमा - thus came from ◇ गिरः - the words ◇ सवितारं - that spread beautifully ◇ सुजिह्वं - as the sweet tongues of flame ◇ पूर्ण - to be filled ◇ गभस्ति - as rays that smote ◇ मीळते - much praised ◇ सुपाणिम् - as the beautiful arms ◇ चित्रम् - as a unique ◇ वयो - body ◇ बृहद् - enlarged ◇ अस्मे - with parts ◇ दधातु - mightily obtained ◇ यूयं - and as the swirls ◇ पात - that descended ◇ स्वस्तिभिः - to a calm and quiet ◇ सदा - for ever ◇ नः - as]

Thus from the divine words came those beautifully spread sweet tongues of flame, as the beautiful arms extended and the rays that smote, filling and getting enlarged as the universe, with the parts that would become its beautiful and unique body. Those swirls descended mightily the universe became calm and quiet, manifesting so for ever.

The sweet tongued voices that originated and spread became the tongues of flame that contained matter and spread from the heaven. The arms of flame that shot out as a result of the invocations that filled the surroundings, became the body of the universe getting enlarged and descending as several turbulences, which then settled down to be a calm and composed universe. In spite of the swirling nature exhibited in the beginnings, the universe ultimately came to a peaceful existence.

From the heaven, an atmosphere containing the diamond like entities extended as held within the arms of a divinity and manifesting till this earth. These arms were flung around as spirals and several objects were thus swirled around. Those were the golden hands that remained entwined which harmed none and were born out of divine prayers and hymns. As if the lightnings that descended from a supreme divinity, as those that reached men and beyond, many got deeply embedded into the food principle that got established. Thus it was that the incessant sounds and the cosmic vibrations that got extended from the heaven in the form of sweet tongues of flame and as the beautiful arms extended, became the universe.

RV 10.149

[(5) पञ्चर्चस्यास्य सूक्तस्य हैरण्यस्तूपोऽर्चन्नृषिः। सविता देवता। त्रिष्टुप् छन्दः]

RV10.149.01 सविता यन्त्रैः पृथिवीमरम्णादस्कम्भने सविता द्यामदृंहत्। अश्वमिवाधुक्षद्धुनिमन्तरिक्षमतूर्ते बद्धं सविता समुद्रम्॥

[सविता - came spreading ◇ यन्त्रैः - restrained and controlled ◇ पृथिवि - as the earths ◇ इम - thus; as ◇ रमण - pleasantly ◇ आद - provided ◇ स्कम्भने - from a pillar ◇ सविता - coming spread ◇ द्याम - moving from the heavens ◇ दृंहत् - connected to ◇ अश्व - widely ◇ वम् - emitted ◇ इव - as if ◇ अधु - steadily ◇ क्षद् - divided ◇ धुनिम् - by sounds of roar ◇ अन्तरिक्षम् - the atmosphere ◇ अतूर्ते - unobstructed ◇ बद्धं - tied to ◇ सविता - and coming spread ◇ समुद्रम् - like an ocean]

Thus as fastened and moved from a pillar, spread the many heavens and the earths, exercising restraint and control while spreading, pleasantly bestowing and getting widely emitted. Steadily getting divided by the roaring sounds and spreading unobstructed, came through an atmosphere which stood like an ocean.

Apparently (in principle) bound to that pillar and knowledgeably spreading from the heaven, became the enlargements which came with roaring sounds, along with restraints and controls and manifesting as the earths that were moved and flung afar. Whatever thus got distributed were later found emaciated, along with an atmosphere that instantly came and stood like an ocean. The expansion and spreading of the universe took place from the heaven to the earth duly maintaining the orientation to the epicentre of the universe, referred here as the pillar. This epicentre was represented by the *yūpa* in the altar space of the *vaidikayajña*. Matter was emitted, distributed and moved from heaven which became emaciated as progressed. The atmosphere, formed instantly along with the flow of the objects, appearing like an ocean with waves to which the objects created were bound. There indeed was a divine restraint in all that happened.

RV10.149.02 यत्रा समुद्रः स्कभितो व्यौनदपां नपात्सविता तस्य वेद। अतो भूरत आ उत्थितं रजोऽतो द्यावापृथिवी अप्रथेताम्॥

[यत्रा - as how came ◇ समुद्रः - in the ocean ◇ स्कभितो - fastened; floated ◇ व्यौन - in many ways ◇ दपां - accumulated and came ◇ नपात् - as descendants ◇ सविता - that came spreading ◇ तस्य - according to those ◇ वेद - as the properties ◇ अतो - that spread ◇ भूरत - steadily, constantly got filled ◇ आ - came ◇ उत्थितं - raised as ◇ रजो - the dust ◇ अतो - that spread ◇ द्यावापृथिवी - from the heaven till the earth ◇ अप्रथेताम् - spread to the proximity]

To whatever extent into an ocean came floating those that in many ways accumulated and came as the descendants that got segregated according to the properties and steadily got filled and spread, those manifested as the heavens, the earths and the dust forms spreading to the proximity.

On surface earth many things floated down the several streams and finally reached the ocean. Many things got accumulated and agglomerated property-wise while moving downstream. In the same way from the heaven many things got manifested floating down the paths of creation and the same way manifested the many properties of this universe. The same type of agglomeration and accumulation took place in the high skies. Those came as the heavens, the earth forms and the dust that pervaded in the atmosphere which stood as if an ocean. There was a suggestion of property-wise segregation and agglomeration in this narration, just as the sands on to the shore. The waveform propagation in the high skies could also be identified from the same words.

RV10.149.03 पश्चेदमन्यदभवद्यजत्रममर्त्यस्य भुवनस्य भूना।
सुपर्णो अङ्ग सवितुर्गरुत्मान्पूर्वो जातः स उ अस्यानु धर्म॥

[पश्च - later ◇ इदम् - thus ◇ अन्यद् - another ◇ अभवद् - till nothing occured ◇ यजत्रम् - as worthy oblations ◇ अमर्त्यस्य - as immortal ◇ भुवनस्य - the universe ◇ भू - came to existence ◇ ना - as from ◇ सुपर्णो - the *Suparṇa* ◇ अङ्ग - parts ◇ सवितुः - mightily spread ◇ गरुत्मान् - as that heavenly bird moved ◇ पूर्वो - from earlier ◇ जातः - as born ◇ स - with ◇ उ - only ◇ अस्य - in that manner ◇ अनु - similar ◇ धर्म - theories]

Later, another theory surfaced that the universe did not only simply come into existence as immortal until those worthy oblations ceased, but had also come into existence as that heavenly bird *Suparṇa* which having born, moved form its earlier position and had mightily come spreading as the universe; that being an account of what really happened.

Yet some and later time reckoning of what occurred was that that beautifully winged heavenly bird *Suparṇa* getting eager, came born, piercing out from the earlier state, shrieked, flapped its wings and flew down from the heaven till this earth to become the universe. It was theorised that the universe came by a set of unprecedented and worthy oblations and there flowed an immortality all over the universe and became the universe. It was also said that this universe came repeatedly born from what ever first born and thus advanced progressively to become so immense.

In the *asyavāmīyasūkta* (RV1.164.46) it will be found stated that there were more than one theory regarding the origin of this universe. Similarly here it was stated that one theory was that this universe came as a series of *yajña*s, starting from the heaven and extending till man. Yet another theory was that the bird *Suparṇa* that remained in the heaven circled and flew down till earth as this very universe. Elsewhere in the *Ṛgveda* it was stated that the large bird *Suparṇa* that remained idle in the heaven for a long period, suddenly shrieked, ran and flew away and came down to the earth endlessly sprinkling objects to become this very large universe. And as stated, there were some more theories on the subject. Whatever these were, it was imperative that these did not contradict or compete with each other.[5]

RV10.149.04 गाव इव ग्रामं यूयुधिरिवाश्वान्वाश्रेव वत्सं सुमना दुहाना। पतिरिव जायामभि नो न्येतु धर्ता दिवः सविता विश्ववारः॥

[ग - moved ◇ अव - downward ◇ इव - as if ◇ ग्रामं - a village ◇ यूयुधिः - setting aide; expanded ◇ इव - as if ◇ अश् - spread ◇ वान् - and moved ◇ वाश्र - lowing; roaring ◇ इव - like that ◇ वत्सं - beloved offspring ◇ सुमना - willingly coming ◇ दुहाना - as milked ◇ पतिः - a husband ◇ इव - like that ◇ जायामभि - born, moved, advanced ◇ नो - as ◇ न्ये - fell into ◇ तु - mightily ◇ धर्ता - came supported by ◇ दिवः - the heaven ◇ सविता - came spread ◇ विश्ववारः - bestowing all treasures]

There were other theories as well. The universe came moving down from the heaven, as a village expanding, distributing everything and in such fashions. The universe came flowing down as the milk willingly extracted from a cow which stood in the heaven, lowing and longing to feed its beloved children. The universe came with those things born and advanced as if from a husband and wife. Then there was this theory that everything simply came supported by the heaven, greatly descending from it and bestowing all the treasures.

No single theory of how the universe manifested was considered supreme and paramount. There were many theories, some biological, some logical and some simply as a series of eventualities. None were set aside as unimportant. Thus the expanding village, the longing motherhood and the divine parentage were subjects much discussed.

RV10.149.05 हिरण्यस्तूपः सवितर्यथा त्वाऽऽङ्गिरसो जुह्वे वाजे अस्मिन्। एवा त्वार्चन्नवसे वन्दमानः सोमस्येवांशुं प्रति जागराहम्॥

[हिरण्यस्तूपः - the golden heap; tuft ◇ सवितः - spread ◇ यथा - appropriately ◇ त्वा - thyself ◇ आङ्गिरसो - as a swirling juice ◇

[5]Till now, we did not notice any 'argument' mounted in any of the accounts that came as part of the *Ṛgveda*.

जुह्वे - tongues of flame ◇ वाजे - energetically ◇ अस्मिन् - as own self ◇ एव - only ◇ आ - manifesting ◇ त्व - thy ◇ अर्चन् - oblations ◇ अवसे - those moved ◇ वन्दमान: - extolled as; respectable ◇ सोमस्य - from the *Soma* ◇ इव - like that ◇ अंशु - a thread ◇ प्रति - into all directions ◇ जागर - wakeful ◇ अहम् - self]

It was said that golden tufts and tongues of flame came from thyself, spreading, holding and swirling juice. It was said that only the very self energetically manifested by thy own oblations and were obtained as whatever that came moving. It was said that the respectable *Soma* became wakeful and came into all directions in thread like manifestations; all of these said as to how the universe manifested.

There were still more theories as to how the universe came into existence. It was said by some that a divinity stood above with his golden hair locks aflame and swirling from his head came the paths of creation. It was said that by the willing oblation of the self only the universe got its contents. Then there was that theory in which everything originated from *Soma* that remained in the heaven and which later flowed down in different paths. From the heaven, that golden embryo and golden heap, shining and energetic hands as the paths of creation got extended to all sides and in three dimensions. The learned extolled that this was *Soma* itself that so came down which bestowed and moved the energetic entities around. The atmosphere that extended from the heaven till the far end of the universe appeared to be an ocean that suddenly had sprung out. In this ocean objects floated and were carried by the waves as urged to move towards the larger earths. The dust like entities got segregated density wise and then regrouped. While these being the phenomena that might have really occurred, there were these other theories on how the universe came into existence.

The remarkable equation of creation and existence that was presented by the *gāyatrīmantra* (RV3.62.10) was a candid and self sufficient statement. It was in recognition of its unique relevance that the *gāyatri* was closely held to chest by the people of India for thousands of years. The closest resemblance to that shining intellect could be claimed by the concept of the *Soma*, which could bring forth the objects and energies. It is not an equivalence but only an observed similarity. This shining and golden transparency, carried the semen virile just as the divine *Savita* inspired all, as an intellect that spread and pervaded everywhere. It was that dalliance and intellect that not only covered the shining paths of creation but extended and spread itself through all the surrounding darkness as well, while the *Soma* remained restricted to the paths of creation. In a way it could be said that all the divinities of *saguṇa* nature prevailed under the divine supremacy of *Savita*, that shining intellect and universal consciousness. ⋆⋆⋆

6

Asyavāmīya Sūkta-The Complex Universe

The complexity of the universe was well brought out by the sage *Dīrghatamas* with this hymn RV1.164 which became famous as the *asyavāmīyasūkataṃ.* While it looked at the creation of the universe from different angles, it also insisted that the universe came only as an agglomerated mix of objects, qualities and spacial composition.

[(52) द्विपञ्चाशदृचस्यास्य सूक्तस्यौचथ्यो दीर्घतमा ऋषिः।
(1-41) प्रथमदोकचत्वारिंशदृचां विश्वे देवाः (42) द्विचत्वारिंश्याः पूर्वार्धस्य वाक् उत्तारार्धस्य चापः (43) त्रिचत्वारिंश्याः पूर्वार्धस्य शकधूमः उत्तरार्धस्य च सोमः (44) चतुश्चत्वारिंश्याः केशिनः (अग्निः सूर्यो वायुश्च) (45) पञ्चचत्वारिंश्याः वाक् (46-47) षड्चत्वारिंशीसप्तचत्वारिंश्योः सूर्यः (48) अष्टचत्वारिंश्याः संवत्सरकालचक्रम् (49) एकोनपञ्चाश्याः
सरस्वती (50) पञ्चाश्याः साध्याः (51) एकपञ्चाश्याः सूर्यः पर्जन्याग्नी वा (52) द्विपञ्चाश्याश्च सरस्वान् सूर्यो वा देवताः। (1-11, 13-14, 16-22, 24-28, 30-35, 37-40, 43-50, 52) त्रिष्टुप् (12, 15, 23, 29, 36, 41) जगति (42) प्रस्तारपङ्क्तिः (51) छन्दांसि]

RV1.164.01 अस्य वामस्य पलितस्य होतुस्तस्य भ्राता मध्यमो अस्त्यश्नः। तृतीयो भ्राता घृतपृष्ठो अस्यात्रापश्यं विश्पतिं सप्तपुत्रम्॥

[अस्य - thus ◇ वामस्य - as propagated ◇ पलितस्य - from a matured ◇ होतुस्तस्य - out of oblations ◇ भ्राता - those co-born ◇ मध्यमो - from the middle ◇ अस्ति - smote away ◇ अश् - spread ◇ न - as ◇ तृतीयो - 3 more ◇ भ्राता - co-born ◇ घृत - sprinkled ◇ पृष्ठो - from a base ◇ अस्य - thus ◇ अत्र - coming till ◇ अपश्यं - nothing visible ◇ विश् - re-entered; entered ◇ पतिं - descended ◇ सप्तपुत्रम् - 7 children]

Thus as propagated from that which got matured, out of oblations and from its middle smote away and spread those co-born, again 3 more as co-born, descending, re-entering as those 7 children that came from firm bases, all the while sprinkling, till nothing was further visible.

The 7 *vyāhṛtis* came from the epicentre of the universe moving outwards and downwards till the very end where nothing further was visible. These 7 *vyāhṛtis* each in turn got divided into 3 parallel circularity's to both sides such that one set moved forward and the other set rebounded backward. This made the universe into 21 distinct regimes. It was within these well established firm bases that matter and energy got sprinkled and remained; under the sovereignty of the ones above. The universe pictured here had a geometry corresponding to one of a sphere which got visualised here as a set of parallel circles which stood at whatever distance. This of course have to be appropriately imagined to be 3-dimensional. It was emphasized here that the description was in the regime level of the shining objects and obviously the others were allotted vassal status. It was not absolutely clear whether the term "*bhrātā*" meant as brothers or multiplets, from this description alone. A meaning that all the 7 *vyāhṛtis* were born simultaneously could be derived in the later case.

RV1.164.02 सप्त युञ्जन्ति रथमेकचक्रमेको अश्वो वहति सप्तनामा।
त्रिनाभि चक्रमजरमनर्वं यत्रेमा विश्वा भुवनाधि तस्थुः॥

[सप्त - as the 7 ◇ युञ्जन्ति - joined to the proximity ◇ रथम् - chariot ◇ एक - one ◇ चक्रम् - wheel ◇ एको - from one ◇ अश्वो

- spread and ◇ वहति - as those carried ◇ सप्त - as 7 ◇ नाम - firmed up ◇ त्रि - 3 as ◇ नाभि - the hub ◇ चक्रम् - a wheel ◇ अजरम् - non-decaying ◇ अनर्वं - unlimited; not obstructed ◇ यत्र - ever so much ◇ इमा - like that manifested ◇ विश्वा - reaching everywhere ◇ भुवन - as the universe ◇ अधि - from above ◇ तस्थुः - that stood still]

A wheel of a chariot, spread from one, with the 7 details to the proximity, firmed up from the hub which stood as three; a wheel which did not decay and which carried away those many that did not get obstructed, let be constructed in such a way as would represent the universe that manifested from above and reached everywhere.

As those 7 that got swung to the proximity, a wheel of 7 separate circularity's, as the wheel of a chariot, with 3 points becoming the hub,[1] would be made to represent that which stood without decay, as an inexplicable arrangement, that started off from the apex above, which apex always remained still. The *Viśvacakṣus* as the epicentre of the universe stood still above, and below to it and around it, the universe appeared to stand as a chariot wheel. 7 circular entities stood as the *vyāhṛtis* and as an arrangement that manifested getting distributed from the centre. As these came for ever and without decay, let an altar be made strong to represent this configuration of the universe. Though these were visualised with such geometric specificity, those could only be taken as of unlimited spacing and size as a composition of the universe. Needless to say that these were spherical, in spite of the description of circles. Whatever might be the distances between these, the configuration of the 7 parallel *vyāhṛtis* and their sub-divisions into 21 remained valid.

RV1.164.03 इमं रथमधि ये सप्त तस्थुः सप्तचक्रं सप्त वहन्त्यश्वाः। सप्त स्वसारो अभि सं नवन्ते यत्र गवां निहिता सप्त नाम॥

[इमं - thus ◇ रथम् - a chariot ◇ अधि - from above ◇ ये - as those ◇ सप्त - 7 ◇ तस्थुः - got positioned ◇ सप्त - 7 ◇ चक्रं - wheels ◇ सप्त

[1]as we would learn later in chapter-9

- 7 ◇ वहन्ति - carrying to the proximity ◇ अश्वा - moved and spread ◇ सप्त - 7 ◇ स्वसारो - specific contents ◇ अभि - advanced ◇ नव - new ◇ अन्ते - till the ends ◇ यत्र - whatever ◇ ग - progressed ◇ वां - propagated ◇ निहिता - coming established ◇ सप्त - as 7 ◇ नाम - specific entities]

Thus a chariot wheel, set out from above, would be positioned with 7 circularity's that would come to the proximity to represent the 7 spreading movements, to represent the 7 distinct contents that these carried, advancing as the new ones that came till the end, to represent whatever got propagated, progressed and got established as these 7 specific sets of entities.

From that extraordinary altitude and from that centre that stood still, the 7 *vyāhṛtis* got formed and existed with one and the same centre, as the 7 distinct circular shapes. These were individualistic (if not independent) elements of the atmosphere which contained 7 different sets of objects and systems of energy that moved and got distributed. Though it could be imagined that these objects got interspersed from one *vyāhṛti* to the next and thereby developed new relations, these *vyāhṛtis* were almost always counted as separate entities.

The Veda often stated the existence of these 7 *vyāhṛtis*, but a specific theory should have emerged as how these came into existence. Did it grow from one smaller one to issue out as another larger one and so on? Or did these come as 7 independent events all commencing from the epicentre, though instantaneously? These questions were answered here. It confirmed that these 7 *vyāhṛtis* came about, all independently and from the same epicentre. It was thus that the objects of one had to mix with the objects of the next, while these crossed the immense spherical spaces. It was thus that new relations were found to develop among these in spite of the imagined individual existence. Thus it was a brief account of all the complex nature of the composition of the atmosphere and the distribution of the regimes thereof.

RV1.164.04 को ददर्श प्रथमं जायमानमस्थन्वन्तं यदनस्था बिभर्ति।
भूम्या असुरसृगात्मा क्व स्वित् को विद्वांसमुप गात्प्रष्टुमेतत्॥

[को - which ◇ ददर्श - issued out as visibilities ◇ प्रथमं - first ◇ जायमान - generated ◇ म - as self ◇ स्थ - remained ◇ अन्वन्तं -followed till the end ◇ यद् - which ◇ अनस्था - came without remaining ◇ बिभर्ति - carrying the desired ◇ भूम्या - came as volumes, earths ◇ असुर - divine ◇ सृगात्मा - arrangement of arrows ◇ क्व - which ◇ स्वित् - oozed out ◇ कोविद् - skilfully ◇ वां - propagated ◇ सम् - got assembled ◇ उप - to below ◇ गात् - progressed ◇ प्रष्टुम् - side by side ◇ एतत् - so advanced]

Which issued out as the first visible, as generated from the self, remained as such, which followed till the end, which progressed without remaining, carried on with increasing volumes, which moved as if a divine set of arrows, which oozed out and skilfully propagated and got assembled to below and did they progress by advancing side by side and shoulder to shoulder?

Which one of these was seen as the first one came, and then as the others, continuously created with whatever measures and distances? Which one of these instantly came carrying all those as desired and shot off as a set of arrows and with what specific volume, then which came along with which and were thus found to advance? What was the order in which these 7 *vyāhṛtis* came into existence. Did it come as one after the other and or as from the shoulders of the earlier one? Did the smallest one come first and then the larger ones sequentially, or was it the other way around? Which all moved by which volume so that it contained this earth in the end? What were their extent and depth? Did all of these come into existence instantly? What was the very nature of this advancement?

Since it was stated everywhere that the heaven was the seat of the seed matter for creation and that it stood adjacent to the *Viśvacakṣus*, like the hub of a wheel, and since the same heaven was the first of the *vyāhṛtis*, its very pre-eminent position and occurrence was never in doubt. The questions could therefore, arise only in the case of the other 6 *vyāhṛtis*. And what exactly was the sequence of their manifestation?

RV1.164.05 पाकः पृच्छामि मनसाविजानन्देवानामेना निहिता पदानि। वत्से बष्कयेऽधि सप्त तन्तून्वि तत्निरे कवय ओतवा उ॥

[पाकः - from the matured ◇ पृच्छामि - established mixed and classified ◇ मनसा - coming from a mind; in principle ◇ वि - divided ◇ जानन् - originated ◇ देवानाम् - as moved from the heaven ◇ एना - thus manifested ◇ निहिता - established as ◇ पदानि - the stages ◇ वत्से - beloved children ◇ बष्कये - young calves ◇ अधि - from above ◇ सप्त - as 7 ◇ तन्तून् - string like lines ◇ वि - divided ◇ तत् - from those ◇ निरे - as separated ◇ कवय - as those depreciated ◇ ओत - interwoven ◇ वा - and moved ◇ उ - indeed]

Got established as manifesting from the matured, upon getting greatly mixed and classified, manifesting as originated and divided (in principle) from a mind, manifesting as moved from the heaven, came those stages, getting established as if the young calves and beloved children of a mother and as the 7 string like lines, indeed each separated, depreciated, moved and remained interconnected to one another.

As if from a divine mind and from a pivotal point and as from the heaven and upon getting matured, the 7 *vyāhṛtis* got pushed away and the objects got mixed one into the other, and so came these distinct stages. As if the beloved children of a mother that stood above and as the 7 strings (rings) that got expanded, the *vyāhṛtis* started off, each one separated from the other, getting emaciated while distanced and all of these only remained interactive to one another. These *vyāhṛtis* came pivoted on to the *viśvacakṣus* and from the heaven. Those were the beloved children of a motherhood that stood at the heaven. Those started off separately one after the other and therefore the larger ones crossed the thresholds of the smaller. Therefore, those (or the objects thereof) got mixed up one into the other. Those were the distinct stages of the atmosphere that expanded as concentric rings. Though these came instantly, but still came only one after the other. Their distances increased while progressed and those appeared emaciated when distanced. And yet the whole of these *vyāhṛtis* stood interactive to one another and to the epicentre. Thus there were several entities in a *vyāhṛtis* that crossed into the regimes of the others. Their interactive nature became complex. The definitions of controls changed. Thus the universe came only as a mix of divided loyalties and with a complex interactive nature. And yet those were the beloved children of a motherhood that stood above. The term "matured" denoted the birth of the *vyāhṛtis*, one after the other. Thus the questions that arose earlier could be considered, fairly answered.

The words to denote the cow that anxiously waited for feeding milk to its children, the milk that was the *Soma* etc., and thus a biological parallel of creation suggested here has come as a theory proposed elsewhere as well. In one such instance, a beautiful and clever picture was presented by way of a calf that knelt down and kneaded her mother for milk, then ran away in circles, came again and drank more milk and circled by a larger distance etc., just to represent not only the larger sizes of the *vyāhṛtis*, but to specify the way the *vyāhṛtis* took off from the centre, each time getting replenished with more vigour. And that was the very subject discussed here.

RV1.164.06 अचिकित्वाञ्चिकितुषश्चिदत्र कवीन्पृच्छामि विद्मने न विद्वान्। वि यस्तस्तम्भ षळिमा रजांस्यजस्य रूपे किमपि स्विदेकम्॥

[अचिकित् - from an unknown ◇ वाञ्चिकित् - came and spread as many known ◇ उष: - dawned ◇ चिद् - from an intellect; a pile ◇ अत्र - only as ◇ कवीन् - from knowledge moved ◇ पृच्छामि - got mixed, classified and established ◇ विद्मने - from intelligence and knowledge ◇ न - as ◇ विद्वान् - moved as the knowledge ◇ वि - divided ◇ यस्त - based on a ◇ स्तम्भ - pillar ◇ षळिमा - as an arrangement of 6 ◇ रजांसि - pounded to dust ◇ अजस्य - and stillborn ◇ रूपे - as the shapes ◇ किम् - many ways ◇ अपि - to the proximity ◇ स्विद् - sweat ◇ एकम् - from that one]

From an unknown came and spread the many known, getting established intelligently, getting mixed and classified by an intellect, with knowledge that moved from knowledge, as the six divided arrangements tied to a pillar, in shapes up to dust forms up to the stillborn and many ways sweat from the earlier ones, to the successive proximity. From the earlier ones smote the new ones, intelligently, till nothing was further born.

From that unknown existence in the heaven, manifested the many known things of the universe as if created with a divine knowledge and intellect. This very knowledge changed from one to other as the universe grew in size. Thus came the subsequent divided 6 *vyāhṛtis*, all as if tied to the pillar that stood at the epicentre. The objects of many forms and sizes stood in each of these *vyāhṛtis*. There were the dust forms and the stillborn, which did not give out anything further. There were those that went on getting created from the earlier ones to be the later ones. With less than a divine intellect and knowledge that correspondingly arose, this complex universe could not have come into existence.

This verse brought forth the concept of the *yūpa* and its position as followed in the *vaidikayajña*. The *yūpa* stood where the *Viśvacakṣus* was supposed to be and represented the epicentre of the universe. Just a *pada* away remained the *uttaravedi* representing the heaven, in a representative fashion, where the first ever of the *yajñas* occurred.

RV1.164.07 इह ब्रवीतु य ईमङ्ग वेदास्य वामस्य निहितं पदं वेः।
शीर्ष्णः क्षीरं दुह्रते गावो अस्य वव्रिं वसाना उदकं पदापुः॥

[इह - till here ◇ ब्रवीतु - indeed moved those circularity's ◇ य - and ◇ ईम् - now; instantly ◇ अङ्ग - as parts ◇ वेद - properties ◇ अस्य - as ◇ वामस्य - as propagated ◇ निहितं - and set up as ◇ पदं - the stages ◇ वे - interwoven ◇ शीर्ष्णः - from an apex ◇ क्षीरं - milk ◇ दुह्रते - as extracted ◇ ग - progressing ◇ अवो - to below ◇ अस्य - as ◇ वव्रिं - the hiding ◇ वस - remaining ◇ अना - faces ◇ उदकं - of water ◇ पदा - in stages ◇ पु: - cleansed]

Those circularity's indeed came till here, as parts of destined properties that got instantly propagated and got positioned and the interwoven stages moved downward, as if the milk extracted from a cow that stood above and these progressed as if the watery faces that remained invisible, which were in fact the cleansed stages of the atmosphere.

Those *vyāhṛtis* came from the heaven till this earth here, along with the objects of predestined properties all mixed up and yet classified. Those *vyāhṛtis* appeared like the invisible and well separated rings that would appear in water upon a disturbance. Those *vyāhṛtis* were extracted from the heaven, downward and at an angle, as if milking a cow. Though the formation of the *vyāhṛtis* was compared with the wave rings that would appear in water, those were 3-dimensional in nature and represented different volumes of the atmosphere. While the rings in water were visible, the stages in the atmosphere were invisible.

In these descriptions and as the contents of most of the verses, statements would be seen incorporated, symptomatic of a description of the 3-dimensionality. In this verse, more clarity was brought about by the description of milking at an angle. How else the 3-dimensionality could be presented by *śabda* and text?

RV1.164.08 माता पितरमृत आ बभाज धीत्यग्रे मनसा सं हि जग्मे। सा बीभत्सुर्गर्भरसा निविद्धा नमस्वन्त इदुपवाकमीयु:॥

[मा - as an arrangement ◇ ता - of those that came ◇ पि - moving ◇ तंरम् - and fording ◇ ऋत - as per rules ◇ आ - manifesting as ◇ बभाज - carefully and repeatedly divided ◇ धि - intelligently ◇ इति - in such manners ◇ अग्रे - till the ends ◇ मनसा - and coming from a mind ◇ सं - assembled ◇ हि - only ◇ जग्मे - constantly moved ◇ सा - coming along with ◇ बीभत्सु - protected and coy ◇ गर्भरसा - pregnant juice ◇ निविद्धा - getting perforated ◇ नम - bowing down with reverence ◇ स्व - self ◇ अन्त - till the end

◇ इद् - only ◇ उप - to below ◇ वाकमीयु - tied to the separate words]

An arrangement of those came moving and fording as per rules, manifesting carefully, repeatedly and intelligently getting divided, manifesting only coming till the ends, as manifested out of a divine mind, constantly progressing and coming from a coy, protected and pregnant juice, which got divided, got perforated and came down till the end bowing down in reverence. All came tied down to the divine words that manifested separately and individually.

The universe came swept around an epicentre and as a result of the confluence of *Agni* and knowledge. An arrangement got swept around a divine mind and it swelled as an immortality and remained vibrant and restless. These came from a pregnant juice which initially remained shy with desires. The paths of creation penetrated and moved till the end as if bent down in reverence and murmuring prayers which all emaciated while progressed and the universe stood pulsating for ever. Thus came the *vyāhṛtis* that were circular, distancing, moving downwards and pulsating. Whatever remained potently at the heaven as a pregnant juice with desire and shyness, later penetrated its envelope and extruded away and downward along with the creations. It provided the immortality to all that were created, though had the same gradually emaciating nature while it progressed to the ends. The sound and vibrations accompanied the process and all happened when a divine knowledge joined hands with *Agni*. The universe appeared as if given birth by a divine mother, a divine father, created out of their mind and intellect and as the immortality that flowed down.

RV1.164.09 युक्ता मातासीद्धुरि दक्षिणाया अतिष्ठद्गर्भो वृजनीष्वन्तः।
अमीमेद्वत्सो अनु गामपश्यद्विश्वरूप्यं त्रिषु योजनेषु॥

[युक्ता - suitably ◇ मा - as an arrangement ◇ त - that ◇ आसीद् - having manifested ◇ धुरि - from an apex ◇ दक्षिणाय - cleverly; efficiently ◇ अतिष्ठद् - pulsating ◇ गर्भो - the wombs ◇ वृजनि -

having separately ◇ इष्वन्तः - as arrows shot out ◇ अमी - not moving ◇ मेद् - fat ◇ वत्सो - beloved offspring ◇ अनु - along with ◇ गाम् - progressed ◇ अपश्यद् - till nothing visible ◇ विश्वरूपि - as a shape that reached everywhere ◇ अं - moved ◇ त्रिषु - as from three ◇ योजनेषु - setting forth ; joined]

As arrangements that suitably manifested and moved cleverly from an apex, as arrows that were shot out from the pulsating wombs, as the offspring that moved till the end where nothing was further visible, as the self (the motherhood) that remained stationary, as those that moved and reached everywhere, came the universe, in principle from those three that stood together.

A principle of wombs and motherhood prevailed from the beginning of creation till the very end, the end where nothing was born and nothing was visible. Every aspect of growth had the appearance of a mountain with its apex as the starting point of creation. Within this stood the beloved children that were born. Simultaneously, the atmosphere came into existence which remained as circularity's extended till the very end, as the 7 stages and each stage getting divided into three. The objects and this atmosphere, indeed came with an inherent 3 dimensionality from the very beginning. The universe appeared to have come from the womb of an appropriate mother and as a clever manifestation that came swiftly from an apex downward and to the surroundings. It manifested from the 3 points on the hub, which acted as the base for the expansion. At the top apex of the mountain like formation of all that were created stood those starting points of creation. At the apex stood a motherhood anxious for her beloved children.

RV1.164.10 तिस्रो मातॄस्त्रीन्पितॄन्बिभ्रदेक ऊर्ध्वस्तस्थौ नेमव ग्लापयन्ति। मन्त्रयन्ते दिवो अमुष्य पृष्ठे विश्वविदं वाचमविश्वमिन्वाम्॥

[तिस्रो - as 3 ◇ मा - an arrangement ◇ तृ - sailed across ◇ त्रीन् - as 3 ◇ पि - moving ◇ तॄन् - again sailing further ◇ बिभ्रद् -

carrying ◇ एक - from one ◇ ऊर्ध्व - at a height ◇ अस्तस्थौ - as smote and taken position ◇ नेम - as several ◇ व - and ◇ ग्लापयन्ति - emaciated to the proximity ◇ मन्त्र - divine uttering ◇ यन्ते - connected to ◇ दिवो - from heaven ◇ अमुष्य - rare and specific ◇ पृष्ठे - bases ◇ विश्वविदं - as the knowledge that reached everywhere ◇ वाचम् - as words ◇ अविश्व - till the end of the universe ◇ मिन्वाम् - moving and pervading]

An arrangement of 3 sailed along, the 3-dimensionality moved along and in principle came moving from those 3 points of origin. What all manifested from the one that stood above got carried along further, smote down and took position, manifested along with the divine uttering which emaciated to the proximity. From the heaven and specific bases, along with knowledge that reached everywhere and the words that moved and pervaded all over, came all till the very ends of the universe.

The universe came as an arrangement of 3-dimensionality and as set-off from the 3, moving and sailing across, out of the divine words uttered connected to the heaven, and progressing from their rare and specific bases so as to reach everywhere. Knowledge and great words came moving from the self and pervaded everywhere. The process of creation all along appeared to have 3 mothers and 3 fathers. For everything from heaven moved from the three and with 3-dimensionality. The objects were 3-dimensional and the space that came along was 3-dimensional. As if fallen away from an apex and as if led by the sounds and vibrations that divided and reached everywhere, the universe swelled and got emaciated when progressing outward. One transformed into another and the contents of the *vyāhṛtis* got interlaced with one another. From one level and place of reference it came to others continuously. Due to the mixing that occurred, objects got interspersed, got agglomerated and new regimes were born. It was the divine sounds and the vibrations which emanated from place to place that brought about the universe as one that occurred instantly. Thus this verse could be interpreted as the 3 dimensionality that first got instituted, as the 3 divisions of the *vyāhṛtis* that got formed from their well established base circularity's and as the 3 points of origin that would get constantly referred to.[2]

RV1.164.11 द्वादशारं नहि तज्जराय वर्वर्ति चक्रं परि द्यामृतस्य।
आ पुत्रा अग्ने मिथुनासो अत्र सप्त शतानि विंशतिश्च तस्थुः॥

[द्वादश - 12 ◇ आरं - spokes ◇ नहि - with nothing ◇ तद् - from that ◇ जराय - emaciated; narrowed down ◇ वर्वर्ति - alternated ◇ चक्रं - a wheel ◇ परि - to the surroundings ◇ द्याम् - moved from heaven ◇ ऋतस्य - as per rules ◇ आ - manifesting as ◇ पुत्रा - the sons that came ◇ अग्ने - from the *Agni* ◇ मिथुनासो - coupled with that ◇ अत्र - then as ◇ सप्त - 7 ◇ शतानि - 100 ◇ विंशति - 20 ◇ च - and ◇ तस्थु - firmed up]

With 12 narrowing spokes and then with gaps (with nothing) as those that came, alternatively as the children of the *Agni* that moved from the heaven according to the rules, all well joined, having firmed up with 720, an immortal wheel thus took shape from the heaven to the surroundings. They came out of divine copulation.

Generally, the geometry of this commentary more or less derived substance from the *śulbasūtras*, that came much later. But the configuration that was narrated here differed with those shapes that came from the *śulbasūtras*. The *rathacakraciti* of *Baudhāyana śulbasūtram* had 32 spokes and a single circular rim and a circular hub. Here the spokes were 12, narrowing to the ends and there were 7 annular segments, that represented the 7 *vyāhṛtis*. It was stated that the spokes cutting through should be inconspicuously merged with the internal annular formations. But there were points common with the *śulbasūtras*. The *puruṣaṃ* measure was stated as 120 for one, and the others are yet to follow. Thus the sizing of the rings progressed in increments of the *puruṣaṃ* measure to represent the 7 *vyāhṛtis*. The width of the annular rings were actually not mentioned but could be assumed as

[2]see chapter-9 on geometry for details.

20, as the narration split the size of 120 into 100 and 20. There were other aspects that differed with the *śulbasūtra*, as well. Here the concept was centred on linear measurements and the circular enlargements were so effected. In the *śulbasūtra* the whole concept of size was centred on areas and thus the *puruṣaṃ* measures were reconfigured 7 times, for enlarging of the sizes. By the time of the *śulbasūtrā*, other magnificent styles of geometrical operations came into existence, so also the considerations of costs and perhaps different purposes. But here the size of the radius of the outer circle might amount to 720 (say, *aṅgulaṃs*), reading the text, which required a large space. The assumption of the measure of *aṅgulaṃs* and the fact that later or at the very Vedic time, the concept of the *puruṣaṃ* measure that was used here, though could not be well confirmed right away, its prevalence is very evident.

From the heaven as if the children born of the *Agni*, the 7 *vyāhṛtis* came all interconnected, along with the sets of objects and energy that remained immortal for ever and let oblations be offered on this altar which represented the universe. For, here we could see the divine manifestation.

RV1.164.12 पञ्चपादं पितरं द्वादशाकृतिं दिव आहु: परे अर्धे पूरीषिणम्। अथेमे अन्य उपरे विचक्षणं सप्तचक्रे षळर आहुरर्पितम्॥

[पञ्च - 5 ◇ पादं - stages ◇ पित् - swelled out ◇ अरं - with spokes ◇ द्वादशा - 12 ◇ कृतिं - created ◇ दिव - from the heaven ◇ आहु: - for oblations ◇ परे - to outward ◇ अर्धे - the middle ◇ पूरीषिणम् - those as filled and set off ◇ अथ - such that ◇ इमे - here thus ◇ अन्य - another ◇ उपरे - below ◇ वि - divided ◇ चक्षणं - from the eye ◇ सप्त - 7 ◇ चक्रे - circularity's ◇ षळर - divine ◇ आहु - oblations ◇ अर्पितम् - be offered]

Executed with 5 steps (stages) and 12 spokes, as one that moved and swelled outward properly filled, the middle clearly set off as separated and maintained with another one coming below be made to commemorate the divine oblations that started from heaven and let the 7 wheels be so conceived that on this stage the oblations could be offered.

The concept of the *uttaravedi* that would be constructed in 5 layers one over the other as followed in the *vaidikayajñas* was confirmed as prevalent in the vedic times. The brick laying specification that the interstices should not fall one over the other was found stipulated. Thus this *citi* will have 12 spokes and 7 annular rings as described earlier, executed in 5 layers and let the offerings be made here remembering the formation of the 7 *vyāhṛtis* that came into existence in the first of creations that ever took place and as the outward expansions from the heaven that occurred. For, here we could see the divine manifestation.

RV1.164.13 पञ्चारे चक्रे परिवर्तमाने तस्मिन्ना तस्थुर्भुवनानि विश्वा।
तस्य नाक्षस्तप्यते भूरिभारः सनादेव न शीर्यते सनाभिः॥

[पञ्च - 5 ◇ आरे - spokes ◇ चक्रे - as circles ◇ परिवर्तमाने - an arrangement swung around ◇ तस्मिन्ना - from that came ◇ तस्थु - and positioned ◇ भुवनानि - the universe ◇ विश्वा - that reached everywhere ◇ तस्य - its ◇ न - as ◇ अक्षः - the epicentre ◇ तप्यते - ablaze with oblations ◇ भूरि - abundantly ◇ भारः - loaded ◇ सनाद् - for ever ◇ एव - only ◇ न - as ◇ शीर्यते - as arteries ◇ स - from ◇ नाभिः - the hub]

Let an arrangement be derived by swinging around as a circle from an epicentre, with 5 segments of the spokes, that took off from the hub, as if the arteries, getting executed to represent the universe that reached everywhere and which stood for ever. Let this be suitable to carry enough weights for offering the oblations in commemoration. Since the precincts of that epicentre was ablaze with the oblations that once occurred, let oblations be offered now in the very centre and the hub.

Matters were clarified but also got complicated. If the annular rings progressed in measures of 120 and 7 times, the largest radius would become 840 and there would have been 6 segments between the rings. But clearly 5 segments were only stipulated and the text appeared to state that the size of the outer ring was 720. These statements would be found correct if the construction possibilities were taken into account. For the 12 spokes with a good size and proportion could not take off from a small hub and should therefore avoid one inner ring. Therefore the spokes would take off from the second annular ring only and would amount to 5 in numbers placed radially outward. The first and second rings would be merged in such a way that there would be no gap between these. This would provide a larger space for the oblations and the outer size of the second ring would be 120 (all as radius). This would become more clear by the 48th verse, by the definitions of the peg points described there and the figure of the *citi* attached there. Altogether, from these explanations, a proposal also arose that this altar would be constructed as a heap tapering up from a broad base in stages defined by the 120 as spacing. It was advised that let the construction be strong and durable, possibly for prolonged oblations and long discussions. It is significant that the *śulbasūtra* specified the total height of the 5 layers as one *jānu* (height up to the knee), for if we construct the *citi* specified here, that height would become the critical upper limit for easy climbing the 5 stages.

As representing the 7 *vyāhṛtis* that formed commencing from the heaven, that which emaciated while progressed outward and which became strongly guarded and protected as a fort and since the universe being conceived as a *rathacakra*, let the offerings be made on this *uttaravedi*. .

RV1.164.14 सनेमि चक्रमजरं वि वावृत उत्तानायां दश युक्ता वहन्ति। सूर्यस्य चक्षु रजसैत्यावृतं तस्मिन्नार्पिता भुवनानि विश्वा॥

[सनेमि - with a rim ◇ चक्रम् - a circle ◇ अजरं - not perishable ◇ वि - divided ◇ वावृत - selectively circumscribed ◇ उद् - raised ◇ ता - coming from those ◇ नयां - lead ◇ दश - stages ◇ युक्ता - suitably configured ◇ वहन्ति - carrying to the proximity ◇ सूर्यस्य - the Sun-like ◇ चक्षु - eye ◇ रजस - with dust ◇ इति - and in such ways ◇ आवृतं - covered ◇ तस्मिन्न - as upon that

◇ अर्पिता - be offered ◇ भुवनानि - as the universe ◇ विश्वा - that reached everywhere]

With a strong and circular rim, from a raised central stage, moving, carrying and led as stages suitably selected and configured, as a wheel that came from that Sun-like eye would be carried on to the successive proximity, keeping in mind that from there came the universe, with dust like objects in many ways scattered and as everywhere and let the oblations be appropriately offered on this stage.

With strong and imperishable circular rims as the ends, divided and led into stages that would be suitably configured, selectively circumscribed and carried to the successive proximity, be covered with dust and other materials, upon which the oblations could be offered. It was from that Sun-like eye and a divine entity that the universe came reaching everywhere. From that eye that shone like a Sun, the universe expanded and got emaciated to the ends, much divided, moved in defined stages and bringing forth the dust forms that reached everywhere. Similarly, let this altar be constructed from a central point with a hub and annular rings of well defined proportions, with clay and small pebble used in the construction for obtaining the rigidity and conformity of shape. Let this altar be constructed suitable for the oblations, reminiscent of that Sun-like shining entity that stood at the centre.

One of the reason for a change in the configuration of the central zone was to facilitate these oblations by providing enough operating room. With the words "*daśa yuktā vahanti*", it could be taken that when the *yajña* would be conducted, a clear concept of which stage (out of the 7) of the growth of the universe was to be represented should be borne in mind. There was a similar statement in the *Baudhāyana śulbasūtram* as well. However, as times passed by, the *uttar-avedis* were configured separately to represent the stages of the enlargements, that too in great detail and with a total number of 21 sizes in a rising order. Moreover, there was an apparent proposal here that this *uttaravedi* be constructed as a heap of 5 layers tapering to the top, in order to resemble the expansion more realistically.

RV1.164.15 साकंजानां सप्तथमाहुरेकजं षळिद्यमा ऋषयो देवजा इति। तेषामिष्टानि विहितानि धामशः स्थात्रे रेजन्ते विकृतानि रूपशः॥

[साकं - simultaneously ◇ जानां - born and moved ◇ सप्तथम् - as 7 that got stationed ◇ आहु - as oblations ◇ एकजं - from a single place ◇ षळिद् - with magnificent ◇ यमा - rules ◇ ऋषयो - as those flowed ◇ देव - from the heaven ◇ जा - generated ◇ इति - in such manners ◇ तेषाम् - from these ◇ इष्टानि - as desired ◇ विहितानि - proportionately ◇ धामशः - in deserving places ◇ स्थ - positioned ◇ अत्रे - from there ◇ रेजन्ते - with trembling ends ◇ वि - divided ◇ कृतानि - as those that created ◇ रूपशः - segregated according to contents]

Those that were simultaneously born and moved, the 7 that got stationed moving from a single source, those that came from the oblations with a set of magnificent rules, those that flowed, those that got generated from the many heavens and from there came as whatever manifested and proportionately stood in their deserving places, and from there came as those that came divided and stood with trembling ends, was the way the universe was created and got segregated according to their contents.

While it came as the 7 circularity's that moved simultaneously from a single source, many objects got stationed, as born out of the oblations that occurred at each place and the oblation were conducted as per the magnificent and divine rules. As the paths of creation that flowed from the heaven and as those that got generated from these paths as desired, came those that got positioned proportionately in deserving places. The *vyāhṛtis* stood as if trembling and resonating. The oblations that occurred were defined by the gods and got commemorated by the sages as they divined it later and to their liking, with due consideration of the stages that were involved. From that singular place called the heaven and the *hiraṇyagarbha* and from that single One that existed, along with the oblations and *yajñas*, the 7 *vyāhṛtis* came into existence. And these contained the objects and the energy of the universe as derived out of the flows that commenced from the heaven. The objects were formed and got much divided, shattered, deformed and transformed as it came about till the very end of the universe. In this process these got segregated within the regimes of the *vyāhṛtis*. Thus there indeed was a series of changes from what first got instantly manifested.

RV1.164.16 स्त्रियः सतीस्ताँ उ मे पुंस आहुः पश्यदक्षण्वान्न वि चेतदन्धः। कविर्यः पुत्रः स ईमा चिकेत यस्ता विजानात्स पितुष्पितासत्॥

[स्त्रियः - from a star like bright spot ◇ सतीस्ताँ - manifested into the *Sat* ◇ उ - only ◇ मे - the self ◇ पुंस - crushed ◇ आहुः - oblated ◇ पश्यद् - as the visibilities; seen ◇ अक्षण् - from the eye ◇ वान् - moved ◇ न - as ◇ वि - divided ◇ चेतद् - intelligently ◇ अन्धः - as darkness ◇ कविर्यः - knowledgeably, energetically ◇ पुत्रः - as sons ◇ स - with ◇ ईम् - then ◇ आ - came ◇ चिकेत - systematically and as desired ◇ यस्ता - came deposited ◇ विजान - shrewdly ◇ अत् - progressing ◇ स - with ◇ पितुष् - moving satisfactorily ◇ पिता - coming swelling ◇ सत् - from *Sat*]

A shining star like spot, manifested into the *Sat* and the self got crushed, oblated and made to move away. All were intelligently divided and moved as the visibilities that came from that eye and as the darkness that stood by the side. Those sons that came from knowledge and then got shrewdly deposited, moved and progressed satisfactorily and had come as swelled to be the universe that manifested from the *Sat*.

The use of the term "*striya: satīstā̃*" could become a serious consideration for the students of history. The process that was described, the words used, indeed resembled a scenario sketched as a woman jumping into the fire. For that which existed as a shining particle, upon its own volition got oblated to manifest as the many different objects of the universe. These children of the *yajña* came into existence upon carefully filtered as the many visibilities that stood around. The universe was divided into the bright paths of creation and the darkness that stood around. The bright objects had multiplied, getting repeatedly born as the sons and grandsons. Those came into existence out of an all pervading knowledge that moved along with the very enlargement of the universe. Somehow the scenario painted was an assembly of sons and grandsons around that fire and oblation.

The darkness described here was perhaps different and more than the darkness that once existed. It was declared at several segments that along with the flow of the paths of creation, along the objects and systems of energy that came till the very end of the universe, a darkness and *vṛtrata* accompanied this growth, both outside and possibly inside the paths of creation. It was stated that this *vṛtrata* outside the paths was resisted and kept at abeyance by the *Soma*. The description here appeared to bring forth the idea that this *vṛtrata* existed both within and outside the shining paths of creation. But still, were these simply dark objects or were these the darkness that surrounded the bright objects? Or were these dark, ominous and invisible?

RV1.164.17 अवः परेण पर एनावरेण पदा वत्सं बिभ्रती गौरुदस्थात्।
सा कद्रीची कं स्विदर्धं परागात् क्व स्वित्सूते नहि यूथे अन्तः॥

[अवः - downwards ◇ परेण - distanced and ◇ पर - distanced ◇ एना - in the manner of ◇ वरेण - enclosures of confirmed ◇ पदा - stages ◇ वत्सं - beloved children ◇ बिभ्रती - carried ◇ ग - quickly moved ◇ उरुदस्थ - in broad paths positioned ◇ अत् - moved ◇ सा - bestowing ◇ कद् - as those things ◇ रीची - set off and piled up ◇ कं - somehow ◇ स्विद् - possibly ◇ अर्धं - halved ◇ परा - further distanced ◇ गात् - and progressed ◇ क्व - to wherever ◇ स्वित् - as secreted ◇ सूते - as those impelled ◇ नहि - or became nothing ◇ यूथे - or a congregation ◇ अन्तः - till the end]

Moving downwards and to distances after distances in the

manner of confirmed stages and enclosures, as the beloved children that got carried away, everything got bestowed and moved from the broad paths that got positioned. Those things stood separated or somehow got piled up, possibly got halved, further distanced and progressed as whatever secreted or as whatever got impelled, became nothing or stood as a congregation. That way manifested the universe with many a constellation getting established till the very end.

The 7 stages of the *vyāhṛtis* that came in circular steps and moved downwards, further got divided upon getting offset to both sides as two subsidiary stages and remained containing different brightnesses and heaps of matter. These processes created different sets of objects and regimes. From these, more objects came as if halved and secreted, which moved away from their earlier positions. This process of halving and secretion somehow continued till different constellations and power centres got firmed up. What was somehow not stated would be that all of these existed, well bound to the overall interactive forces with which the universe always existed. The vibrations as the shivers that divided and moved, the secretions of lesser dynamic values, the dependency chain as the children and the well maintained conditions of equilibrium etc. narrated the properties and phenomenal nature of this progress. Several equations of existence thus came into force. The description was part of the presentation of the interspersed nature of what manifested as a result and the complexities there-of.

RV1.164.18 अव परेण पितरं यो अस्यानुवेद पर एनावरेण।
कवीयमानः क इह प्र वोचद्देवं मनः कुतो अधि प्रजातम्॥

[**अव** - downward ◇ **परेण** - and to distance ◇ **पितरं** - swelled and forded ◇ **यो** - somehow ◇ **अस्य** - as ◇ **अनुवेद** - the sub-set of properties ◇ **पर** - moving away ◇ **एना** - in that manner ◇ **वरेण** - as enclosures ◇ **कवीयमानः** - with knowledge of diminishing measures ◇ **क** - what ◇ **इह** - here ◇ **प्र** - to the surrounding ◇ **वोचद्** - as words ◇ **देवं** - from the heaven; gods ◇ **मनः** - it could be imagined ◇ **कुतो** - from which that ◇ **अधि** - stood above ◇

प्र - to the surroundings ◇ जातम् - as those born]

While moving downward and to distances, swelling and fording and somehow manifesting as the many properties and their sub-sets, while moving in the manner of enclosures and as the knowledge that went on diminishing, what came here to the surroundings as the words comparable to those that came from the heavens, it should be imagined, when those were born to the surroundings from what stood above?

As to below and away to distances, the universe got swelled along with corresponding sub-sets of properties and as the arrangements that manifested to both sides with diminishing levels of knowledge. What were the words that came, from which gods that stood above and how it could be imagined to have manifested to institute those things which spread to the surroundings? What as, from whom and from which the universe manifested? What swept everything to the surroundings and to below? How the objects acquired corresponding properties and moved offset equally and intelligently to both sides? Whose words caused these creations and these arrangements? Were there different divinities that could be named for the words that manifested in different stages or did these come from the first ever source? Did these words all by itself change or did the definitions and the nature of the cosmic vibrations remain the same or did these manifest differently as per the occasions? How these matters beyond description could be explained completely? But these phenomena indeed took place as could be imagined.

RV1.164.19 ये अर्वाञ्चस्ताँ उ पराच आहुर्ये पराञ्चस्ताँ उ अर्वाच आहुः। इन्द्रश्च या चक्रथुः सोम तानि धुरा न युक्ता रजसो वहन्ति॥

[ये - whatever ◇ अर्व - quickly ◇ अञ्चस्ताँ - got swirled ◇ उ - certainly ◇ पराच - and distanced ◇ आहुर्ये - favorably positioned by oblations ◇ पर - later ◇ अञ्चस्ताँ - again got swirled ◇ उ - certainly ◇ अर्वाच - moved quickly ◇ आहुः - out of oblations ◇ इन्द्रश्च - from *indrata* ◇ या - moving ◇ चक्रथुः - cyclically ◇ सोम - from the *Soma* ◇ तानि - and from those ◇ धुरा - the contents and burden ◇ न - as ◇ युक्ता - appropriately ◇ रजसो - pounded to dust ◇ वहन्ति - and carried off to the proximity]

Whatever quickly got swirled and moved and got confirmed to distances and so got positioned by favourable oblations, again got swirled and moved and took confirmed positions and those came quickly moved out of oblations and from those *indratas* that repeatedly and cyclically manifested and were at the same time the contents and burden that moved from the *Soma*, reduced to appropriate dust forms and got carried away repeatedly to the proximity.

An unknown thing manifested as a shining particle of matter and energy, and became the immensely moved circularity's and cyclonic progresses that were swung around and away from such points of origins. These became arrangements that progressed at corresponding speeds. The *Soma* upon getting afflicted and moved, paths of creation and objects were issued out and moved away fróm the heaven as the burden that came down as well as the dust forms that manifested along with it. Alternately most of these appeared like dust when compared to the immense universe. At the same time the statement could also be regarding the swirling dust forms that went around in the universe. But in the end the universe appeared as a well organised wheel that took off from the epicentre and in reality from that shining particle that first manifested in the heaven. And yet this very process repeated several times.

The physical and phenomenal aspects of the creation of the universe was described by the above verses such as the formation of the *vyāhṛtis* and the swirling actions that were discernible in the formation of the universe and even in the formation of the objects. The description now turned to some of the other points of view of how the universe came about.

RV1.164.20 द्वा सुपर्णा सयुजा सखाया समानं वृक्षं परि षस्वजाते।
तयोरन्यः पिप्पलं स्वाद्वत्त्यनश्नन्नन्यो अभि चाकशीति॥

[द्वा - two ◇ सुपर्णा - good branches; birds with beautiful wings

◇ सयुजा - that stood together ◇ सखाया - as friends ◇ समानं - a symmetrical ◇ वृक्षं - tree ◇ परि - to the surroundings ◇ षस्व - by own wisdom ◇ जाते - as those born ◇ तय् - moved ◇ उ - firmed up ◇ अन्य - as others ◇ पिप्पलं - like a *Pipul* tree ◇ स्वा - through the atmosphere ◇ द्व - in two ways ◇ -त्ति - presented ◇ अनश् - for ever ◇ न - as ◇ न्यो - seated ◇ अभि - to the proximity ◇ च - as ◇ अक - afflictions ◇ शि - and happiness ◇ इति - like that]

From that extraordinary *Pipul* tree which stood with two beautiful branches that originated from the same point in friendship, from that tree that stood equitably out of the heaven, upon getting eaten and becoming nothing, in that extraordinary food principle, came the happiness and benevolence of the universe as out of afflictions that steadily progressed to the surroundings.

Two birds with beautiful wings proceeded together as friends on a *Pipul* tree that symmetrically stood to the surroundings, as those born by own wisdom, proceeding and progressing differently, sweetly and steadily consuming, apparently till disappearing, progressing to the successive proximity and bestowing happiness from a set of afflictions.

Like a *Pipul* tree that stood with two beautiful and symmetrical branches spread to the surroundings in friendship, by own wisdom born, firmed up as those and moved as the others through the atmosphere, got seated to the proximity and these could be presented in two ways, one as afflictions and the other as the happiness that manifested. The happiness (the excellence's) and the afflictions occurred (those bad elements as well) always manifested side by side. There were two streams of manifestation of the good and the bad standing side by side. Those were the products and paths of creation and the darkness that simultaneously manifested.

Thus, the very terms of this verse could be read to mean the structure of the multiple meanings of the *Ṛgveda*, which was nothing accidental, but its very nature and style. So it would manifest here in this verse, in this hymn and in many places through the *Ṛgveda*.

This *Pipul* tree stood with two branches to opposite sides coming from the same junction as if they were bosom friends. This tree stood at heaven projecting outward. This tree represented consumption by that extraordinary food principle which not only ate but created nothingness in the process, manifesting as the routes through which the universe grew with the objects that accompanied. It became the benevolences of the universe that stood happily. In fact there were many such trees pointed into different directions as this. The branches and leaves were the routes and positions through which the universe grew, the objects that were created moved and every one of these branches took off to both sides symmetrically. This symmetry would be the very subject here. This progress of the expansion of the universe was on that extra ordinary food principle which not only ate but created emptiness. This food principle was well presented in the *puruṣasūkta*.

The present hymn by its first part, narrated the manner in which the seven *vyāhṛtis* took shape and how the same got divided into three. The Veda often stated that the expansion of the universe maintained a sense of equilibrium and symmetry to both sides when it originated from the heaven and whenever the process got repeated from the many later heavens. It was this principle that was described here, getting compared to the branches that took off from the same junction and getting compared with the several sub-divisions of these branches in like manner. The term "*Suparṇa*" came considerably confusing with the bird of the same name that got described in many places and even in this very hymn. But there could not be two birds such as one sitting eating and the other without eating, in the heaven. In fact based on *Suparṇa*, the bird, that remained at the heaven and which flew down as much as to reach this earth, one important icon of the *uttaravedi* of the later times was instituted.

It was *Suparṇa* the bird, therefore, that got configured as the *uttaravedi* of 7.5 times the *puruṣaṃ* measure in area, in the *vaidikayajña*, as if equating it to the area of the heaven. Therefore, the *Suparṇa* here could not be that particular bird. In fact the next two verses retained the same meaning of the tree and branches with term *Suparṇa* used appropriately.

It will be found stated in the 46th verse that there existed more than one theory of how the universe came about and went on to mention 4 of these. One of those was an almost biological process enjoining with the presentations of the *puruṣasūkta*. Thus *asyavāmīyasūkta* as a whole presented a theory that the objects and phenomena of the universe manifested only much interspersed into several places. Likewise the description also resorted to a style of ideas enmeshed into one another. What was scrupulously avoided was contradictions at all levels.

At the same time, a set of meanings, that two friendly birds progressed along the branches of this extra ordinary *Pipul* tree in search of ripen fruits in identical fashion also came as a valid imagery of the same progress of the universe with a left right state of equilibrium. Thus "*dvā suparṇa*" could as well be two birds representing this progress. It would become valid as depicting the symmetrical manner in which the universe enlarged and progressed, whereas, as the tree it described the symmetrical fashion in which the paths of creation stood. Thus the verse almost advocated basically a biological process and the scenario made out was not different in both ways of interpretation.

RV1.164.21 यत्रा सुपर्णा अमृतस्य भागमनिमेषं विदथाभिस्वरन्ति।
इनो विश्वस्य भुवनस्य गोपाः स मा धीरः पाकमत्रा विवेश॥

[यत्रा - from wherever ◇ सुपर्णा - those beautiful branches; birds *Suparṇa* ◇ अमृतस्य - as immortal ◇ भागम् - parts ◇ अनिमेषं - vigilantly ◇ विदथाभि - knowledgeably progressed ◇ स्वर् - through the atmosphere ◇ अन्ति - to the proximity ◇ इनो - strongly ◇ विश्वस्य - reached everywhere ◇ भुवनस्य - as the universe ◇ गोपाः - coming protected ◇ स - with ◇ मा - as an arrangement of ◇ धीरः - courage; as bestowed from an intellect ◇ पाकम् - got matured ◇ अत्रा - from there ◇ विवेश - divided and entering; re-entering]

From wherever those beautiful branches took off and manifested as the immortality and as the parts that vigilantly and knowledgeably progressed through the atmosphere to the proximity and manifested as the powers that reached everywhere in the universe, from there these came again as the protected arrangements that came matured from an intellect and got several times divided and also re-entered.

This tree of beautiful branches, represented the immortality and the progress of courage and stability provided, which ultimately manifested as a protected universe. A courageous progress that did not turn back and which consisted of the shining objects that moved watchfully, reached everywhere as matured, remained strong, many times got divided and many times re-entered. The divine words of prayers, the sounds and the cosmic vibrations not only accompanied this process, but were found to manifest re-defined as divided and re-entered, just as the progress of growth that occurred.

There also existed the other strain of meanings of this bird *Suparṇa* trotting from branch to branch of the *Pipul* tree in search of ripen fruits. The concept of a movement of the bird till the very end of the tree, as an imagery of the biological growth of the universe centred on the food principle would be equally relevant, though all the terms did not contribute to this stream of description. Thus there were more that one way and different extents to which the text could be read, yet sticking to the mainstream ideas.

RV1.164.22 यस्मिन्वृक्षे मध्वदः सुपर्णा निविशन्ते सुवते चाधि विश्वे। तस्येदाहुः पिप्पलं स्वाद्वग्रे तन्नोन्नशद्यः पितरं न वेद॥

[यस्मिन् - on whichever ◇ वृक्षे - trees ◇ मध्वदः - tasting the sweetness ◇ सुपर्णा - the birds *Suparṇa* ◇ निविशन्ते - as those settled down till the ends ◇ सुवते - as beautifully; enveloped ◇

च - and ◇ अधि - from above ◇ विश्वे - reached everywhere ◇ तस्य - from that ◇ इद् - indeed ◇ आहुः - the oblations ◇ पिप्पलं - the *Pipul* tree ◇ स्वा - through the atmosphere ◇ द्व - to both ◇ अग्रे - ends ◇ तन्नो - from those ◇ नश् - as emaciated ◇ अद्यः - as ◇ पि - expanded ◇ तरं - and forded ◇ न - as ◇ वेद - the properties]

On whichever tree these birds *Suparṇa* manifested and settled down, from there and till the ends came those enveloped nature as moving from above and reaching everywhere in the universe and indeed as the oblations that progressed, just like that *Pipul* tree that stood in the atmosphere with two ends, as emaciated in properties while expanded and forded.

The universe came as if that bird *Suparṇa*, which tasting the fruits of the *Pipul* tree trotted down the branches much intoxicated. The universe came as that *Pipul* tree that came from the *Soma* and stood filled and swelled and stretching itself to the very bottom and equally to both sides from the heaven and in which process it emaciated towards the ends. The universe came as the enveloped paths of creation and the oblations that stood spread like the *Pipul* tree and which brought about the many properties as well as a principle of destruction. The verse thus had almost three streams of presentation of that single event. It was not the insufficiency of one but the necessity to look at the origin of the universe from different perspectives that was proposed. This description, therefore, brought in the suggestions of the theories that existed. In a way it declared that a single route of description of a single system of phenomena would not completely express the complex process of creation.

Both as the tree that stood at heaven with its branches pointed downwards and as the bird that tasted the sweetness of the fruits of the *Pipul* tree, the interpretations from the beginning of this set of verses were amply confirmed as relevant, by this verse. Here, the term *Suparṇa* only meant a bird of beautiful wings and not that bird which became the icon of the *uttaravedi* of the *yajña*. Moreover, here it was the very method and style of the *Ṛgveda* of depicting the 3-dimensionality as a 2-dimensional sketch. It was from that high heaven that the creations flowed to the surroundings and to below so as to reach up to the earth and naturally the tree that depicted the paths would stand inverted.

These descriptions and comparisons in terms of a biological process or contents ended here and the subject would be now presented from yet another angle of view.

RV1.164.23 यद्गायत्रे अधि गायत्रमाहितं त्रैष्टुभाद्वा त्रैष्टुभं निरतक्षत।
यद्वा जगज्जगत्याहितं पदं य इत्तद्विदुस्ते अमृतत्वमानशुः॥

[यद् - which ◇ गायत्रे - strode off as the *gāyatri* ◇ अधि - from above ◇ गायत्रम् - again as *gāyatri* ◇ आहितं - manifested as desired ◇ त्रैष्टुभाद् - as *triṣṭubh* ◇ वा - and ◇ त्रैष्टुभं - again *triṣṭubh* ◇ निरत - deeply ◇ क्षत - broken down ◇ यद् - which ◇ वा - moved away ◇ जगज्जगत् - as constellation after constellation ◇ या - that progressed ◇ हितं - as desired ◇ पदं - stages ◇ य - and ◇ इत् - indeed ◇ तद् - as that ◇ विदुस्ते - as those attended by an intellect ◇ अमृतत्वम् - an immortality ◇ आ - manifested ◇ नशु - and moved]

Which moved as the *gāyatri* that came from the *gāyatri* that manifested above, got repeatedly cut up as *triṣṭubh* after *triṣṭubh* as desired, became the constellation after constellation that progressed and became the stages that came as desired. Indeed these came from an intellect that moved along for ever and thus the universe had become immortal.

The miraculous divine sounds of prayers came from above and an arrangement progressed according to the divine wishes. The arrangements of 3-dimensionality came moved and then got divided into *triṣṭubh*, again into *triṣṭubh* and thus got placed downwards. The calamities that got many ways born moved repeatedly and got resurrected from those states, intelligently aiming at an instant immortality. Which strode off from above as the 3-dimensionality and again as the 3-dimensionality, manifesting as desired, were deeply broken down as *triṣṭubh* and again as *triṣṭubh* as desired. Constellation after constellation, and several stages manifested in this way and as desired to become an immortality that spread widely.

The narration moved to another presentation of the birth of the universe. The universe came into existence from the *gāyatri* and the sound that manifested as the primordial cosmic vibrations of appropriate value and upon acquiring the 3-dimensionality, moved along with it. It got systematically divided into 3 × 8 and then again and again to 4 × 11.[3] Much further it came the same way, much moving till the end. All came into existence as if calamities, several times repeated. All were placed many ways into many positions. The 7 *vyāhṛtis* that was found manifested, its further divisions and the objects that were cast off all over the universe, thus came into existence in the same pattern. The progress of enlargement of the universe getting so divided, intelligently proceeded to the very end with the sole aim of providing conditions of a perpetual immortality. The shining intelligence that stood above and pervaded as everywhere in the universe oversaw to the advent of the sound and the cosmic vibrations to appear wherever necessary to assist these processes. This very intellect moved along with the outward formation of the multiple *vyāhṛtis*. Thus it touched this earth and at the same time established an immortality everywhere.

RV1.164.24 गायत्रेण प्रति मिमीते अर्कमर्केण साम त्रैष्टुभेन वाकम्। वाकेन वाकं द्विपदा चतुष्पदाऽक्षरेण मिमते सप्त वाणीः॥

[गायत्रेण - as *gāyatri* ◇ प्रति - that came in all directions ◇ मिमीते - getting established from what was got established ◇ अर्कम् - as Sun-like things came ◇ अर्केण - Sun-like things ◇ साम - from an immature state, uniformly ◇ त्रैष्टुभेन - broken down in *triṣṭubh* ◇ वाकम् - as the word ◇ वाकेन वाकं - words that came after words ◇ द्विपदा - as doubled ◇ चतुष्पदा - and quadrupled ◇

[3] In chapter-9, the term "*triṣṭubh*" would be found interpreted as the fraction of 2/3 and therefore indicting yet another order of divisions.

अक्षरेण - not decayed ◇ मिमते - established with imagination ◇ सप्त - the 7 ◇ वाणी - notes of music]

The *gāyatri* that prevailed into all directions and those things that got established from those which were earlier established, the Sun-like objects that came from the Sun-like objects, uniformly broken down in *triṣṭubh*, the words and the words that came from the words, doubled and quadrupled and not decayed, thus everything was established with imagination, like the 7 notes of music. It was the repeated manifestation of sound and cosmic vibrations that brought forth the universe.

Progressing in all directions, with the 3-dimensionality that got established from the 3-dimensionality that was earlier formed, as the Sun-like entities that moved from the Sun-like entities, from an immature state getting matured and broken down in *triṣṭubh* were the ways in which the universe came. By the words and the words that came after words, as doubled and quadrupled, essentially as not decayed and destroyed, the universe got established according to the divine imaginations. The *vyāhṛtis* stood and resonated like the 7 musical notes. Manifesting with the *gāyatri* that came into many directions, repeatedly got positioned as the Sun-like brilliance. From an immature state getting matured by the sounds, getting pounded in *triṣṭubh* by the words, progressed as the words that came from words and in twos and fours became an immortality that got established. By the term *gāyatri* all by itself, a concept that the creation started with the cosmic vibrations and upon establishing the 3-dimensionality was firmly put forward. The metrical science of *chandas* was brought in as the way of describing the systematic divisions. What first remained immature was energised by the words and sounds, got matured and became the 7 *vyāhṛtis* that moved and got firmly established. The movement of these stages were in terms of doubling distances. The divine words traveled with the creations in appropriate dimensions. That shining divinity defined by the *gāyatri* pervaded as everywhere and established and sustained the universe.

The contents of the above two verses and terms used like "*traiṣṭubhāḍvā traiṣṭubhaṃ*" and many descriptions of the process of creation that hitherto appeared, indicated a theory of a fractal universe. That would include not only the process of multiplication and expansion in physical terms, but there is also a clear proposal of a fractal geometrical structure of the universe. It would also appear that by the term "*gāyatri*", the three points of origin on the periphery of the heaven, based on which the geometry of the *Ṛgveda* got configured was also under reference.

RV1.164.25 जगता सिन्धुं दिव्यस्तभायद्रथंतरे सूर्यं पर्यपश्यत्।
गायत्रस्य समिधस्तिस्र आहुस्ततो मह्ना प्र रिरिचे महित्वा॥

[जगता - as those that got born and progressed ◇ सिन्धुं - and flowed ◇ दिव्यस्त - as divine brightness ◇ भा - shining ◇ यद् - in many ways ◇ रथंतरे - gladly progressing like a chariot ◇ सूर्यं - the Sun-like ◇ परि - to the surroundings ◇ अपश्यत् - till nothing further visible ◇ गायत्रस्य - progressed as the 3-dimensionality ◇ समिधः - equally bestowed ◇ तिस्र - as 3 ◇ आहुः - oblations ◇ ततो - as those from those ◇ मह्ना - coming elatedly ◇ प्र - to the surroundings ◇ रिरिचे - repeatedly evacuated ◇ महित्वा - as the greatness that progressed]

Those that were born and progressed, those that flowed and shined like a divine brightness, progressed jubilantly in many ways like a chariot, as the Sun-like objects that came to the surroundings till nothing was further visible. Progressing as the 3-dimensionality and progressing from that three which stood equally, all came elatedly to the surroundings from the oblations. As those that came from those, repeatedly evacuating, became a greatness that progressively got instituted.

Through the 3-dimensionality that manifested, through the *vyāhṛtis* and its 3 divisions that got established, the bright paths of creation got formed and the Sun-like objects came into existence. These were found progressing, repeatedly manifesting from the divine words that came to the surroundings until the very ends and until nothing was further born or visible. From that which stood initially as a Sun-like brightness moved like a chariot that was gladly and enthusiastically led. It brought in the 7 *vyāhṛti*s and their subdivisions of 21. That initial brightness, upon oblations became the individual definitions of the *vyāhṛti*s and the objects under them. The term flowing could be indicative of *Soma* as well. The term "*samidhastisra*" could refer to the equitable nature of the 3-dimensionality, the three points on the horizon of the heaven or the 3 sub-divisions of the *vyāhṛti*s. The progress was compared to the speed, enthusiasm and flourish of a racing chariot. The above three verses described the metrical divisions, the expansions and movements in geometric progression that came into the process of creation.

RV1.164.26 उप ह्वये सुदुघां धेनुमेतां सुहस्तो गोधुगुत दोहदेनाम्।
श्रेष्ठं सवं सविता साविषन्नोऽभीद्धो घर्मस्तदु षु प्र वोचम्॥

[उप - downwards ◇ ह्वये - as oblations ◇ सुदुघां - easily milked and moved ◇ धेनुमेतां - as a nourishing beverage that extracted ◇ सुहस्तो - by expert hands ◇ गोधुगुत - kneaded and flowed ◇ दोहदेनाम् - came distressed by desires ◇ श्रेष्ठं - as excellences ◇ सवं - squeezed ◇ सविता - came spreading ◇ स - till ◇ अविषन्नो - nothing pervaded ◇ अभीद्धो - inflamed ◇ घर्मस्तद् - with internal heat ◇ उ - indeed ◇ षु - from a pregnant state ◇ प्र - to the surroundings ◇ वोचम् - by words]

A nourishing beverage flowed down from the oblations occurred as the milk kneaded and extracted easily by expert hands and the excellence's that came moved upon getting distressed by desires. Those that got squeezed out and spread till nothing further pervaded, and those things delivered from a pregnant state came out of an internal heat that had manifested. The divine words came to the surroundings and the universe manifested from a divine motherhood that stood above.

From that which remained distressed with desires, a nourishing beverage was obtained as extracted by expert hands and became the excellence's that moved by repeated squeezing, spreading and manifesting till nothing pervaded further. Getting delivered from an inflamed pregnant state with an internal heat generated by the divine words, all manifested to the surroundings. Those were the divine extractions, continuously issued out as the shining things and energies emitted out. It was as if the shy nipples of a cow getting pulled out, kneaded and milked, that from what remained in the heaven, a continuous extraction was effected and the shining paths of creations and the energies flowed incessantly. It was the first of cosmic vibrations that reverberated in the *Soma* that made it flow down as the paths of creation. It was as if a motherhood was stationed at the heaven, initially not yielding and yet later giving everything. Once again the downward angle of propagation was impressed upon. The description not only represented the beginning of the process of creation, but also the later processes that followed from many heavens.

RV1.164.27 हिङ्कृण्वती वसुपत्नी वसूनां वत्समिच्छन्ति
मनसाभ्यागात्। दुहामश्विभ्यां पयो अघ्न्येयं
सा वर्धतां महते सौभगाय॥

[हिङ्कृण्वती - making severe lowing sounds ◇ वसु - an excellence ◇ पत्नी - came down ◇ वसूनां - as many excellences ◇ वत्सम् - the beloved children ◇ इच्छन्ति - as desired; willed ◇ मनस - from a mind ◇ अभ्या - advancing ◇ गात् - progressing ◇ दुहाम् - as milked out, as internal heat ◇ अश्व् - spread ◇ विभ्यां - divided to the proximity ◇ पयो - as a juice ◇ अघ्न्य - from a cow; not quenched ◇ इयं - thus ◇ सा - coming with ◇ वर्धतां - came as enlargements ◇ महते - and great ◇ सौभगाय - well being]

From an excellence that stood above, many excellence's came descended as desired and moved to the proximity, progressing from an un-quenched internal heat. Spreading from a mind, getting divided to the proximity and as a juice that got enlarged, a great well-being got provided. These all came as if from a cow that stood above making lowing sounds beckoning its beloved children, secreting milk which it could no longer contain, due to the severe internal heat that it felt.

All manifested as if from a divine couple that stood above, ever anxious of their beloved children. A divine and powerful sound accompanied the creation from the very beginning and it appeared to manifest as the anxious beckoning from a mother who stood above. It pictured a cow beckoning her children to her proximity with severe lowing sounds. It developed an intense desire to feed due to its swollen udders and wanted to discharge the milk which would be the nourishment to its offspring's. It lowed its head and mightily beckoned. When the desire for creation and welfare of the objects manifested in a mind, the internal heat that so swelled within, got compelled to discharge and along with the high sounds of cosmic vibrations that came to the surroundings, the universe got created. The enquiry for immortality by a process of evolution began with the seed matter that was the *Soma*. The *Soma* was compared to the milk of the cow as the nourishment that was eager to flow down, which then indeed flowed down to sustain everything below the heaven and below the subsequent many heavens.

RV1.164.28 गौरमीमेदनु वत्सं मिषन्तं मूर्धानं हिङ्ङ्कृणोन्मातवा उ। सृक्वाणं घर्ममभि वावशाना मिमाति मायुं पयते पयोभिः॥

[गौर - from a whiteness ◇ मि - that stood ◇ इम - thus ◇ इद् - only ◇ अनु - a set of ◇ वत्सं - beloved offspring ◇ मिषन्तं - got sprinkled till the end ◇ मूर्धानं - shaking and lowing the head ◇ हिङ्ङ्कृण् - repeatedly making lowing sounds ◇ उन्मात - madly shaking the head ◇ वा - moved ◇ उ - indeed ◇ सृक्वाणं - with mouth twisted ◇ घर्मम् - internal heat ◇ अभि - to the proximity ◇ वा - moving with ◇ वश - immense desire ◇ अना - breathing hard ◇ मि - established ◇ मा - as arrangements ◇ अति - great ◇ मायुं - roaring; magically ◇ पयते - as those moved ◇ पयोभिः - filled with a juice; as a reservoir]

A whiteness had come moved and progressed and the beloved children had manifested from that as from a bull which stood with staring eyes, head lowering and shaking. making lowing sounds, stepping forward breathing hard and madly progressing, getting into a further aggravated state, roaring with desires and pouring out the seed matter. The universe came into existence with such furious emotions and with paths of creation flowing down from the heaven.

The creation of the universe in the beginning had those fierce and maddening moments as well. While those chains of objects, if issued forth along with the white or invisible transparency of the *Soma* and got sprinkled from it, just a moment before there were the loud roars and maddening desires that enabled it. Thus those were forcefully executed deeds. Those were the frothing whiteness that spewed around. The internal heat that was accrued in a long time was found discharged to become the immense heat and objects of the universe. The cosmic vibrations of an extreme nature were necessary for the creation of this large a size. These vibrations not only multiplied the temperature but made the 3-dimensional movement outward possible. If events of severity were observed in the first of creations, a matching upheaval and desire marked its commencement. And this desire suddenly arose, got revved up and the process of creation started.

The verses 26, 27 and 28 presented a biological angle to the process of creation. It talked about the cow, the bull, milk, anxiety, nourishment etc. as parts of the concept. It also described the internal heat that longed for the interactive bond with those created. Above all the last verse introduced the subject of whiteness which would be taken up in the next verse.

RV1.164.29 अयं स शिङ्क्ते येन गौरभीवृता मिमाति मायुं ध्वसनावधि श्रिता। सा चित्तिभिर्नि हि चकार मर्त्यं विद्युद्भवन्ती प्रति वव्रिमौहत॥

[अयं - thus ◇ स - as ◇ शिङ्क्ते - those as marched ◇ येन - somehow ◇ गौरभीवृता - enveloped with a whiteness ◇ मीमाति - as a great arrangement that came into existence ◇ मायुं - roaring; magically ◇ ध्वस - destruction ◇ न - as ◇ अवधि - well as non-destruction ◇ श्रिता - came side by side ◇ सा - bestowing ◇ चित्तिभिः - thoughtfully; from a mind ◇ नि - to below ◇ हि - only ◇ चकारं -as from a creator, bestowed shining ◇ मर्त्यं - as mortal; till man ◇ विद्युद् - rising from knowledge ◇ भवन्ती - as those occurred ◇ प्रति - in all directions ◇ वव्रिम्˙- unseen ◇ औ - indeed ◇ हत - destroying]

Thus, as those that marched together in many ways, enveloped with a whiteness and as the great arrangements that came into existence magically and roaring, destruction and non-destruction manifested side by side, thoughtfully getting bestowed from a mind to below. The Creator, bestowed those shining things till man, which arose from knowledge and moved in different directions and along with that many unseen and indeed destroying forces also came co-born.

Though the creations progressed in many ways, out of an immense desire, roaring and sprinkling till the end, all were enveloped with the *Soma* that came along. The thoughtful delivery, and the interspersed existence and the progress till man were all guided by the *Soma*, that invisible transparency. Those were the paths of creation that resembled a lightning. Then there were those objects that hid or destroyed. There were thus objects and groups of power centres that were not only visible, but invisible as well, while some others silently destroyed many. Along with that whiteness that got spewed and reached all the way down to this earth, man and beyond, a darkness came descended in equal extents. Which were those invisible objects and would these get described?

RV1.164.30 अनच्छये तुरगातु जीवमेजद्ध्रुवं मध्य आ पस्त्यानाम्।
जीवो मृतस्य चरति स्वधाभिरमर्त्यो मर्त्येना सयोनिः॥

[अनच्छये - those in a state of turbidity ◇ तुरगातु - speedily progressed ◇ जीवमेजद् - moved from existed things ◇ ध्रुवं - fixed ◇ मध्य - middle ◇ आ - coming ◇ पस्त्यानाम् - as moving away from a stable ◇ जीवो - as living ◇ मृतस्य - and dying ◇

चरति - as those moved; locomotive ◇ स्वधाभि - advancing from the self bestowed ◇ अमर्त्यो - immortal ◇ मर्त्येन - and mortal ◇ सयोनि - from the same womb; as from the wombs]

From the existing things speedily progressed, out of a state of turbidity moved and manifested, from fixed middles got blown away as if vacating from a stable. Those living things and dying things, those that moved to and fro, all of them got bestowed from the self, advancing both as mortal and immortal till man and all of those came from the same womb.

Those found interspersed and moved quickly, were found to take fixed positions. Many came moved from there as alive, dead or as those that lost all their strength. Many came, in principle, from many wombs that manifested, to reach man and this earth. Though all were issued forth from the heaven that was the *hiraṇyagarbha*, some were found active and lively where as the others were dead or inactive. These came mixed and got mixed and at times took temporary positions as if in a stable. Later their places of occupancy became empty, again as a stable. The living as well as the dead came to these stables, but to go away. Thus there was two class of objects that first took temporary positions. One was the live ones which were capable of generating and delivering new things, essentially meaning those hot objects. The others were the dead and cold ones. Both would split into many and move away, making the stable empty. Yet there remained a loyalty and a longing felt to the stable. More over, each of the products of the hot objects that came by splitting would again undergo the divisions till the end of that chain of divisions and existences. The description here compared well with the term "*sāśanānaśane*" of the *puruṣasūkta*, as the concept presented here was that many power centres of the universe became basically empty and acted only as the controlling points. The description would also get corroborated by what was stated in the verse RV 1.89.9 (See Chapter-7). This process of creating apparently empty points of origin started from each epicentre and continued in several stages until the earth. These fields of influence acted as a chain of dependencies from that origin of all events, till the very end. Every womb or the point of origin was capable of producing different streams of good and bad as well as the many and sets of creation and the invisible ones that harassed the ones created came from the same source in each stage.

Thus the geometrical organisation of the universe have two distinct aspects and therefore the objects that stood under these regimes were subjected to a several types of mixing. Yet both of these system elements were the essential parts of the universe. What was stated as invisible could also be the chain of emptiness. Those were therefore not simply emptiness, but were the field forces and influences, formed as a result of individual evacuations of objects and energy systems. This concept was reiterated in several places in the Vedic texts, by direct statements as well as by obvious inferences. As compared to the modern elaborate field theories, these statements might appear as simply suggestions made. But here these were not simply suggestions as the statements wanted to convince us the existence of not the random fields, but a chain of such fields extending from the point of origin till the far end of the universe. Therefore it should be construed that a theory was clearly and forcefully mooted.

RV1.164.32 य ईं चकार न सो अस्य वेद य ईं ददर्श हिरुगिन्नु तस्मात्। स मातुर्योना परिवीतो अन्तर्बहुप्रजा निर्ऋतिमा विवेश॥

[य - and ◇ ईं - now ◇ चकार - bestowed brightly shining ◇ न - as ◇ सो - with ◇ अस्य - appropriate ◇ वेद - properties ◇ य - and ◇ ईं - then ◇ ददर्श - and as those found bestowed ◇ हिरुगिन्नु - only as broken down driven away and then ◇ तस्म - from those ◇ अत् - moved ◇ स - as ◇ मा - an arrangement ◇ तुर्योना - as from a supremacy, to the four sides ◇ परिवीतो - surrounded ◇ अन्तर् - from inside ◇ बहुप्रजा - having come as many progeny ◇ निर्ऋति - destroyed ◇ मा - as arrangements ◇ वि - divided ◇ वेश - and occupied as newly settled]

And then many got bestowed brightly shining with appropriate properties, as those that were found bestowed broken down and driven away from those that had come earlier, as arrangements that moved from a supremacy, as the arrangements that came to the four sides and from the inside to the surrounding outside, as those that got divided, destroyed and as those that came newly settled.

Thus that which came brightly shining and with many properties till here from the self as segregated and spread to the surroundings and manifested from a motherhood, were found to have born in abundance as exploded to the surroundings and as manifested from a series of calamities that had occurred. The interpretations made with the previous verse got corroborated here. It was from a single motherhood that both the bright and not so bright objects of the universe were born. It was from a single source that the benevolence and the malevolence got created. From that same motherhood came those things that stood separated and those things that came in different categories. The emptiness and the fields thus came co-born with the bright objects and their paths. Right from the beginning and with reference to the point of origin, these fields were generated along with the objects. In every instance of an object or a closely held system being disturbed, divided and moved, the very same brought about the emptiness in the respective original locations. This continued till this earth and the ends. The incidences were triggered by calamities (instantaneous occurrences for apparently no reason) that struck the original locations, which divided the system and threw them apart. But the processes emaciated when progressed to the end of the universe. And yet the calamities that occurred at chosen moments could not be disassociated from the process of creation.

RV1.164.33 द्यौर्मे पिता जनिता नाभिरत्र बन्धुर्मे माता पृथिवी महीयम्। उत्तानयोश्चम्वो३र्योनिरन्तरत्रा पिता दुहितुर्गर्भमाधात्॥

[द्यौः - as the heavens ◇ मे - repeatedly ◇ पि - moved ◇ ता - as those came ◇ जनिता - born as those came ◇ नाभिः - from the hub; from the navel ◇ अत्र - that way ◇ बन्धुः - as related ◇ मे - that repeated ◇ मा - arrangements ◇ ता - from those ◇ पृथिवी - as earths ◇ महीयम् - greatly pervaded and enlarged ◇ उत्तानयोश्चम् - risen and spread ◇ उ - indeed ◇ योनिः - from the womb ◇ अन्तरत्र - from inside ◇ पि - moved ◇ ता - as those ◇ दुहितुः - heated internally ◇ गर्भम् - from a pregnant state ◇ आ - manifested ◇ ध - bestowed ◇ अत् - and moved]

The heavens that repeatedly got manifested, those manifested and moved through the hub and a navel, those that stood correspondingly related, those that repeatedly manifested to become the arrangements of earth forms and thus got enlarged by arising and spreading, all of these indeed came from what stood inside the many wombs and got manifested as bestowed and moved from such hot pregnant states.

The body of the universe got enlarged from the heaven, instantly spreading and becoming the arrangements of many relatives that extended up to the earth. The chords of growth extended many ways through a 3-dimensionality. Arrangements came, as growths from wombs that got internally hotted up and from these many things swelled up. From the womb of the heaven the objects moved with 3-dimensionality incessantly swelled into different directions. Identical processes got repeated till this earth and the process was nothing confined to the heavens in the high skies. There were thus several such wombs that got hotted up and several children born. These went on to such an extent that the objects could be only termed as relatives and not direct descendants. There was thus a thinning of the interactive nature and bond between the objects and the different fields. And yet that universal interactive existence that the *gāyatri* proclaimed would prevail apropriately. The sequence of conception of human beings and the quadrupeds, getting created by continuously getting fed and nourished by the navel chord was compared with the sequential events of formation of different objects of the universe.

At the same time there was a suggestion here that, though in the earlier verses the narration was more centred on the point of origins and their chains, the actual delivery of the objects occurred from the heavens and the many hubs of creation of the universe. The relevancy of the point of origin was a matter of orientation and not the physical manifestations and their attributes. Therefore the term "*nābhi*" was meant in two ways.

RV1.164.34 पृच्छामि त्वा परमन्तंपृथिव्याः पृच्छामि यत्र भुवनस्य नाभिः। पृच्छामि त्वा वृष्णो अश्वस्य रेतः पृच्छामि वाचः परमं व्योम॥

[पृच्छामि - interspersed and acceptably established ◇ त्वा - from thyself ◇ परम् - to the most distant ◇ अन्तं - ends ◇ पृथिव्याः - as the earths ◇ पृच्छामि - interspersed and acceptably established ◇ यत्र - whichever that came ◇ भुवनस्य - as the universal ◇ नाभिः - hubs; navel ◇ पृच्छामि - interspersed and acceptably established ◇ त्वा - from thyself ◇ वृष्णो - sprinkled ◇ अश्व - spread ◇ वस्य - remained ◇ रेतः - as the semen virile ◇ पृच्छामि - interspersed and acceptably established ◇ वाचः - as words ◇ परमं - the great ◇ व्योम - atmosphere]

Everything came from thyself to the most distant ends as interspersed and established; interspersed and established came the many earths from whatever hubs or navels that appeared; interspersed and established came from thyself, getting sprinkled, getting spread and so remained; interspersed and established came the semen virile and the words that manifested along with the great atmosphere.

The universe was established only as interspersed and mixed, while coming into existence from thyself. It was so while the many navels and hubs of the universe were formed. So these were while got sprinkled, divided and got distributed from the semen virile. So it was when manifested as the divine words and so it was while came as the supreme atmosphere. The universe as a whole came as a mixture and much interspersed from the beginning to the end. Even when it all commenced from the hub or navel, or when it was divided repeatedly by the words, or when it moved through the supreme atmosphere, all got severely mixed. As a result, there were several levels of interactive relations between those created. Even the sounds and vibrations that appeared as a divine necessity here and there in the process had the same nature of being mixed. The navel referred here could be taken as the hub of the chariot wheel to which structure the universe was often compared, and which repeatedly appeared as the many growth centres in the course of creation.

The presentation here reflected the very character and nature of approach of this hymn. The main theme of this hymn, all by itself was that the process of the first of creations could not be described, at any rate, by any single theory and could be attempted only by looking at it as a mix of several conjugate theories. When such and more than one theory got combined and got co-related, a reasonable set of explanations might ensue which would appear satisfactory. Just as the objects and the systems that were born interspersed, these theories would also be mixed to one's satisfaction. The very process of *ādisṛṣṭi* was indeed most inexplicable.

RV1.164.35 इयं वेदिः परो अन्तः पृथिव्या अयं यज्ञो भुवनस्य नाभिः। अयं सोमो वृष्णो अश्वस्य रेतो ब्रह्मायं वाचः परमं व्योम॥

[इयं - thus ◇ वेदिः - as the *vedis* ◇ परो - till afar ◇ अन्तः - till the ends ◇ पृथिव्या - came as the earths ◇ अयं - thus ◇ यज्ञो - as the *yajñas* ◇ भुवनस्य - of the universe ◇ नाभिः - navels, hubs ◇ अयं - thus ◇ सोमो - from the *Soma* ◇ वृषणो - got sprinkled ◇ अश् - spread ◇ वस्य - and remained ◇ रेतो - as the semen virile ◇ ब्रह्म - that got much enlarged ◇ अयं - thus ◇ वाचः - the words ◇ परमं - supreme ◇ व्योम - atmosphere]

Thus when manifested as the *vedis* (platforms by way of the heavens) till afar and till the very ends, when manifested as the earth forms that got formed by the *yajñas* that occurred, thus when manifested as the hubs and navels of creation that got formed all over the universe, thus when got sprinkled as the *Soma* and the semen virile, thus when got much enlarged through the supreme atmosphere, everything was coming into existence from the words supported by the *Brahma*.

The words that came from the *Brahma* accompanied the

process of creation from the beginning till the end. It was these words, that manifested which went on getting enlarged, which established the universe. Thus a supreme atmosphere came into existence, from the heaven till the end of the universe. The space just below (for that matter at left, right or above) the *Viśvacakṣus* was referred as the *vedi*, where the process of creation took material forms. The *uttaravedi* of the *vaidikayajña* was, therefore, supposed to be the very heaven and was accorded an exalted status and became the podium where the oblations would be offered. Just as the first of the *yajña* started at the heaven, in the *vaidikayajña* the main oblations would be offered at the *uttaravedi*. In the *śulbasūtras* the altars were often referred simply as the *vedis*.

Here, the nature of a mixture and the interspersed state was stated as a universal phenomenon that got extended from the heaven till it reached the earth, i.e, when came as several events, or when came as many chains or when came as much divided. This process while traversing through the supreme atmosphere created many extensive groups of different objects connected to different power centres. Even the atmosphere came into existence in an interspersed style due to the mixing and abutting of the *vyāhṛti* limits into one another. Besides, even when the seed matter progressed as the regime of the *Soma* this principle of mixing was visible. This would directly refer to the evolutionary mutations that went on with the living matter of this earth, which possibly could be seen reflected in the progress and expansion of the universe itself.

RV1.164.36 सप्तार्धगर्भा भुवनस्य रेतो विष्णोस्तिष्ठन्ति प्रदिशा विधर्मणि। ते धीतिभिर्मनसा ते विपश्चितः परिभुवः परि भवन्ति विश्वतः॥

[सप्त - 7 ◇ अर्ध - half ◇ गर्भा - interior; middle ◇ भुवनस्य - as the universal ◇ रेतो - semen virile ◇ विष्णोः - equally spread ◇ तिष्ठ - got stationed ◇ अन्ति - to the proximity and ◇ प्रदिशा - in all directions and regions ◇ विधर्मणि - as distributed around ◇ ते -

as those ◇ धीतिभिः - from an intellect as well as ◇ मनसा - from a mind ◇ ते - as those ◇ विपश्चितः - intelligently differentiated ◇ परिभुव - the surrounding atmosphere ◇ परि - all around ◇ भवन्ति - occurred those ◇ विश्वतः - that reached everywhere]

From that half and middle of 7 of the universe, from a pregnant state of 7 1/2 measures, equally spread the semen virile and got stationed to the proximity and in all directions and regions, as distributed around those that came from an intellect and a mind, getting intelligently differentiated and coming to the surrounding atmosphere as those that manifested and reached everywhere.

From this well defined place, in the very middle of the 7 *vyāhṛtis*, the *Soma* came flowed to the proximity as the seed matter, remained wherever it chose and eventually got emaciated while progressed. Not only the space became large and less occupied but the size and thermal properties of the objects also got reduced, while the universe came expanded. The presence of a divine mind and the prayers that ensued as the sounds and the cosmic vibrations accompanied the process. Though this related to the concept of description of spaces and places in 2-dimensional terms, these were obviously 3-dimensional.

The term "*saptārdha*" meaning 7.5 as well as the "the middle of 7" could equally apply in this case. For not very clearly known reasons (that is, from the descriptions, hitherto, which would get modified in chapter-9), the *uttaravedi* of the *vaidikayajña* would measure to an area of 7.5 square *puruṣaṃ*.[4] Here, however, the area of the heaven or the *hiraṇyagarbha* would become 7.5, if the terms were so interpreted and perhaps the very concept that the later period adopted rested on this or similar expressions.

In these verses certain key words like "the hub", "womb",

---

[4]But there are indeed clear statements in the *Ṛgveda* itself that the area of the heaven being equated to 7.5 square *puruṣaṃ* by coming up with a figure of 108000, (RV 1.126.03 & 04) which however, did not get corroborated here, by any of the descriptions that appeared hitherto.

"words" and "hymns" were used to formulate the theories and these theories in turn cascaded into one another to become an adjunct new one, to get carried on as the descriptions of the interspersed nature of creation.

RV1.164.37 न वि जानामि यदिवेदमस्मि निण्यः संनद्धो मनसा चरामि। यदा मागन्प्रथमजा ऋतस्यादिद्वाचो अश्नुवे भागमस्याः॥

[न - as ◇ वि - divided ◇ जानामि - the birth places established ◇ यदि - whatever as ◇ वेदम् - property as manifested ◇ अस्मि - as parts ◇ निण्यः - miraculously ◇ संनद्धो - equipped; prepared ◇ मनसा - coming from a mind ◇ चरा - moved to and fro ◇ मि - established ◇ यद् - whichever way ◇ आ - as manifested ◇ मागन् - the self tortuously moved ◇ प्रथमजा - born as the first ◇ ऋतस्याद् - according to rules ◇ इद् - only ◇ वाचो - with words ◇ अश् - spread ◇ नु - indeed as ◇ वे - woven ◇ भागमस्या - with the parts coming]

The divided places of birth that got established, whatever property that manifested and whatever parts that miraculously came into existence, those came from a mind and got established or moved to and fro from the self and those came tortuously moved from those that came born first. Thus whichever way those manifested, those came only from the divine words that manifested according to divine rules. Indeed so came those that stood like the interwoven parts of the universe.

The sound and the cosmic vibrations were universally relevant, wherever matter traveled. These astonishing vibrations first manifested in the heaven when all stood as one and were found to act the same way in the later processes. Those things which were first born, later moved to new places. When those got divided and got distributed, the motive force behind all these acts could only be this sound and the vibrations that appropriately manifested. The definitions that emanated from a mind, a point of origin, and those words that appropriately came for the later manifestations, defined everything. It divided what existed and distributed to the surroundings and thus appeared to be a process of continuous evacuation. All appeared as if guided and carried out by a divine mind.

RV1.164.38 अपाङ् प्राङेति स्वधया
गृभीतोऽमर्त्यो मर्त्येना सयोनिः। ता शश्वन्ता विषूचीना
वियन्ता न्यऽन्यं चिक्युर्न नि चिक्युरन्यम्॥

[अपाङ् - swirled downward ◇ प्र - to the surrounding ◇ अङ - swirled ◇ इति - in such manners ◇ स्वध - from the self ◇ या - moved ◇ गृभीतो - holding to ◇ अमर्त्यो - immortal ◇ मर्त्येना - and mortal manifested from ◇ सयोनिः - the same womb ◇ ता - as those ◇ शश्व - that hopped and jumped ◇ अन्ता - till the end ◇ विषूचीना - going apart in different directions ◇ वियन्ता - as an array till the end ◇ नि - to below ◇ अन्यं - as others ◇ चि - from a heap ◇ कि - whatever ◇ उः - confirmed ◇ न - as ◇ नि - to below ◇ चि - from a heap ◇ कि - whatever ◇ उः - confirmed ◇ अन्यम् - as others]

Swirled downward and swirled to the surroundings as whatever that moved from the self, moved as those that came immortal and mortal, those came till man and beyond man, manifesting from the same womb, as those that hopped and jumped till the end, went apart in different directions, became an array that came till the end of those that manifested to below and got confirmed as others. From a heap of whatever manifested, manifested again to below, coming and getting confirmed as whatever others to become the universe.

We have known the universe as having come into existence with a geometrical definition of the 7 *vyāhṛtis* around the epicentre and the objects that came along. These were imagined as concentric circles for the sake of convenience. We knew that it was a representation of spherical entities but we carried on with the ideas. But things were not that simple. These *vyāhṛtis* and the universe were born as if swirled around an axis and a point, simultaneously outward and downward and the spherical shape was complex. Modern cosmologists would love to hear this. They believed that a spherical universe (if it is really so!) could be mathematically perfect, only if a circle was repeatedly turned around three mutually perpendicular axis.[5] Here, it amounted to be the same as the swirling action proposed was around as well as downward, but executed simultaneously. Any way, the presentation requirement was the same. It was for this reason that the term extraordinary was repeated. But more complexities could be derived from the narration. The statement that all these happened from the same womb meant that the rotations did not take place with respect to the epicentre, but with reference to a plane called heaven which in turn was a spherical entity that stood very near to the epicentre. This astounding statement clearly indicated the precise thinking of the Vedic sages. It was no wonder they kept away from the concept of a perfect sphericity and brought in the state of resonance into the description repeatedly. The principle and a philosophy that we could recognize here would be that a point would not be capable either to get converted as a sphere nor deliver the enormous masses and energy with which the universe was conceived. But it was necessary that even when the axis of rotation passed through the centre, the very action must be centred on a plane slightly away from it, and thus presupposing a small space to have existed. Be it known that the Vedic minds would not be satisfied by simply comparing the universe to a watermelon!

RV1.164.39 ऋचो अक्षरे परमे व्योमन्यस्मिन्देवा अधि विश्वे निषेदुः। यस्तन्न वेद किमृचा करिष्यति य इत्तद्विदुस्त इमे समासते॥

[ऋचो - the serene prayers ◇ अक्षरे - immortal ◇ परमे - as supreme ◇ व्योमन् - atmosphere ◇ यस्मिन् - whatever ◇ देवा - as the heavens ◇ अधि - from above ◇ विश्वे - reaching everywhere interconnected ◇ निषेदुः - placed as to below only ◇ यस् - upon being frothed up ◇ तन्न - as from That ◇ वेद - the properties ◇ किम् - which ◇ ऋचा - prayers ◇ करिष्यति - became operational ◇ य - or ◇ इत् - moved ◇ तद् - from those ◇ विदुस्त - stood

[5] At least that is what this author gathered.

applicable ◇ इमे - here ◇ समासते - equally relevant]

When everything came from the serene and auspicious prayers, as the immortal supreme atmosphere and as the many heavens that reached everywhere from above, interconnected, as those that frothed up from the existing ones and descended with many properties, which of the serene and auspicious prayers became operational or in other words to what extent were these applicable or did these come equally relevant and valid while reaching here?

It was clear that the first of creations started out of divine hymns, the sounds and cosmic vibrations that manifested in the heaven. But when the creations moved through the supreme atmosphere, were the hymns the same or did their values change? Or to what extent the concept of these hymns came relevant? Did the divinity above influence the properties that manifested much below and much away? Did the motive and dividing forces and their nature, which came in the form of the sounds and vibrations, ever change or did these go on changing? Did the places that were reached influence and re-evaluate these? Let us wait for the answers for these questions, from the Vedic text itself.

RV1.164.40 सूयवसाद्भगवती हि भूया अथो वयं भगवन्तः स्याम।
अद्धि तृणमघ्न्ये विश्वदानीं पिब शुद्धमुदकमाचरन्ती॥

[सूयवसाद् - as good pasturage ◇ भगवती - happily and prosperously ◇ हि - only ◇ भूया - coming into existence ◇ अथो - and then ◇ वयं - as interconnected ◇ भगवन्तः - prospered till the end ◇ स्याम - as the powers ◇ अत् - that moved from □ धि - an intellect ◇ तृणम् - grass ◇ अघ्न्ये - not destroyed ◇ विश्वदानीं - delivering as everywhere ◇ पिब - moved intelligently ◇ शुद्धम् - as the clean ◇ उदकम् - water ◇ आचरन्ती - came moved to and fro and to the proximity]

As those that came into existence happily and prosperously from a good pasturage, as those that prospered and stood interconnected till the end, as the powers that moved from an intellect which did not harm even a shoot of grass, everything got delivered intelligently as everywhere, manifesting from the *Soma*, just as the water had manifested and moved to and fro and to the proximity.

The body of the universe came into existence as the shining objects that rested and moved well guided, manifesting downwards from above as beautiful and powerful, getting delivered everywhere and getting emaciated and thus all appeared to be a clean arrangement of the *Soma* that came to the proximity, like water on this earth. From the very beginning, whatever issued forth and took positions or moved were all well guided and beautiful. This continued to the very end, having manifested from the *Soma*, as comparable to the existence of water on earth. The process of emaciation of the *Soma* and the distribution of the created objects were akin to water and objects born on this earth. The water also gave birth to various life forms, nourished them and took to forms of emaciation in its existence such as becoming its vapour and got distributed to extreme ends and all over the earth. The existence of the *Soma* was none too different.

RV1.164.41 **गौरीर्मिमाय सलिलानि तक्षत्येकपदी द्विपदी सा चतुष्पदी। अष्टापदी नवपदी बभूवुषी सहस्राक्षरा परमे व्योमन्॥**

[**गौरीर्** - with whiteness ◇ **मिमाय** - those as wished ◇ **सलिलानि** - floating as if in water ◇ **तक्षति** - greatly fashioned out as ◇ **एकपदी** - one stage ◇ **द्विपदी** - two stages ◇ **सा** - and so on ◇ **चतुष्पदी** - four stages ◇ **अष्तापदी** - demarcated till the end of all stages ◇ **नवपदी** - as new stages ◇ **बभूवुषी** - born out of heat ◇ **सहस्र** - as 1000 ◇ **अक्षरा** - permanent ◇ **परमे** - supreme ◇ **व्योमन्** - atmosphere]

As a whiteness that manifested and as those that floated in the ocean of an atmosphere as wished, greatly fashioned out in stages of 1, 2 and 4 and demarcated till the end of all stages, as the new stages that got formed, were so born out of heat in a thousand ways, to remain in the supreme atmosphere that came and stood for ever.

Moved as an arrangement of whiteness that came as the

paths of creation and manifesting as those born out of divine wishes, all were born and had risen out of an enormous heat to become the new stages in the supreme atmosphere. As arrangements of matter and energy that shined, sets of objects of the universe appeared as if floating in an ocean. There were several flows of white paths of creation. The new stages, getting born in a geometric progression of 2 and 4 till the end of the supreme atmosphere, became the immortal arrangements that came into existence. The distances between the stages should be reckoned in thousands and also should be reckoned as increased in a geometric progression till the very end. The universe while got enlarged a thousandfold, it emaciated a thousand ways. The increase in size of the altars proposed in the *vaidikayajña* would be kept to an arithmetic progression and later in this hymn the same progress would be presented compounded to a manageable size. This was a matter of convenience and the text here said that the actual progress of the universe was a geometric progression.

RV1.164.42 तस्याः समुद्रा अधि वि क्षरन्ति तेन जीवन्ति प्रदिशश्चतस्रः। ततः क्षरत्यक्षरं तद्विश्वमुप जीवति॥

[तस्याः - as those that ◇ समुद्रा - came through that ocean ◇ अधि - from above ◇ वि - divided ◇ क्षरन्ति - successively emaciated ◇ तेन - likewise ◇ जीवन्ति - successively survived ◇ प्रदिश - in all directions and regions ◇ शतस्रः - in hundreds ◇ ततः - as those that came from those ◇ क्षरति - greatly emaciated ◇ अक्षरं - and non - decayed ◇ तद् - from That ◇ विश्वम् - that reached everywhere ◇ उप - to below ◇ जीवति - as those survived]

As those that came through this ocean (of an atmosphere) from above, divided and successively emaciated, likewise successively survived and moved into all directions and regions, repeating a hundred times as those that came from those, then got greatly emaciated, remained non-decayed and became those that reached everywhere in the universe from That (the *Sat*), progressing downward and remaining as those that survived.

The progress was divided into two stages. One as come from the heaven above to the proximity much divided. The next stage was as spread from such locations to all mutually perpendicular directions in which case also the divisions and emaciation having taken place. But some of these remained and moved as not emaciated as well. These were identical processes that progressed through the atmosphere, referred here as the ocean, manifesting from the Supreme Truth. The objects moved as if over waves in this ocean of an atmosphere. The emaciation would be of two types, one of the objects and their size and the other by the increasing distances between them. In this spherical universe, there could not be any of the cardinal directions. Therefore, the four directions were those that came from a point to forward, backward, upward and downward. Movements and growth in such directions, made the universe a complex structure, correspondingly populated and indeed very large.

RV1.164.43 शकमयं धूममारादपश्यं विषूवता पर एनावरेण।
उक्षाणं पृश्निमपचन्त वीरास्तानि धर्माणि प्रथमान्यासन्॥

[शकमयं - those emitted ◇ धूम - as smoke and dust ◇ मा - arrangement ◇ रा - issued out ◇ द - granted ◇ पश्यं - visibilities; as seen ◇ विषूवता - manifested as spread in all directions ◇ पर - and distanced ◇ एनावरेण - as confirmed enclosures ◇ उक्षाणं - sprinkled ◇ पृश्निम् - as the spots ◇ अप - downward ◇ च - and ◇ अन्त - till the end ◇ वीराः - courageously; issued and moved ◇ तानि - from that ◇ धर्माणि - as per the rules ◇ प्रथम - the first ◇ अन्यासन् - positioned as the others]

The arrangements of smoke and dust that got emitted out, derived as the invisible darkness that got revolved, the circular enclosures that manifested and distanced, the spots that got sprinkled downwards till the end, those that courageously got positioned and those that came as the others from the first came; all of these manifested according to divine rules.

From those that first came, arrangements of lesser ones,

many a dust forms and other objects also had come, getting sprinkled and appearing like dots and spots and these processes came descended till the very end. From the earlier established ones those came courageously and obeying the rules of creation. Those came as conclusive arrangements that came without turning back and as those that sub-served the earlier ones. Thus there were many sub-systems of the universe, obtained by division, which stood in equal measure to both sides, i.e, symmetrically, from their respective points of origin. The division and growth of the universe into all the four directions and around from wherever an object earlier stood, took place and these became subservient to the ones above and thus several hierarchical orders had manifested.

RV1.164.44 त्रयः केशिन ऋतुथा वि चक्षते संवत्सरे वपत एक एषाम्। विश्वमेको अभि चष्टे शचीभिर्ध्राजिरेकस्य ददृशे न रूपम्॥

[त्रयः - as 3-dimensionality ◇ केशिन - hair locks ◇ ऋतुथा - as the seasons that stood◇ वि - divided ◇ चक्षते - those from the eye ◇ संवत्सरे - of the years ◇ वपत - as those sheared off ◇ एक - from one ◇ एषाम् - in that manner ◇ विश्वम् - reaching everywhere ◇ एको - one by one ◇ अभि - advancing ◇ चष्टे - noticeably ◇ शचीभिः - mightily as well as ◇ ध्राजिः - impulsively ◇ एकस्य - from one ◇ ददृशे - 'as the visibility burst off ◇ न - as a ◇ रूपम् - shape]

The body of the universe had come into existence as the 3-dimensionality manifested and as the paths that stood like the hair-locks falling from a head, as the seasons that stood divided in an year, as the ones that got sheared off from a single one and reached everywhere, as those that progressed one by one noticeably, mightily and impulsively and those were the visibility that burst off from a single one.

As the thick bunches of hair-locks that fell down from a head above, and as those things that manifested at appointed times, as the ones that stood separate from the others, as those many that manifested from a single entity and reached everywhere, the universe came instantly expanded.

From those epicentres getting divided and manifesting at selected moments, came the off-springs that stood in groups, severed and separated one by one and as if manifested from one place to all places. Those came and stood from each of those eyes to the successive proximity. The universe could also be compared to the year and the seasons that stood without strict divisions. As an arrangement overseen by an eye that saw all, the universe appeared to have got instituted as a flow in 3-dimensions from a space to the ones below it. The incessant flows appeared from many sources, like the hair locks falling from a head. In spite of the much divided nature of the manifestations, the interlaced state was totally inevitable. This incomparable universe thus came instantly, forcefully and reaching everywhere, but as occurred at selected moments. The nature of the calamitous occurrences that was earlier presented was reminded. This description would also remind another one description where these locks of hair was stated to be burning. In comparison, here the *Agni* was excluded from the descriptions. From the many eyes and epicentres, the paths of creation flowed and the objects were so stationed till the very end of the universe.

RV1.164.45 चत्वारि वाक्परिमिता पदानि तानि विदुर्ब्राह्मणा ये मनीषिणः। गुहा त्रीणि निहिता नेङ्गयन्ति तुरीयं वाचो मनुष्या वदन्ति॥

[चत्वारि - to all four sides ◇ वाक् - as the words ◇ परिमिता - that came regulated ◇ पदानि - as the stages ◇ तानि - and from those ◇ विदुः - intelligently ◇ ब्राह्मणा - expanded; known as came from the *Brahma* ◇ ये - whatever ◇ मनीषिणः - intellect and consciousness ◇ गुहा - as the caves ◇ त्रीणि - of 3 ◇ निहिता - firmed up ◇ न - as ◇ इङ्गयन्ति - swirling around to the proximity ◇ तुरीयं - from the fourth state of mind ◇ वाचो - the words ◇ मनुष्या - till man ◇ वदन्ति - it was often said]

As the words that came from *Brahma*, as the words that came from all the four sides, out of whatever intellect and consciousness that might be, the universe got intelligently established in regulated stages extending till man, which men often understood and stated as a creation in the fourth state of mind. Along with these manifestations, a set of 3-dimensional caves, created by swirling to the proximity, were also born.

People realised the words that manifested for the birth of the universe differently. Some said that it came from the words of *Brahma* Himself while others said that those were the words that came from whatever intellect and consciousness that prevailed in the surroundings. Yet others believed that these words came out of the *turīyāvastha* of a divine mind. Because whatever occurred were of such unique nature and could only be surmised as came by a divine intervention. For those very divine words became the atmosphere, the objects and the energy systems of the universe. These were the ways in which the universe was born, said the learned sages of yore. Along with the *vyāhṛtis* that came in regulated stages, those 3-dimensional dark caves were also born. Those were found created by a process of swirling around to the proximity. Are we seeing a description of the "black holes" here? It was dark because it was described as a cave, in which nothing was visible. It was created by a rotating action, and most importantly to the proximity, which meant that their sizes were not large. This also meant to be something that was different from the darkness that once prevailed. Though no further description of their properties were forthcoming, one could not possibly discount the presence of further validating statements in the vast *Ṛgvedasaṃhita* itself. The four directions mentioned here are once again, forward, backward, upward and downward.

At the same time the 3-dimensional caves could be read as the conic bulk forms that came as the division of the atmosphere and its contents and could be the growth pattern of the individual segments which also contained the specific paths. These conic forms were often described as mountainous shapes. The description of the regulated steps and stages of expansion could be associated with this conic sections. All the same there was that darkness and emptiness in the caves which possibly added an enigma to the theory.

RV1.164.46 इन्द्रं मित्रं वरुणमग्निमाहुरथो दिव्यः स सुपर्णो गरुत्मान्। एकं सद् विप्रा बहुधा वदन्त्यग्निं यमं मातरिश्वानमाहुः॥

[इन्द्रं - by *Indra* ◇ मित्रं - by *Mitra* ◇ वरुणम् - by *Varuṇa* ◇ अग्निम् - by *Agni* ◇ आहुः - with oblations ◇ अथो - and then ◇ दिव्यः - the divine ◇ स - as ◇ सुपर्णो - the *Suparṇa* ◇ गरुत्मान् - that great heavenly bird ◇ एकं - from one ◇ सद् - as the *Sát* ◇ वि - divided ◇ प्रा - coming to the surroundings ◇ बहुधा - as many that got positioned ◇ वदन्ति - many ways said ◇ अग्निं - or as by *Agni* ◇ यमं - as per the rules ◇ मातरिश्वानम् - from a pregnant fire that smoldered ◇ आहुः - and oblations]

It was stated by the Veda that the universe came out of the oblations and was created by *Indra*, *Mitra*, *Varuṇa* and *Agni* and also that it came as *Suparṇa*, the bird that earlier remained in the heaven and that it was it's creation. It was also stated that the universe came to the surrounding much divided from *Sat*, as from the One and only One, and also that it came from the oblations and by *Agni*, that smoldered within a divine motherhood and as that which took place according to the rules. It was further stated that the universe came from a motherhood along with the associated afflictions inherent to such manifestations. Lastly it was stated that the universe came simply as an arrangement that sprung out from one to become the many to the surroundings.

It would be more correct to say that there were many theories about the birth of the universe and not one. Some said that it was a divine occurrence brought about by the divinities like, *Indra*, *Mitra*, *Varuṇa* and *Agni* and out of oblations. Others said that it was the very bird *Suparṇa* that remained in the heaven that came as an arrangement downward which got extended up to this earth and so became the universe. Yet others said that all came from the one and only one *Sat* and became many to the surroundings, sticking to a theory of a simple physical occurrence. Again some said that it was the manifestation of an immense heat and temperature as *Agni* that started all, objects and energy getting flung to the surroundings. It could be said that all theories were of equal importance. It clearly demonstrated that the Vedic people were comfortable with many theories on the subject co-existing, even if they differed to certain extent. It would be sufficient if theories did not come in conflict with one another and enough that the description did not contradict one another.

Between the 45th and the 46th verse, it would appear that 7 or more different theories of how the universe was created were presented. However the 45th verse, merely presented the 3 ways in which the sounds and vibrations were believed to have manifested, as the root cause and effect of all that manifested later. The 46th verse narrated the physical processes that subsequently happened, which became known as the way the universe was created. Behind the many processes that were imagined, the theme of the prayers and hymns that reverberated as the sounds and vibrations addressed to the self, would appear central.

RV1.164.47 कृष्णं नियानं हरयः सुपर्णा अपो वसाना दिवमुत्पतन्ति।
त आववृत्रन्त्सदनादृतस्यादिद्घृतेन पृथिवी व्युद्यते॥

[कृष्णं - dark and wicked ◇ नियानं - descending as led and ◇ हरयः - distanced in a rapid course ◇ सुपर्णा - the bird *Suparṇa* ◇ अपो - descended ◇ वसाना - with a circular facial opening ◇ दिवम् - from heaven ◇ उत् - rising ◇ पतन्ति - falling to the proximity ◇ त - as those that ◇ आ - came ◇ व - as ◇ वृत्रन् - the *vṛtrata* ◇ सद् - and from that ◇ अनादृतस्य - those disrespectful ◇ आदिद् - only bestowed ◇ घृतेन - as sprinkling ◇ पृथिवी - the earths ◇ वि - divided ◇ उद् - rising ◇ यते - proceeding]

The bird *Suparṇa* descended from the heaven, after taking off, descending into a circular paths in a rapid course to the successive proximity, bestowing those that got sprinkled as the earths, which came many times divided, rising, proceeding and all the time distancing from those dark and wicked things that stood open mouthed, those disrespectful things that came from the *vṛtrata*.

The bird *Suparṇa* that remained in the heaven, avoiding the things with dark, wicked and attracting openings, flew from the heaven downward and circumnavigated further down, creating many places of divine excellence, gushing forth and sprinkling immortality till this earth. It was the bird *Suparṇa* that remained at the heaven that swooped down and manifested as the universe. It took off from heaven downward and circumnavigated repeatedly and in increasing sizes of circularity and thus created the universe by way of sprinkling several excellences. It became the very universe with its 3-dimensional features. This description somewhat enjoined with the 38th verse by a similarity of action to certain extent. But this verse stated other important matters. What were the things that this bird *Suparṇa* avoided? Those which stood dark, ominous and with entrances that attracted or in other words, what stood with gaping mouths. This description also enjoined with the 45th verse and the suggestion contained here compared well with the "black holes" that the present day physicists proposed. Some of the readers might conclude that this was stretching things too far. The question put to them would be that why the term "*kṛṣṇaṃ niyānaṃ harayaḥ*" came here at all? All that was stated could exist without these words and would have amounted to be a good description of the birth of the universe, as one of the theories. Besides the term "*vṛtra*" was used in the descriptions. It was a favorite theme of the *Ṛgveda* that the bright paths of creation under the canopy of *Soma* repelled the darkness and kept them at abeyance. The description here clearly had two purposes. One was to present the way the bird flew down to become the universe. The other was to present that this dark phenomenon existed as the very reflection of the act of this bird. What better way to describe an invisible entity than this? Or was it only the darkness that swirled along with the bright paths?

RV1.164.48 द्वादश प्रधयश्चक्रमेकं त्रीणि नभ्यानि क उ तच्चिकेत।
तस्मिन्त्साकं त्रिशता न शङ्कवोऽर्पिताः षष्टिर्न चलाचलासः॥

[द्वादश - with 12 ◇ प्रधय - segments; as expanded ◇ चक्रम् - a wheel ◇ एकं - from one ◇ त्रीणि - as three ◇ नभ्यानि - hubs etc. side by side ◇ क - whatever ◇ उ - firmed up ◇ तद् - from that ◇ चिकेत - appropriately ◇ तस्मिन् - from those ◇ साकं - simultaneously, along with that ◇ त्रिशता - 300 ◇ न - as ◇ शङ्कवो - the pegs ◇ अर्पिताः - fixed ◇ षष्टिः - 60 ◇ न - as ◇ चला - moving ◇ चला - and moving ◇ सः - like that]

A wheel as an expanded shape with 12 segments, starting with three that got firmed up on the hub, which stood side by side, appropriately conceived with 300 peg points, using 60 pegs which would get positioned, moved, again would get positioned and in such a way, be executed suitable for the oblations.

Some of the descriptions of this *citi*, which had a close resemblance to the *rathacakraciti* were made with the verses 11th to 14th. Some more descriptions were added here, which for some reasons did not get placed earlier and together. From the earlier descriptions, it was clear that this should represent the 7 *vyāhṛtis* by shape. It was also stated that this would have 12 spokes and the 7 annular rings to represent the 7 *vyāhṛtis*. Out of the 7, the innermost one would be solid and the spokes were supposed to commence from its outer periphery. If so, each spoke would have 6 segments, but the earlier verse stated that the spokes would have only 5 segments. It was also pointed out that if the central space representing the heaven were constructed small and if the spacings of 1 *puruṣaṃ* started from its edge, as per the basic format, neither the spokes could take off effectively, nor there would be enough space for the functions of the oblations. Besides the overall size was conceived as 720. Therefore the second annular ring and the first circular disc would be near and adjacent, almost merging and measuring as limited to a radius of 1 *puruṣaṃ*. This would also agree with the statement of "*pañcāre cakre*" that was made earlier.

The number of pegs and peg points mentioned would surely indicate the methodology of construction. The 3 × 5 segments of the spokes and their 4 pegs each would make the count of 60. This would be expected to provide the format of a quarter of the wheel. It appeared that some shifting of the pegs would be necessary, which in any way was proposed. The most interesting statement would be that the total number of such peg points would come to 300. This in other words meant that there would be no peg in the very centre, since if it was, the total would have been an odd number. But this agreed with the general approach of the Vedic people which avoided perfect circles, and perhaps even precise centres. This philosophy in approach would be found repeated in the sophisticated configuration of the *rathacakraciti* described by *Baudhāyana*. In order to catch up with the statement of 300 peg points, the tabulation given here would help.

Table 6.1: Table of Pegs

1	Spoke segments	15 × 4 × 4	240
2	On annular rings	7 × 2 × 4	56
3	As a central square	4	4
	Total		300

Therefore without any particular centre, a small square would be executed first. Its diagonals extended would be the lines that demarcate the quarter segments. On these, as on a single line 14 peg points would come. The enclosed visual would make the altar shape sufficiently clear. Obviously the annular segments would not be exactly circular. The use of stone and dust were indicated earlier, to smooth-en the shape and perhaps fill the gap between the first disc and second annular ring.

It was possible that the intention here was a general and yet accurate presentation of the *citi* and we would observe

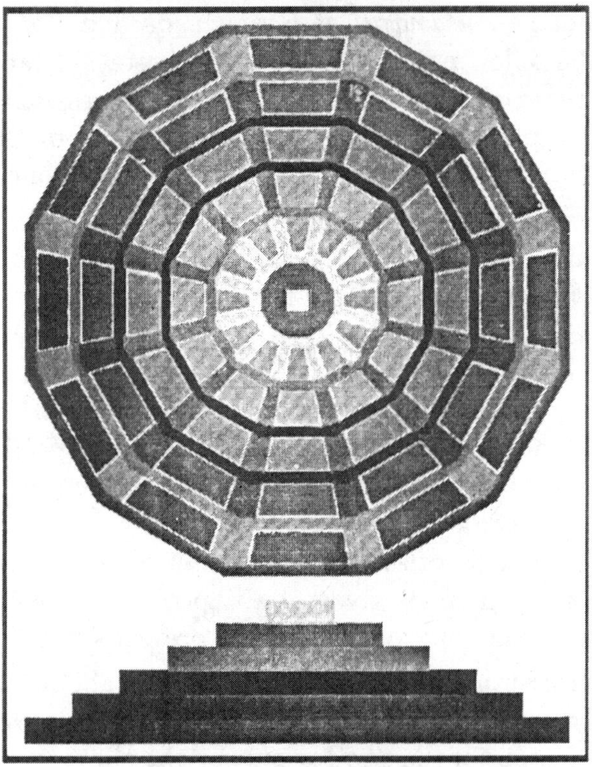

Figure 6.1: The Altar of RV1.164

that it did not come up to the standards of accuracy and descriptive content of the later *śulbasūtra*. The *rathacakraciti* of *Baudhāyana* while followed the same approach of a basic small square in the centre, touched the zenith of perfection and style. At the same time it should be pointed out that his style, language and terminology were somewhat similar to the Vedic text.[6] Perhaps here we might be seeing an early stage of geometry and mathematics, though it could not be over emphasized as this would not agree with the statement of 7, 21 and 101 that had already occurred in several places in the *Ṛgveda*, and which have to be construed to belong to a higher level of geometry and arithmetic. These conclusions could be

[6]Just the impression gathered by the author

drawn from the *śulbasūtras* of *Baudhāyana* and *Kātyāyana*. Besides, the following account of a interpretation variant of the same verse would reveal a stunning cleverness and accuracy of the geometry and its prevalent status during the very Vedic period, which would appear to set aside the conclusions drawn on the basis of this *citi* alone.

Though a *citi* with the above details appeared to be accurate, a nagging doubt would still persist. Because the term "*trīṇi nabhyāni*" did not get sufficiently represented in the above accounts. The use of various numbers such as 3, 12, 20, 100, 300, 60, 720 etc in the verses RV1.164.11 and RV1.164.48, pointed to a work out of $(300+60)\times60\times60\div12 = 108,000$. Did it indicate the secrets of the concept of 7.5 *puruṣaṃ* and 108,000 square *aṅgulam* in any way? Possibly yes. A presentation of some of the many geometry that appeared in the *Ṛgveda* is given at Chapter-9 and would also discuss the geometry proposed by the present verse.

After presenting some common theories about the creation that were prevalent in those times and after furnishing some more details of the circular *citi*, by the above verses, the narration now turned to the concluding part of this hymn.

RV1.164.49 यस्ते स्तनः शशयो यो मयोभूर्येन विश्वा पुष्यसि वार्याणि। यो रत्नधा वसुविद् यः सुदत्रः सरस्वति तमिह धातवे कः॥

[यस्ते - frothed up from a heap ◇ स्तनः - of a breast ◇ शशयो - as those that hopped and jumped ◇ यो - whatever ◇ मयोभूर्येन - causing much pleasure ◇ विश्वा - as reaching everywhere ◇ पुष्यसि - as blossomed out ◇ वार्याणि - as the great excellences ◇ यो - whatever ◇ रत्नधा - bestowed as the diamonds ◇ वसुविद् - benevolently ◇ यः - and ◇ सुदत्रः - granted as good gifts ◇ सरस्वति - carrying the juice; like the river *Sarasvati* ◇ तम् - emaciated ◇ इह - reached here ◇ धातवे - as the objects that stood on a string ◇ कः - by whom?]

From what stood like breasts and a fuming heap, those pleasant things that hopped and jumped, whatever reached everywhere, as the excellence's that blossomed out and whatever thus got bestowed like diamonds gifted and benevolently granted, were carried by the juice of the semen virile that flowed like river *Sarasvati*, got emaciated and had reached here as those objects that stood on a string. These were so created by whom?

Who it was that approached a motherhood, imparted afflictions to that heap of potentialities that became the excellence's of the universe that hopped and jumped out of it? Then who distributed these excellence's that came as several benevolences and became the glittering objects of the upper skies and further got carried down up to this earth along the paths of creation that carried the semen virile? Who made this interactive universe which emaciated towards the end verily possible? Who prepared the *Soma* that remained immature into a state of a continuous flow from the heaven along with those created, down and away and until here?

A mature and eager woman-hood, the breasts that swelled with the milk as the nourishment ready to flow, the bewitching diamond necklaces worn around the neck (just below the head and so, heaven) presented yet another visual of a damsel ready for procreation and tending. It was this readiness in conjugation with a divine intervention, that the process of creation took off, manifesting as the universe, interwoven, interactive and which so remained for ever.

RV1.164.50 यज्ञेन यज्ञमयजन्त देवास्तानि धर्माणि प्रथमान्यासन्।
ते ह नाकं महिमानः सचन्त यत्र पूर्वे साध्याः सन्ति देवाः॥

[यज्ञेन - as the *yajña* ◇ यज्ञम् - and *yajña* ◇ अयज् - moved ◇ अन्त - till end ◇ देवा - from the heavens ◇ अस्तानि - smaller ones blown away ◇ धर्माणि - as per the rules ◇ प्रथम - from that came first ◇ अन्य - as the others ◇ आसन् - having taken position ◇ ते - those ◇ ह - distanced ◇ नाकं - as the sky ◇ महि - great ◇ मानः - measures ◇ सचन्त - with the benedictions till the end ◇ यत्र - from those ◇ साध्याः - coming subdued ◇ सन्ति - from the *Sat* ◇ देवः - and the heaven]

Born out of *yajña* after *yajña*, till the end where all *yajña* had ceased, born and having come from those that stood as the heavens, born according to the rules, further having come from those that came first, blown away and much distanced as the great arrangements that came from the heavens and out of the benedictions that got offered, got subdued towards the end and the universe thus came only from those that came just earlier and manifested only from the *Sat* and from the first of heavens.

Perhaps it was not known what existed earlier and also what manifested as the first. But as *yajña* conducted as per divine rules and the repetition of the same, continuous and great arrangements came into the universe till the very end, by which time all *yajña* had ended. In this creation of the universe, there was a chain of manifestations from whatever existed earlier which started in the heaven and the *Sat* and continued till the very end. There were divisions and movements in each instance, just as it occurred from the heaven. Those were the divine gifts that were delivered as per divine rules. That was the manner in which the universe became enormous to bring this earth and beyond into existence. It was the cyclic repetitions of the *yajña* and the heavens that created this immense universe.

RV1.164.51 समानमेतदुदकमुच्चैत्यव चाहभिः।
भूमिं पर्जन्या जिन्वन्ति दिवं जिन्वन्त्यग्नयः॥

[समानम् - equal to and ◇ एतद् - and just as ◇ उदकम् - the water ◇ उच्च - from a height ◇ इति - in many manners ◇ अव - downwards ◇ चाहभिः - sequentially; incessantly advanced and distanced ◇ भूमिं - in the earth ◇ पर्जन्या - from the clouds ◇ जिन्वन्ति - got impelled to the proximity ◇ दिवं - from the heaven ◇ जिन्वन्ति - got impelled to the proximity ◇ अग्नयः - with the *Agni*]

Just as the water that flowed on the earth moving and advancing downward incessantly from above springing out from the clouds to the proximity, from the heaven sprang out (the *Soma*) to the proximity to create the earths and those that sequentially got formed, with the help of *Agni*.

A parallel was drawn between what happened from the heaven and what happened at the earth. In both the *Agni* was found to participate, and both started chain processes of creations. From the heaven, the *Soma* flowed down to become the universe, coming with the *Agni*, to become the several earth forms and this earth was formed at the end of such a chain of events. From the atmosphere in the earth, water got sprinkled downward as drops, upon the advent of lightning. Thus all those created moved downward, possibly meaning by a divinity always remaining above and several bright objects got positioned below the heaven and above the earth.

Both the flow of the *Soma* from the heaven and the water from the clouds had the benefit of the participation of *Agni*. If it was a series of oblations that happened from heaven which extended everything downwards, it was the lightning that brought about the rainfall. Just like the lightning, the path of creation had that brilliance, divided and emaciated structure. Both descended by the will of God and both spread as per His wishes.

RV1.164.52 **दिव्यं सुपर्णं वायसं बृहन्तमपां गर्भं दर्शतमोषधीनाम्।
अभीपतो वृष्टिभिस्तर्पयन्तं सरस्वन्तमवसे जोहवीमि॥**

[**दिव्यं** - the divine ◇ **सुपर्णं** - *Suparṇa* ◇ **वायसं** - led and assembled ◇ **बृहन्तम्** - till the enormous ends ◇ **अपां** - downward ◇ **गर्भं** - from its egg ◇ **दर्शतम्** - as the visibilities ◇ **ओषधीनाम्** - and the plant kingdom ◇ **अभीपतो** - descending to the proximity ◇ **वृष्टिभिः** - also sprinkling ◇ **तर्पयन्तं** - as the satisfactions that came till the ends ◇ **स** - as ◇ **रस्वन्तम्** - the juice that came till the end ◇ **अवसे** - without stopping ◇ **जोहवीमि** - as the sequential oblations established]

That divine bird *Suparṇa* which remained at the heaven led and assembled this body, as that which came from an egg, to be the visibilities that came up to the plant kingdom, descending to the proximity and also sprinkling those satisfactions that came till the end, carrying the juice and semen virile, while the sequential and non-stop oblations established everything in the universe.

More than one concept was presented here. That beautifully winged *Suparṇa* which remained at heaven flew down till earth sprinkling the objects both visible and invisible. The universe was thus set up, instantly. It was as if that bird carried the semen virile till this earth which swept over the flora and fauna of this earth and remained here for ever. In other words and apparently, it was that bird that brought down the *Soma*. The *Soma* flowed down and away from the heaven creating several distinct paths of creation. It was also said that the universe was established by a series of oblations and with the aid of *Agni*. This sprinkled the objects and entities visible and invisible. It was also conceived that the universe appeared to have a road map of progress of that heavenly tree with beautiful branches that spread much and extended much deep. The trees and the flora of this earth got constantly replenished from the *Soma* existing as an unseen plenum. Just as there were the visible objects, the invisible ones also came into existence. The description of *garuḍa* carrying the *amṛt* down to earth as described in our mythology appeared to come out of this and similar narrations.

This last verse appeared to glide over several theories, not particularly insisting on a single sequence of presentation. Here we could see the bird *Suparṇa*, the tree with the branches spread, the *Soma* that flowed, the *Agni* and the oblations. An all important question of the first appearance of life forms in the universe got answered as one that *Suparṇa* brought until the flora and fauna. The verse also suggested that this very hymn altogether have such a structure of interspersed ideas. Just as the universe that came with interspersed entities and with different schemes of sharing power.

Known as the *asyavāmīyasūktaṃ*, this collection of verses was termed by many as one of the most sophisticated presentations of the *Ṛgveda*. It has several constructional features which might be found unique, though perhaps might also be consistent with other parts of the enormous text of the *Ṛgveda*. Many of the verses had two components and at times two streams of ideas that were expected to merge or cascade. This in a way represented the very interspersed and interlaced universe that it tried to present. This collection of verses also presented the geometry of an altar comparable to the *rathacakraciti* of later times.

An acknowledgment that different theories existed regarding the birth of the universe was not only interesting, but highly educative to those who try to understand the *Ṛgveda*. Here it was stated that at least 4 theories co-existed in the Vedic times. The collection as a whole seemed to present all these 4 in turn. Perhaps the verses 20, 21 and 22 required some special mention. At first the verse presented the biological approach, and introduced the *annabhāva*. The biological angle itself was presented as the tree that stood at heaven and as the birds that trotted along the tree. Verse 21 almost suggested that the very bird *Suparṇa* got transformed as the universe. Carefully selected objects and living things appeared to be the favorite subjects for metaphors of narration. The cow that longed for its off-springs and the raging bull that stood majestically making lowing sounds were thus made capable to represent the hidden and obvious desires of the process of creation. Altogether in many places in this hymn, there was a smooth transition of theories. As it touched many aspects of the creation of the universe, it had the look of an overall appraisal of existing theories, but indeed as an independent and sophisticated presentation of complex phenomena, all by itself. The 46th verse would appear like a brief tabulation of these theories. The darkness that was mentioned here appeared to be different, since specific terms were used to denote the "opening that attracted" etc. Many statements of these dark and evil forces could be found in many places in the *Ṛgveda*, the hymn RV1.032 of *Hiraṇyastūpa* being a good example. ⋆⋆⋆

7

Other Ṛgveda Mantras on Cosmology

The *mantras* that came to us from a very long past and held much in reverence were also found to be serene descriptions of the creation and existence of the universe. It was indeed possible that there would be parallel sets of other meanings for these *mantras* presented here; but it so happened that this study was more focused on the physical manifestations of creation.

RV 1.99

It is unusual that a hymn consisted only of one single verse and this is but such a one, very much dear to many of us. Obviously it must have been considered not only auspicious but significant as well.

[(1) एकर्चस्यास्य सूक्तस्य मारीचः कश्यप ऋषिः। अग्निर्जातवेदा अग्निर्वा देवता। त्रिष्टुप् च्छन्दः॥]

RV1.99.01 जातवेदसे सुनवाम सोममरातीयतो नि दहाति वेदः
स नः पर्षदति दुर्गाणि विश्वा नावेव सिन्धुम् दुरितात्यग्निः॥

[जातवेदसे - by the *Jātavedas* ◇ सुनवाम - with rejuvenated powers ◇ सोमम् - as the *Soma* ◇ अराति - till nothing was bestowed ◇ इयतो - as spread ◇ नि - to below ◇ दह - getting burnt ◇ अति - greatly ◇ वेद: - as properties ◇ स - along with ◇ न: - as ◇ पर्षद् - as showered from a bunch of grass ◇ अति - greatly ◇ दुर्गाणि - as a set of forts ◇ विश्वा - reaching everywhere ◇ नाव - a boat ◇ इव - like ◇ सिन्धुम् - flowing ◇ दुरित - those that came out of afflictions ◇ अत्यग्नि - great *Agni*]

The universe appeared like a highly protected set of fortifications, spreading till nothing was further bestowed, created by *Jātavedas* out of a rejuvenated *Soma*, with properties obtained by extreme afflictions. Objects got showered as if from a bunch of grass, created by high degrees of burning brought by the *Agni* and those that came like the boats floated down and reached everywhere. Thus the universe was comparable to a wheel with large spokes and a rim that stood as a fortification.

The universe came into being as phenomena that could only be termed as extreme. The term "*jātaveda*" which generally meant to be the *Agni* could have an extent of meanings more than that. The description here likened the shape of the universe to that of the chariot wheel of a very large size with a number of spokes. This comparison was often resorted to when the universe was intended to be presented as a highly protected place. It should be presumed that the annular rim was likened to the walls of a fortification and the likening could be to the universe as a whole but more likely to a stages of expansion.

It was from the *Soma* and upon the advent of the *Agni* and the onset of a set of afflictions that the creation of the universe commenced. There was a high level of burning as the objects and energy poured out and flowed downwards. Those objects showered down from the paths of creation which stood like a bunch of grass. The flow of matter like boats docking to several places en-route reached up to the very end of the universe. The *Soma* that remained at the *hiraṇyagarbha* for an unknown period not only provided the first objects and energy of creation but flowed along with the objects downward and up to the very end of the universe and remained potent for all times to come. The *Soma* remained an invisible brightness and a transparency that contained the *bījasatta* for creation and so it stood for ever. It was an intense burning activity that defined the birth of the objects and energy of the universe.

The matters presented here was nothing new in comparison to many similar presentations elsewhere in the Veda. However, there were two aspects of this hymn which appeared to have been meant to be impressed upon. One was that whatever happened was with extreme intensity and the other was the detailed consideration of the term "*jātaveda*". The process of creation that ensued ever since the advent of *Agni* into the *Soma* was indeed of extreme severity. The term "*jātaveda*" could be read as those born from the Veda or along with the Veda. The meaning of the term "*veda*" was given as - sacred knowledge, property, goods, etc. However, the meaning that would be most appropriate here would perhaps be the basic cosmic vibration which was termed as the "*śabda*". The meaning of the term "*jātaveda*" thus could not be limited to "*Agni*" but would also therefore mean the space and time and whatever came born. This interpretation of the term "*veda*" as "*śabda*", however, would be indirect. While the *veda* was divine knowledge its physical manifestation in the first of creations was as *śabda*, the fundamental cosmic vibrations. Since the dividing line between this cause and effect could be termed as thin, it was suggested that the term *veda* could be directly read as the *śabda*. Out of the several and very detailed considerations of the different aspects of the creation of the universe that appeared in the Veda, two distinct theories were presented earlier by way of the *puruṣasūktam* and the *nāsadīyasūktam*. While one followed the route of the growth of the universe as one that happened with the *annabhāva*, the other invested all values in the initial *Agni*. Both in a way almost circumvented the root cause and formation of the primary space, time and energy.

As the entire *Ṛgveda* could be construed as providing various definitions of that Supreme Divinity proper, the question that whether the term "*jātaveda*" was a divine entity or was a term of *ādhibhautika* significance might not matter. Here it was the phenomenon that would be considered as the first choice. Thus it was theorised that in order to commence the creation, space, time and energy, the root cause and phenomenon was the fundamental cosmic vibrations that manifested, tending to be a physical entity. It was these cosmic vibrations that were elsewhere described as chanting of hymns, murmur and roar depending upon the stage of creation that was described. Even so, the presence of a divinity proper who was variously described as *Jātavedas*, *Vācaspati* etc. would be found imperative depending upon the descriptive contents of the context and perhaps it was really so meant.

It was often heard that the Veda was only *śabda*. Here it was proposed that the term *veda* had also the definite meaning of *śabda*. Whether such a meaning existed in the dictionary, *nirukta*, etc. or not, it was required here. It was also proposed that its validity will be tested not with meanings set up by later times, but by confirmation or negation of it with the contents of the Veda itself. Or in other words as an internal consistency sought and obtained. At one point of time the anxiety that was felt for communicating the complex notions of creation and existence of the universe was given expression by the *yajña* principles and practices, in addition to the voices of wisdom. But it appeared that the words that "the Veda was only *śabda*" was uttered in frustration and despair, if not then, at a later time. A command could have been issued that let the Veda be maintained at least as the *śabda* and it was this command that we saw carried out fervently ever since. On the other hand, the creative genus of the *śabda* or the primordial cosmic vibrations not only manifested as the properties and objects of the universe, but could manifest before us again in like fashion to come up as new properties and new streams of creations.

A modern thought that whether the process of creation of the universe started as a speck in a divine consciousness or as a physical entity in the form of a speck of matter and energy was perhaps nothing new and had been critically studied by the Vedic sages. The *śabda* was extolled ever since and by the time it reached us and by now became a simple statement that the Veda is *śabda*. Perhaps no other voice came to us as fervently and as forcefully as this. In all these contexts the term could be either the cause or the effect, but essentially only denoted by "*jātaveda*" as such. It could be assumed that it was for this special reason and by way of providing a platform for discussion that this hymn contained only just one verse. The need might also have been severe, just as the severity of occurrences expressed by the verse.

RV 1.89

[(10) एकोननवतितमं सूक्तं (1 - 10) दशर्चस्यास्य सूक्तस्य राहूगणो गोतम ऋषिः। विश्वे देवा देवताः। (1 - 5, 7) प्रथमादिपञ्चर्चां सप्तस्याश्च जगति (6) षष्ठया विराड्स्थाना (8 - 10) अष्टम्यादितृचस्य च त्रिष्टुप् छन्दांसि॥]

RV1.89.01 आं नो भद्राः कृतवो यन्तु विश्वतोऽदब्यासो अपरीतास उद्भिदः। देवा नो यथा सदमिद् वृधे असन्नप्रायुवो रक्षितारो दिवेदिवे॥

[आ -manifested ◇ नो -as ◇ भद्राः - an auspicious benevolence ◇ कृतवो - having created to the proximity ◇ यन्तु - guided; regulated ◇ विश्वतो - as reaching everywhere ◇ अदब्यासो - incessantly ◇ अपरीतास - irresistibly ◇ उद्भिदः - burst forth ◇ देवा - from heavens ◇ नो - as ◇ यथा - duly coming ◇ सदम् - for ever ◇ इद् - only ◇ वृधे - getting enlarged ◇ असन् - and remained ◇ न - as ◇ प्रा - coming to the surroundings ◇ युवो - youthful things; stood together ◇ रक्षित - protected ◇ अरो - speeding from ◇ दिवेदिवे - as heavens and heavens]

An auspicious benevolence manifested and those that came

created reached everywhere below irresistibly bursting forth and incessantly coming from many heavens, to be here for ever. Upon getting enlarged with those youthful things that came to the surroundings, all remained protected, speeding from the heavens and heavens.

Those excellence and benevolence manifested by getting created in a regulated manner, incessantly and irresistibly reaching everywhere, were speeding from the heavens and heavens. An incessant process of creation started from the heaven, shining objects exploded into the surroundings, the groups of such objects stood together and the universe expanded to the ends until nothing further was generated. The heavens manifested from the heavens and the excellence and benevolence spread everywhere by fording distances in a protected manner and the universe came into existence in a regulated fashion. As a series of unbroken events, an enormous space came into existence with many a shining object. As a process that cyclically got repeated, the universe grew with many heavens and many objects that were still capable of producing.

RV1.89.02 देवानां भद्रा सुमतिर्ऋजूयतां देवानां रातिरभि नो नि वर्तताम्। देवानां सख्यमुप सेदिमा वयं देवा न आयुः प्र तिरन्तु जीवसे॥

[देवानां - from heavens, moved as ◇ भद्रा - the protected excellences ◇ सुमतिः - and benevolence ◇ ऋजूयतां - directly manifested and progressed ◇ देवानां - from heavens, moved ◇ रातिः - generously; graciously ◇ अभि - advanced ◇ नो - as ◇ नि - to below ◇ वर्तताम् - and so remained ◇ देवानां - from heavens, moved ◇ सख्यम् - with friendship ◇ उप - to below ◇ सेदि - emaciated; exhausted ◇ मा - arrangements ◇ वयं - of the body that ◇ देवा - from the heavens ◇ न - as ◇ आयुः - extended ◇ प्रति - in all directions ◇ रन्तु - in paths ◇ जीवसे - successfully remained]

The protected excellences moved from the many heavens, the benevolences manifested directly and progressed from the many heavens. A generosity and graciousness got advanced, descended and so remained. A friendship moved from the many heavens, many arrangements of emaciation occurred and the body of the universe manifested from the many heavens with the paths of creation getting extended from such heavens and the universe remained successful for ever.

As the excellence and benevolence that moved and directly progressed from the heavens, and as those that progressively forded away till the end, the universe came into existence. Thus acceptable entities that stood in friendship moved from the heavens, as an existence of those that remained well connected to one another and the surroundings. Those were arrangements that gradually emaciated and a shining body of the universe came into existence. The hot objects stood their ground along with those that shined sympathetically and thus the universe appeared to have been guided by divine directions. It became gradually emaciated as it enlarged. Those were divine progresses, growths and then emaciation. Those expansions were marked with increasing distances and decreasing densities of occupation.

RV1.89.03 तान् पूर्वया निविदा हूमहे वयं भगं मित्रमदितिं दक्षमस्रिधम्। अर्यमणं वरुणं सोममश्विना सरस्वती नः सुभगा मयस्करत्॥

[तान् - those, moved ◇ पुर्वया - from the earlier ◇ नि - to below ◇ विदा - in principle ◇ हूमहे - as great oblations ◇ वयं - a body ◇ भगं - by *Bhaga* ◇ मित्रम् - *Mitra* ◇ अदितिं - *Aditi* ◇ दक्षम् - cleverly ◇ अस्रिधम् - unfailingly ◇ अर्यमणं - *Aryama* ◇ वरुणम् - *Varuṇa* ◇ सोमम् - the *Soma* ◇ अश्विन् - *Aśvin* ◇ आ - coming as ◇ सरस्वती - *Sarasvati* ◇ नः - as ◇ सुभगा - well being ◇ मयस्करत् - as great pleasures]

The body of the universe came as those that moved from what earlier existed, by great oblations and in principle by manifesting cleverly and unfailingly, with the *Soma* flowing down like the river *Sarasvati* to become a great well being and pleasure that was brought about by *Bhaga*, *Mitra*, *Aditi*, *Aryama*, *Varuṇa* and *Aśvin*.

Thus it came beautiful, friendly, intimate and came unfailingly from the *Soma*. Getting divided, spreading and moving over the roaring waves of the cosmic ocean, manifesting from the divine sounds and cosmic vibrations, became a great coexistence. What existed earlier as the *Soma* in the heaven, by the divine oblations manifested as this structured universe, in 3 dimensions. As the incessant steps of creation, the paths of creation containing the semen virile flowed down to bring about the many forms of happiness and pleasures around. An error free cleverness thus created everything. As a divine wish, the sounds and the primordial cosmic vibrations appeared whenever and wherever necessary. Those paths of creation appeared like the river *Sarasvati*, that which distributed the good things around and along its journey.

RV1.89.04 तन्नो वातो मयोभु वातु भेषजं तन्माता पृथिवी तत् पिता द्यौः। तद् ग्रावाणः सोमसुतो मयोभुवस्तदश्विना शृणुतं धिष्ण्या युवम्॥

[तन्नो - from That ◇ वातो - moved those (as if by a wind) ◇ मयोभु - pleasantly ◇ वातु - moved strongly ◇ भेषजं - a magic potion ◇ तन् - from That ◇ मा - as an arrangement ◇ ता - of those coming as ◇ पृथिवी - the earths ◇ तत् - from That ◇ पिता - came swelling ◇ द्यौः - as the heavens ◇ तद् - from That ◇ ग्रावाणः - as the mountains ◇ सोम - the *Soma* ◇ सुतो - having squeezed out ◇ मयोभुवः - magically originated ◇ तद् - those ◇ अश्विना - having come spread and divided ◇ शृणुतं - with prayers ◇ धिष्ण्या - and an intellect ◇ युवम् - joined]

From That got strongly moved and came those, carried by a wind and as a magic potion that pleasantly flowed. From That came an arrangement of those that manifested swelling from the heavens. From That came the earths, from That came the mountains and all those that manifested upon getting squeezed out of the *Soma*. Those that magically originated from the combined manifestation of the divine prayers and an intellect, came divided and spread to reach everywhere.

From the heaven, from the *Sat* and from the *Soma*, the stages of creation emanated and those were later repeated several times to the surroundings and to below from the points of creation that repeatedly manifested. As a magic potion, that would sustain life the *Soma* flowed down along with those that were created. Those paths of creation got divided several times. As the heavens that manifested from the heavens, the creation progressed with the paths taking off and branching away from those new heavens. The mountain like abodes of those created got formed around each of those heavens. Those were the shapes that got formed from the heaven to the next of heavens. Those were the conic bulk containers of those created which stood around. Yet these processes were attributable to the presence of a divine mind, intellect and the primordial cosmic vibrations.

The essential elements of creation in the form of a fatherhood, a motherhood, the womb as the heaven and the *hiraṇyagarbha*, the space to grow as the atmosphere, the semen virile in the form of the *Soma* were apparently mentioned here. However, "nature" and the "*Agni*" could also be identified as the motherhood of creation from many a description. The overall shape of growth from the points of creations was compared to mountains or conic sections with their apex at the heaven, just short of the epicentre in the beginning and later several of these taking off from such centres of origin, in multiple directions. There were several repetition of this process. An unseen wind blew through the *Soma* as the forces that would propagate the objects to wherever necessary.

RV1.89.05 तमीशानं जगतस्तस्थुषस्पतिं धियंजिन्वमवसे हूमहे वयम्। पूषा नो यथा वेदसामसद् वृधे रक्षिता पायुरदब्धः स्वस्तये॥

[तम् - emaciated ◇ ईशानं - supremacy as moved ◇ जगतः - as those born, progressed ◇ तस्थुषः - risen from those which stood ◇ पतिं - fallen ◇ धियंजिन्वम् - energizing meditation ◇ अवसे - that moved without remaining ◇ हूमहे - as great oblations ◇ वयम् - a body ◇ पूषा - purified and classified ◇ नो - as ◇ यथा

- coming with corresponding ◇ वेद - properties ◇ साम - that moved equally ◇ सद् - from *Sat* ◇ वृधे - enlarged; grew ◇ रक्षिता - guarded ◇ पायुः - protected ◇ अदब्धः - uninterrupted ◇ स्वस्तये - to a state of tranquility]

A supremacy went on getting emaciated, those born and progressed rose and fell from those that had already come into existence and those moved on without stopping. They were duly energized by meditation and the great oblations that occurred. The body of the universe manifested as those that got purified and classified into appropriate properties, growing equally from the *Sat* to become a well guarded and well protected state and uninterruptedly manifesting to a state of ultimate tranquility.

Before the commencement of the creation, a state of inaction and immobility existed, which was also stated as "non-existence". The invigorating thoughts of an unseen divine mind then manifested and great oblations ensued which enlarged the body of the universe from the *Sat* and an embryonic state. Objects got moved as if by a downward draught of a wind and made this filtered, cleansed and protected universe. What came into existence was found to have come as a continuous flow of protection extended from the heaven till far away. In these processes, rising, falling, speeding, remaining, fading, cleansing and filtering took place as required. What was so static and immobile earlier, became a dynamic order. Well protected by the heaven above, the explosive growth then settled down to a stable state. Thus it was that a delivery got metered out from divine knowledge by a divine intellect. Since it was claimed to have reached a final state of tranquility, it would follow that the movement that we see around us, in the high skies or on the surface of our earth did not constitute the definitions of that perpetual dynamic order and the everlasting time-space correspondence. Those movements that we see would not disturb those early and fundamental definitions.

RV1.89.06 स्वस्ति न इन्द्रो वृद्धश्रवाः स्वस्ति नः पूषा विश्ववेदाः।

स्वस्ति नस्तार्क्ष्यो अरिष्टनेमिः स्वस्तिनो बृहस्पतिर्दधातु॥

[स्वस्ति - stable; calm ◇ न - as ◇ इन्द्रो - *indrata* ◇ वृद्धश्रवा - coming with great speed ◇ स्वस्ति - stable; calm ◇ नः - as ◇ पूषा - cleansed and segregated ◇ विश्ववेदाः - property that reached everywhere ◇ स्वस्ति - stable; calm ◇ नस्त - a hole or gap ◇ क्ष्यो - what remained ◇ अरिष्ट - safely ◇ नेमिः - as the rim ◇ स्वस्तिनो - stable; calm ◇ बृहस्पतिः - greatly descending ◇ दधातु - obtained as well decided moves]

From that stable and calm point and from the *indrata* came with great speed. From that stable point, got cleansed and got segregated as the property that reached everywhere. From that stable shining point which stood at the hub with a bore, safely and in a stable way, moved up to the rim, greatly descending with well decided moves and became this stable and quiet universe.

That point referred to as the *Viśvacakṣus* was presented as a stable, immobile and fixed entity around which the universe appeared to form as a *rathacakra*. From the heaven near this centre (or a center somewhere in the middle of the heaven) and from a shining particle of matter and energy, moved everything with great speed and became everything of the universe. The *nābhi* of the wheel formed only with a small gap from this axis. The *nemi* was far away and greatly fallen. The universe thus appeared to be a protected place as originated from this fixed point. Thus the first of *vyāhṛtis* and the hub of the universe was only with a gap from the centre and the rim was much below. Here, the two dimensional *rathacakra* should be visualised but also with a distinct 3 dimensionality, since the rim is very much below. Many of the verses thus had 3 dimensionality packed into the description with appropriate words of suggestion. The description also contained a reference to the mighty bird that once remained in the heaven.

RV1.89.07 पृषदश्वा मरुतः पृश्निमातरः शुभंयावानो विदथेषु जग्मय। अग्निजिह्वा मनवः सूरचक्षसो

विश्वे नो देवा अवसा गमन्निह॥

[पृषद् - as spots ◇ अश्न् - spread ◇ वा - moved by ◇ मरुतः - by a wind ◇ पृश्नि - spotted things ◇ मा - arrangement ◇ तरः - that forded ◇ शुभं - beautiful; auspicious ◇ य - as ◇ अवानो - descending ◇ विदथेषु - from knowledge ◇ ज - born ◇ गमय - as broad paths ◇ अग्नि - *Agni* ◇ जिह्वा - tongues of flame ◇ मनवः - as if ◇ सूर - the Sun-like ◇ चक्षसो - eye ◇ विश्वे - reached everywhere ◇ नो - as ◇ देवा - the heavens ◇ अवसा - without stopping ◇ गमन् - progressed ◇ इह - till here]

As the spots that moved away and spread as if by a wind, as the arrangements of spotted things that forded away, as the beautiful and auspicious things that descended from knowledge, as those born from the broad paths of creation, as the tongues of flame extended from that eye of Sun-like shine and reached everywhere; came all from the many heavens, progressing without stopping till here.

The paths of flames shot out from a Sun-like entity, objects moved away like spots and drops, the heavens stood around and to below and thus the universe grew to its limits. What existed in the heaven got severely pounded and got distributed around as objects, which in comparison with the universe appeared like mere drops. It was a constantly moving enlargement that took place with reference to the epicentre which stood shining like a Sun. While it was a delivery from the heaven, it remained geometrically aligned to the epicentre, called the *Viśvacakṣus*. Thus a set of benevolences came into existence from divine knowledge. The reference to the drops was perhaps meant as the liquid state that most of these originally possibly were. Here, the description covered not only the processes that started from the first of heavens, but covered those that took place from the subsequent many heavens. In the middle and brim of such heavens stood the shining points of origin.

RV1.89.08 भद्रं कर्णेभिः शृणुयाम देवा भद्रं पश्येमाक्षभिर्यजत्राः।
स्थिरैरङ्गैःस्तुष्टुवांसस्तनूभिर्व्यशेम देवहितं यदायुः॥

[भद्रं - from the auspicious ◇ कर्णेभिः - ears progressed ◇ शृणुयाम - with the powers of audibility ◇ देवा - as the heavens ◇ भद्रं - and the auspicious ◇ पश्य - visibilities ◇ इम - thus ◇ अक्ष् - pervading ◇ अभिः - advancing forward ◇ यज - as oblations ◇ त्राः - protected ◇ स्थिरैः - from the firm ◇ अङ्गैः - parts ◇ तुष्टु - satisfactory, happy ◇ वां - propagated ◇ स - with that ◇ तनूभि - parts of body ◇ व्यस्ह - that spread ◇ इम - like this ◇ देवहितम् - as per the will of God ◇ यद् - in whatever way ◇ आयुः - came extended]

From those auspicious ears manifested the many heavens, progressed with the powers of audibility, became the auspicious visibilities that advanced forward and pervaded to become the satisfactory and happy parts of the body that got established. Those got propagated, spread from the protected oblations and became those that got extended in many ways till here; all by the will of God.

It was by the divine sounds in the form of prayers addressed to the self, it was by what was heard in those heavens which acted as the ears, that the many heavens, the splendid visibilities and the paths of creation got established and the many objects propagated to far off distances. Thus the universe came into existence with healthy body parts that moved over the waves originated from respective apex points. And yet it was the will of a Supreme Divinity that made these things possible. From the heaven and that auspicious ear, with the creative powers obtained from audibility, many heavens moved to the proximity and many auspicious visibilities advanced out of the oblations that came along with sufficient strength. They got stationed as those that moved from an axle and from the firm shoulders of the satisfactory stages that later got formed, manifesting several times to provide the parts of the body of the universe. The growth got divided and spread to both sides as per the will of God to wherever it got extended.

The heaven became the auspicious ear since the power of audibility was first experienced there. From that eye and epicentre the visibilities got first born. Out of the *yajñas* the 3 dimensionality was established. From those stabilised and pleasant shoulders of the well established stages, came a body to the proximity and pervaded as per the will of God and just as those came about. It was well known that the first of creations commenced by the divine sounds and the primordial cosmic vibrations that arose as the praises and prayers. Out of those sounds of praise that arrived in the ear (heaven) which made it auspicious, the universe was born by a series of auspicious *yajñas* that occurred. Whatever happened at the heaven that stood near were visible from that eye of the universe. Moreover, the process was repeated from the many heavens that stood around and below. All that were created stood only below and around the *Viśvacakṣus* which saw all.

It was heaven, the first stage of creation that was variously described as *hiraṇyagarbha, mayobhuva, viśvatomukha*, and the golden ear, on different occasions. It was from this heaven that matter and energy of the universe got impelled and pervaded as everywhere. From the heaven, which became auspicious by hearing the divine praises that poured in, and as a result of the *yajñas* that ensued incessantly along, the 3 dimensionality got established and moving in multiple directions, several heavens were born which acted as further stages of creation. From the shoulders of these auspicious stages, creation progressed as it occurred. The principle of the multiple heavens in a hierarchical order was presented by the term "*divedive*" which would appear in many places.

RV1.89.09 शतमिन्नु शरदो अन्ति देवा यत्रा नश्चक्रा जरसं तनूनाम्।
पुत्रासो यत्र पितरो भवन्ति मा नो मध्या रीरिषतायुर्गन्तोः॥

[शतम् - as 100 ◇ इन् - advanced ◇ नु - then ◇ शरदो - as the Autumn season ◇ अन्ति - to the proximity ◇ देवा - as heavens ◇ यत्रा - in how so many ways ◇ नश्चक्र - cyclically destroyed ◇ जरसं - decayed ◇ तनूनाम् - manifested as the body parts ◇ पुत्रासो - as sons ◇ यत्र - how so many ◇ पितरो - as fathers ◇ भवन्ति - became ◇ मा - arrangement ◇ नो - as ◇ मध्या - the middle ◇ रीरिषद् - released and destroyed, became void ◇ आयुः

- got extended ◇ गन्तो - moved till the end]

Advancing by a hundred fold to the proximity, from the heaven till the end from whichever stood like a pleasant Autumn, many ways came, destroyed or cyclically decayed, the body parts moved as sons that were born, many of them becoming fathers and thus several arrangements came to the proximity, in the process of which the middle became void by evacuation. These processes got extended till the end and so the universe came progressed.

The universe manifested with a 100 repetitions of what took place in the first of heavens till the end. The paths of creation shot out of the heavens as a bunch of grass reeds that would shoot out, with bent down ends and dropped the entities like seeds getting dropped. The universe thus became enlarged by hundreds of countless cycles that appeared and emaciated. As the shafts of brightness that shot out to the proximity from heaven (possibly also referring to the *vyāhṛtis*) came the universe, the body becoming faded and emaciated to the ends. The objects born as sons became fathers and produced new ones and ever so many such cycles were repeated, yet progressively got emaciated. In each of these developments and multiplications, the centres of the respective events became empty of matter and became points of merely interactive influence. This almost conformed with the meaning of the term "*sāśanānaśane*" mentioned in the *puruṣasūktaṃ*, where "*naśane*" was interpreted as disintegration and thereby the emptiness that was created. The universe was thus conceived to have multiple centres of influence spread over the immense volume. The subject of this potential, influential emptiness was not limited to the higher levels of the universe, but was extended everywhere. Besides the words chosen gave the impression that all the sons did not become fathers, but only countless ones really did. All objects and properties did not get divided but many so did.

RV1.89.10 अदितिर्द्यौरदितिरन्तरीक्षमदितिर्माता स पिता स पुत्रः।
विश्वे देवा अदितिः पञ्च जना अदितिर्जातमदितिर्जनित्वम्॥

[अदिति - great; immense ◇ द्यौः - heavens ◇ अदिति - great ◇ अन्तरिक्षम् - atmosphere ◇ अदिति - great ◇ माता - mothers ◇ स - with ◇ पिता - fathers ◇ स - and corresponding ◇ पुत्रः - son ◇ विश्वे - reached everywhere ◇ देवा - from the heavens ◇ अदितिः - great ◇ पञ्च - five ◇ जना - came generated ◇ अदिति - great ◇ जात - born ones ◇ अदिति - great ◇ जनित्वम् - principle of birth]

With great heavens, a great atmosphere, great mothers, likewise great fathers and correspondingly great sons made the universe great, born with the 5 elements of a great birth based on the great principle of birth.

From the one that did not bestow manifesting as the heaven, from the one that did not bestow manifesting as the atmosphere, from the one that did not bestow becoming a mother, manifesting as fathers and corresponding sons, reached everywhere and the universe was born immense and great in these 5 ways and as a great principle of birth that took place.

Here 5 essential elements of a birth (*sṛṣṭi*) was declared. It was stated that when all these 5 elements could be termed great, then it essentially denoted the *ādisṛṣṭi*. Firstly, the seed principle came as the (*hiraṇyagarbha*) that was heaven. Secondly the space into which it gave birth became the atmosphere that extended from the heaven till the earth and was named as the *antarikṣa*. Thirdly, a divinity manifested as the father. Fourthly, the *Agni* and nature as such was the mother and lastly those born as sons came constituted as the universe and as the 5 essential elements of the great *ādisṛṣṭi*. When such 5 great elements got assembled, a great universe was born, which could only be described as the great principle of birth and a great birth that really took place. All of these got manifested from the one that did not bestow for a long time. The verse thus provided or contributed to the meaning of the term " *prapañca*" by which the universe was always known. Further it was also implied that if the term "great" was removed, an ordinary birth or any birth (*sṛṣṭi*) would be defined. Here the term "great" therefore, took the meaning of divinity as such, an immense size or an extremely benevolent and sublime nature as visualised. The etymology of the term "*prapañca*" was made clear and as expressed here, it did not take shape from the 5 earthy elements, that was the usual description. The term "great", therefore, might be construed as the excellence and enormity of the universe. The term "*pañca janā*" was also found interpreted as the 5 elements and the 5 senses, but the descriptions contained in this verse indicated the particular set of meanings that got presented here.

However, the generally well known 5 principles would be indeed relevant if reckoned in appropriate universal measures and dimensions, of which the human realisation might come in the form of the earthly *pañcabhūta*s. The *Praśnopaniṣat* listed the 16 principles by which the universe could be understood, all of these taken to a universal level. In fact, it could be said that the *Ṛgveda* resorted to a description style which derived from the elements of these 16 principles at all times. By whatever means, extent and intensity the Vedic sages realised everything around them including the inexplicable nature of the Supreme Divinity and the birth of the universe, the expressive components of the description would necessarily manifest as the 16 principles which the *Praśnopaniṣat* called the *ṣoḍaśakalā*.

This hymn had found place in the daily prayers of many, from time immemorial and indeed was a beautiful description of creation and existence of the universe. It neither elaborated the intensity of the accompanying phenomena, nor the matter and energy by way of reference to the *Soma* or *Agni* and perhaps not even the very nature of the 5 principles in detail. The creation and existence were not much differentiated. But the geometry of the universe was sufficiently stated and the emptiness that occurred everywhere was confirmed. The interactive universe and its sublime and benevolent nature of creation and existence was however very much visible all through the words. Probably for this reason the hymn was found much adorable. It was also possible that quite a different set of meanings could also be read into the words of this hymn as portions of which are found repeated in the other Vedas as well.

RV 7.41

This set of verses are well known as *bhāgyasūkta*. It could be seen that the description and the subject kept to an elegant style just as the term *Bhaga* indicated and got extolled.

[(7) स्पतर्चस्यास्य सूक्तस्य मैत्रावरुणीर्वसिष्ठ ऋषिः (1) प्रथमर्चो अग्नीन्द्रमित्रावरुणाश्विभगपूषब्रह्मणस्पतिसोमरुद्राः (2 - 6) द्वितीयादिपञ्चानां भगः सप्तम्याश्चोषसो देवताः प्रथमर्चो जगती (2 - 7) द्वितीयादिषण्णाञ्च त्रिष्टुप् छन्दसी]

RV7.41.01 प्रातरग्निं प्रातरिन्द्रं हवामहे प्रातर्मित्रावरुणा प्रातरश्विना।
प्रातर्भगं पूषणं ब्रह्मणस्पतिं प्रातः सोममुत रुद्रं हुवेम॥

[प्रातरग्निं - moved forward from the *Agni* ◇ प्रातरिन्द्रं - moved forward from the *Indrata* ◇ हवामहे - as great oblations ◇ प्रातद् - moved forward from ◇ मित्रावरुण - *Mitrāvaruṇa* ◇ आ - manifested ◇ प्रातद् - moved forward from ◇ अश्विन् - the *Aśvin* ◇ आ - coming ◇ प्रातद् - forward ◇ भगं - a beautiful ◇ पूषणं - well nourished ◇ ब्रह्मणस्पतिं - and greatly descended ◇ प्रातद् - to the surroundings with ◇ सोमम् - the *Soma* ◇ उत - connected to ◇ रुद्रं - horrendous ◇ हुव - sounds ◇ इम - thus]

Thus moved forward from the *Agni*, moved forward from the *Indrata*, the great oblations that were taken forward by *Mitrāvaruṇa*, manifesting and moving forward by the *Aśvins* and coming forward as a beautiful, well nourished universe that greatly descended to the surroundings along with the *Soma* and the horrendous sounds that came with it.

From the heaven and with the *Soma*, horrendous oblations of the self occurred. The universe grew around a shining particle of matter and energy and around the *Agni*. Around the 3-dimensionality that was established and around the matter and energy that came moved with roars, the universe got further expanded. This enlargement occurred around whatever came moved as divided and distributed and whatever came beautiful, well cleansed and filtered. There was movements away from the centre, several branching of all of those that were created and the enlargement continued. The divine sounds and the cosmic vibrations manifested around everything that potentially remained. As those beautiful things moved and as if blown by an unseen wind the universe was continuously expanding with properties getting widely distributed. The universe thus came into existence as several physical phenomena and at the same time was counted as a set of divine occurrences. The horrendous oblations that first occurred became the oblations that spread extensively. Such were the ways the universe manifested and in such ways the divinities appeared.

RV7.41.02 प्रातर्जितं भगमुग्रं हुवेम वयं पुत्रमदितेर्यो विधर्ता।
आध्रश्चिद्यं मन्यमानस्तुरश्चिद्राजा चिद्यं भगं भक्षीत्याह॥

[प्रातः - as those to the surroundings ◇ जितं - conquering ◇ भगम् - beautiful ◇ उग्रं - ferocious ◇ हुव - calls ◇ इम - thus ◇ वयं - a body ◇ पुत्रम् - with offspring's ◇ अदितेः - great ones ◇ यो - somehow ◇ वि - divided ◇ धः - and issued ◇ ता - came as those ◇ आध्र - weakened ◇ चिद् - as if ◇ यं - supported ◇ मन्य - in principle ◇ मानः - as arrangements ◇ तुरः - quickly; promptly ◇ चिद् - as if ◇ रा - bestowed ◇ जा - coming born ◇ चिद् - as if ◇ यं - supported ◇ भगं - beautiful ◇ भक्षीत्या - known as the food principle ◇ ह - distancing]

As those that came to the surroundings conquering, as those that manifested beautiful and ferocious, as those that came upon divine beckoning, a body manifested with great offspring's, got many ways divided and issued out, as those that supported the weaker ones, and in principle as the arrangements that moved promptly, bestowed, born and supported by that beautiful food principle that manifested to distances.

The beautiful body of the universe thus came out of horrendous oblations and conquering around to manifest as the great children that progressed or stood divided, the weak ones getting duly supported. An arrangement of these came instantly, as issued out from the existing or born anew, supported by a divine mind and as those that moved to the distances on the food principle. The contents of the universe manifested in many different ways and with different properties. Thus there were those that conquered, vanquished, and those that greatly moved. There were those that looked weak, the others that supported the weaker ones and still others that became prosperous. Some acquired their properties by new birth while the properties of the others got depleted. And yet others totally disappeared by consumption by still others. Thus came the regal progresses of bright and beautiful objects. Those were the energetic offspring's of the self. It was supposedly a quick progress from one, believed to have remained initially weak and inert in the heaven.

RV7.41.03 भग प्रणेतर्भग सत्यराधो भगेमां धियमुदवा ददन्नः।
भग प्र णो जनय गोभिरश्वैर्भग प्र नृभिर्नृवन्तः स्याम॥

[भग - by the *Bhaga* ◇ प्रणेतः - guided as ◇ भग - beautiful ones ◇ सत्य - from Truth ◇ राधो - issued and stationed ◇ भग - beautiful ◇ इमां - and thus coming ◇ धियम् - from an intellect ◇ उद् - risen ◇ अवा - to the proximity ◇ ददन्न - as bestowed from the bestowed ◇ भग - beautiful ◇ प्रणो - to the surroundings ◇ जनय - generated ◇ गोभिः - progressed and ◇ अश्वैः - spreading many ways ◇ भग - beautifully ◇ प्र - to the surroundings ◇ नृभिः - till man and further ◇ नृ - from man ◇ अन्तः - till the end ◇ स्याम - as the powers that would be; correspondingly; approximately]

Guided by *Bhaga*, those beautiful ones manifested from Truth, got issued and stationed as the beautiful arrangements that came forth, born and moved from an intellect, arising to the proximity, getting bestowed from those got bestowed earlier, as the beautiful ones that spread and progressed to become the beautiful surroundings till man and from man till the end, approximately, as could be reckoned.

As the beautiful excellence's led from the heaven by *Bhaga*, as the benevolences and pleasures that these became, the universe came from the eternal Truth. As the beautiful arrangements that spread and progressed, as the ones bestowed from the earlier ones and progressed, these excellence's were extended till earth, man and beyond man, till the very end of the universe. It was thus the deeds guided by a divine intellect, a delivery from the eternal Truth and manifestation of several excellence's from earlier existed excellence's that really occurred. It occurred as the eternal food principle that came till the earth, which supported the evolutionary cycles. It manifested as ever so beautiful a series of occurrences.

RV7.41.04 उतेदानीं भगवन्तः स्यामोत प्रपित्व उत मध्ये अह्नाम्।
उतोदिता मघवन्सूर्यस्य वयं देवानां सुमतौ स्याम॥

[उत - interconnected ◇ इदानीं - instantly ◇ भगव - glorious ◇ अन्तः - till the end ◇ स्यामोत - apparently as if woven like a net ◇ प्र - to the surroundings ◇ पित्व - swelling ◇ उत - as connected to ◇ मध्ये - the middle ◇ अह्नाम् - instantly (as if days) ◇ उत - connected to ◇ उदिता - as those risen ◇ मघवन् - happily ◇ सूर्यस्य - like a Sun ◇ वयं - a body ◇ देवा - from the heavens ◇ नां - as moved ◇ सुमतौ - with an equitable disposition ◇ स्याम - and strengths]

The universe came into existence instantly, interconnected, beautiful and glorious till the end, as if woven like a net that came and stood swelling to the surroundings, as those that instantly and happily arose like a Sun and as the days that would recur, from the middle of an existing one, moving in an equitable manner, as connected to the heavens and manifesting with appropriate strengths.

Led and delivered as a beautiful body with parts that stood interconnected to one another, moved from the respective centres of creation maintaining their perpetual relations, the universe became a place of happiness, of equitable dispositions and of corresponding strengths. It got established as moved from the heaven, as those which shined like a Sun, maintaining an orientation with the epicentre. The objects moved instantly to distances and took positions in proportion to the strengths with which those were born and broadcast. The entire expansion took place totally interactive and became a happy co-existence. The bountiful gifts that came from the many heavens, maintained their relationship with their respective centres of origin. These cyclic process of creations repeated several times to the surroundings and to below.

RV7.41.05 भग एव भगवाँ अस्तु देवास्तेन वयं भगवन्तः स्याम।
तं त्वा भग सर्व इज्जोहवीति स नो भग पुरएता भवेह॥

[भग - beautiful ◇ एव - only ◇ भ - shining ◇ ग - progressed ◇ वाँ - and propagated ◇ अस्तु - as those came into existence ◇ देव - from heaven ◇ अस्तेन - smote strongly ◇ वयं - as a body ◇ भगव - glorious ◇ अन्तः - till the end ◇ स्याम - with strengths ◇ तं - emaciated ◇ त्वा - from thyself ◇ भग - beautifully ◇ सर्व - as always ◇ इज् - honorably ◇ ज - born ◇ उ - only ◇ हवि - from oblations ◇ इति - like that ◇ स - with ◇ नो - as ◇ भग - by *Bhaga* ◇ पुर - from earlier advanced ◇ एता - approached ◇ भव - occurred ◇ इह - till here]

Those that came into existence from the heaven came only as strongly smote away, progressed only as the shining and beautiful ones to become the glorious body of the universe. With the strengths emaciating to the ends, those got honorably born and moved beautifully, always manifesting out of the oblations. It was *Bhaga* who made those things happen in this way. All got manifested, advancing from what existed earlier and getting created till here.

It was by oblations of sufficient strength that the shining entities came into existence to become parts of the universe which appeared to become a beautiful fortress. It was as if a sublime divinity that existed at heaven moved and spread everything to become this immense universe. In the process, while some of the hot and shining objects remained so, many got transformed to diminished and emaciated states. The universe itself, while very much shined in the central regions, became lean and of lesser lustre in the processes of expansion. The strength of oblations defined the shine and beauty of the objects that were created. It was always a progress from whatever earlier existed to become the newer and later ones. Those objects were the products of oblations that came repeated several times.

RV7.41.06 समध्वरायोषसो नमन्त दधिक्रावेव शुचये पदाय।
अर्वाचीनं वसुविदं भगं नो रथमिवाश्वा वाजिन आ वहन्तु॥

[सम् - equally ◇ अध्वराय - incessantly ◇ उषसो - as those dawn ◇ नमन्त - bowing down till the end ◇ दधि - churned ◇ क्र - extracted ◇ अव् - as satisfactory ◇ एव - only ◇ शुचये - as those shining ◇ पदाय - stages; steps ◇ अर्वाचीनं - from the just earlier ones ◇ वसुविद् - bestowing wealth ◇ अं - moved ◇ भगं - beautiful ◇ नो - as ◇ रथम् - a chariot ◇ इव - like that ◇ अश्वा - moved and spread ◇ वाजिन - energetically, speedily ◇ आ - coming ◇ वहन्तु - indeed bearing a burden till the ends]

As those born equally, incessantly and bowing till the end, churned and extracted as the satisfactory ones, only as those shining stages, as those that came from the just earlier ones, moving and bestowing wealth and beauty, moving and spreading like a speeding chariot carrying the burden, indeed so manifested the universe till the ends.

The universe came from the heaven as if a brilliant Sun had arisen, the rays striking downward at an angle, along with the swirling paths of creations and well piled up stages that expanded to the surroundings and to below. Those were the *vyāhṛtis* that came as rays flashed. Along with came the curling paths of creation from the heaven and several stages of several heavens. The universe was bestowed as a set of benevolences and was made beautiful, by the dawning of new objects incessantly, getting synthesized like butter from milk and remaining interconnected to one another. Those progresses were in clear and swift steps that piled up and matter moved and got distributed in many directions like the spokes of a chariot wheel. The universe finally appeared like a protected fortress. The steady progress was also like the swiftly drawn chariot with horses that proceeded from the heaven till the end.

Here, a reason for the five stages in which the *uttaravedi citi* of the *vaidikayajña* would become more clear. While the five stages are more attributable to the seven *vyāhṛtis*, the paths of creation and the repeated manifestation of objects were also considered to fit into a major pile up of five.

RV7.41.07 अश्वावतिर्गोमतीर्न उषासो वीरवतीः सदमुच्छन्तु भद्राः। घृतं दुहाना विश्वतः प्रपीता यूयं पात स्वस्तिभिः सदा नः॥

[अश्वावतिः - greatly spreading and descending ◇ गोमतीः - progressing from speech and worship ◇ न - as ◇ उषासो - as those dawned ◇ वी - set in motion ◇ रवत् - by sounds ◇ ई - only ◇ सदम् - for ever ◇ उच्छन् - exhibiting great ◇ तु - powers ◇ भद्राः - auspicious excellence ◇ घृतं - sprinkled ◇ दुहान - as those milked out ◇ विश्वतः - reaching everywhere ◇ प्र - to the surroundings ◇ पी - swelled ◇ ता - coming as those ◇ यूयं - by thyself ◇ पात - protecteded ◇ स्वस्तिभिः - as the peace ◇ सदा - that came for ever ◇ नः - as]

Those greatly descended and spread. Those dawned and were set in motion, always getting delivered, exhibiting great powers. From a height and till the end came the auspicious excellence's as sprinkled from those that got milked out and thus reached everywhere. Those that swelled to the surroundings, came protected by Thyself and became the peace that got established for ever.

The universe was known to have dawned and enlarged from the high heaven downward, moving, distributing and rushing objects with gusto and courage to become an excellence and a benevolence, that came and stood for ever. It moved out as afflictions and sprinkling to everywhere and swelled to the surroundings with extreme agitations and yet became a protected well being that came and stood for ever. There never was a hesitation in the progress of growth of the universe and the agitated state was a natural consequence of multi-directional expansion, division and sprinkling. At the end of all these turmoils, the universe came into a great state of peace and well being that manifested for ever.

The universe came into existence from the *Brahma*, got well expanded, the *Soma* got divided and the oblations occurred continuously. A shining particle of matter and energy had manifested, duly enlivened by the *Agni*. The *Soma* got severely divided, the 3-dimensionality got established and the process of creation moved away with roaring sounds. New objects were born while some got destroyed. The matter that moved became the distributed benevolences and well being of the universe. Those became the pleasant existences that reached up to man and beyond. With the hot and bright things above, this earth remained as an object of lesser hotness and with an ambiance that promoted various life forms. The universe thus appeared to be a well protected fortress. With new dawning as well as destruction, the universe expanded as a chariot raced and yet was one that manifested in clear steps and stages. Thus the universe was known to have originated from a great excellence to become several excellences that got piled up, which all co-existed interactive to one another.

RV 10.09

[(9) नवर्चस्यास्य सूक्तस्याम्बरीषः सिन्धुद्वीपस्त्वाष्ट्रस्त्रिशिरा वा ऋषिः। आपो देवताः। (1 - 4,6) प्रथमादिचतुर्ऋचां षष्ठयाश्च गायत्री (5) पञ्चम्या वर्धमाना गायत्री (7) सप्तम्याः प्रतिष्ठा गायत्री (8 - 9) अष्टमीनवम्योश्चानुष्टुप् छन्दांसि]

RV10.09.01 आपो हि ष्ठा मयोभुवस्ता न ऊर्जे दधातन।
महे रणाय चक्षसे॥

[आपो - downward ◇ हि - alone ◇ ष्ठा - got stationed ◇ मयो - as a pleasant ◇ भुवस्ता - space manifested ◇ न - as ◇ ऊर्जे - with energy ◇ दधा - coming into existence ◇ तन - as those offspring's ◇ महे - great ones ◇ रणाय - happily ◇ चक्षसे - from the eyes]

As the most pleasant space that got stationed downwards and far away, and as those great happy entities that got delivered energetically, all came into existence from the eyes that stood above.

Cast downwards from the *Viśvacakṣus*, the primary space of *mayobhuva* (heaven or the atmosphere) came formed. The first form of energy and great afflictions commenced and culminated in the formation of the universe. Those pleasant objects that were created could be seen from the all seeing eye that stood above all. At the same time the flow of the objects could be said to have taken place out of the rigours and afflictions that took place in the heaven. This very process was repeated several times, delivering the objects to the surroundings and downwards from the many heavens.

As another meaning; the flowing water was seen capable of delivering the energy and pleasant things of this earth. The water was termed great due to its ability to deliver energy and life to the surroundings. It sustained the cycles of dissolution and birth of several life forms.

RV10.09.02 यो वः शिवतमो रसस्तस्य भाजयतेह नः।
उशतीरिव मातरः॥

[यो - somehow ◇ वः - like ◇ शिवतमो - the most excellent ◇ रसः - juice ◇ तस्य - from that ◇ भाज - divided ◇ यते - those progressed ◇ ह - and distanced ◇ नः - as ◇ उशतीः - most desirable ◇ इव - like that ◇ मा - an arrangement ◇ तरः - that forded along]

Somehow, that most excellent juice and semen virile got divided, smote down and moved, as an ardent and desirable arrangement of great affections that forded along and distanced till here. The *Soma*, that most excellent elixir ardently flowed down and delivered the pleasant objects of the universe to the satisfaction of all. Thus the creation moved till the end of the universe.

Alternately; whichever, as a juice got well received, whichever got divided as many and were thus born as desired, had come out of water, that eternal motherhood that manifested on earth. Ever since water acted like a liquid and juice that would give birth and sustain many things of this earth. It was the very reason and substance of all diversity seen on the surface of the earth.

RV10.09.03 तस्मा अरं गमाम वो यस्य क्षयाय जिन्वथ।
आपो जनयथा च नः॥

[तस्मा - from that came ◇ अरं - suitably, readily ◇ गम - progressed ◇ अम - with strengths ◇ वो - as whatever ◇ यस्य - efforts; in many ways ◇ क्षयाय - as those emaciated ◇ जिन्व् - recouped; as impelled ◇ अथ - then ◇ आपो - downwards ◇ जनय - born as those ◇ अथा - then coming again ◇ च - and so ◇ नः - on]

From That progressed with suitable strength and powers, emaciated and recouped in many ways, descending, getting born, then manifesting again from those that came manifested; so it went on.

From the *Soma* many came born to below, in great diversity. While some perished or became of lesser values, the others prospered and got regenerated. Sequentially yet instantly, these came from one to become the other and so the creation progressed. The reference could equally apply to the gradual emaciation of the contents of the universe as it progressed outward.

As another meaning; this water appropriately moved, conquered the regions of this earth and became the substance from which many things were born. With a divine intention and desire, the water spread all over the earth and into the immediate atmosphere. The water pervaded through the surface earth and the atmosphere in many ways and acted as a receptacle of the seed principle, as that which promoted the food principle.

RV10.09.04 शं नो देवीरभिष्टय आपो भवन्तु पीतये।

शं योरभि स्रवन्तु नः॥

[शं - an excellence ◇ नो - as ◇ देवीः - a goddess ◇ अभिष्टय - with endearing praises ◇ आपो - descended; downward ◇ भवन्तु - occurred indeed to the limits ◇ पीतये - as those swelled ◇ शं - excellence ◇ योः - somehow ◇ अभि - advanced; to the proximity ◇ स्रवन्तु - flowed compulsively ◇ न - as]

What was a serene and shining excellence, winning over a goddess with endearing praises, descended indeed to the limits as occurred, and those swelled to be many excellences, somehow advancing and compulsively flowing to the proximity.

What was earlier a serene excellence, got divided most violently, descended incessantly, flowed strongly and swelled to become the many excellences of the universe. As if a goddess that stood in the heaven was fondly embraced many excellence were obtained which descended as a flow till the ends of the universe. A serene excellence that remained protected, became several excellences that swelled through the atmosphere and flowed as the paths of creation. That which existed directly below the *Viśvacakṣus*, as the *Soma*, later became the paths and the objects that were created for ever.

As another meaning; the water that existed as a protected excellence became the quencher of thirst and manifested as a basic substance that flowed to the proximity. The one excellence thus became several excellence and a basic source and medium for creation and growth. Flowing downstream and spreading all over, water helped in spreading life forms everywhere.

RV10.09.05 ईशाना वार्याणां क्षयन्तिश्चर्षणीनाम्।
आपो याचामि भेषजम्॥

[ईशाना - a supremacy manifested ◇ वार्याणां - as the excellence's manifested ◇ क्षय - emaciating ◇ अन्ति - to the proximity ◇ चर्षणीनाम् - from the eyes ◇ आपो - downwards ◇ याच् - entreatingly ◇ आमि - fading away ◇ भेषजम् - as a magic potion]

From a supremacy manifested a magic potion as an excellence, that moved and emaciated to the proximity, coming from the eyes (epicentres) and moving downwards entreatingly and then fading away.

A magic potion came regulated by a supremacy and then progressed downwards; the vigour got emaciated and then disappeared totally. Those created descended downwards bowing down entreatingly and as if paying homages to the divinity that stood above. Those regulated supremacy became lesser and lesser in value, as the universe expanded and ultimately was reduced to a state of nothing born further. That magic potion flowed downwards as the *Soma* and that thick flow dwindled as it descended with many branches. That which was found to control, regulate, influence all aspects of creation and act as an answer to all problems as the seed substance, emaciated in the high skies while it progressed.

As yet another meaning; the water became a sustaining magic potion tasting of which made the adjoining fields productive and thus acted as the basic medium that supported all life forms. The association of different elements that would get born as the living things of the earth was promoted by water.

RV10.09.06 अप्सु मे सोमो अब्रवीदन्तर्विश्वानि भेषजा।
अग्निं च विश्वशंभुवम्॥

[अप्सु - as a liquid form ◇ मे - went on exchanging ◇ सोमो - the *Soma* ◇ अव् - that got expelled ◇ र - bestowed ◇ वि - getting divided ◇ इद् - only a ◇ अन्तर् - from the inside ◇ विश्वानि - reaching everywhere ◇ भेषजा - as a magic potion ◇ अग्निं - with *Agni* ◇ च - and ◇ विश्व - as the universe ◇ शं - auspiciously ◇ भुवम् - manifested]

As a liquid form that went on exchanging, the *Soma* got expelled, bestowed and got divided from the inside, reaching everywhere as a magic potion and along with the *Agni*, brought forth the universe as an auspiciously instituted excellent entity.

As water or as that divine liquid called the *Soma*, an elixir got distributed, from the inner regions and until the very end of the universe as a magic potion that moved along with the *Agni*, bringing forth all the benevolences of the universe. Here the comparison of water to the *Soma* got confirmed. Those were declared as alike in becoming the magic potion that spread all over their regimes. For the *ādisṛṣṭi*, it was the *Agni* that caused the afflictions and which manifested as the motive force that spread the *Soma* along with its creations to the very end of the universe. It was the same *Agni* that caused the water to take different forms and spread all over the earth. And it was from water that many life forms took shape and spread. It was into this same water that the seed principle returned, to be reborn again.

RV10.09.07 आपः पृणीत भेषजं वरूथं तन्वे मम।
ज्योक्च सूर्यं दृशे॥

[आप - downward ◇ पृणीत - overflowing ◇ भेषजं - as a magic potion ◇ वरूथं - stationing as protected ◇ तन्वे - parts of the body ◇ मम - by the self ◇ ज्योक् - extending ◇ च - as ◇ सूर्यं - Sun-like ◇ दृशे - visibilities]

As a magic potion that overflowed downward and as the protected parts of the body getting stationed everywhere, the self came extended along with the Sun-like visibilities.

That which overflowed downward like a magic potion, became the protected parts of the self getting extended till the end of the universe with Sun-like entities. The *Soma* came overflowed from its original place and acted like a magic potion, creating several Sun-like shines that were well protected and visible till the end. Thus the *Soma* came as a shining excellence that had flowed downward.

As another meaning; it was long ago that the water descended to this earth from the Sun and acted as a magic potion for creation. This was observed and confirmed by many, after due deliberations. This water that scattered, spread and provided, in the course of a long period, protected its regimes of creation.

RV10.09.08 इदमापः प्र वहत यत्किं च दुरितं मयि यद्वाहमभिदुद्रोह। यद्वा शेप उतानृतम्॥

[इदम् - thus ◇ आपः - downward ◇ प्र - and to the surroundings ◇ वहत - as those carried ◇ यत् - progressed ◇ किं - in all manners ◇ च - and ◇ दुरितं - afflictions and injuries ◇ मयि - magically ◇ यद् - somehow ◇ वाहम् - carrying and moving ◇ अभि - progressed to the proximity ◇ दुद्रोह - persistent and bad mischief ◇ यद् - which ◇ वा - moved ◇ शेप - (thinned) as a tail ◇ उत - connected ◇ आ - coming ◇ नृतम् - as a dance]

Thus as those carried downward and to the surroundings and which progressed in all manners, as the afflictions and injuries imparted, somehow magically carrying and moving and thus while progressed to the proximity, was also found to bring forth persistent and bad mischief into existence, which all came related to one another, and which all thinned like a tail, appearing like the cyclic dances of creation.

The *Soma* moved downward from its place, got subjected to afflictions and injuries, carried persistent animosities, got emaciated in many ways and appeared like a cyclical dance of creation that occurred. Those transformations appeared to take place very slowly, like the small taper of a tail.

As another meaning; thus water flowed downwards carrying and absorbing the mischief and evil as well and appeared like a cyclical dance of creations and transformations. The transformation of water into its different forms like the ice to vapour was described as a slow process and a process which could repeat or even revert. It was compared to a folk dance with hands crossed and moving in circles which would also retrace the steps. The term "*śepa*" was artfully employed here as a technical term, locally formalized, to represent an easily visible acute angle as if the tapering tail of an animal.

RV10.09.09 आपो अध्यान्वचारिषं रसेन समगस्महि पयस्वानग्न आ गहि। तं मा सं सृज वर्चसा॥

[आपो - descending ◇ अधि - from above ◇ आ - coming ◇ नु - only ◇ अच् - moved ◇ आरिषं - manifested as the afflictions ◇

रसेन - as a liquid ◇ सम - equally ◇ गः - progressing ◇ महि - to be great ◇ पयस्वान् - as a concentrated concoction ◇ अग्न - with the *Agni* ◇ आ - came ◇ ग - and progressed ◇ हि - only as ◇ तं - emaciated ◇ मा - an arrangement ◇ सं - assembled ◇ सृज - as discharged ◇ वर्चसा - with great might]

As the afflictions that descended and moved from above, as an elixir and a liquid form that progressed along, as a concoction that was concentrated by the *Agni*, came those arrangements that progressed, emaciated and got assembled mightily discharging from above.

As an agility that was shot out and as a magic potion that flowed downward, the universe came into existence with the help of the *Agni* and manifesting from the *Soma*. The universe came about from the *Soma* as an enlargement with an equitable balance to both sides. The *Soma* was refined and made into a concoction by the *Agni*. In this journey, a gradual emaciation of the space had occurred by the reduction in density of objects and their occupancy. Many objects got enlarged by collision and compounding.

As another meaning; the water that was derived out of the *Agni* flowed and moved and got subjected to pressures, existed in liquid forms, attained depths and yet also got expanded to its vapour state. A process of thinning and thickening always existed. It moved always in one form or the other and thus received the distinction of being unique and immortal.

It was found that this hymn could be interpreted in two levels, one as a description of the *Soma* which participated in the *ādisṛṣṭi* and the other as the water that pervaded all over the earth. The nature of the water was seen reflected in the principle of the *Soma*. Both of these were described as the immense potentiality for creation and sustenance. In both interpretations, the description remained to be general and equal in nature. Both the descriptions were, in a way, based on an *annabhāva* that was most necessary.

The first 3 verses are invoked while taking bath and the hymn altogether would become part of the *mantra* set, meant for purification of water. The fourth verse would be used for smearing the *dhūLībhasma* over our body parts. It could be realised that these functions in a way were retracing the very process of *ādisṛṣṭi*. While water was poured from the head downwards with the above *mantra*, it somehow traced the steps of the *ādisṛṣṭi*, where matter and the *Soma* flowed downwards from the apex. Similarly it could be surmised that the custom of wearing the *dhūLībhasma* with the *mantra* "*śaṃ no devīrabhiṣṭaya..*" could have come to us from the Vedic period itself. This approximately spherical universe has its centre as the *Viśvacakṣus* and all the creations took place slightly away from it and commencing from the *viśvatomukha* or heaven. The traditional concept of the third eye of *Śiva* located at the forehead and above the eye-brows happens to clearly agree with the geometry of the *Puruṣa*. It was from here that the 7 *vyāhṛti*s commenced which was subdivided into 3 each. Thus wearing the *dhūLībhasma* is essentially retracing the concept of the 7 *vyāhṛti*s and its 3 divisions each from the forehead downwards till the feet. Just as the verse stated, one excellence became several excellence's that came descended.

All the hymns interpreted here are also *mantras*, held much in reverence. The common characteristics of these *mantras* were that these were sweet utterances and contained no harsh terms and did not describe events as horrifying sequences. It would appear that many of the present day ritualistic practice just slipped through the periods of the *brāhmaṇa* and other thought and literary forms quite unimpaired or with very less modifications. What was specifically meant here was that certain amount of clarity of the Vedic history could be recognized in these descriptions. ★★★

8

Origin of the Universe-In Atharvaveda

In this chapter, 5 hymns of the *Atharvaveda* are being discussed. The subject of the origin of the universe and the quest for the secrets of nature could be a subject of *Atharvaveda* as well.[1]

AK1.01

[(4) चतुर्ऋचस्यास्य सूक्तस्याथर्वा ऋषि। वाचस्पतिर्देवता। (1 - 3) प्रथादितृचस्यानुष्टुप् (4) चतुर्थ्या ऋचश्च चतुष्पद विराड्उरोबृहति छन्दसि]

AK1.01.01 ये त्रिषप्ताः परियन्ति विश्वा रूपाणि बिभ्रतः।
वाचस्पतिर्बला तेषां तन्वो अद्य दधातु मे॥

[ये - as those ◇ त्रिषप्ताः - 21 ◇ परियन्ति - to the surroundings and proximity ◇ विश्वा - reached everywhere ◇ रूपाणि - a shape ◇ बिभ्रतः - carrying ◇ वाचस्पतिर्बला - by the powers of *Vācaspati*

[1]Though this segment was placed at end of the book, it was actually written at an early stage.

◇ तेषां - and from those ◇ तन्वो - as the parts ◇ अद्य - like that ◇ दधातु - powers obtained indeed ◇ मे - changing hands]

As the 21 (circularity's) that came to the surroundings and to the successive proximity and thus reached everywhere, a shape was carried on by the powers of *Vācaspati*, with the parts manifesting from those already manifested and with the powers indeed went on changing hands.

Thus the shape of the universe manifested as the 21 spacial distributions that came to the surroundings with correspondingly obtained contents and thus got positioned progressively, by the powers of *Vācaspati*. The shape of the universe became 21 circular enlargements from the epicentre of the universe by first taking position as the 7 and then getting split into 21. The commands that emanated from *Vācaspati*, out of his mind and by the powers of his hymns, created the universe. Here and through the earlier chapters like the *puruṣasūktaṃ*, an approximately spherical universe got defined, of which any cross section through the centre would look like 7 parallel circles (*vyāhṛtis*), each again subdivided into sets of three.

AK1.01.02 पुनरेहि वचस्पते देवेन मनसा सह ।
वसोष्पते नि रमय मय्येवास्तु मयि श्रुतम्॥

[पुनरेहि - it was only later ◇ वचस्पते - as the words descended ◇ देवेन - from the heaven ◇ मनस - and a mind ◇ सह - strongly ◇ वस् - remained ◇ ओष्पते - with temperature diminished ◇ नि - to below ◇ रमय - pleasing ◇ मय् - moved ◇ य - and ◇ इव - as if ◇ अस्तु - remained; permitted ◇ मयि - as a conjuration ◇ श्रुतम् - it was said]

It was only later and as a second set of occurrences that the words that descended from the heaven, from a mind, and from those that came strongly and remained, became those with diminishing temperatures, to the extent of a pleasing level, as if a conjuration that came progressed, it was said.

The universe could be said to have come into existence in two stages. First, many heaven like entities were produced as a divine occurrence with the power of the divine words uttered. From those that so came, a secondary process manifested in which from the existing ones and many new ones moved to the surroundings as well as descended and this was then known as the magic that further occurred. In the beginning, extreme heat and temperature manifested as the powers of creation. But in the second set of occurrences, these temperatures came to lesser and pleasing levels. First it was in the mind of the *Vācaspati* that the very thought for the creation of this universe occurred. *Vācaspati* created the universe with his mind energised and hotted up. This was well known and had been passed on as a *śruti* to our times. The very beginning of creation as well as the subsequent events were considered as a sort of magic that occurred.

AK1.01.03 इहैवाभि वि तनूभे आर्त्नी इव ज्यया।
वाचस्पतिर्नि यछतु मय्येवास्तु मयि श्रुतम्॥

[इह - from here ◇ इवाभि - as those advanced ◇ वि - divided ◇ तनु - parts of the body ◇ उभे - to both sides ◇ आर्त्नी - as the ends of bow ◇ इव - like that ◇ ज्यया - with bow string ◇ वाचस्पतिः - moved and descended ◇ नि - to below ◇ यच् - somehow ◇ शतु - sheared ◇ मय् - progressed ◇ य -and ◇ इव - like that ◇ अस्तु - remained ◇ मयि - as a conjuration ◇ श्रुतम् - it was said]

Then what came as the parts of a body, upon getting sheared as if the two ends of a stringed bow, moved as well as descended in such a manner that it was acclaimed as another conjuration that came progressed.

The basic order and shape of the universe was first achieved as 7 *vyāhṛtis* and later those were subdivided and offset symmetrically to both sides to get a larger number of systems in 7 sets of 3. The appearance of this two offsets were as if the two ends of a bow with reference to the arrow in the middle. By this and the previous hymns, it was described that a sort of conjuration took place in two stages. The first was at the heaven, near the very centre of the universe and the second was a set of acts that split the 7 *vyāhṛtis* into 21.

It was from *Vācaspati* that the divine words originated and therefore these events were his own creations.

One could easily observe the ideas that later got ingrained into the Indian traditions such as the $7 \times 2 = 14$ worlds that we would speak about. Without the systematic delineation of the 21 sizes and the circularity concepts detailed in the Vedas and the *śulbasūtras*, this statement would be read simply as 14. Because as per the statement here, the 7 were split both ways into two only. It is true that the birth of the universe was indeed an instantaneous occurrence. But within this very process there was a differentiation of time and space and everything occurred with their own specific dimensions and order. What first occurred was the conjuration at the heaven that set off the process of creation which also established the 7 *vyāhṛtis*. This was followed by the division from the middle of the *vyāhṛtis* and formation of the 21 subsets. These occurred at different levels and for each, there came into the surroundings those specific divine sounds and the cosmic vibrations.

AK1.01.04 उपहूतो वाचस्पतिरुपास्मान्वाचस्पतिर्ह्वयताम्।
सं श्रुतेन गमेमहि मा श्रुतेन वि राधिषि॥

[उपहूतो - beckoned by ◇ वाचस्पतिः - *Vācaspati* ◇ रूप - a shape ◇ अस्मान् - as parts that got blown ◇ वाचस्पतिः - as the words that descended ◇ ह्व - crookedly swirled ◇ यताम् - and progressed ◇ सं - got assembled ◇ श्रुतेन - by the words of prayers heeded to ◇ गमेमहि - moving to great distances ◇ मा - as arrangement ◇ श्रुतेन - of the words of prayers ◇ वि - divided ◇ राधिषि - as delivered from above]

The parts came descended as beckoned by the *Vācaspati*, divine words descended, those paths progressed swirled and crooked, the arrangements brought about by the words of prayers travelled long to great distances; the words of prayers that descended from above which were capable of division, and it was thus that the body of the universe got divinely manifested.

It was the divine words uttered, which came as purposeful set of prayers that caused the creation of the universe. It was a set of swirling actions that descended from the heaven and moved to the distances that brought the universe into existence. Those were the paths of creation that flowed down and to the surroundings. By the divine invocations that came from the *Vācaspati*, what earlier existed was severed into parts and the universe was created there-of. The reason, desire and the resource for the manifestation of the universe thus came from the *Vācaspati*. Without clearly enunciating the participation of *Agni* or the process of oblations, the cause of creation was thus initially posited on the divine entity of *Vācaspati*. This could be taken as not without purpose. It was the favourite theory of modern science that the creation of the universe started in the form of an intense heat that first manifested. From the Vedic period till today, we await with much anticipation for the confirmation whether it was the space or the *Agni* that manifested first. Earlier in this narration, both the theories were presented as the *puruṣasūkta* and the *nāsadīyasūkta*. With the contents of this *sūkta*, the concept that it was the primary cosmic vibrations that first manifested which in turn provided the ambiance and energy for the *Agni* and space to manifest was once again asserted. But significantly, the statement was well connected with the geometry of the universe and the theory was set up as applicable to all stages of creation.

There was repeated references to the *śruti* in the above narration which could perhaps mean that what occurred here was a re-statement of known facts. The word doubled as the sounds and vibrations as well as a reference to known facts. The placement of this hymn as the first one of the *Atharvaveda* could be termed as salutary in nature. The subject has been very much presented through the *Ṛgveda* texts. However, the statement that the systems of the first holocaust were later split in the middle and what got created got multiplied and got positioned, was perhaps a significant statement, though details of this were furnished in the *asyavāmīyasūkta*. It was clear that the seven *vyāhṛti*s were seen as seven circular geometrical sets of notional entities which were later divided and offset to both sides and at the same time were those that retained their relations to the centre. There was a small conflict of interest between this presentation with the 21 enlargements that the *śulbasūtra*s prescribed. In the *śulbasūtra* texts the 21 enlargements were in 7 equal sets of three and the first size of 7.5 *puruṣaṃ* was declared as *prathamaṃ* and the enlargements commenced from there. The term *prathamaṃ* therefore denoted the geometrical first and not the chronological first. The circularity principle has been so much stated repeatedly all through these hymns that no other shape of the universe could be ever thought of.

There was yet another important aspect of the existence of this universe which was somewhat made more clear here. The creation of the universe started from the *hiraṇyagarbha*. Instantly this universe grew and took shape as 7 *vyāhṛtis*. Next, these seven *vyāhṛtis* got split in the middle and became the 21 circularity's. That is, the growth outward was terminated by forces that swept through as to both sides from each of the *vyāhṛti*s. Therefore, there was a second set of inward set of forces and then it was again counterbalanced with an outward set of forces. It was like this that the universe acquired the state of resonance ever since. The universe was therefore, named the *jagat* with the interactive forces and different regions of individual influence coming into existence and individually resonating for ever.

AK 1.32

[(4) चतृचस्यास्य सूक्तस्य ब्रह्म ऋषिः। द्यावापृथिव्यौ देवते। प्रथमातृतीयाचतुर्थिनमृचामनुष्टुप् (2) द्वितीयायश्च ककुम्मत्यनुष्टुप् छन्दसी]

AK1.32.01 इदं जनासो विदथ महद् ब्रह्म विदिष्यति।

न तत्पृथिव्यां नो दिवि येन प्राणन्ति वीरुधः॥

[इदं - thus ◇ जनासो - having born ◇ विदथ - from an existing knowledge ◇ महद् - becoming great ◇ ब्रह्म - and much enlarged ◇ विदिष्यति - knowledge greatly broadcast ◇ न - as ◇ तत् - from that ◇ पृथिव्यां - as the many earths manifested ◇ नो - as ◇ दिवि - heavens; shining ◇ येन - somehow ◇ प्राणन्ति - as those came to the proximity and the surroundings ◇ वीरुधः - moved and positioned as broken into many]

Thus having born from an existing knowledge, became great and got much enlarged by knowledge that got greatly broadcast, manifested as the many earths and the many heavens that moved, as those that many ways came to the proximity and to the surroundings and as those that moved and got positioned upon getting broken into many.

Thus under the great directions of the *Brahma*, many regions were born, getting extended as the earth forms that sprouted from the heaven and which spread to the surroundings. Further, from the potential ones, great expansions had taken place subsequently. These came as divided into several regions of influence and successively populating the proximity and the surroundings. These phenomena prevailed, from the heaven till this earth. Matter was thrown around as if from a sprouting fountain, from each of this locations. Those were the manifestations that came from divine knowledge and as divine efforts.

AK1.32.02 अन्तरिक्ष आसां स्थाम श्रान्तसदामिव।
आस्थानमस्य भूतस्य विदुष्टद्वेधसो न वा॥

[अन्तरिक्ष - the atmosphere ◇ आसां - manifested and positioned ◇ स्थाम - and got positioned as the strengths ◇ श्रान्त - that sequentially emaciated ◇ सदाम् - moved as for ever ◇ इव - in the same manner ◇ आस्थानम् - from those places ◇ अस्य - as those ◇ भूतस्य - born ◇ विदुष्टद् - mercilessly ◇ वेधसो - cutting down ◇ न - as ◇ वा - moved]

When many got strongly positioned in the atmosphere and when their strengths got sequentially emaciated and remained so for ever, from the same points of origin, a set of forces that would mercilessly cut down had also got generated which came moving along with those created.

Upon the formation of the first stage of creation and the atmosphere there-of, the creation progressed further with reducing strengths till the end and so remained for ever. But from the same points of origin, those bad elements that would cut down their enemies had also born with equal might, which appeared to be lying in wait for the weak ones or for the emaciation of powers that would take place.

AK1.32.03 यद्रोदसी रेजमाने भूमिश्च निरतक्षतम्।
आर्द्रं तदद्य सर्वदा समुद्रस्येव श्रोत्याः॥

[यद् - somehow ◇ रोदसी - from the heaven to the earth ◇ रेजमाने - as hot and bright systems ◇ भूमिश्च - as earths ◇ निरतक्षतम् - deeply damaged ◇ आर्द्रं - secreted ◇ तद् - from those ◇ अद्य - as ◇ सर्वदा - issued out to everywhere ◇ समुद्रस्येव - only as an ocean ◇ श्रोत्याः - quickly flowing]

As the hot and bright systems and the earth forms that came into existence in many ways from the heaven up to this earth and as the ones derived by getting deeply damaged and secreting from the existing ones; everything got issued out as everywhere, as if rushing into an ocean.

The primary set of objects came into existence as individual bodies, the groups and the constellations, getting divided repeatedly and from those many secreted to small distances as other earth forms and several other objects. Those objects propagated through the atmosphere which stood like an ocean with waves. All the objects did not move out forcefully to distances, but some of them stood near to their origins with less motive power, as if secreted to the neighbourhood.

AK1.32.04 विश्वमन्यामभीवार तदन्यस्यामधि श्रितम्।
दिवे च विश्ववेदसे पृथिव्यै चाकरं नमः॥

[विश्व - reaching everywhere ◇ मन्याम् - as arrangements moved ◇ अभीवार - consecutive circularity's ◇ तद् - that ◇ अन्यस्याम्

- one after the other moved ◇ अधि - from above ◇ श्रितम् - attached to ◇ दिवे - the heavens ◇ च - and ◇ विश्ववेदसे - as the propertied that pervaded as everywhere ◇ पृथिव्यै - as the many earths ◇ चाकरं - and suitable shines ◇ नमः - bowing]

For the arrangement of consecutive circularity's that came moved and reached everywhere, for those that moved one after the other from above, for the properties that pervaded everywhere attached to the heavens above, for the many earths and suitable shines that manifested, let that divinity be saluted bowing down with utmost reverence.

From that Supreme Divinity that stood above, came the *vyāhṛtis*, came the many heavens that stood below, came the many earth forms and the many properties. From the shoulders of the heaven came those shining objects of the universe, the many paths of creation and several systems of energy. For the creation of the universe, That as the divinity that stood above be venerated with folded hands. The universe then extended and gradually got emaciated to the ends. But more than this, who remained here with his head in the location of heaven, his shoulder as the edge of the heaven and his feet reaching the very end of the universe? Who stood here with folded hands bowing to that Supreme Divinity?

Under the guidance of the *Brahma*, all things of this universe from heaven to earth were born, as commenced from the heaven itself. What was created acquired various positions from the heaven to earth, the atmosphere and the density of occupation gradually getting reduced while so progressing outward. The objects and systems got mercilessly split and damaged in the process. Like this and as secreted from these, several smaller routes of creation and objects got formed. All that were created from the heaven to the very end of the universe, venerated *Brahma* for these divine manifestations.

AK 2.12

[(8) अष्टर्चस्यास्य सूक्तस्य भरद्वाज ऋषिः। द्यावपृथिव्यादिबह्वयो देवताः। (1, 3 - 6) प्रथमर्चस्तृतीयादिचतसृणाञ्च त्रिष्टुप् (2) द्वितीयायाजगती (7 - 8) सप्तम्यष्टम्योश्चानुष्टुप् छन्दांसि]

AK2.12.01 द्यावापृथिवी उर्व१न्तरिक्षं क्षेत्रस्य पत्न्युरुगायोऽद्भुतः।
उतान्तरिक्षमुरु वातगोपं त इह तप्यन्तां मयि तप्यमाने॥

[द्यावापृथिवी - as the heavens and earths ◇ उर्वन्तरिक्षं - as the vast atmosphere ◇ क्षेत्रस्य - as the fields ◇ पत् - descended ◇ नि - to below ◇ उरुगायो - progressed in broad paths ◇ अद्भुतः - miraculously ◇ उत - connected ◇ अन्तरिक्षम् - the atmosphere ◇ उरु - very large ◇ वात - wind ◇ गोपं - that protects ◇ त - those ◇ इह - till here ◇ तप्यन्तां - with temperature till the end ◇ मयि - surprising ◇ तप्यमाने - level of temperatures]

The heavens and earths that got positioned, the vast atmosphere that got extended from the heaven till this earth, the fields that descended to below, the broad paths of progress that came miraculously connected to the atmosphere, the winds that widely spread and the protections that reached till here were all brought about by those different temperatures that reached till the end, which had come from an earlier surprising level of temperature.

At the heaven an enormous temperature of great strength had manifested to form a wide expanse of the atmosphere extending from the very heaven to this earth. This temperature also enabled the movement of the hot objects till the end of the universe. Therefore, the temperature that manifested was capable of two distinct functions; one of providing all the hotness of the objects and those objects that came moved and secondly to create the wide atmosphere itself. The universe altogether appeared to be an arrangement brought about by the heat and temperatures that came in different measures wherever required. Thus it was a wonder that the universe was born in all these ways and yet remained totally calm and interactive. No specific objects such as the earth forms came into this description. There was only the atmosphere, the invisible field forces and the various levels of temperatures. It was theorised that one enormous temperature caused and became the objects and the multiple level of temperatures of everything in the universe. It also brought those invisible field forces as well.

AK2.12.02 इदं देवाः शृणुत ये यज्ञिया स्थ भरद्वाजो मह्यमुक्थानि शंसति। पाशो स बद्धो दुरिते नि युज्यतां यो अस्माकं मन इदं हिनस्ति॥

[इदं - thus ◇ देवाः - from the heaven came ◇ शृणुत - with audibility ◇ ये - whatever ◇ यज्ञिया - *yajñas* ◇ स्थ - got established ◇ भरद्वाजो - quickly spreading ◇ मह्यम् - as great ◇ उक्थानि - as word uttered ◇ शंसति - highly auspicious ◇ पाशो - string ◇ स - with ◇ बद्धो - tied ◇ दुरिते - as those afflictions ◇ नि - to below ◇ युज्यतां - appropriately moved ◇ अस्माकं - as the many parts ◇ मन - in principle ◇ इदं - till here ◇ हिनस्ति - only as the co-travelled]

Thus from the heaven, the audibility manifested and with the many forms of *yajñas*, the universe got established with those that quickly spread and as those that came from the great words uttered, to become the auspicious deliveries that occurred. But along with these came those that would tie down the objects as if with a string and impart afflictions. Thus many parts descended, in principle manifesting appropriately and moving as co-travellers.

While it was the divine sounds of the words of prayers uttered with a pronounced audibility along with the many forms of *yajñas* that everything got manifested as the good things of the universe, along with it a set of miseries also got unleashed which would tie down the ones created and impart severe afflictions. Yet those were only the essential parts of creation and were considered as having come into the universe as co-travellers. While the creation progressed with divine intentions and essentially interactive to one another, it had to face the afflictions imparted along with it. It could be termed, on the one hand, as the knots of responsibility connected to a series of afflictions that commenced from the heaven and on the other, there came those mischievous entities which harmed the ones created. Thus the bad and evil manifested with equal might along with the excellences of the universe. Yet the universe was known to have divinely progressed with a pronounced visibility and audibility throughout its growth. It was the phenomenal and divine cosmic vibrations that enabled everything, including the manifestation in different forms.

AK2.12.03 इदमिन्द्र शृणुहि सोमप यत्वा हृदा शोचता जोहवीमि।
वृश्चामि तं कुलिशेनेव वृक्षं यो अस्माकं मन इदं हिनस्ति॥

[इदम् - thus ◇ इन्द्र - as *Indra* ◇ शृणुहि - indeed well known ◇ सोमप - as the drinker of *Soma* ◇ यत्वा - moved and progressed ◇ हृदा - from the heart ◇ शोचता - as ignited ◇ जोहवीमि - and as oblations ◇ वृश्चामि - set up as desired ◇ तं - emaciated ◇ कुलिशेनेव - only by an Axe ◇ वृक्षं - a tree ◇ यो - somehow ◇ अस्माकं - as many parts moved ◇ मन - in principle ◇ इदं - till here ◇ हिनस्ति - only as dependents; co-travellers]

Thus from the *Indra*, indeed well known as the drinker of the *Soma*, came moved and progressed, the hearts getting ignited, as the oblations that progressed, set up as desired and then emaciated, as if a tree cut up by an Axe and the many parts so moved, all in principle manifesting till here as dependents and co-travellers.

It was with the manifestation of a shining particle of matter in the heaven and into the *Soma* that existed there that the process of creation started. It commenced with the heart that was the heaven being ignited and as oblations that happened to the surroundings. The *Soma* was made into several segments as desired getting segmented as if a tree would be chopped by an Axe and the chips would fly off. The purpose in turn was to state that the growth of the universe would take inexplicable routes from the heaven. But did we see someone appear as the partaker of the *Soma*, as the one who danced with exhilaration, as the one who led the ways? Did we see a cosmic dance of a creator?

AK2.12.04 अशीतिभिस्तिसृभिः सामगेभिरादित्येभिर्वसुभिरङ्गिरोभिः। इष्टापूर्तमवतु नः पितृणामामुं ददे हरसा दैव्येन॥

[अशीतिभिः - with 18 ◇ तिसृभिः - and with 3 ◇ सामगेभि - with *Sāma* songs ◇ आदित्येभिः - as the Sun like ◇ वसुभिः - as excellences ◇ अङ्गिरोभिः - as churned and swirled to both sides ◇ इष्टापूर्तम् - out of satisfactory oblations ◇ अवतु - mightily pushed ◇ नः - as ◇ पितृणाम् - moved from a paternity ◇ आमुं - exciting an unripe state ◇ ददे - continuously obtained ◇ हरसा - energised ◇ दैव्येन - by divinities]

As the 21 that moved, as the *Soma* that was energised by the *Sāma* songs, as the Sun-like excellences manifested, as the paths swirled to the surroundings, as the satisfactory oblations that got pushed to distances, as those born from a paternity and out of an unripe existence after getting energised, as those obtained from those already stationed, this universe came as a divine manifestation.

By the *Brahma, Āditya, Vasu* and *Aṅgiras* and as solemn *yajñas*, a progress occurred as if effected by many divinities, all descending and moving from that divinely shining juice. From a divine paternity, a divine progress occurred as the 7 *vyāhṛtis* and its subdivisions that came descended and moved from the heaven. It was the *sāma* songs that aroused the idle *Soma* to become that divinely shining juice that flowed down. It was by the *Agni* and the oblations that these excellences found the necessary energy to move and transform. In spite of the flying pieces of the chopped up tree and a process commenced though that way, the expansion of this immense universe took place in measured ways and as a calculated progress.

AK2.12.05 द्यावापृथिवी अनु मा दीधीथां विश्वे देवासो अनु मा रभध्वम्। अङ्गिरसः पितरः सोम्यासः पापमार्छत्वपकामस्य कर्ता॥

[द्यावापृथिवी - as the heaven and earths ◇ अनु - and their sub-sets ◇ मा - an arrangement ◇ दीधीथां - of brilliant things that got stationed and moved ◇ विश्वे - reaching everywhere inter-connected ◇ देवासो - from the heavens ◇ अनु - with sub-sets ◇ मा - an arrangement ◇ रभध्वम् - held to and emaciated ◇ अङ्गिरसः - as the juice swirled ◇ पितरः - moved and forded ◇ सोम्यासः - from the *Soma* ◇ पापम् - evil ◇ आर्छत्वं - mischievous nature ◇ प - protected ◇ कामस्य - as desired ◇ कर्ता - coming from the very creator]

When an arrangement of the heavens and the earth forms and their sub-sets came, when the brilliant things got stationed and moved reaching everywhere in the universe, essentially interconnected, whenever the arrangements of those and their sub-sets got swirled from the heavens, moved, forded and emaciated from the very *Soma*, then, from there and along came from the very creator, the evil and mischievous things and those desirable protections. Both of these streams of creation invariably got manifested.

Though the universe came into existence primarily as swelled to the surroundings from the *Soma*, separate sub-divisions had occurred, each under the one above, and there were separate upheavals in each stage. In this process, while some were maintained as it was, the others got destroyed or got mutilated. The universe could only be termed as occurred by appropriate movements and taking new positions and it came as the good deeds and protection offered on the one hand, while on the other and at the same time, manifesting as the evil wandering objects that disrupted these progresses. While the paths of creation, known as pure, took off from the heaven, the darkness and the sinful ones that emanated from it, also inevitably came into existence.

AK2.12.06 अतीव यो मरुतो मन्यते नो ब्रह्म वा यो
निन्दिषत्क्रियमाणम्। तपूंषि तस्मै वृजिनानि सन्तु
ब्रह्मद्विषं द्यौरभिसंतपाति॥

[अतीव - only extreme ◇ यो - whatever ◇ मरुतो - as a wind ◇

मन्यते - considered ◇ नो - as ◇ ब्रह्म - enlarged ◇ वा - and moved ◇ यो - whatever ◇ निन्द् - abhor-able ◇ इषत् - and inquisitive ◇ क्रियमाणम् - processes ◇ तपूंसि - burning down ◇ तस्मै - entities ◇ वृजिनानि - those deceitful things ◇ सन्तु - as the mights from सत् ◇ ब्रह्मद्विषं - that resisted any enlargement ◇ द्यौ - from the heaven ◇ अभि - to the advancement ◇ संतप - scorching heat ◇ अति - great]

Though considered as manifested, moved and got enlarged by an extreme wind, though considered as those abhorable and inquisitive processes and entities that would burn down and annihilate, those deceitful things that resisted all enlargements, yet all of these came as the powers that emanated from the *Sat*, advancing from the heavens and from that phenomenal scorching heat that manifested.

Extreme conditions were the hallmark of the progress that commenced with the manifestation of an extreme temperature in the beginning. There was opposition to progresses and yet objects and powers descended from the heaven, from the *Sat* and from that scorching heat. Those shameless entities and the products of the *vṛtrata* encroached into the paths of creation, hunted down the objects and wantonly destroyed them. Those hateful things acted against all expansions.

AK2.12.07 सप्त प्राणानष्टौ मन्यस्तांस्ते वृश्चामि ब्रह्मणा।
अया यमस्य सादनमग्निदूतो अरंकृतः॥

[सप्त - as 7 ◇ प्राणानष्टौ - as those came to the surroundings and became nothing ◇ मन्यस्तां - reckoned as those manifested ◇ ते - from those ◇ वृश्च - selectively ◇ आ - coming and ◇ मि - getting established ◇ ब्रह्मणा - getting expanded ◇ अया - and moved ◇ यमस्य - as per the rules ◇ सादनम् - as those stood together ◇ अग्निदूतो - the *Agni* as a messenger ◇ अरंकृत - and so stood decorated]

Manifesting to the surroundings as the 7, reckoned as those that came from those, coming and getting established selectively, moved and thus expanded as per the rules and stood together as decorated, were effected by the *Agni*, which appeared on the scene as a messenger.

The atmosphere stood as the 7 *vyāhṛtis* that moved away from the epicentre and got sub-divided into 21. At the same time the paths of creation swirled from the heaven and objects got selectively placed as here and there. All these manifested from the heaven with the aid of *Agni*, which appeared as a harbinger, throughout the process of creation. It was thus that this universe expanded and stood decorated by a divine set of rules.

AK2.12.08 आ दधामि ते पदं समिद्धे जातवेदसि।
अग्निः शरीरं वेवेष्ट्वसुं वागपि गछतु॥

[आ - came ◇ दधामि - bestowed pushing forward, emaciating ◇ ते - as those ◇ पदं - stages ◇ समिद्धे - as equally stationed ◇ जातवेदसि - as the properties that manifested ◇ अग्निः - from *Agni* ◇ शरीरं - as a body ◇ वेवेष्ट्वसुं - interactively coming as desired excellences ◇ वाग् - as words ◇ अपि - to the proximity ◇ गछतु - obtained with might]

Thus came those that got bestowed as the stages pushed forward and emaciated, as those that equally got stationed, and as the properties that manifested from *Agni* to become a body which after repeatedly manifesting, stood sufficiently interactive. All of these were so obtained by the words that came to the proximity to manifest as the desired excellences of whatever might that would be.

It was basically the *Agni*, matter and the space that was born out of the divine words that were uttered and this subsequently became the well beings that got set up, as the contents of the seven *vyāhṛtis*. The interactive nature of all that came to become the universe was instituted by the objects and systems of energy of appropriate properties and levels of intensity. It was a temperature of sufficient magnitude to form the hot objects of appropriate strength and to create the vast atmosphere which enabled the spreading of the objects till the end. And what a wonder it became? All that were created was attached to each other as if tied by a rope.

Upon manifestation of a shining particle of matter into the *Soma* and into the heaven, the *Soma* itself was strewn around and as out of a series of *yajñas*, matter descended to become this vast universe. As if originated from a divine father, and as large upheavals, the 7 *vyāhṛtis* and the 21 divisions were established. Cruelties and forces of destruction which acted against the expansion also manifested with equal might. Still the universe took the form of 7 clear *vyāhṛtis* and its subdivisions which remained in a state of quietude and perpetual resonance. It was the sound and vibrations manifesting as the cause and effect that enabled the creation of *Agni*, space, time and all the contents of the universe.

AK2.35

[(5) पञ्चर्चस्यास्य सूक्तस्याङ्गिरा ऋषिः। विश्वकर्मा देवताः।(1) प्रथमर्चस्यः बृहतिगर्भा त्रिष्टुप् (2 - 3) द्वितीयातृतीययोस्त्रिष्टुप् (4 - 5) चतुर्थोपञ्चम्योश्च भुरिक्त्रिष्टुप् छन्दांसि]

AK2.35.01 ये भक्षयन्तो न वसून्यानृधुर्यानग्नयो अन्वतप्यन्त धिष्णयाः। या तेषामवया दुरिष्टिः स्विष्टिं नस्तान्कृणवद्विश्वकर्मा॥

[ये - those ◇ भ - lustre ◇ क्षयन्तो - emaciated to the ends ◇ वसून्यान् - loosing the excellence ◇ ऋधुः - growing ◇ यान् - lead by ◇ अग्नयो - the *Agni* ◇ अन्वतप्यन्त - with the available heat till the end ◇ धिष्णयाः - with intellect ◇ या - moved ◇ तेषाम् - from those as moving ◇ अव - to below ◇ या - and moving ◇ दुरिष्टिः - with decreasing strengths of oblations ◇ स्विष्टिं - as successful *yajña* ◇ नस् - successively ◇ तान् - thinning down ◇ कृणवद् - moving from a high position ◇ विश्वकर्मा - accomplished everything to its due place]

As those which went on losing lustre while progressed and emaciated to the ends, as those which lost the excellence while moved, the universe grew as led by the *Agni* and whatever available heat, moving intelligently till the ends, and as helped by a divine intellect. Those that came from the earlier ones became a body that was derived in decreasing strengths of oblations and yet as the successful *yajña*s that occurred which while moving from the high positions had successively thinned down and had brought everything to its due place.

Everything came from the *Soma* led by the *Agni* and intelligently devised. Objects took positions as settled down, moved out from there and grew to the proximity and to distances till the end of the universe, as if guided by a divine intellect. Parts were secreted out of the sacrifices and oblations, as the afflictions occurred and thus got gifted to become the body of the universe. Prior to that, the *Soma* that existed was pierced, violated and later made to reach everywhere, taken through the paths of creation. There were several such streams of creation that moved from the heavenly abode of the *Soma* from which matter got moved. All occurred as directed by the *Viśvakarma*, as if led by the nose ring.

AK2.35.02 **यज्ञपतिमृषय एनसाहुर्निर्भक्तं प्रजा अनुतप्यमानम्।**
मथव्या अन्त्स्तोकानप यान्राध सं नष्टेभिः सृजतु विश्वकर्मा॥

[**यज्ञ** - from *yajña* ◇ **पतिम्** - descending ◇ **ऋषय** - flowed ◇ **एनस** - as mischievous ◇ **आहुः** - oblations ◇ **निर्भक्तं** - keeping away from participation ◇ **प्रजा** - born to the surroundings; as offspring's ◇ **अनुतप्यमानम्** - with lesser temperatures ◇ **मथव्या** - upon agitation and division ◇ **अन्त्** - bound to ◇ **स्तोकान** - a spot of spark ◇ **पयान्** - flowed ◇ **नरा** - till man ◇ **अध** - and then ◇ **सं** -as assembled ◇ **नष्टेभिः** - and as lost ◇ **सृजतु** - as the mights discharged ◇ **विश्वकर्मा** - created as everything to its due place]

As the *yajña*s that descended, paths that flowed and as the processes that mischievously kept away from the oblations, many were born to the surroundings as offspring's with gradually reducing temperatures, much agitated and divided, bound to the spots of brightness that appeared and flowing from those till man, in a process with mights accrued or lost and so got created bringing everything to its due place.

As a series of *yajña*s, the afflictions there-of, the movement, the agitation and division, many were born and got placed in many places. The processes continued downward with lesser temperatures. All these started from that spot of brightness that appeared in the heaven. That included even those that obstructed such progresses. As the offspring's of lesser temperature, many descended from sacrifices as those that flowed to the surroundings and below. It was when a dry spark of energy and matter appeared in the *Soma* that the process of creation commenced. Many that were created appeared to become large by assembly, union and many disappeared. Many were displaced and thrown out from their original positions.

AK2.35.03 अदान्यान्त्सोमपान्मन्यमानो यज्ञस्य विद्वान्त्समये न धीरः। यदेनश्चकृवान्बद्ध एष तं विश्वकर्मन्प्र मुञ्चा स्वस्तये॥

[अद - as the food principle ◇ अन्यान् - that mutated ◇ सोमपान् - as with drinking of *Soma* ◇ मन्यमानो - the arrangements in principle ◇ यज्ञस्य - of the *yajña* ◇ विद्वान् - moved from knowledge ◇ समये - well regulated ◇ न - as ◇ धीरः - courageously; from an intellect ◇ यद् - whatever ◇ एनश्च - as mischief ◇ कृवान् - got created and moved from above ◇ बद्ध - bound to ◇ एष - similarly ◇ तं - emaciated ◇ विश्वकर्मन् - created as bringing everything to its due place ◇ प्र - to the surroundings ◇ मुञ्चा - as released ◇ स्वस्तये - a state of calm]

A food principle went on mutating, a process of drinking of the *Soma* and the arrangements obtained out of the *yajña* in principle had moved from a divine knowledge, getting regulated by an intellect. The mischief that came unleashed had come moved only bound to what stood above and everything had emaciated to the surroundings. In these ways, all were brought to their due place and thus came to a state of calm and quietude.

The *yajñas* that were instituted courageously with the appropriate knowledge, commenced with the partaking of the *Soma* which nevertheless remained non-depreciated. There were several chains of such *yajñas* which progressed unremittingly. Here two conflicting attitudes stood side by side.

Firstly, the partaking of the *Soma* while became the stimuli for creation did not deprive the knowledge and intelligence to prevail. And then it did not forget to connect a happiness and well being to whatever got made. The *Soma* while became the energiser was also the very seed matter for creation. Though the *Soma* was consumed, it remained in-exhausted. In the later *vaidikayajña*, the *Soma* was partaken and at the same time offered as oblations in a like fashion, as if enacting the original sequence of the *yajña* of nature.

AK2.35.04 **घोरा ऋषयो नमो अस्त्वेभ्यश्चक्षुर्यदेषां मनसश्च सत्यम्। बृहस्पतये महिष द्युमन्नमो विश्वकर्मन्नमस्ते पाह्य१स्मान्॥**

[घोरा - as violent ◇ ऋषयो - flows ◇ नमो - bowing down; down an incline ◇ अस्त्वेभ्य - that shot off to the proximity ◇ चक्षुः - from an eye ◇ यद् - whatever ◇ एषां - as quickly established ◇ मनसश्च - from a mind ◇ सत्यम् - and the *Satya* ◇ बृहस्पतये - greatly enlarged descending ◇ महिष - most powerfully ◇ द्युमन् - from the heaven ◇ नमो - bowed down with respect ◇ विश्वकर्मन् - to *viśvakarma* ◇ नमस्ते - pays respect ◇ पाहि - as the protected ◇ अस्मान् - parts]

As violent flows shot off to the proximity and down an incline from an eye, as those that quickly moved from a mind and from *Satya*, getting greatly enlarged and powerfully descending from the heaven, bowing down respectfully, bringing everything to its due place, as the protected parts got stationed and in such ways since the universe manifested, let homages be respectfully paid to *Viśvakarma*, the creator.

From that fixed eye, from a divine mind, from *Satya* shot out a violent flow down an incline as occurred, greatly descending to become a greatness. Those that steeply moved from the heaven manifested in clear steps and measures, as the protected entities that came from what existed earlier. Flowing violently from the heaven where the *Satya* manifested, the objects of the universe greatly descended. The epicentre of the universe stood near to this heaven and saw all. A shining food form manifested and the *Soma* traveled along with the objects, accomplishing all and protecting all. The phenomena of birth and mortality got extended from the very beginning of creation till the end. An incessant flow occurred from the heaven which scattered the objects as everywhere. The fixed eye remained not only as the epicentre of the universe but oversaw what all happened. It was here and from here, the heaven, that the concept of visibility first originated. It was with the presence of a mind and its action that the process of creation started.

AK2.35.05 यज्ञस्य चक्षुः प्रभृतिर्मुखम् च वाचा श्रोत्रेण मनसा जुहोमि। इमं यज्ञं विततं विश्वकर्मणा देवा यन्तु सुमनस्यमानाः॥

[यज्ञस्य - as the *yajñas* ◇ चक्षुः - that progressed from an eye ◇ प्रभृतिर्मुखं - from the face of all beginnings ◇ च - and ◇ वाच - by words ◇ आ - manifested ◇ श्रोत्रेण - as the audibility ◇ मनसा - from a mind ◇ जुहोमि - as established oblations ◇ इमं - thus ◇ यज्ञं - as *yajña* ◇ विततं - that spread ◇ विश्वकर्मन् - bringing everything to its due place ◇ आ - came ◇ देवा - from the heavens ◇ यन्तु - with whatever mights ◇ सुमनस्यमानाः - and in appropriate dimensions and measures]

As the *yajñas* that moved from that eye and from the face of all beginning, as the divine words and the audibility that manifested, everything got established by oblations to become the universe that spread till here, manifesting and bringing everything to its due place. The *yajñas* that spread from the heavens in appropriate dimensions and measures had established everything and had brought this much acceptable universe.

Commencing as a *yajña* and becoming a series of *yajñas* that were widely placed, the universe became very large. The platform of heaven for the first of the *yajñas* stood very near to the epicentre. A divine guidance established favourable dimensions to all events, objects and the very size of the universe. A mind upon getting hotted up, along with the divine words that were uttered and heard, the process of creation commenced. This first set of vibrations brought forth the temperature and space that were essential. Perhaps the statement of "*bhadraṃ karṇebhi śṛṇuyāma devā* - - " could be remembered here. Where the visibilities got first manifested, where the sounds of divine words were first heard, and where a divine mind was first noticed, from there the process of creation of the universe started. From there as a *yajña* and as many series of *yajña*s this universe grew to its immensity.

The universe was created from the *Soma* and by the *Agni* as a series of *yajña*s, the brightness getting diminished as it expanded. Upon the manifestation of a dry spark into the *Soma*, matter was generated and swept away from the centre to distant places with sequentially lesser temperature levels. An *annabhāva* could be discerned in the growth of the universe. The creation started with the exultation of partaking of the *Soma* while the very *Soma* provided the seed principle. Thus the words that were heard, and a mind kept hotted up, a divine guidance manifested and made the universe a great benevolence.

AK6.122

[(5) पञ्चर्चस्यास्य सूक्तस्य भृगुऋषिः विश्वकर्मा देवता (1 - 3) प्रथमादितृचस्य त्रिष्टुप् (4 - 5) चतुर्थापञ्चम्योर्ऋचोश्च जगती छन्दसी]

AK6.122.01 एतं भागं परि ददामि विद्वान्विश्वकर्मन्प्रथमजा ऋतस्य। अस्माभिर्दत्तं जरसः परस्तादच्छिन्नं तन्तुमनु सं तरेम॥

[एतं - arriving as ◇ भागं - the parts ◇ परि - to the surroundings ◇ ददामि - repeatedly bestowed and established ◇ विद्वान् - moving from the knowledge ◇ विश्वकर्मन् - as everything to its due place ◇ प्रथमजा - manifested as the first born ◇ ऋतस्य - as per the rules ◇ अस्म - parts ◇ अभिः - advanced ◇ दत्तं - obtained ◇ जरसः - emaciated ◇ परस्ताद् - progressed ◇ अच्छिन्नं - as unbroken ◇ तन्तुमनु - as if strings ◇ सं - assembled; stood together ◇ तर - forded ◇ इम - like that]

As the parts that arrived to the surroundings, upon getting established by repeatedly getting bestowed to bring everything to its due place, as those that moved from knowledge, as those that manifested from the first born according to the rules, as the parts that emaciated and yet progressed as unbroken strings, as those that got assembled and stood together and as those that forded to safe places, the universe came into existence.

The process of creation as commenced by the *Viśvakarma* as an activity that came from knowledge and according to the divine rules, continued by delivering to the proximity from the parts that already existed, as those that decayed, emaciated and disintegrated. A knowledge capable of accomplishing everything accompanied the creation to whatever extent it went. Out of those parts that came into existence, some got further afflicted and became many that issued out to the surroundings and these processes continued.

AK6.122.02 ततं तन्तुमन्वेके तरन्ति येषां दत्तं पित्र्यमायनेन।
अबन्ध्वेके ददतः प्रयच्छन्तो दातुं चेच्छिक्षान्त्स स्वर्ग एव॥

[ततं - as those from those ◇ तन्तु - as a string ◇ मनु - in principle ◇ एके - the ones ◇ तरन्ति - forded to the proximity ◇ येषां - efforts moved ◇ दत्तं - obtained ◇ पित्र्यमायनेन - as moved from a paternity ◇ अबन्ध्वेके - as separated from the ones ◇ ददतः - as those repeatedly obtained ◇ प्र - to the surroundings ◇ यच्छन्तो - whatever acceptable ◇ दातुं - apportions ◇ चेत् - the mind ◇ शिक्षन् - dictated ◇ स - bound to ◇ स्वर्ग - the heaven ◇ एव - only]

Those that came from those, those that moved as a string in principle, the ones that forded to the proximity, the many efforts progressed; all these were obtained as moved from a paternity. Separated from the ones that came earlier and in this manner repeatedly came to the surroundings, with whatever acceptable apportions a divine mind dictated and always bound to the heaven that stood immediately above.

The process of creation still continued, sequentially and as a string in principle. Only from such objects that potentially stood such as the heavens, these string like continuities progressed. Those then progressed as a chain of a father, his son and his son till the very end. It was thus that the many earth forms came into existence. Only out of such hot and powerful objects that could get divided or issue out, could new things be derived. Along with these strings of manifestations in the form of the paths, of creation and the objects born, chains of silent field forces also manifested and remained.

AK6.122.03 अन्वारभेथामनुसंरभेथामेतं लोकं श्रद्दधानाः सचन्ते। यद्वां पक्वं परिविष्टमग्नौ तस्य गुप्तये दंपति सं श्रयेथाम्॥

[अन्वारभे - as those one after the other ◇ थाम् - manifested and positioned ◇ अनुसंरभ - clasping to each other; shoulder to shoulder ◇ इथाम् - in such manner manifested ◇ एतं - derived ◇ लोकं - a world ◇ श्रद् - heartily ◇ दधानाः - issued out and positioned ◇ सचन्ते - as oblations till the end ◇ यद् - many ways ◇ वां - propagated ◇ पक्वं - matured ◇ परिविष्टम् - attended around ◇ अग्नौ - by many *Agni* forms ◇ तस्य - from that ◇ गुप्तये - secretly ◇ दंपति - as wished by the lord above]

Those that got positioned and moved one after the other, those that moved in a manner of shoulder to shoulder, manifested heartily as the universe. Those that were issued out and positioned by the oblations that came till the end, those that many ways propagated, surrounded by the many forms of *Agni* and having got matured by it, progressed, as if secretively wished by the Lord above, came manifested as the universe.

Blowing arduously, protected intelligently, consuming exceedingly, got into far flung positions and from there moved as the oblations that came till the end which were found to courageously deliver and these came from such mature minds, attended by the *Agni*, with the temperatures totally hidden, reduced or mixed as it happened. The regions and the group of objects that came into existence from the heaven on the food principle, as intelligently devised and as if blown by an unseen wind, positioned many things to long distances.

The process of creation progressed from those objects by way of the oblations and by the act of the *Agni* to bring about objects with varying levels of temperature. Those that got matured in their positions, delivered new things to the surroundings. Those were progresses that never turned back.

AK6.122.04 यज्ञं यन्तं मनसा बृहन्तमन्वारोहामि तपसा सयोनिः। उपहूता अग्ने जरसः परस्तात्तृतीये नाके सधमादं मदेम॥

[यज्ञं - as the *yajñas* ◇ यन्तं - moved regulated ◇ मनसा - from mind ◇ बृहन्तम् - getting enlarged till the end ◇ अन्वारोहामि - that got established ascending one by one ◇ तपसा - along with heat ◇ सयोनिः - from the same womb ◇ उपहूता - set aflame ◇ अग्ने - by many levels of *Agni* ◇ जरसः - as emaciated ◇ परस्ताद् - came forward as ◇ तृतीये - as the 3 ◇ नाके - heavens ◇ सधमाद - as a ceremonial drinking party ◇ मद - exhilarated ◇ इम - fashion]

As the regulated *yajñas* that moved from divine minds, which got enlarged in ascending orders and which established one after the other till the end, as manifested from the many wombs with many levels of heat, as created by many forms of *Agni* that came moved forward and emaciated, were the ways in which the universe came into existence. From the three that stood in the heaven the universe appeared to have manifested. The creation came moved with exhilaration, as if derived from a drinking party.

Just as it happened originally in the heaven with that ceremonial participation of the *Soma* and the exhilaration it produced, the same and similar things happened vide the *yajñas* that occurred down the line and till the end. From those many points of creation, from those wombs of creation, with the participation of *Agni*, matter gushed forth which later decayed or emaciated. The expansion that took place from the three points in the heaven had repeated many a time. And yet there was altogether a celebration in the process of creation.

AK6.122.05 शुद्धाः पूता योषितो यज्ञिया इमा ब्रह्मणां हस्तेषु प्रपृथक्सादयामि। यत्काम इदमभिषिञ्चामि वो अहमिन्द्रो मरुत्वान्त्स ददातु तन्मे॥

[शुद्धाः - clear and shining ◇ पूता - manifesting as purified ◇ योषितो - with chanting of hymns ◇ यज्ञिया - as by *yajñas* ◇ इमा - thus came ◇ ब्रह्मणां - moved by *Brahma* ◇ हस्तेषु - arms of ◇ प्र - to the surroundings ◇ पृथक् - widely separated ◇ सादयामि - and emaciated and established ◇ यत्काम - progressing as desired ◇ इदम् - thus ◇ अभिषिञ्चामि - sprinkled from the swirling arms ◇ वो - and indeed ◇ अहम् - as the self ◇ इन्द्रो - and as from *indrata* ◇ मरुत्वन्त्स - propagated by a wind ◇ ददातु - successively issued out ◇ तन्मे - from *Sat* by a series of changes]

Manifested as purified and as the clear shines that came with the chanting of hymns and as the *yajñas* that progressed. As moved by the hands of *Brahma* that got extended to the surroundings, as the arms of creation that stood widely separated and which came progressively emaciated, those things progressed as desired. As broadcast from those swirling arms, and indeed as the self that moved along with the *indrata*, as if propagated by a wind, the universe came into existence. It had come from *Sat* and as the effects brought in by a series of changes.

It was as an act of the *Brahma* with knowledge accompanied that the universe manifested, got much enlarged and gradually emaciated to the end. The chanting of hymns or with the cosmic vibrations that first arose, the process of creation was given a start. Out of a particle of brightness, all got manifested as purified and a series of *yajñas* descended to the surroundings. It was thus that the creation progressed and matter got sprinkled and firmed up till the end. The objects that were created remained divided and yet remained bound to their sources with whatever forms and levels of strength.

The universe came as a chain of actions that commenced from the heaven as a series of *yajñas*. The objects gradually became smaller with the density of occupancy gradually diminishing when expanded outwards. Possibly, our earth was one of the objects that came positioned in the 7th *vyāhṛti*. The enlargement of the universe was like enormous bursts off, matter getting scattered to the surroundings, with objects of varying levels of temperature. Though repeatedly moved from such hot sources, the 3-dimensional features were maintained at all the times. The universe was born with *Soma* providing the seed substance and acting as the very provider of the intoxication needed for creation. This creation came from knowledge and at the hands of *Brahma*, that Supreme Divinity.

It was the divine words that acted as the very reason and substance of this universe. With the advent of *Agni*, those temperatures as well as the space and time got sufficiently instituted, just as the term *Jātaveda* proclaimed. From that basic phenomenal entity called the *Agni*, with its many dimensions and measures, its combinations and evolutions, basic matter and their several combinations took to finite forms. The Veda clearly believed so and contributed to this theory, strongly. But the Veda invested the primordial reasons for the very manifestation of the cosmic vibrations into the divine words. The Veda stated that everything in the universe manifested and existed only with an interactive nature of varying degrees of intensity. Statements of those invisible power centres, those hot objects and the swirled up paths of creation not only described the sequences of a unique series of events, but also suggested the sources of the all prevalent gravitational forces of the universe. There might be a necessity to identify them and delineate them into conceptual theories that would satisfy the present generation of people. There are no mathematical equations written and no arguments mounted here, for the Veda dwell in fundamental hypothesis and conclusions, obviating all arguments. ★★★

9

Geometry in the Ṛgveda

The Chapter-6 on the *Asyavāmīyasūkta* defined a wheel with 12 radial segments and several annular rim segments, in general resembling a *rathacakra*. The *rathacakra* represented a protected and fortified universe and it was also identified as representative of the spherical shape and geometry of the universe. It will be found from this chapter that this shape not only represented the time and space simultaneously, as a presentation of the ecliptic it also contained an all important geometrical symbol and concept of the Vedas. Some of the examples of clear Vedic statements on such geometrical formations and its association with the zodiac would be presented here.

In RV1.164

In the *Asyavāmīyasūkta* of the *Ṛgveda*, the verses 11, 12, 13, 14 and 48, described a circular formation with 12 spokes. So let us revisit these verses in general and examine the verse RV1.164.48 in particular, for the separation of the 48th verse from those of the 11th to 14th must have had a special significance and purpose.

RV1.164.48 द्वादश प्रथयश्चक्रमेकं त्रीणि नभ्यानि क उ तच्चिकेत।
तस्मिन्त्साकं त्रिशता न शङ्कवोऽर्पिताः षष्टिर्न चलाचलासः॥

[द्वादश - with 12 ◇ प्रथय - segments; as expanded ◇ चक्रम् - a wheel ◇ एकं - from one ◇ त्रीणि - as three ◇ नभ्यानि - on hubs ◇ क - whatever ◇ उ - firmed up ◇ तद् - from that ◇ चिकेत - appropriately; thoughtfully ◇ तस्मिन् - with those ◇ साकं - along with that ◇ त्रिशता - 300 ◇ न - as ◇ शङ्कवो - the pegs ◇ अर्पिताः - fixed ◇ षष्टिः - 60 ◇ न - as ◇ चला - moving ◇ चला - and moving ◇ सः - like that]

Let a wheel with 12 sectors, with the 3 points on the hub, be devised thoughtfully, incorporating those, with 300 pegs, moving 60 and using those for fixing and moving again until it is suitable for propitiation and oblations gets constructed.

This verse read along with the verses 11 to 15 of RV1.164, basically described a *rathacakraciti* with multiple concentric annular rings, which in turn represented the 7 *vyāhṛtis* of the universe. On the other hand or along with it, the 48th verse directly pointed to a unique geometrical construction. The verse essentially brought forward the numbers 12, 3, 300 and 60. It suggested to use the number 60 variously and which permitted us the following derivation.

$(300 + 60) \times 60 \times 60 \div 12 = 108,000$

The above calculation happened to be the value in seconds of one *rāśi* of the *rāśīcakra*.[12] This would tempt us to bring in the notion that time was equally represented in the *rathacakra* formations, or for that matter in all the *uttaravedi* altar shapes. Once we feel certain that the idea mooted here

[1]It is clear that during the Vedic period, a circle was reckoned in terms of 360 major divisions and further divisions of 60 and 60, whether these were named as degrees, minutes and seconds or not. Such naming that happened here is in accordance with present day requirements.

[2]Here a reference could be made to RV 4.20.08 which dramatically mentions about the *rāśis*, which further emboldens the geometrical presentations here.

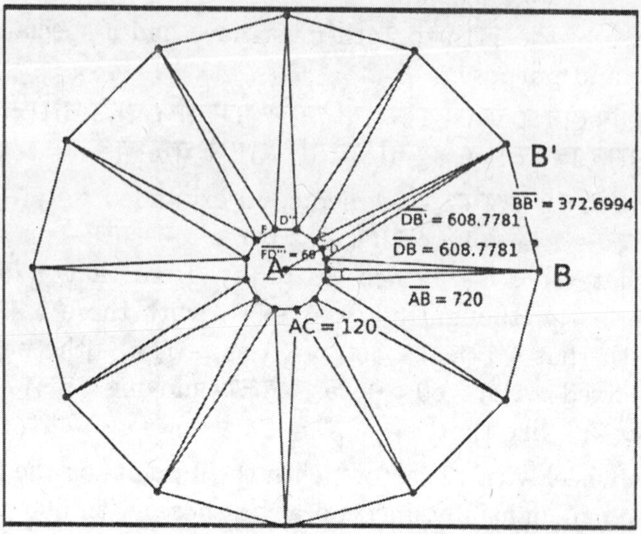

Figure 9.1: The *Rāśīcakra* of RV1.164.48

could be correct, every word of the above verse would come more alive and more meaningful. Let us see how it would enfold before us as a very beautiful geometrical construction. In the verse RV1.164.11, the use of numbers 100, 20 and 720 was mentioned. The methods of construction, using the ropes with loops on ends and wooden pegs were always relevant and in fact those were perhaps the only tools used during the Vedic times. Here, two figures will be shown, the first being the *rāśīcakra* (Fig 9.1) complete and the second showing the basic construction methodology, taken to a Vedic ambiance.

It could be noticed that this unique formation was achieved by rope markings of 120, 720 and suitable manipulation of the same. The diagram could be drawn as follows and as shown in the Fig 9.2. Draw a line AB = 720. Make peg marks C at a distance of 120 from A and F as the midpoint of line AB. Draw two circles as shown with AF as radius and get the intersection point G. Draw a construction line passing through point G, which would happen be at 30° to line AB. Obtain point D, with AD as 120. Join the line CD and mark

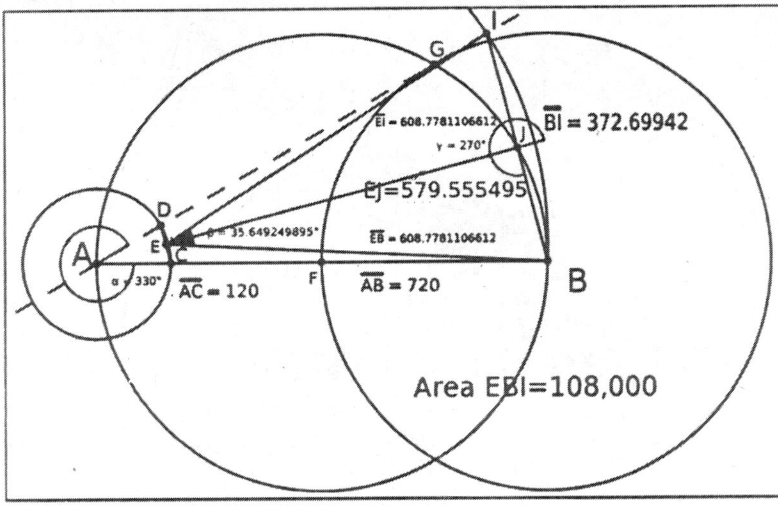

Figure 9.2: The Configuration of RV1.164.48

its midpoint E. With E as centre and EB as radius, draw an arc to cut the line AG extended at I. Now draw the triangle BEI. This triangle would return an area of 108,000! It is also interesting to note that all the line lengths of this triangle would be found irrational as well and that the sum of the 12 sides at the inner circle amounted to $12 \times 60 = 720$!!

Now the methodology of construction and the area resulted, demanded some studies. In order that the area would be a rational quantity, and since the side BI returned an irrational value (372.6994249476), it followed that the vertical dropped from point E, i.e, EJ would also be of irrational value (579.5554957734). Interestingly, the point J fell on the intersection of the basic circle and line BI.

However, we know that the area is indeed 108,000 since a triangle CBB' would also have the same area. But since a triangle with a centre-line symmetry is the very subject here, an infinite nature would be found carefully carried forward and this would immensely satisfy a Vedic enquiry. For the Vedic proposal was that an element of irrationality always got attached to all types of realities.

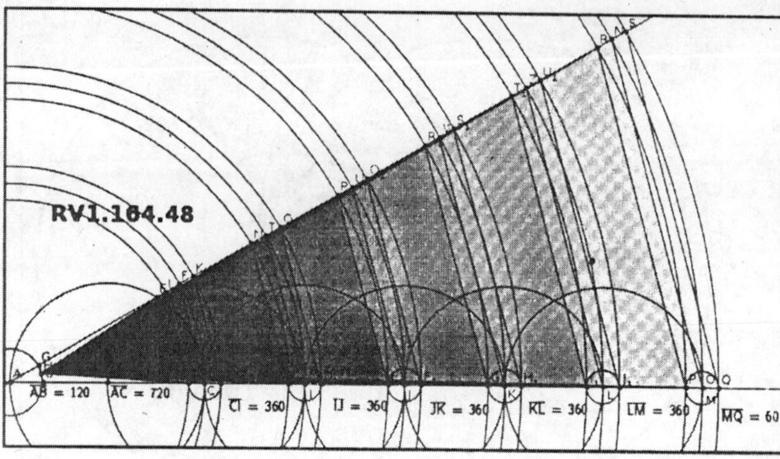

Figure 9.3: The Expansions Geometry of RV1.164.48

Table 9.1: Areas of sectors of RV1.164

	vyāhṛti	Area	*puruṣamātra*	(+)	(++)
1	First	108000	7.50	10.5	4.5
2	Second	259200	18.00	15	4.5
3	Third	475200	33.00	19.5	4.5
4	Fourth	756000	52.50	24	4.5
5	Fifth	1101600	76.50	28.5	-
6	Sixth	1512000	105.00	-	-

However, the verse meant mouch more. Hitherto, only the first *vyāhṛti* got conceived from this verse with 108,000 as the area of the sector. But the numbers mentioned could be made use of, to geometrically conceive all the seven *vyāhṛtis*, in the following manner. Earlier the *vyāhṛti* circle got formed by a circle with a radius of 720. This could be taken upwards with an increment of 360 to geometrically conceive all the 7 *vyāhṛtis* (the first *vyāhṛti* being the heaven with a radius of 120). Further, the offset to both sides could be defined by offsets of 60. See Fig 9.3. From the tabulation given here, it will be found that the area of sectors progressed in a definite incremental arithmetic progression. Geometry was getting used for firming up the ideas in tune with human realizations. In other words, taking it from a largeness and wilderness to a methodical smallness.

In RV1.035

This hymn was found to contain two geometrical presentations, one in RV1.035.06 and another in RV1.035.08. The one of RV1.035.08 will be detailed here.

RV1.035.08 अष्टौ व्यख्यत्ककुभः पृथिव्यास्त्री धन्व योजना सप्त सिन्धून्। हिरण्याक्षः सविता देव आगाद्दधद्रत्ना दाशुषे वार्याणि॥

[अष्टौ - as 8 ◇ वि - divided ◇ अख्यत् - as known ◇ ककुभः - distinguished ◇ पृथिवि - earth forms ◇ आ - came ◇ त्री - as 3 ◇ धन्व - the 5th sign ◇ योजना - joined ◇ सप्त - 7 ◇ सिन्धून् - flows ◇ हिरणाक्षः - from the golden eye ◇ सविता - spread ◇ देव - heaven ◇ आ - came ◇ ग - moved away ◇ दधद् - issued out ◇ रत्ना - as diamonds ◇ दाशुषे - arose as auspicious visibilities ◇ वार्याणि - eminently]

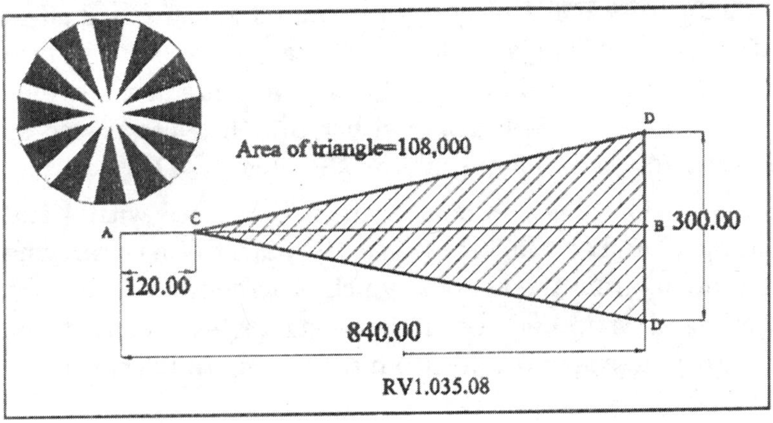

Figure 9.4: The Configuration of RV1.035.08

As configured by 8, 3, 5 and 7 and as the flows that happened from that golden eye (epicentre), from the heaven those distinguished earth forms spread, visible and known as those that got issued out and glittered like diamonds as those that eminently arose.

This description configured as 8 x 3 x 5 x 7 = 840 and its division into 7 to get 120. First a line AB would be made 840 long and point C would be 120 from point A. The line length of BD would be 150 and line CD would be now mirrored as CD'. The triangle CDD' would have an area of 108,000. The wheel could be completed by rotation of the segment with reference to point A as shown in Fig 9.4.

In RV2.018

Let us next consider the hymn of RV2.018, in which the verses 1 to 6 indicated a geometrical constructions.

RV2.018.01 प्राता रथो नवो योजि सस्निश्चतुर्युगस्त्रिकशः सप्तरश्मिः।
दशारित्रो मनुष्यः स्वर्षाः स इष्टिभिर्मतिभी रंह्यो भूत्॥

[प्रात -As those that came to the surroundings ◇ आ - coming ◇ रथो - as a chariot wheel ◇ नवो - with 9 ◇ योजि - combined ◇ सस्निश्चतुर्युगस्त्रिकशः - obtained as 4 and 3 joined ans shuffled ◇ सप्तरश्मिः - as 7 rays ◇ दश - as a stage; 10 ◇ अरित्रो - taken forward ◇ मनुष्यः - till man ◇ स्वर्षा - as the contents that came through the sky ◇ स - along with ◇ इष्टिभिः - progressed as desired ◇ मतिभी - thoughtfully ◇ रंह्यो - eagerly ◇ भूत् - born]

A charriot wheel be made with 9, combined with 4 and 3, using 10 and as the 7 rays taken forward till man carrying the contents from the heaven, which progressed thoughtfully, eagerly and as desired. Let it represent the expansion of the universe as a progress made from the heaven to the earth and man.

The verse described a *rathacakra* formation with 7 annular rings and brought in the area of 108,000 by:

4 x 3 x 9 x 1000 = 108,000

It also suggested a measurement of 720 by mentioning "man". But the verse did not yet go into the details of construction.

RV2.018.02 सास्मा अरं प्रथमं स द्वितीयमुतो तृतीयं मनुषः स होता। अन्यस्या गर्भमन्य ऊ जनन्त सो अन्येभिः सचते जेन्यो वृषा॥

[स - Thus ◇ अस्मा - with parts ◇ अरं - suitably ◇ प्रथमं - from the first ◇ स - and then ◇ द्वितीयम् - the second ◇ उतो - connected to ◇ तृतीयं - the third ◇ मनुषः - till man ◇ स - thus ◇ होता - with oblations ◇ अन्यस्या - from the other ◇ गर्भमन्य - from the inside as the other ◇ ऊ - indeed ◇ जन् - born ◇ अन्त - till the end ◇ सो - such that ◇ अन्येभिः - all others ◇ सचते - stood together ◇ जेन्यो - noble origin ◇ वृषा - and manhood]

Thus as the existences that suitably came from the first to the second, connected to the third and so progressed till man, distancing interconnected all along, to become another one coming from the inside of the earlier one, indeed born so till the end as the others, those that stood together, all getting manifested from a genuine manhood. There were repeated manifestations from what came earlier into existence and as progressed from the inside of the earlier coming to the outside.

The verse, however, also touched upon the construction of the shape mentioned in the first verse of this hymn, by referring to 3 starting points that would come one after the other to form the hub of the wheel, the rim of which would be as big as to reach the earth. It also said that in each case, the expansions will take place one by one from the inside (meaning the three points that had got defined) to outside.

RV2.018.03 हरी नु कं रथ इन्द्रस्य योजमायै सूक्तेन वचसा नवेन। मो षु त्वामत्र बहवो हि विप्रा नि रीरमन् यजमानासो अन्ये॥

[हरी -Carrying ◇ नु - instantly ◇ कं - from the apex ◇ रथ - as a chariot◇ इन्द्रस्य - from the *indrata* ◇ योजम् - jointly ◇ आयै - moved ◇ सूक्तेन - with verses ◇ वचसा - and words ◇ नवेन - as 9 renewed ◇ मो - as arrangements got confirmed ◇ षु - by conception ◇ त्वाम् -moved from thyself ◇ अत्र - from there ◇

बहवो - swelling to distances ◇ हि - indeed ◇ वि - divided ◇ प्र - around ◇ आ - came ◇ नि - to below ◇ रीरमन् - willingly bestowed ◇ यजमान - as the arrangements the *yajamāna* ◇ असो - brought into existence ◇ अन्ये - as others]

Carrying those things that came instantly from the apex as if a chariot that moved away from the *indrata*, as the ones moved along with the verses and words, as the new ones that got confirmed moving from thyself, from there swelling to distances and coming divided to the surroundings and below as willingly bestowed and as the arrangements that the *yajamāna* brought into existence as evolved.

The geometry of the *rathacakra* stood as referred. How the formation will get enlarged and would get confirmed as separated from one another was also indicated.

RV2.018.04 आ द्वाभ्यां हरिभ्यामिन्द्र याह्या चतुर्भिरा षड्भिर्हूयमानः।
आष्टाभिर्दशभिः सोमपेयमयं सुतः सुमख मा मृधस्कः॥

[आ - came ◇ द्वाभ्यां -progressed as 2 ◇ हरिभ्याम् -progressed carrying the; (5); multicoloured ◇ इन्द्र - from *indrata* ◇ याह्या - as journeyed ◇ आ - and manifested ◇ चतुर्भिरा - coming repeatedly as 4 ◇ षड्भिः - and 6 ◇ हूयमानः - as the well regulated oblations ◇ आष्टाभिः - progressed as the well marked; 8 ◇ दशभिः - stages; 10 ◇ सोमपेयम् - drinking the *Soma* ◇ अयं - thus ◇ सुतः - extracting ◇ सुमख - as vigorous sacrifices ◇ मा - and arrangements ◇ मृधस्क - getting forsaken from an apex]

Came progressed as a set of two that manifested and journeyed from the *indrata*, coming repeatedly as 4, 6, 8 and 10 being the stages that came clearly marked and as what was thus brought upon extracting and drinking the *Soma*, and as the arrangements that were brought by vigorous sacrifices, which went on getting forsaken as those came progressed from the apex.

It indicated a progress of a geometry with clearly demarcated stages that would come as 4, 6, 8 and 10. The details will become clear as the narration progresses.

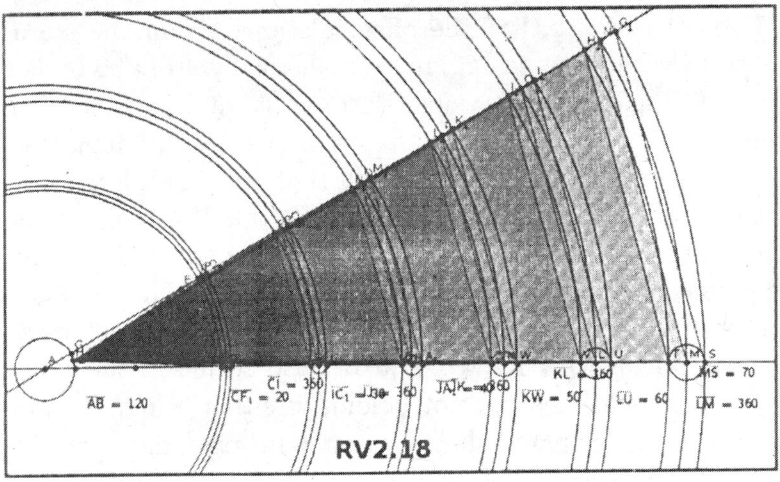

Figure 9.5: The Configuration of RV2.018

RV2.018.05 आ विंशत्या त्रिंशता याह्यर्वाङा चत्वारिंशता हरिभिर्युजानः। आ पञ्चाशता सुरथेभिरिन्द्र आ षष्ट्या सप्तत्या सोमपेयम्॥

[आ - Came ◇ विंशत्या - as 20 ◇ त्रिंशता - as 30 ◇ याहि - journeyed and ◇ अर्वाङ् - advanced ◇ आ - came ◇ चत्वारिंशता - as 40 ◇ हरिभिः - as the ones that got carried; (5) ◇ युजानः - jointly ◇ आ - came ◇ पञ्चाशता - as 105 ◇ सुरथेभिः - as the good chariot ◇ इन्द्' - from the *indra* ◇ आ - came ◇ षष्ट्या - as 60 ◇ सप्तत्या - known as the seven that came ◇ सोमपेयम् - drinking the *Soma*]

Came as 20, came as 30, came as 40, 50 and 60, advancing as journeyed forward, as the well connected five stages that came carried, to be 105 as a shape that came united. The *indra* who strode a good chariot brought the seven *vyāhṛtis* after drinking the *Soma*.

The seven *vyāhṛtis* came from the *indrata* as a *rathacakra* shape that stood in the skies. It was also proposed to use the numbers 20, 30, 40, 50 and 60 to arrive at a size of 105. The geometric configuration resulted is shown in Fig: 9.5

The configuration is similar to what was presented in

RV1.164.48, except that the offset distances from the main *vyāhṛtis* went on increasing, more realistically, from 20 to 80. This confirms the earlier observation that it is not the dimensions of the occurrences that was tried to be depicted; but is was the underlying principle that was considered uppermost. In other words, it did not matter if two opinions were expressed on the same subject and it mattered only to the extent of its ability to make matters clear. Thus the geometry often stood in the background of the ideas that were proposed along with it. It could be also surmised that this very geometrical idea did not belong to either *Dīrghatamas* or to any one in particular. It could be presumed that it came from unspecified origins.

RV2.018.06 आशीत्या नवत्या याह्यर्वाङा शतेन हरिभिरुह्यमानः।
अयं हि ते शुनहोत्रेषु सोम इन्द्र त्वाया परिषिक्तो मदाय॥

[आशीत्या - Came as 80 ◇ नवत्या - as 9 ◇ याहि - from what existed earlier ◇ अर्वाङ् - advanced forward ◇ आ - came ◇ शतेन - as 100 ◇ हरिभिः - carrying; (5) ◇ उह्यमानः - getting transported ◇ अयं - thus ◇ हि - only ◇ ते - those ◇ शुनहोत्रेषु - that swelled from the oblations ◇ सोम - as the *Soma* ◇ इन्द्र - from the *indrata* ◇ त्वा - from thyself ◇ अया - moved ◇ परिषिक्तो - as poured out to the surroundings ◇ मदाय - delightfully]

Came as 80, moved as 9, came advancing forward from there came as 100 and 5, getting carried and transported and thus only as those that swelled from the oblations and stood as the ones that came from the *Soma* and from the *indra* who delightfully poured out to the surroundings; all as moved from thyself.

The geometry of the *rāśīcakra* that ensued was simple and returned an area of 107957.28 by using circles with 120, 720 and three more circles with 90 as radius, as shown in Fig:9.6

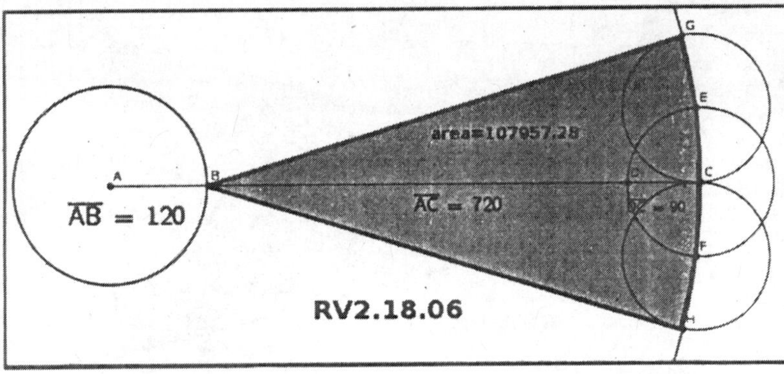

Figure 9.6: The Configuration of RV2.018.06

In RV4.058

It appeared that this verse coming as RV4.058.03, evaded proper interpretation, as mentioned by many. It was obvious from the terms used that geometry and astronomy could be its contents and yet what did it say?

RV4.058.03 चत्वारि शृङ्गा त्रयो अस्य पादा द्वे शीर्षे सप्त हस्तासो अस्य । त्रिधा बद्धो वृषभो रोरवीति महो देवो मर्त्यां आ विवेश॥

[चत्वारि - Crossing ◇ शृङ्गा - from an apex ◇ त्रयो - with 3 ◇ अस्य - as ◇ पादा - the steps ◇ द्वे - 2 ◇ शीर्षे - heads ◇ सप्त - at 7 ◇ हस्तासो - *hasta* got positioned ◇ अस्य - as ◇ त्रिधा - to 3 ◇ बद्धो - bound ◇ वृषभो - powerfully ◇ रोरवीति - and broad shoulders ◇ महो - became great ◇ देवो - from the heaven ◇ मर्त्यां - till man ◇ आ - coming ◇ विवेश - interconnected]

With a crossing apex and along with 3 and making this as the base, from which the steps taken with 2 apexes each at a distance of 7 *hasta*, triangular in appearance, (a *citi*) be made to represent the progress that was made from the powerful and broad shoulders of the heaven till man, all suitably interconnected.

Baudhāyana's words that the earlier *uttaravedis* used to be simple triangles and trapeziums could be remembered

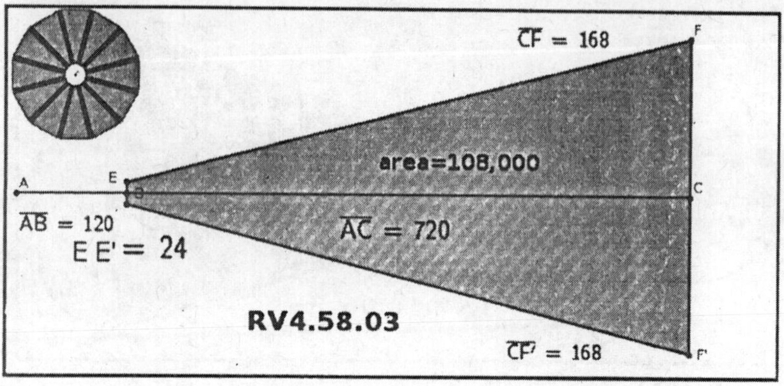

Figure 9.7: The Geometry of RV4.058.03

here. If it was a triangle that was presented vide RV1.164.48, here it came as a trapezium. Here A is the starting point of the drawing. Draw a line AC 720 long since it was stated that it reached man and his surroundings. The verse specifically mentioned *catvāri* as indicating a junction. It then mentioned 3, 2, 7, *hasta* or 24. Along the same line make peg mark B at 120 from A, as derived from referring to 'man'. It was amply clear that a boundary was specified by $7 \times 24 = 168$. Points F and F' is at a distance of 168 fromthe base line as shown in the Fig 9.7. At C draw the vertical line CF as 168 and mirror it with respect to the baseline. At Point B, mark two peg points E and E' at a distance of 12 each since the term *pāda* would mean as 12. Now complete the trapezium E'EFF' and it will return an area of 108,000. The is calculation shown below will confirm this.

$$(24 + 336) \div 2 \times (720 - 120) = 180 \times 600 = 108,000$$

In RV5.027

Another depiction of the expansion into the seven *vyāhṛtis* without the three sub-divisions is given by the following three verses.

RV5.027.01 अनस्वन्ता सत्पतिर्मामहे मे गावा चेतिष्ठो असुरो मघोनः। त्रैवृष्णो अग्ने दशभिः सहस्रैर्वैश्वानर त्र्यरुणश्चिकेत॥

[अनस्वन्त - breathed out up to the end ◇ सत्पतिः - descending from the *Sat* ◇ मा - arrangements ◇ महे - great ◇ मे - moved from the self ◇ गावा - progressing away ◇ चेतिष्ठो - as very clear ◇ असुरो - and divine ◇ मघोन - bountiful gifts ◇ त्रैवृष्णो - with the 3 as the source of strength ◇ अग्ने - with *Agni* ◇ दशभिः - as stages progressed ◇ सहस्रैः - by 1000 ◇ वैश्वानर - emaciate till man ◇ त्र्यरुण - from the 3 reddish spots ◇ चिकेत - carefully]

As the great arrangements that descended from the *Sat* and emaciated to man, as the very clear, divine and bountiful gifts that came from the *Agni*, the self moved from the 3 powerful source in stages that progressed to be 1000, as carefully created from the three reddish spots.

RV5.027.02 यो मे शता च विंशतिं च गोनां हरी च युक्ता सुधुरा ददाति। वैश्वानर सुष्टुतो वावृधानो अग्ने यच्छ त्र्यरुणाय शर्म॥

[यो -Whatever ◇ मे - moved from the self ◇ शता - as 100 ◇ च - and ◇ विंशतिं - twenty ◇ च - and ◇ गोनां - resolutely moved ◇ हरी - as 5 ◇ च - and ◇ युक्ता - suitably ◇ सुधुरा - progressing well ◇ ददाति - as those obtained in large measures ◇ विश्वानर - being everywhere until man ◇ सुष्टुतो - praised as ◇ वा - moved ◇ वृधानो - and enlarged ◇ अग्ने - by the *Agni* ◇ यच्छ - as whatever ◇ त्र्यरुणाय - moved from the 3 red spots ◇ शर्म - as a refuge]

And whatever moved from the self as 100 and 20 and resolutely moved as 5 progressing well and suitably, as those auspiciously obtained as everywhere up to man, were got enlarged by the *Agni* as whatever that progressed from the 3 reddish spots to become the refuges.

The use of 100 and 20 and progressing in 5 stages to the 1000 from the 3 points was impressed upon. It represented the auspicious benevolence that pervaded till man, all effected by the divine *Agni*. The man and earth remained somewhere in the rim region of the universe.

RV5.027.03 एवा ते अग्ने सुमतिं चकानो नविष्ठाय नवमं त्रसदस्युः।

यो मे गिरस्तुविजातस्य पूर्वीर्युक्तेनाभि त्र्यरुणो गृणाति॥
[एवा - thus only ◇ ते - as those ◇ अग्ने - the *Agni* ◇ सुमतिं - with a kind disposition ◇ चकानो - shining ◇ नविष्ठाय - till the youngest ◇ नवमम् - as new ones ◇ त्रसदस्युः - quivering and emaciating ◇ यो - whatever ◇ मे - got evolved ◇ गिरस्तुविजातस्य - and got powerfully created by the words ◇ पूर्वीः -from what existed earlier ◇ युक्तेन - suitably ◇ अभि - progressed ◇ त्र्यरुण - from the 3 red spots ◇ गृणाति - and got sprinkled]

Thus came those from the *Agni* and from a kind disposition, shining till the youngest as new ones that got assembled, as whatever that came moved from the self quivering and emaciating, as empowered by words that moved along and as manifesting from what existed earlier, suitably progressing from the 3 reddish spots, as the objects that got very much sprinkled.

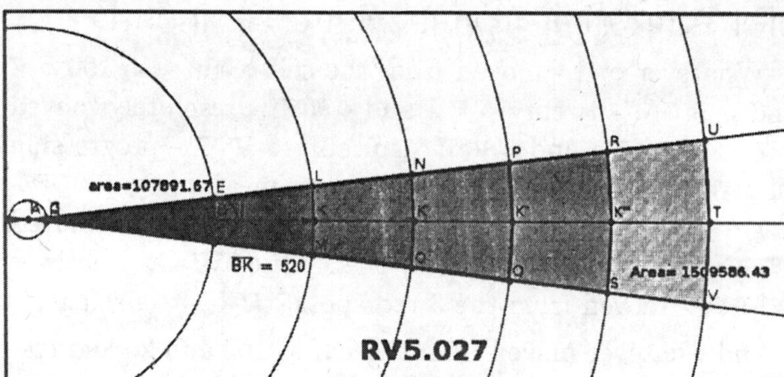

Figure 9.8: The Expansions Geometry of RV5.027

The three verses detailed above was found to relate the expansion of the seven *vyāhṛti*s in yet another way. The sizes 100, 20 and 5 were clearly told to be used imaginatively. The first circle was of 100 radius and the first *vyāhṛti* circle was of 1000 radius. The ends were defined by a circle of radius 120, resulting in the area of the first *vyāhṛti* as 107891.67. The next circles were with an increment in radius of 520, resulting in the area of the last *vyāhṛti* as 1509586.43. See Fig:9.8 The corresponding area of sector and their increment is shown in the table below.

Table 9.2: Areas of sectors of RV5.027.03

	vyāhṛti	Area	*puruṣamātra*	(+)	(++)
1	First	107891.67	7.492	10.47	4.4985
2	Second	258672.46	17.963	14.970	4.4985
3	Third	474232.33	32.93	19.468	4.4985
4	Fourth	754571.28	52.400	23.967	4.4985
5	Fifth	1099689.31	76.367	28.465	-
6	Sixth	1509586.43	104.832	-	-

In RV5.029

This hymn appeared to present triangular shapes and trapeziums each amounting to an area of 108,000 to represent the ecliptic or the zodiac. According to the Indian system, the zodiac would be reckoned divided as the 12 months and also as the 27 days.

RV5.029.06 नव यदस्य नवतिं च भोगान्त्साकं वज्रेण मघवा विवृश्चत्। अर्चन्तीन्द्रं मरुतः सधस्थे त्रैष्टुभेन वचसा बाधत द्याम्॥

[नव - With 9 ◇ यदस्य - somehow with ◇ नवतिं - 90 ◇ च - and ◇ भोगान्त्साकं - like the hood of a snake ◇ वज्रेण - (27th part of the ecliptic) and as crossing ◇ मघवा - bountiful gifts (15th star) ◇ विवृश्चत् -spread out ◇ अर्चन्ति - as offerings to the proximity ◇ इन्द्र - from the *indrata* ◇ मरुतः - as if by a wind ◇ सदस्थे - stood together ◇ त्रैष्टुभेन - as 2/3 ◇ वचसा - along with words ◇ बाधत - and afflictions ◇ द्याम् - from the heaven]

Let a configuration be made using 9 and 90, crossing lines spread out and using the ratio of 2/3, and the star of *magha* being the 15th using 15, to represent the 1/27th part of the ecliptic which would appear like a hood of a snake. Let it represent the spreading that took place from the *indrata* as if carried out by a wind. Let it represent the divine words uttered, the offerings made and the afflictions that commenced from the heaven.

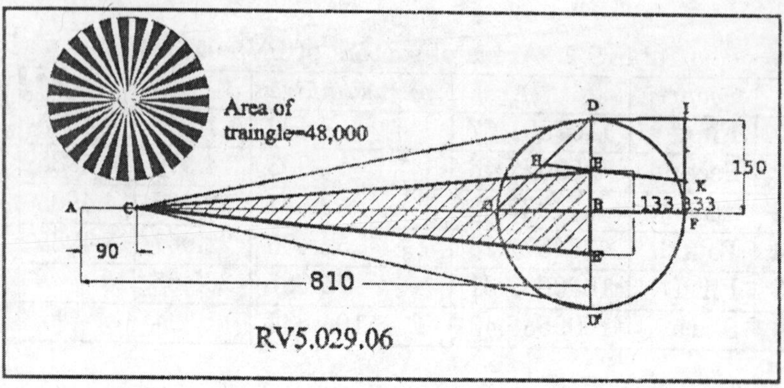

Figure 9.9: The Configuration of RV5.029.06

Let line AB be 810 long. Mark off point C at 90 from A. Line DD' would be 300 long and the triangle CDD' would amount to an area of 108,000. In order to represent the 1/27th value of the ecliptic (*rāśīcakra*) the following area value should come.

$1,296,000 \div 27 = 48000$

Here the term "*traiṣṭubhena*" should be read as 2 times 1/3rd and accordingly an accurate fraction of 100 amounting to 66.66...7 should be configured. For this, draw circle DD' as diameter which would provide the points F and G. Draw line FI parallel to BD and divide this line into 3 and to get point K. Now join D and G and find its midpoint as H. Join H to K and the intersection point E would be used along with its mirrored E' to get the triangle CEE'. The area of this triangle would be 48,000. Such a wheel having 27 segments could be seen at Fig 9.9.

RV5.029.07 सखा सख्ये अपचत्तूयमग्निरस्य क्रत्वा महिषा त्री शतानि। त्री साकमिन्द्रो मनुषः सरांसि सुतम् पिबद्वृत्रहत्याय सोमम्॥

[सखा - With friends ◇ सख्ये - and friendship ◇ अपच् - from a raw state ◇ अत् - moved ◇ तूयम् -powerered by ◇ अग्निः - the *Agni* ◇ अस्य - as ◇ क्रत्वा - resolutely moving ◇ महिषा - with great strength ◇ त्री - as 3 ◇ शतानि - 100 ◇ त्री - and 3 ◇ साकम् - as the apex ◇ इन्द्रो - *indra* ◇ मनुषः - till man ◇ सरांसि - flowed at angles ◇ सुतम् - getting extracted ◇ पिबद् - drinking ◇ वृत्र - the *vṛtrata* ◇ ह - kept aloof ◇ त्याय - as known ◇ सोमम् - by the *Soma*]

From that which remained in a raw state, invigorated by the *Agni*, came those friends and many friendships, resolutely and with supreme strength, with 3, 100 and 3 variously used, the *indra* remaining at the apex, flowing at angles and reaching to man and this earth. The *Soma* upon getting squeezed and much drunk, flowed down and it kept the *vṛtrata* aloof.

From point A draw line AB = 900. Mark off C at 150 from A. Mark D at 144 from point B and join the line CD. Mirror the Line CD to the opposite side to get line CD'. The triangle CDD' would amount to the value of 108,000. Next the wheel could be completed by revolving the segment around point A (See Fig 9.10).

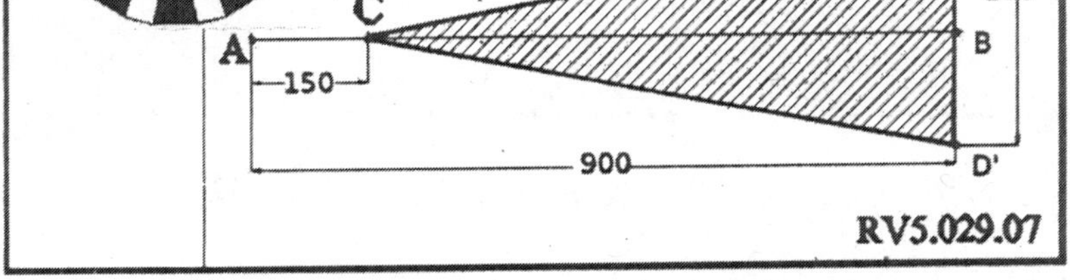

Figure 9.10: The Configuration of RV5.029.07

RV5.029.08 त्री यच्छता महिषाणामघो मास्त्री सरांसि मघवा सोम्यापाः। कारं न विश्वे अह्वन्त देवा भरमिन्द्राय यदहिं जघान॥

[त्री - 3 ◇ यच् - somehow ◇ शता - with 100 ◇ महिषाणा - powerful contents ◇ मघो - gifted ◇ माः - arrangements ◇ त्री - of 3 ◇ सरांसि - crossed and flowing ◇ मघवा -as bountiful gifts moved ◇ सोम - from the *Soma* ◇ इय् - spread ◇ अपाः - and so obtained ◇ कारं - ceated (with wickedness) ◇ न - as ◇ विश्वे - reached everywhere ◇ अहु - by oblations ◇ अन्त - till the end ◇ देवा - from the heavens ◇ भरम् - filled with ◇ इन्द्राय - moved from the *indrata* ◇ यद् - somehow ◇ अहिं - as a snake ◇ जघान -from the hips]

Somehow with 3 and 100 and from the three as the month that flowed crossing, moved the bountiful gifts (15), from the *Soma* spread and obtained those which were created as wickedness of this universe and which moved as if snakes coming from the hips. These too came from the heaven and the *indrata* and filled this universe.

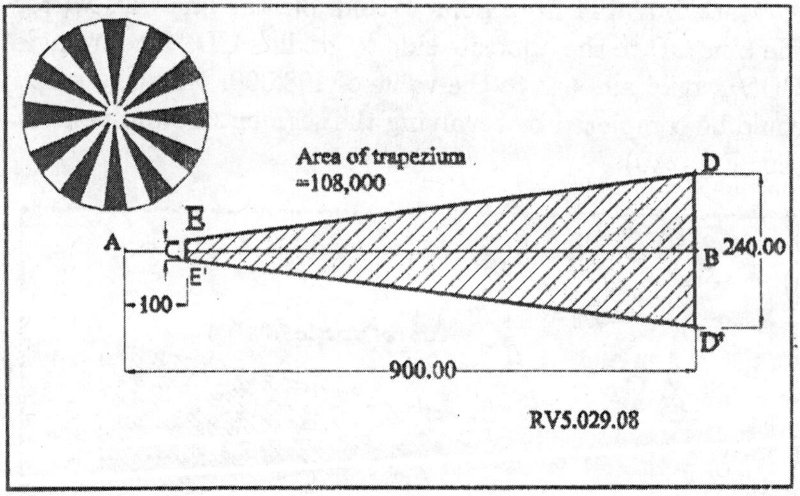

Figure 9.11: The Configuration of RV5.029.08

In other words, using 3 and 100 variously along with 15, configure a shape to represent this narrative. Therefore, make line AB = 900 and mark off point C at 100. Make line CE as 15 and BD as 120. Mirror the line DE as D'E'. The trapezium DEE'D' would return an area value of 108,000. It was stated that this represented a month or a *rāśi*. The wheel could be now completed by swinging around point A, as shown in Fig 9.11. Thus the hymn RV5.029 presented the use of triangles and trapeziums to represent the ecliptic.

In RV8.046

RV8.046.22 षष्टिं सहस्राश्व्यस्यायुतासनमुष्ट्रानां विंशतिं शता।
दश श्यावीनां शता दश त्र्यरुषीणां दश गवां सहस्रा॥

[षष्टिं - 60 ◇ सहस्र - 1000 ◇ अश्वि - divided and spread ◇ अस्य - as ◇ अयुत - mixed ◇ असनम् - and seated ◇ उष्ट्रान - as a camel's back ◇ अं - moved ◇ विंशतिं - as 20 ◇ शता - and 100 ◇ दश - stages ◇ श्यावीनां - moved bold and dark ◇ शता - as 100 ◇ दश - stages ◇ त्रि - 3 ◇ अरुषीणां - strategic points ◇ दश - stages ◇ गवां - progressed ◇ सहस्रा - to 1000]

This essentially stated to use the numbers 60, 100, 120, and 1000 to configure a shape which will have a slope as if a camel's back. It suggested stages defined by 60. The dark zones and the bright zones of creation should configure in the resultant shape. It was this way that the universe came with bright regions of the created and the dark zones of the unknown.

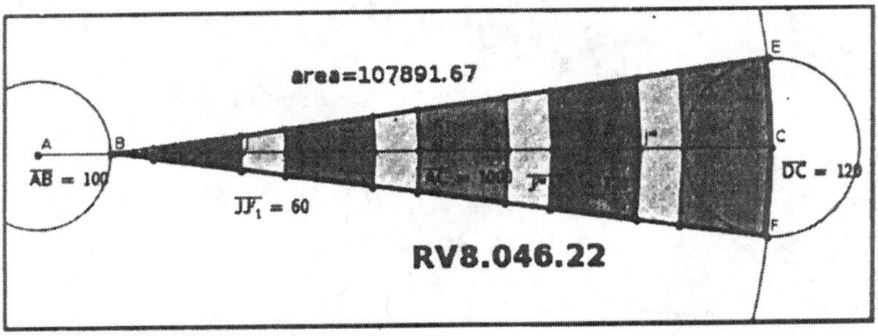

Figure 9.12: The Configuration of RV8.046

First draw a line AC, 1000 long and mark a point B at a length of 100 from A. Draw a circle from point A with 1000 as radius and then two circles with 100 and 120 as radius from points B and C. Point D is 120 inwards from point C. Lines joining E and F to A will cut the inner circle at H and G. Draw a line joining H and G and its midpoint is I. A segment from A and as AECFA will measure to 107,891.67 in place of the targeted 108,000. In this case, the area was compromised as 107,891.67, as shown in the Fig:9.12.

100 + (120 + 60) + (120 + 60) + (120 +60) + (120 + 60) + (120 + 60) = 1000

Further five stages are configured with 120 and 60 wide as shown in the figure. With these five stages an altar will be constructed as shown in Fig:9.13.

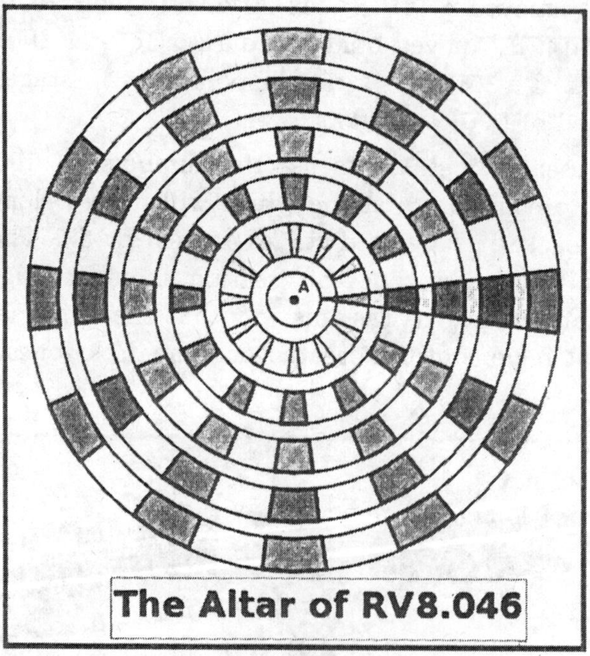

Figure 9.13: The Altar of RV8.046

It appears that two, three or more methods of conceiving the geometry must have been prevalent during those days. One was for the purposes of constructing an altar for oblations. That was what got depicted here at RV8.046 and as shown in Chapter 6. The other was for depicting the geometry of the expansion as the seven *vyāhṛtis*. The third was for depicting the 21 sizes that came offset fro the seven *vyāhṛti*. RV10.90.15 starting with "*saptāsyāsan paridhayas-trisapta samidhā kṛta* .." was thus a summary statement of this kind. The fourth and the most frequent ones in the *Ṛgveda* could be those for conceiving the nature of a basic expansion with a target of achieving 108,000 by different methods.

In RV10.052

The three verses of this hymn presented here was another way of conceiving the basic expansion into the seven *vyāhṛtis*.

RV10.052.04 मां देवा दधिरे हव्यवाहमपम्लुक्तम् बहु कृच्छ्रा चरन्तम्।
अग्निर्विद्वान्यज्ञं नः कल्पयाति पञ्चयामं त्रिवृतं सप्ततन्तुम्॥

[मां - as the arrangements ◇ देवा - that came from the heavens ◇ दधिरे - on churning, coagulation ◇ हव्यवाहमपम्लुक्तम् - carrying the products of oblation as hidden ◇ बहु - many ◇ कृच्छ्रा - that came inflicting pains ◇ चरन्तम् - moved till the end ◇ अग्निः - as *Agni* ◇ विद्वान् - moving with knowledge ◇ यज्ञं - and *yajña* ◇ नः - as ◇ कल्पयाति - moving in all possible ways ◇ पञ्चयामं - as 5 progression ◇ त्रिवृतं - 3 circles ◇ सप्त - 7 ◇ तन्तुम् - chords]

Along with the arrangements that came from the heavens, as the products of oblation and coagulation, came those many hidden ones which inflicted pain and those that moved till the end along with *Agni*, and those that moved along with knowledge and as moved from the *yajña*, and moved in all possible ways and indeed as the 5 progressions of 3 circularity's and as the 7 chord-like continuities.

10.052.05 आ वो यक्ष्यमृतत्वं सुवीरं यथा वो देवा वरिवः कराणि।
आ बाह्वोर्वज्रमिन्द्रस्य धेयामथेमा विश्वाः पृतना जयाति॥

[आ -Came ◇ वो - either as ◇ यक्षि - speedily ◇ अमृतत्वं - as the immortality ◇ सुवीरं - with superior courage ◇ यथा - suitably ◇ वो - or ◇ देवा - from the heavens ◇ वरिवः - as streams ◇ कराणि

- arms ◇ आ - came ◇ बाह्वोर् - as hands ◇ वज्रम् - of lightning (15th) ◇ इन्द्रस्य - from the *indrata* ◇ धेयाम् - getting placed ◇ अथ - along with ◇ इम - thus ◇ आ - coming ◇ विश्वाः -reaching everywhere ◇ पृतना - as strife ◇ जयाति - greatly successful]

Came speedily as if the immortality that moved courageously and in suitable ways from the heavens, or as the streams that branched and came as the arms of lightning (15th and so 15) of *indra*, getting placed, along with becoming the arrangements that reached everywhere, as a strife that was greatly successful.

RV10.052.06 त्रीणि शता त्री सहस्राण्यग्निं त्रिंशच्च देवा नव चासपर्यन्।
औक्षन्घृतैरस्तृणन्बर्हिरस्मा आदिद्धोतारं न्यसादयन्त॥

[त्रीणि - As 3 ◇ शता - came as 100 ◇ त्री - and 3 ◇ सहस्राणि - as 1000 ◇ अग्निं - the *Agni* ◇ त्रिंशच्च - as 30 ◇ देवा - from the heavens ◇ नव - as new (9) ◇ चासपर्यन् - seated around ◇ औक्षन् - came pouring down ◇ घृते - like sprinkled ghee ◇ अस्तृणन् - scattered ◇ बर्हि - as the bunches of grass ◇ अस्मा - the parts ◇ आदिद् - coming ◇ होतारं - from suitable oblations ◇ न्यसाद् - positioned to below ◇ अयन्त - as moved ◇]

As 3, 100, 3, 1000, as 30 and as new (9), along with the *Agni*, got seated to the surroundings of the heavens, came pouring down, got sprinkled like ghee and got scattered, (with the paths of creation that stood) as if bunches of grass, as the entities that indeed came untiringly till the end from suitable oblations and taking position to below.

In short, we have to make the configurations by the numbers 3, 9, 15, 30, 100 and 1000. It is clear from the verse RV10.52.04 that the expansion of the 7 *vyāhṛti* and its subdivision into 3 has to be configured. The basic configuration that gave the area of 108,197.22 was obtained by a first circle of radius 100 and the second circle of 900 radius and 9 circles of 15 radius. The next *vyāhṛti*s were offset at a rate of 465. See Fig 9.14.

The resultant area configuration is shown in the table below:

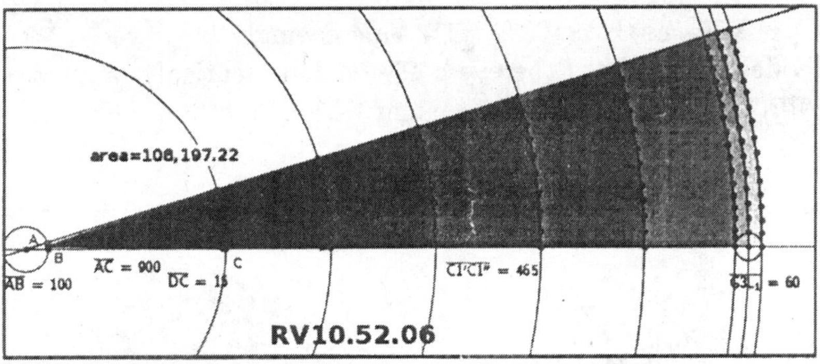

Figure 9.14: The Expansions Geometry of RV10.052.06

Table 9.3: Areas of sectors of RV10.52.06

	vyāhṛti	Area	*puruṣamātra*	(+)	(++)
1	First	108197.22	7.51	10.49	4.50
2	Second	259276.84	18.00	14.99	4.51
3	Third	475178.98	33.00	19.50	4.50
4	Fourth	755999.42	52.50	24.00	4.51
5	Fifth	1101720.82	76.51	28.51	-
6	Sixth	1512331.49	105.02	-	-
7	Sixth-minus	1455710.71	101.09	-	-
8	Sixth-plus	1570064.54	109.03	-	-

In RV10.055

This hymn contained yet another presentation of geometry by the following verse. Though the geometry here would be found similar to that of RV8.046, the trapezium measurements are different. But these validated each other and validated the approaches taken in the interpretations.

RV10.055.03 आ रोदसी अपृणादोत मध्यम् पञ्च देवाम् ऋतुशः सप्तसप्त। चतुस्त्रिंशता पुरुधा वि चष्टे सरूपेण ज्योतिषा विव्रतेन॥

[आ - Came ◇ रोदसी - from the heaven till the earth ◇ अपृणाद् - from a state of not bestowing ◇ ओत - weaved from ◇ मध्यम् - the middle ◇ पञ्च - as 5 ◇ देवा - moved from the heavens ◇ ऋतुशः - as the good seasons (less 6) ◇ सप्तसप्त - as 7 and 7 ◇

चतुस्त्रिंशता - as 3x4x100 ◇ पुरुधा -increasingly bestowed ◇ वि - divided ◇ चष्टे - from the eye ◇ सरूपेण - in identical manners ◇ ज्योतिषा - shining ◇ विव्रतेन - using various methods]

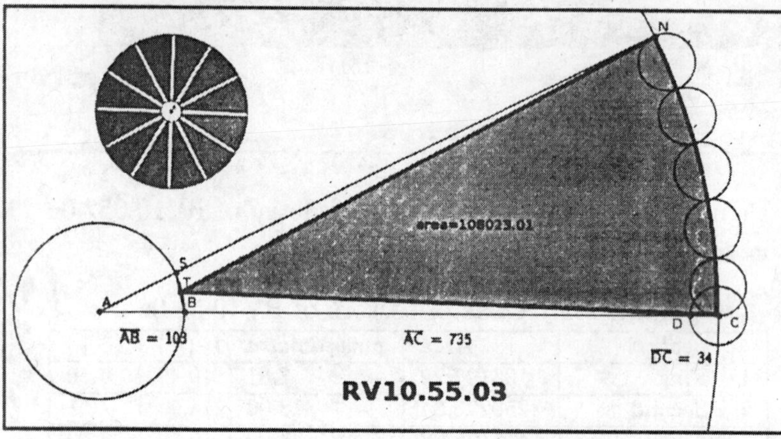

Figure 9.15: The Configuration of RV10.055

Those came from the heaven till the earth from a state of not bestowing, as 5 and as connected to the centre, like the good seasons, with 7 and 7 and 3, 4, 100, upon getting repeatedly divided from the eye (epicentre), as the shining things that got spread out. The universe got filled with the objects and those stood in groups and as different regions. To represent this aspect, let an altar be made as follows and as shown below:

It was stated to use the numbers 3, 4, 5, 7 (used twice) and 100 variously to obtain the necessary configuration. In the Fig 9.15, the first circle is of 103 radius, the second circle is of 735 radius, and 5 circles are swung over the arc. The area obtained is 108,023.01. The measurements are obtained as shown below:

$100 + 3 = 103$

$(7 \times 100) + (7 \times 5) = 735$

In RV4.26

Here is another verse (RV4.26.03) which contained an interesting geometry.

RV4.026.03 अहं पुरो मन्दसानो व्यैरं नव साकं नवतीः शम्बरस्य ।
शततमं वेश्यं सर्वताता दिवोदासमतिथिग्वं यदावम्॥

[अहं - the self ◇ पुरो - moving forward ◇ मन्दसानो - as the happiness ◇ व्यैरम् - the divided flows of a liquid form ◇ नव - 9 ◇ साकं - along with ◇ नवतीः - 90s ◇ शम्बरस्य - as a bottom of a pestle ◇ शततमम् - in hundredth ◇ वेश्यं - regions connected ◇ सर्वताता - providing all happiness ◇ दिवो - to the heaven ◇ दासम् - indebted ◇ अतिथिग्वं - offering refuge ◇ यद् - in many ways ◇ आवम् - descending]

It is the usage of terms like *nava*, *navatī* and *śatatamaṃ* that told us that there could be a concept of geometry hidden in the words. Any geometrical presentation based on these should use 9 and 90 as well as 100, and come up with not only an acceptable geometry but an acceptable Vedic idea as well. The details of construction are as below, using the following measurements.

$90 + 9 + 9 = 108$

$90 \times 9 = 810$

Draw aline AC = 810 and on this mark point B at a distance of 108 from A as shown in Fig 9.13. Mark D at 9 away from point C. Draw a circle from point A with AC as radius and yet another circle with AB as radius. Draw a small circle from point C and CD as radius. Set off 8 full circles (a matter of trial and error) progressively from point C as shown, to obtain point T. Join the line AT. Mirror the details to obtain point T'. The lines AT and AT' cut the circle of 108 radius at points V and U respectively. Make the line UV and mark its middle point W. Divide the distance VW and UW into two to get points Z and Z1 respectively. Create a region as Z1-Z-T-T'-Z1, along the arc of T-T'. This will return an area of 108009.8726 (The corresponding figure is not shown).

But in this construction, the term "*śatatamaṃ*" meaning an operation by the hundredth was not hitherto carried out and the area resulted was not entirely satisfactory. Therefore, now the value of 108 is to be adjusted, upward for the reason that we obtained a higher area value. More of trial and error established a measurement of 108.11 which returned an area of 108000.0496 which we could now take as satisfactory, being accurate to the extent of 0.0000459%. See Fig:9.16.

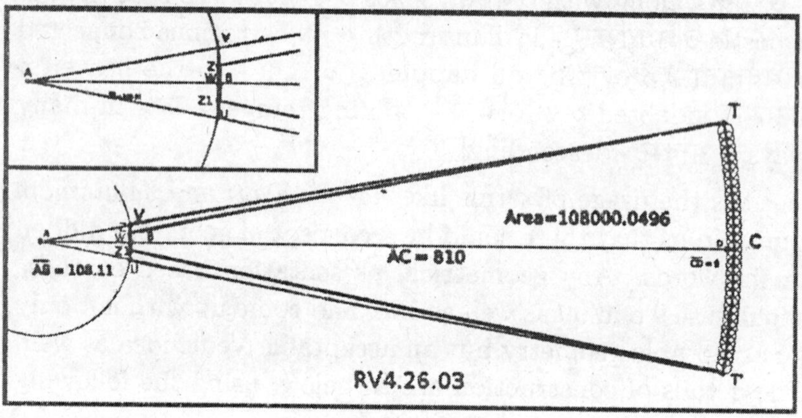

Figure 9.16: The Configuration of RV4.026.03

For one thing, it is a geometrical configuration described by very few words. Then it contained a tuning operator proposed by the term "*śatatamaṃ*". Thirdly, the very accuracy of the area value is simply astonishing. This configuration could have been the fore-runner of the *droṇaciti* described by the *sūtra* 18 of *Baudhāyana*. It once again appeared that the *Ṛgveda* was firmly anchored on geometrical principles along with the divine matters and the cosmology of the universe.

In RV10.90

It is now necessary to look into the *puruṣasūkta* as the first four verses indicated the presence of a geometrical configuration of the *rāśīcakra*. The term "*daśāṅgulam*" that appeared in the first verse, the term "*jyāya*" in the third verse etc. pointed to a geometry.

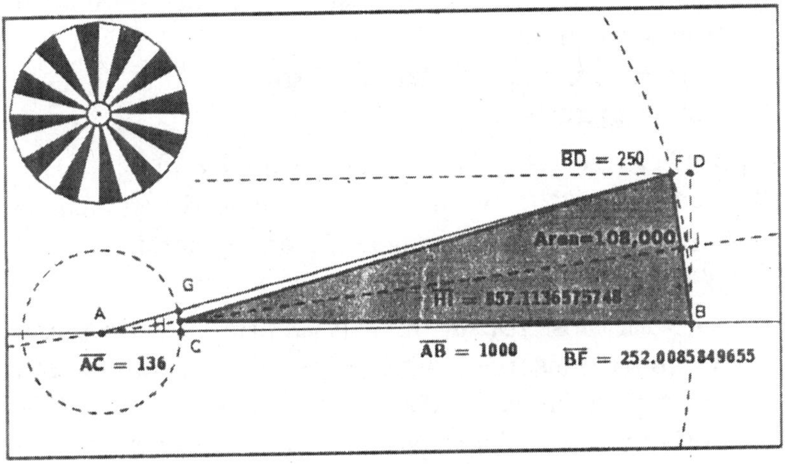

Figure 9.17: The Configuration of RV10.90

From the interpretation of the said verses, *sahasraśīrṣā* would be 1000 from the centre, and *puruṣa* would be 120 from the centre. The value of 120 will be now modified to 136 as follows:

daśāṅgulam - 10 ; *ati ati ṣṭha* - 3 + 3 = 6 ie, the three digits of the finger taken twice. This will be 120 + 10 + 6 = 136. From the term "*pada*, the value of 250 will be taken.

Therefore in figure B (Fig 9.17), AB will be 1000 and AC will be 136. Draw the corresponding circles. Set up a parallel line ED at a distance of 250 from AB. This line cuts the circle at point F. Join the points A and F by a line. This line cuts the inner circle at G. Join the line CG and mark its midpoint H. The triangle HBF will return an area of 108,000. This configuration in a way solved the riddle of the *daśāṅgulam*, though the other literary meanings of the same presented in the relevant chapter stood valid.

In RV4.030.21

It was not geometry alone that received the attention of the sages. Arithmetic notions could also be found skillfully added to the ideas in order to communicate effectively. Here is an example of such an instance.

RV4.030.21 अस्वापयद्दभीतये सहस्रा त्रिंशतं हथैः।
दासानामिन्द्रो मायया॥

[अस्वापयद् - obstructing the sleep ◇ द - giving ◇ भीतये - fear ◇ सहस्रा - a 1000 ◇ त्रिंशतं - with 30 ◇ हथैः - divided and balance remained ◇ दासानाम् - progressively becoming nothing ◇ इन्द्रो - from इन्द्रत ◇ मायया - moving like an apparition]

Along with those fearful things that prevented sleep and moved as apparitions, the creation of the universe progressed in emaciating orders, as if 1000 is divided by 30 and as balanced of the visible. There was a severe diminishing order in the remainder which could be mathematically (in principle and not in measures and counts) presented as below using 1000 and 30:

Table 9.4: A series

Balanced	1000	1	0.001	0.00001	0.0000001
Dividend	33.3	0.0033	0.000033	0.00000033	0.0000000033
Product	999	0.999	0.00099	0.0000099	0.000000099
Balance	1	0.001	0.00001	0.0000001	0.000000001

It proves to show that not only the decimal systems were well within the ambit of their knowledge, purposeful and intelligent operations were also usual. As regards the birth of the universe, the gradual emaciation to the ends should be taken valid for all the phenomena. The mathematical operation shown need not be terminated here and could be taken further by addition of more of 3 to 33.3 etc. which would show endlessly larger and larger depreciation rates. Therefore the usage of term "*sahasrā*" has much more significance.

It could be concluded that the *Ṛgveda* employed geometrical concepts as essential parts of the descriptions, for the very purpose of deriving theoretical strength from accurate and incontestable presentations. The geometry of the *Ṛgveda* was found to have nothing to do with the earth bound entities and realities. Neither was those furnishing any of the dimensions and absolute details of this universe. While the geometry presented in this chapter was based on the precession of the ecliptic, the numbers came to conceptualize the geometry accurately. The numbers, like 3, 7, 21, 100, 105, 1000 etc. in other instances and in other chapters, also came to indicate the nature of a progress and to demonstrate the tendencies observed. The calculations of the ecliptic were based on the fundamental division of the circle into 360 and 60's, arriving at a *rāśi* value of 108,000. As a result the precession rate was $1^o/72$ years or 48 seconds per year and correspondingly the Great Cycle Time got configured as 27000 years. In comparison the modern science have somewhat concluded on a value of 25920 years based on the precession rate of 50 or 50.21 seconds per year. However, its predictability over a period of 27000 years might come correct, only with an assumption that there is nothing that would disturb the present structure and more pertinently, nothing external would influence it to any degree. In the very principle, the *Ṛgveda* differs with this notion. Therefore, it could be presumed that according to the *Ṛgveda*, it did not matter whether the precession rate is 48 seconds per year or 50 seconds per year. The only intention was that the concept should come as a basic principle, universal in nature. Indeed a mathematical order was proposed but a universal interactive nature with attendant possible influences and variations were also proposed with equal emphasis. Therefore, it is relevant only to discuss the relative principles without insisting on absolute values. In the very principle, the *Ṛgveda* differs with this notion. Therefore, it could be presumed that according to the *Ṛgveda*, it did not matter whether the precession rate is 48 seconds per year or

50 seconds per year. The only intention was that the concept should come as a basic principle, universal in nature. Indeed a mathematical order was proposed but a universal interactive nature with attendant possible influences and variations were also proposed with equal emphasis. Therefore, it is relevant only to discuss the relative principles without insisting on absolute values.

Then what was the nature of this Vedic enquiry? Briefly put, it was a search for connecting a cosmic phenomena, adopting a finite number and area of 108,000, creating a semblance of rationality from a set of values and achieving all, out of very clear and simple geometric steps. However the irrational nature might surface at any moment, in any of the study of such realities.

How could the ropes with loops on ends and a few wooden pegs, configure and reveal these astonishing levels of accuracy and conceptual perfection? How could a theory be so neatly wedded to geometry? How could a so called primitive set of Vedic people bedazzle us like this? ⋆⋆⋆

10

The Vedic Cosmos

Some of the hymns of the *Ṛgveda* and a selected few of the *Atharvaveda* that appeared to deal with the cosmology of the universe were presented through the earlier chapters, the interpretation being based on their physical (*bhautika*) content. Those revealed that the Vedic sages had an in-depth awareness of the cosmological principles that were found to surface in other civilizations at a much later time. At the same time, the vivid accounts of the physical nature of creation came only with the divine aspects, very much stressed.

Thus the *puruṣasūkta* [PS] presented the concept of the *Puruṣa*, the cosmic man, who along with the *Prakṛti* brought the universe into existence. This hymn dwell-ed on the physical aspects of creation and did not much emphasize on the participation of the *saguṇa* divinities. A regenerative process closely linked with the common birth and the dissolution, was visible in the descriptions. These physical processes would not have progressed without a divine participation. The *puruṣasūkta* refrained from directly and conspicuously mentioning the *Agni*. It did not declare the presence of *Agni* and at same time left us with no option than to conceive it in the processes that were described. In comparison, the *nāsadīyasūkta* introduced *Agni* directly and in the very beginning as the very *Śakti* element that would enable all the processes of creation.

The *nāsadīyasūkta* [NS] of seven verses, gave an account of the state of the unknown before the creation and then went on to state what could have happened immediately after. While the PS described the physical process of origin of the universe and the subsequent events, the *nāsadīyasūkta* supplied the properties of such events, though these took to differing ideological approaches. An intense original heat and temperature provided all the energy required for the first of creation and this heat manifested in every stage of creation. In the NS, the *Agni* was at the centre stage of all events. A remarkable statement was that space and time could start only along with the first of creations, just as the light and darkness could only be. The creation process, the three dimensional space and the advent of time were thus stated as instantaneous occurrences. It appeared that the subject of where to install that super temperature that the modern cosmologists and physicists contemplated and confronted with, did not trouble the Vedic set. They envisaged a supreme space and a matter of unknown properties into which an original tiny matter of equally unknown properties and values of having manifested, the universe could spring up to the later and present state. All the same, they declared the existence of unfathomable subjects to which we did not have access.

Both PS and NS agreed to the absence of external introductions into the space born and declared that everything happened within itself. While the PS took to a route of instantaneous growth by production of matter and energy in a process of self multiplication, the NS postulated a higher level of energy and matter at the introductory stage. However, the NS also stated of the *annabhāva* and the *śabda* just as the PS did. But further statements did not appear to firmly establish this factor, in spite of the statements of derivative generation. The NS resorted to a straight forward description and a state of awe was visible throughout the description. This awe was somehow not very visible in the PS, which went on describing the creation of the different classes of objects of the universe, in a matter of fact fashion.

The hymn RV10.130, more or less embraced the principles of both PS and NS. [1] The subject of the seven *vyāhṛtis*, its division to 21 were conceptually formulated. It said that the *Agni* manifested out of and along with the *śabda*, both emanating from a divine mind. In the *sūkta* RV10.154, it was proposed that the universe was born out of an intense heat that came roaring. The hymn RV10.190 of just 3 verses, said that from the unknown *Sat*, manifested the first known and became *Satya*. The opposing qualities, one of entities, specific routes of creation and the other of darkness that surrounded all, were brought into focus. The Truth contained the first of all cause and effect and was visible and thus tenable to description. The first steps of creation could indeed take off from here. The hymn had yet another purpose of suggesting the presence of an ethereal substance implied by the description of the cosmic ocean which could then support such notions as the "murmur" and "roar" described elsewhere, suggesting the necessity of a medium.

RV10.81 and RV10.82 stated that it was not known from which this universe came and into which it was born, but stated that all was born as a result of the oblation of what remained near to the point of origin. There was a hundred repetitions of what happened at the heaven and there was serious mixing of what were born. However, it was stated that the domain, extent and limits of the universe was not known. What supported the universe was not known. Out of what substance the universe got created was not known. The point of origin itself manifested from a womb of extreme darkness and the growth proceeded equitably in all directions. What was thus born were hot, cold, big, small or dusty as it came about, compounded with their union or fragmentation.

---

[1]It is not implied here that any particular *sūkta* borrowed ideas from another.

The *Soma* initially remained in the heaven as inactive and then suddenly got awakened and became a flow of objects and the energy of the universe. The *Soma* became the seed principle as well as the very exhilaration for creation. Along with the paths of creation that contained the *Soma*, came the darkness that surrounded it. The *Soma*, an unseen brightness held this darkness at abeyance. It fought with the *vṛtrata* that appeared at every proximate region. The *Soma* provided not only the seed principle for creation but into this all could dissolve upon individual dissolution. It was from an ever existing divine mind that the divine sounds manifested for the first time. These divine sounds were the cosmic vibrations and were thus instrumental in the division and propagation of matter throughout the universe.

In the Hymn RV3.62, the famous *gāyatrīmantra* and its abiding deity of *Savita* were presented. It also presented the essential nature of several divinities. It is a complex subject, with the line of demarcation not very clear. When would an object or a phenomenon become divine? One of the assumption would be that when something that could not be expressed and explained by rational thoughts and by a language, then a concept of divinity comes in automatically. We assume that only the *Brahma* came as God Supreme (which itself was not stated with absolute certainty and clarity) as per the Veda. The *gayatrīmantra* stated that a brightness and intellect pervaded through the universe. It was through this, the interactive nature prevailed. An inquiry into a single line equation of existence was a favourite subject for such a long time and it is so even today. A statement that would define all that happened and all that would possibly happen (*sans* predictions) is still anxiously awaited. That has not yet happened in spite of the enormous tools that the modern astrophysicists and cosmologists have assembled. But it appeared that the *gāyatri* put forward a concept much nearer to the target than anything else and till now.

In the first of creations of the universe and in the existence ever after and in the complex phenomena that always accompanied, an all prevalent interactive nature was anointed, with all the qualities of a very concise equation. It was stated that none could transcend the dictum proclaimed by the *gāyatri* and thus it appeared to be one of the most scientific and complete statement on this subject that ever occurred. Though almost equivalent concepts could have been mentioned by the modern scientists in so many words, the fact that the statement of the *gāyatri* came from such a long time back and ever remained a divine utterance to the people of India could be termed as a matter of great pride. It somehow validated our claims of a long time of existence, a scientific pursuit and made us feel important. The *gāyatri* seems to recommend a structured existence for all. In a way this rule touched even the dissolution of the universe by the fact that at that critical moment of implosion a supreme command would call back everything to naught.[2]. The name of the divinity called *Savita* to a certain extent could be compared with the concept of the divine *Soma*. It was more or less confirmed that the brilliant and excellent intellect of *Savita* remained at a higher level in the hierarchical order of divinities. From the hymns on the divinity of *Savita*, it came about that it could be either *nirguṇa* or *saguṇa*. It was described essentially as a brightness and intellect that reflected on all of those that existed. It prompted, promoted and inspired the *saguṇa* divinities into action.

RV1.164 stated that there were more than one theory regarding the birth of the universe and all of them were considered relevant. This hymn stated that many of the manifestations in this universe came only as mixed and interspersed and the poet resorted to an identical route of description. It gave the details of a circular *citi* with seven annular rings to represent the seven *vyāhṛtis*. RV1.164.48 explained the concept of 108,000 sq. *aṅgulam* used in the construction of the *uttaravedis*, though this geometrical concept could be found

[2]Though not found stated in the *Ṛgveda*

much repeated in the Vedas. In addition, the same verse stipulated one geometrical concept of the expansions of the seven *vyāhṛtis*. These belied any assumption or proclamation that the geometry during the Vedic period was simple and primitive. The most significant theory put forward by this hymn was that since these circularity's manifested one after the other in an ascending order, the larger ones traversed through the smaller ones and therefore systems and objects got mixed up. For this reason, there could be several mixed loyalties spread among several systems. It emphasized the manifestation of darkness and talked about those evil ones that came from it. It also proposed that due credence should be given to the theories that the manifestation of the universe was almost a biological process. The bull that bellowed and the cow that stood anxiously waiting for its calves, that bird *suparṇa* etc. came as part of such theories. It stated that in the process of creation of so many good things of the universe, most inevitably those annihilating forces were also raising their heads.

RV1.99 meant that the term "*jātaveda*" pronounced the concept that the *śabda* was the primordial cosmic vibrations itself. RV1.89 was a beautiful and elegant description of the process of creation which came as a divine occurrence and stated that the universe was made into ever so great a place where all co-existed in apparent peace. It described the voids that were generated in the processes of creation and in the processes of multiplication. RV7.41 was yet another elegant description of the universe. It claimed that the universe was created and maintained as a magnificent place which accommodated all. RV10.09 suggested that the *Soma* was well comparable to the water on the earth. Both acted as a repository of the seed principle and both flowed downwards from wherever it earlier existed. These were described as the magic potion of life and the semen virile that flowed down from the heaven. Upon local dissolution, all returned to these eternal sources.

In the very first hymn of the first *kāṇḍa* of *Atharvaveda*, it was stated that "*vāk-śabda*" and thereby the cosmic vibrations that came from a divine mind was the first of reasons for the process of creation. The universe took to the form of the seven *vyāhṛtis*, subsequently each got divided into 3, equal to both sides and became 21 circular (spherical) formations. The very act brought in a state of perpetual resonance for ever. The care and perfection with which the entire sequence was planned was astonishing. These sub-divisions occurred to each of the seven *vyāhṛtis* and thereby it was implied that the individual forces were of lesser value than that which caused the original expansion. Further, the state of resonance was separately installed in seven levels whereby though there were clearly drawn boundaries, the objects came interspersed to one another of the *vyāhṛtis*, just as stated in the *asyavāmīyasūkta*. It implied that one large resonant force in the seventh *vyāhṛti* was not capable of all the pulsating state of the entire universe. Thus the significance of the concept of " *ananta*" in the description of the universe would be found to fade away.

The hymn AV1.32 mainly stated that the universe took form from the heaven (*hiraṇyagarbha*) to the surroundings as formations that also greatly came descended and became emaciated by the time it grew to its full extent. The systems of energies also took to the same format of gradual reduction to the end regions. The hymn AV2.12 said that as if by an unseen wind the universe took large strides to grow into its immense size. The one who partook the *Soma*, divided the very *Soma* and separate streams of creations took shape. Coming into existence as a series of tumultuous events, sun-like objects were scattered around into the seven *vyāhṛtis* and into the 21 divisions. The hymn AV2.35 stated that from the fixed axis and from the *Soma* that remained nearby, the creation flowed downwards constantly accompanied and rightly persuaded by the divine words. The hymn AV6.112 stated that the creation took place as a chain of events that emanated from knowledge and made possible by the *Viśvakarmā*.

Chapter-9 presented certain selected verses wherein geometry was found essentially ingrained. These verses dwelt on the theories of the ecliptic, its division into 12 *rāśis*. The angularity of a *rāśi* was computed to a value of 108,000, which was the area of the *uttaravedi* since the Vedic times. Though these verses were singled out from the enormous *Ṛgveda* text, the concept of geometry could be taken as widespread through out the Veda. References to the 3 points designated as positioned at the edge of the heaven, or that space from which the creation started, could be recognised in many verses of the *Ṛgveda*.

The universe

The inquiry about how the universe came, started several millennium ago and appeared to be still continuing with new vigour. Ever new theories abound the modern science and cosmology and strong arguments were found put forward claiming correctness of each. These modern inquiries had the backing of extensive facilities of observation, experiments, mathematical analysis, all well founded on earlier established and confirmed facts. Though much difference of opinions occurred, nevertheless these progressed forcefully. But none of these could surprise us as much as the contents of the Vedic text would do. For, what in modern times got theorized could be termed as proportionate to what we have accumulated as knowledge and facilities. On the other hand and in comparison, the theories put forward by the Vedic texts, appeared to come out of vacuum. It would be found convenient to accept the dictum that the Veda is *apauruṣeya* than to believe that these came from rational thought processes. For, the profundity of the thought processes of the Vedic sages, would confound the modern mind in no small measure.

The highly poetic descriptions, presentation methodology, the arrangement of words enabled to be read with multiple meanings, expert coining of technical terms though of localised significance, and above all creating a world of *śabda* could be termed simply out of this world. Perhaps we could never understand the mind of the Vedic sages, who in spite of knowing and declaring that many of the matters of the creation and existence of the universe as beyond comprehension, still ventured to deeply think about it, come out with several theories and place them into our realms of knowledge. For this, we find that their mind traveled into a vastness and to that point beyond everything, that which touched the Supreme Divinity.

Geometry of the Universe

To us everyday the Sun rose in the east and set in the west. Struck by its regularity and power, realising its attributes and causal nature to all that happened on earth, we prayed to this God to guide us in our efforts. Thus we faced East at Sunrise and with folded hands looked upward. We have no difficulty to get ourselves oriented with a basic sense of direction which we resolved into 4 cardinal directions, its sub-divisions or the ecliptic as desired. In the night many stars appeared like glittering diamonds and many of them could be located or identified with some accuracy. But for the Vedic sages, the universe was not these things alone. They too gazed at a point far away and they knew that they had to see up to an epicentre of all events and named it as the *viśvacakṣus*, the eye of the universe. It was the primary location of a divinity and a divine mind. If the universe that they saw came from this epicentre or if it had any part to play in the process of creation, then it could not have been a lopsided universe that emerged from there. It could not have exercised any partiality in any direction. And then what would be direction itself when there was nothing in the beginning of it all? It could have grown in a thousand directions from this epicentre. But a question arose as to how a mere point and nothingness could pour out this vast universe? The parts of the universe that they saw, all by itself, came as enormous and beyond comprehension.

But it was from that space heaven, located at or near the *viśvacakṣus* that the events of creation started, prompted and overseen by a Supreme Divinity. This heaven stood slightly away from the *viśvacakṣus* just as the hub of a chariot wheel would do from its centre and this epicentre remained motionless. This heaven was the first divine platform of creation and could be stated as located just below, above, left or right as one wished and circular or spherical as further wished. For we, men of this earth, it would be better to see the epicentre much above and far, in some or the other direction from us such that we could describe the events that followed with an impressed sense of direction and conveniently as downwards and till us. But was there not a universal law about what all could have happened in the beginning of the universe? Could they see the reflections of the same now, in this earth, their surroundings and in man's own existence? Or was there a different set of laws of existence then, at those points of time of such considerations than what we saw it now? Most unlikely. There could have been many types of manifestations and establishment of different properties and there could have been several mutations that brought about totally different objects and properties in course of time. But there had to be a set of common laws, applicable then and applicable now. Was there a single equation that covered all the events and phenomena that started with the creation, till now? If a totally interactive universe was imagined, there could not have been a serious discontinuity to disrupt over any period of time and over any of the cosmic incidences. In the meanwhile no catastrophic disorder could be imagined to have taken place, which would hide those original events or obliterate the perpetual marks left. There could not have been a discontinuity to the space and time correlations that started in the very beginning. Therefore, it would be appropriate to imagine many aspects of the first of creations with comparable events and phenomena of the earth that they saw now, duly scaled to universal dimensions. But these things were more related to the language and expressions and not the seeing proper which had already taken place in a state of *turīyāvastha* of the discerning minds. All of these could not be communicated. What could be effectively communicated had to be confined to the 16 principles with which human beings realise everything, which were also known as the *ṣoḍaśakalā*.

As we see a 3-dimensional universe in existence, a 3-dimensionality had to be born first. This 3-dimensionality would have to be presented as 2-dimensional extracts while being described. At any rate, it would not be possible to describe the 3-dimensionality as such and in full. What would be described of this 3-dimensionality would be presented as descriptions in terms of the 2-dimensional visuals. Therefore, when a circle was described, it could be a sphere. When a tree was described as standing in the heaven, there were several such trees that stood in all the 1000 directions. When a sun-like shine beamed towards earth, it beamed in all directions. When *suparṇa* the bird circled down to the earth, so did many, in many directions. When a mountain stood with its apex at the heaven and base towards the earth, so did a 1000 mountains in all directions. From the heaven the seven circular *vyāhṛtis* got formed with the *viśvacakṣus* as the apparent epicentre and the last of *vyāhṛtis* reaching up to the end of the universe. The *viśvacakṣus* remained with a floating gap from the rest of the universe or vice versa. The binding force of all was a universal consciousness and intellect which shined proportionately all over the universe.

The seven *vyāhṛtis* were the basic geometrical order of the universe, the first of which near the *viśvacakṣus* being called the heaven, *viśvatomukha*, *mayobhuva*, *hiraṇyagarbha* etc. In the seventh *vyāhṛti*, this earth and similar objects remained.[3] Though the universe would become so large at the

[3]Curiously, whether our solar system came in the seventh *vyāhṛti* or not, did not come specified by the statements. The earth was more prominent as the location of the perceiver, than anything else.

very instant of its birth, immeasurably large, it could not be classified as infinite or ever expanding. The universe indeed started expanding from the very moment it was created, instantly and up to the seventh *vyāhṛti*. Then this expansion was controlled by a unique event. Each of the seven *vyāhṛtis* got divided into three, one part remaining and the parts on both sides moving instantly to opposite sides equally; ascending and descending. Thus the seven *vyāhṛtis* became 21 distinct spheres of entities. The universe shook all over(?) and came to a state of perpetual resonance. Those events created the definitions of the distinct geometrical organisations of the universe.

The sphericity of the universe was thus only approximate on two counts. For one, the perpetual resonance and the pulsating nature that came about would not accommodate a permanent exactitude. For another, there was a floating gap between the *viśvacakṣus* and the heaven. Besides, though it was picturised that the *vyāhṛtis* took form as circularity's with respect to the *viśvacakṣus* or the heaven near by, it was also stated that the universe was formed with its paths of creation swirled around and downward with respect to its nominal axis, which itself was defined as a space of small size![4] It was for this reason that the term axis doubled as the eye. And that too simultaneously and in what all directions? Therefore, the *vyāhṛtis* also got formed in a complex manner. The *vyāhṛtis* were parallel circularity's for the sake of convenience in descriptions of geometric representations, but those *vyāhṛtis*, at the same time, also descended progressively from the heaven in a complex manner. However, the formation of the universe could be described only with more and more of details.

What geometry described above amounted to be the broad structural organisation of the universe in the shape of the seven *vyāhṛtis* and the subdivisions of 21. Those were the

---

[4]So it was stated in the *asyavāmīyasūkta*.

geometric bases of the atmosphere through which different hierarchical orders took off in all directions, from the subsequent many heavens. Those were, in a way, the classification of the intensity and density levels of a descending order. Those should be in turn got extrapolated into appropriate spherical regimes. But the *ādisṛṣṭi* had more of geometrical orders. For one, there was a sense of symmetry in whatever that happened. Thus all manifestations came equally to both the left and the right, whichever ways and routes the creation progressed. It maintained the universe in a state of equilibrium for ever. The final sate of equilibrium had many minor component states of equilibrium. The creations took off from the small space of the heaven in all directions with this sense of equilibrium, in main trunk routes which were then repeatedly sub-divided into several branches in the same manner. Thus the line sketch of the routes resembled those symmetrical pipul trees that stood on the edges of the heaven into all directions. Not only these stood so, 3-dimensionally so, these all manifested simultaneously, instantly and as extended till far off places like this earth.

Thus the Vedic sages clearly envisaged a spherical universe of incalculably large dimensions which had a vague epicentre rather than an absolute centre. The sages conceived this most enigmatically and at the same time efficiently. One of the reason that the universe was compared to the *rathacakra* was to clearly enunciate the concepts that went into the nature of the epicentre. They used the inevitable clearance between the wheel hub and the axle to represent and locate the epicentre vaguely floating. If a wheel rotated (the universe of course did not rotate) the very centre could not be termed as rotating. It was under a constant urge to rotate and this urge got transmitted through the limbs of the wheel to the very end. Perhaps this was the very genesis of the interactive nature that pervaded everywhere. It agreed with the concept of the perpetual resonance in which the universe remained. The universe got tense from the moment the

3-dimensionality got instituted and thereafter the space and time correlation never broke down. An interactive intellect came into force from the very moment of creation, goes on through the existence and would collapse at the moment of dissolution, if at all. The space and time correlation would be valid so long as that state of resonance imparted values and maintained a dynamic order.

Just as the epicentre-heaven geometric relation was unsteady, the same concept was useful for defining the sphericity of the universe. In more than one occasions it was stated that the universe took this shape by a swirling action simultaneously executed with reference to several axises (or not) and as if from a small space acting as the base. An action of rotation, around and downwards, the much repeated terms of the *Ṛgveda*. The vagueness of the location of the hub with reference to the axle was thus very convenient and agreed with other notions. The whole of geometry and the principles that were readable into the texts thus stood complementary to one another. The sages conceived these with an unbelievable and stunning correctness.

The Objects and Phenomena

Once, nothing existed in the universe, not even the smallest of anything. Was there a darkness prevailing as somewhere? That was also not known. It was known that a divine mind and an everlasting "will" only existed for ever. The time had not manifested and therefore how long this divine mind and the supreme will remained was not known or relevant. Knowledge itself was not relevant as there was nothing first or second. The space and 3-dimensionality had not formed yet. The energy and light was not there and so there was no darkness that could be named. Then suddenly a particle of a bright and shining matter manifested as into somewhere and this place came to be known as the heaven. It was called the *hiraṇyagarbha*, as it now contained this golden embryo. It was called the *viśvatomukha*, as it was the very mouth and face of creation where the sacred hymns reverberated. It was called the *mayobhuva*, as this became the first pleasant space from where the magical birth of the universe took place.

It could not be stated with absolute certainty what subsequently happened by which the universe became enormous. There were different theories on this and each of them appeared to be true. These matters had received the prolonged attention of many learned seers. Though a consensus possibly did not emerge, there were several matters on which all agreed. The first of these would be that nothing external, other than what first came into existence automatically, ever participated or contributed to the growth of the universe. The universe became so enormous and so powerful with a variety of bright and hot matter as well as small and big objects, all by its own. The objects got widely distributed till this earth with varying levels of heat, which emaciated gradually during the outward distribution. Thus the inner core area of the universe was intense both in contents, density and thermal levels which were then found to gradually diminish in the outward direction. There were objects that were flung afar with a high motive force and there were objects that got formed as secreted from the main stream. Thus there were strong and apparently independent systems of objects and several combinations of their interactive existences. Those weaker secreted entities stood loyal to their parent bodies. There were swirling furies and secreting soberness side by side. There were objects that got sprinkled continuously from the paths that took off from whatever came potentially first formed. There were thus a thousand configurations to reckon.

One of the predominant theory was that it was into the *Soma* that the primordial bright particle of matter first manifested. The *Soma*, which contained the elixir of seed substance was lying as a heap, inert and immature for an unknown period. Along with the bright particle that manifested into the *Soma*, from a divine mind the *śabda* having emanated, these surrounded the very same *Soma* meaningfully and intently. This divided the *Soma* into many and that much streams of creation flowed downwards and outwards from the heaven. Thus it reached the very end of the universe. The *Soma* remained transparently enveloping the creations for ever. The *Soma* thus provided the seed substance to all of creations and acted as a ready receptacle for individual dissolution. On earth the *Soma* provided immortality of another kind by sustaining life forms which went into the evolutionary cycles. It was as if it held *Vanaspati* in reverence.

Along with the bright and the opaque bodies that were created, along with the *Soma* that flowed down, a darkness had also come born. This darkness was kept at abeyance from the paths of creation by the enveloping nature of the *Soma*. The dark zones were yet other conic sections of volumes or whatever other shapes and volumes, that came surrounding the path of creations. For, the *antarikṣa* extending from the heaven to the very end of the universe was born along with the bright objects which remained within the long plenums of the *Soma* and it was side by side to these that the darkness came born and remained. In fact the *vyāhṛtis* were the organisational and structural format of the *antarikṣa*. This darkness was known as the *vṛtrata* that surrounded the paths of creations. Within the plenum of the *Soma*, whatever darkness that manifested was kept at abeyance or destroyed by the bright objects themselves. And yet there were dark and ominous entities of unknown properties here and there, that looked like the caves of darkness that attracted, and which the bright objects deftly avoided. These dark entities were formed by a swirling action about their own individual axis and who could tell what it contained and how to describe the invisible? But those were there and those might's encroached into the paths of creation. Those captured many of the created and destroyed them beyond recognition.

The universe was thus born from an excellence that remained in heaven as several excellence's that manifested to the surroundings and downwards. The *ādisṛṣṭi* could not, however, be termed as a pleasant and smooth only occurrence brought about by a Supreme Divinity. It had its moments of exhilaration provided by the *Soma*, but also had those moments of anxiety not only in the very beginning but extended to the very end of the several progresses. Those were steady progresses that did not turn back, but the objects also had to face setbacks and destruction. There were happy agglomerations and tearing hungers side by side. There were regal sovereign-ties and those evil ones that conquered and destroyed. And yet, ultimately all settled down to a happy and benevolent state.

In the beginning nothing of the four dimensions of space and time as well as energy existed. All came created upon the advent of that bright particle of matter into the heaven. Therefore, it was from the heaven, very near to the *Viśva cakṣus*, that the 3-dimensionality took form. It was only along with this 3-dimensionality that time was born. Simultaneously the *Agni* had manifested into that bright particle of matter and from it the universe grew instantaneously to the surroundings. But first, it was the divine sounds and the cosmic vibrations that enabled all. It was this *śabda* that became the *Agni*. It was this *śabda* again that matured the *Soma* and then divided it into many. It was the *śabda* assuming appropriate levels that manifested as the three dimensions and thus came containing the cause and effect of everything from the beginning. It was the *śabda* that propagated the objects by providing a motive force in wave form. Those were the divine sounds that came from the *Brahma*, the Supreme Divinity. Those were the cosmic vibrations that manifested and spread. These *śabda* came in appropriate and sufficient levels, whenever and wherever necessary. It was divine by origin, by nature and could manifest anywhere.

There were more than a couple of theories of how the universe grew to its immense size right after the manifestation of that shining particle of matter. In one of these, the universe grew from that infinitesimal matter to its very enormity with the *annabhāva*. According to this theory, that very particle consumed itself and grew to a larger size on a food principle. The very particle contained the cause and effect which went on multiplying in a geometric progression. The cause and the effect grew larger and larger instantly. These created nothingness at many stages of original occupancy. The birth and the progress of expansion of the universe and the manifestation of everything were reposed on a *yajña* principle and heat and temperature came sufficiently and as it occurred. These *yajñas* took place under divine guidance and according to the divine rules. It envisaged a process of a totally interactive self multiplication, an omniscient presence of divinity and the constant accompaniment of the *śabda*.

Yet another proposition was that it was the manifestation and association of the *Agni* into that shining particle of matter that the larger processes of creation took place. The value of the heat that manifested was almost equivalent to the sum total of all the contents of this universe. But this theory had also an element of the *annabhāva* and the very same *śabda* as parts of the cause and effects. Therefore, the value equivalence that was mentioned could not be categorically assigned to the very beginning of the process. This theory had mentioned about the roaring sounds that came in the initial stages of expansion. All the same, in principle it declared an explosive growth due to an extreme heat and temperature that appeared in the very beginning of creation.

There were other theories as well. One of them stated that this universe came as executed by several divinities under the guidance of a Supreme Divinity. Another theory stated that this universe was born out of the mind of a Supreme Divinity in His own state of *turīyāvastha*! Yet others proposed that the universe was created by *suparṇa*, the bird that originally remained in the heaven and which circled and flew down till this earth and created the immortal objects. It was sprinkling the *amṛt* and an immortality till the end. However, there was a general agreement on many matters of these theories of how the universe came and many aspects of the phenomena that occurred during the creation. The universe came into existence due to the will of a Supreme Divinity, and a divine guidance always took care of all that happened and all that came born. All the objects and energy systems of the universe remained in an interactive state from the very beginning of creation. The universe emaciated as it progressed outwards in all respects. The universe upon creation appeared as a protected fort, well barricaded. The universe grew in different directions simultaneously. Nothing external ever participated in the process of creation. All agreed on these matters.

The theory of how these seven *vyāhṛtis* came into existence could be a bit perplexing. Did the first one get formed and from it's shoulder the second one came offset? Or did those all manifest simultaneously from the epicentre in increasing sizes? Or was there a reverse order starting from the seventh and inward, though still oriented to the same epicentre? Since it was the heaven that formed first, it could be assumed that the 2nd and 3rd larger came later and in that order. Obviously objects of the succeeding *vyāhṛtis* got interspersed and mixed with the objects of earlier ones and ever so many new hierarchical orders were established. Those got reorganized in several directions from where those stood. The space where those earlier stood became an emptiness and a center of power. All occurred according to a set of supreme and divine rules and as directed by an ever present interactive nature defined by a super consciousness; all occurred according to the will of a Supreme Divinity.

During the birth of the universe and its existence ever after, there indeed was an exalted and shining divine intellect and a super consciousness that constantly guarded the interests of the whole of the universe. This totally interactive intellect inspired the lesser intellects that could be associated with the distributed entities which stood alone or in groups. This very super consciousness might be at the same time deriving values from the distributed intellects proportionately.

It was this super intellect that sustained the universe. It was all powerful and nothing could step out of its influence and command.

Divinity

This commentary is essentially a delineation of the physical aspects of the origin of the universe, i.e, its creation and then its existence. The divine aspects were closely enmeshed into the descriptions and there was neither any effort to set aside those aspects nor it was possible to do so. So many names which were derived from the physical nature of objects and processes concurrently manifested as divinities as well. Those physical specifics could not simply exist as such without a divine nature attached to them. Most of such divinities such as *Indra, Mitra, Varuṇa* were predominantly *saguṇa* in nature. It was those physical objects and processes that could not stand alone and for the manifestation of which candid explanations could not be furnished by the languages used, even by those venerable sages, that could be believed to have been allotted a divine status.

The Supreme Divinity of *Brahma* stood as *nirguṇa* in principle, which at any rate was a well accepted concept. It seemed that the very functions of creation and existence were relegated to *saguṇa* divinities such as *Indra, Mitra, Varuṇa* and others and their specific functions were very much discernible. Not only they performed in the upper skies near heaven, but they also manifested themselves much down below till this earth, whenever and wherever necessary. However, the Supreme *Brahma* provided the very reason and perhaps much more, but did not direct the events to follow. This function was apparently carried out by the divinity named *Savita*, which stood inexplicably both as *saguṇa* and *nirguṇa* at the same time. While the *saguṇa* concepts were marginally traceable in the concept of *Savita* it was more emphatically described as an excellence and a brilliant intellect that pervaded the universe. The functions of *Savita* began right from the moment of the first of manifestations, commencing with the origin of those words of prayer and the cosmic vibrations which set off the very process of creation. Later, its very omniscient presence inspired everything that followed. In the beginning no space or time were recounted to be present and apparently only *nirguṇatva* prevailed at the source.

As this dalliance and intellect of *Savita* spread and pervaded everywhere, such phenomenon as the sounds and vibrations could manifest anywhere, to start off a new modification of the existing. While it was the very birth of stars, planets etc. that took place in the beginning, later in places like this earth it showed its presence as the evolutionary processes and biological mutations. Above all, it was the very intellect and interactive nature that defined the processes of creation and existence and perhaps it was for this reason that it was described as an excellent dalliance. It was this that got described as the super consciousness that prevailed all over the universe. But this super consciousness and intellect were not enough for material manifestations. The very physical functions, therefore, were always carried out by the *saguṇa* divinities.

This almost suggested a hierarchical order of the divinities. In this hierarchical order, the Supreme *Brahma* stood above all and right below would be the divinity called *Savita*. Still below in the hierarchical order would appear all the *saguṇa* divinities. There were still more and many divinities that got mentioned in the texts, but perhaps the *sūkta* RV3.62 had the purpose of stating the major considerations that went into the concepts of specifically chosen divinities. The concept of God and the overall nature of divinity presented here completely agreed with the faiths and beliefs that we have today. The God is omniscient and omnipotent and His presence would be felt in everything around us. The *advaita Brahma* stood over all and as everywhere. In order to realise His nature, it is not enough to simply believe so, but have to understand this very universe, including its birth and all the complexities of that original set of events. The sages proposed that the perceiver being stationed on surface earth, would get better informed if the description followed a system of narrating everything as things happened from the heaven till the earth. It was proposed to use selected objects and phenomena that could be seen on earth to describe the cosmic events and those unique set of occurrences that resulted in the universe. It tried to realise the God in terms of earthly realities.

The presence of God in all the objects, living and non-living and the phenomena all around us and extending up to the heaven could be realised through that supreme brilliance and intellect, defined and extolled by the *gāyatri*, which pervaded as everywhere. While the exalted heaven physically remained at such height and distance away from this earth, its very qualities and nature were extended till this earth and beyond, by the extended arms of the *Soma*, which enveloped all. Besides there came into existence a series of heavens, till this earth from where the creation continued. It was the *Soma* that remained in the heaven that flowed to us, as the first of creations to provide the many heavens and then again from each of these heavens, bringing many as manifested till here. The fundamental nature and properties of objects and energy could at any time manifest from this *Soma* and return to this all encompassing receptacle, which is virtually the extended arms of the heaven. Thus we are surrounded by the virtues of the heaven and it was for this reason that the universe was often praised as an excellence all by itself. That supreme intellect and dalliance, though universally present and has a higher status than anything in the universe, still could be taken to have commuted more directly through the paths of creation and through the presence of *Soma*. It embraced all objects animate and inanimate.

Dynamics of the Universe

It was described that the universe came out of an unknown and possibly out of nothing or out of an inexplicable something. Initially and almost instantly, the creation started as if in chaotic conditions. But according to the descriptions, it did not ultimately result in a state of chaos but only resolved into a state of calm and quietude. There were swirling furies as the paths of creation descended, not only in the beginning, but extended and continued till the very end and yet that did not create disorder or say rotate the universe. The space and time were instantaneously born from the very beginning of creation, as from the heaven and with an orientation to the epicentre. This epicentre could not be termed as the very centre of an absolutely spherical universe, but was the thematic middle of a universe which looked like a huge watermelon. And yet from this epicentre and the near abouts the geometry of the universe took form and shape. While the nature of the processes of creation, the properties of the objects and the energy that poured out and even the way the entire creation was viewed at were, if different and many, the geometry of the universe remained the same.

If a nature, a structure and a hierarchical order of divinity was proposed, the objects and systems of energy which were collectively referred to as the bright paths, were also of identical hierarchical order. It was the very bright and the very dense that stood in the inner core region and the lesser and emaciated ones that spread to the surroundings and in all directions. And then there was those chains of invisible fields that extended from the points of origin into the surroundings which descended the same way. It was interesting to notice that a distance or an uncertainty was always maintained between these power centres or epicentres and the paths containing the objects. At the same time the original centre, and the subsequent epicentres were not absolutely and geometrically pin pointed. Some of those perhaps stood qualified to be called as "fields". Those were the fields that extended as a chain from the epicentre till the end. Not only there were several stray convergences into the fields from the objects around, but the fields were also coupled interactively with the higher and lower fields. The term " *śūnyata*" was found carefully avoided in the Vedic descriptions and there was no such proposal nor corresponding definitions, hitherto.

These fields were not specifically proposed as states of gravitational pulls and repulsions. These were not specifically qualified as anything in particular, but were termed as invisible. Their qualifications though were not specifically defined, could still be with a parallel structure and order of divinity. Perhaps that supreme brilliant excellence and intellect defined by the *gāyatri* provided the attributes of these fields as well. The super consciousness not only embraced the chains of shining objects but the chains of invisible fields as well. It provided the definitions of all manifestations, for it was thus that the very creation started from heaven. In that particular instance it covered the point or field of origin as well as the heaven where *saguṇatva* first manifested. It prevailed the same way till the very end. Therefore, a divine communion got itself extended from the very beginning, till the very end. It was for the perceiver to identify and speculate on the attributes of any and all.

The dynamic order of the universe was not posited on a wildly speculated geometry. The universe was indeed an approximate spherical entity of enormous and yet conclusive size. A division of this geometrical structure according to their levels of intensity was proposed by the seven *vyāhṛti*s. It was further proposed that these seven *vyāhṛti*s were subdivided into 21 for controlling the expansion once and for all, among other things. The universe thus came into a pulsating state and of perpetual resonance. In spite of the statements of the gradual emaciation and a continuous expansion, a perpetually expanding universe was not envisaged at all. The space and time correlation that originally manifested along with the 3-dimensionality needed to be ever relevant. It was not enough that the universe contained objects and systems that moved or orbited, but this correlation had to be firmly reposed on the overall nature and existence of the universe. That proposal was thus strongly bonded to the very geometry of the universe. If the universe expanded and contracted in seven levels, after attaining an apparent perpetual level of growth, if it resonated perpetually, the space-time-energy correlation would sustain for ever. Perhaps in the matter of associating the very geometry of the universe to this correlation, the Vedic sages scored a point over the modern scientific proposals, at least in respect of a finality of a conceptual element.

The process of creation could be broadly and tentatively divided into two stages; the first being the instantaneous growth that took place which decided the extents of the universe. At this stage and point of time, the objects, energy, the fields and the very atmosphere got extended from the heaven till the very end as co-born. The second stage was the continuous evolutions from what came first into existence. Here, a parallel could be drawn between what happened at the universal level, to what happened on earth. The creation and the destruction that we observe in the high skies were placed in the second or further category. These were compared to the evolutionary process that we see in the plant and animal kingdom of this earth. Those were of secondary nature as far as the dynamics of the universe was concerned. Those did not affect the primary definitions. It was the will of God, a supreme intellect and the super consciousness that gave a start to the process of creation. It was the will of God that came pervaded along with the expansion of the universe, which sustained the universe. Therefore, the dissolution would be nothing but the collapse and withdrawal of this supreme intellect and excellence and a command to return.

Gravity

It could be observed rather curious that from all the descriptions and observations that came out in the foregoing chapters, that an account enabling the formulation of a theory of gravity practically did not surface, directly identified and stated; or so it would seem in the first instance. Naturally of course, nothing came up with the name of "gravitational force". But, it might be possible that the fundamental nature of gravitation was indeed presented by a set of terms, ideas and description of the details of the formation of the universe. The Veda indeed presented that universal interactive nature and the constant exchange of inspirations in no uncertain terms. It described the chain of dependencies and the empty fields of influence, if not in mathematical terms, clearly as descriptions of events and phenomena. The very geometry of the universe was tied up to this interactive forces and its strong and weak levels but never failing to mention these and the divine inspirations that went with it. The declared epicentre of the universe, the primary stage of creation, the paths of creation that were swirled around and the resonating circularity's could not detach themselves from the very interactive nature, stated as prevalent everywhere. In spite of the statement that those paths of creation got swirled around the epicentre from the heaven, that interactive nature just slipped through these actions. That perhaps described the fundamental nature of gravitation, as it invisibly slipped through space and matter alike.

Though we recognise the effects of gravitation as rectilinear and parallel tendencies, what could be its configuration in a universal level and were those universally the same? Traditional Indian thought system always implored us to believe that whatever we experience on this earth with the 5 principles of sight, audibility etc., should be appropriately reconfigured when it was applied in a universal level, though of course this aspect was often found glossed over. It could be therefore, surmised that, since we experience the forces of gravitation today and since a space-time concordance was found to prevail unobstructed from the beginning of the universe, there could be nothing to prevent in imagining that gravity was very much present from that very beginning. It was for this reason that the space-time concordance was posited, for ever, on a resonating geometry of the universe. Since the universe commenced from the heaven, got enormously enlarged and ultimately stood resonating in a dynamic order, it was claimed that the space-object-time-energy correlation remained with a single sequence of continuity and validity. In other words, if a property as the gravity and its effects were now recognizable, a component of this would have been discernible in the very early beginning. Thus it could be argued that the gravity was a subject latent and present through the Vedic texts, though not specifically named so. Its presence from the very beginning of the universe is very obvious.

But the detailed description of the process of creation, perhaps hid any direct ideas of gravitation. The geometry of the universe consisting of the seven circularity's and its sub-divisions and the multi-pronged paths of creation juxtaposed one over the other or remaining with inexplicable complexities of mixing, could be claimed to have prevented a clear decipherment of statements on the nature of gravitational forces. In spite of the near sphericity and an apparent clarity about the geometry of the universe to which the Vedic theories always took, the details of the formation of a geometrical order provided a severe complexity to its very structure. And it was through this geometry that the twisted and multi-branched paths of creation spread. There was mixing and mixing as the *asyavamīyasūkta* explained and the gravitation has to be identified without excluding these aspects. But it was clearly stated that the interactive nature and the universal exchange of inspirations filtered though this complex structure and we, on bringing the subject to the present times, have to identify the basic principles of gravitation from these descriptions.

The pertinent question is that how did this gravitation manifest at all. Here, the basic question is that, did the Veḍa realise the gravitational forces at all? Next only the question arises of how it came. But the Veda never side stepped this issue, stating that such matters were divine and beyond human comprehension, but only described the events and phenomena as they saw it and then it would become our duty, if so desired, to identify from the text, and make these into such things as to suit the contemporary requirements. It would be a matter of language, realisations and expressions and no description in the Veda prevented us to do so. The modern theories of quantum gravitation presumably stated that the first of attractive and repulsive forces later manifested as the gravitation and the material properties of everything in this universe. No such candid statement could possibly come from the Veda. The Veda described only the events and phenomena as principles and ostensibly declared everything in terms of absolute truth. In a way, it claimed accuracy of the statements and justified their validity. The elements of speculation that could be alleged to the statements and their veracity could not be easily challenged. The totality of all the concepts brought forward could not be defamed by any common rationality. Had a definition of a sense of specific spacial directions ever been stated in the very beginning of these cosmic events, what we observe today as the gravitational forces could not have been identified with any matching phenomenon in the beginning of all. Thus the universality of the *gāyatrīmantra* could be realized only upon detailed consideration of the many facets of creation viewed from different angles. It could be about more than the shining intellect that pervaded everywhere and which exchanged information up to the minutest of existences. It was identified as the gravity that spread all over the universe in an identical manner, permeating and percolating through all objects and existences.

The Numbers Principle

Along with the clear concepts of geometry with which the Vedic texts got interpreted here, a need also arose to recognize the principles of numbers, often presented by numbers as such and on other occasions, by certain words and terms in association with a phenomenon. This would be a subject not easy to bring forward in full detail. The state of nothingness, the numbers 1, 2, 3, 5, 7, 8, 21 etc., were not merely used to indicate values but could be invested with deeper set of meanings. While the numbers and the mathematics are used by us today as part of information and as tools of arguments, we would not be able to recognise any argument as such in the *Ṛgveda* texts. The statements of the Veda were either as hypothesis or as conclusions. In the Veda, the numbers could not be identified as a statement of size or quantity, but as part of a presentation of tendencies of phenomenal values. The absolute nature of numbers were not expected to be identified with any of the physical realities of the universe. While seven were the *vyāhṛtis*, it was only as a principle and not in absolute terms. While "*dvipade catuṣpade*" was the way the universe enlarged and progressed, those numbers did not indicate any value of either size or of the distance. The birth and explosive expansion of the universe would not conform to the absolute terms and equations of mathematics, as far as the Vedic notions were concerned; may be likewise in terms of modern science as well. At the same time the universe manifested only in terms of certain principles which by themselves were so complex that it could be better realized as distinctly divine.

The statement of mountain like formations from the heaven could be vaguely compared to the unique pyramidal squares of $1^2 + 2^2 + 3^2 + ... + 24^2 = 70^2$. But, if the additions continued approximate equivalence could be found at the basic integers of 48 (=195) and again at 192 (=1542). These occurrences, though approximate in value, corresponded to the *dvipade catuṣpade* formation commencing from 24. Today we could not claim that this really was so meant by the sages and it could be just an accidental coincidence. And still such terms could have been used only with deeper significances than those directly readable to the text. Besides, once again, an absolute value correctness could not be the Vedic style and the nature of the universal scales. Yet another, indeed very significant meaning of the term *dvipade catuṣpade* was the absence of a term *tripade* in between. An expansion and an organisation with nothing in the centre, was found as a strong Vedic concept and in the case of the proposed geometrical organisation, as a squaring or as a cubical tripling function there could not be any object in the absolute centre. Therefore the squares and cubes of odd numbers would not qualify for the present assessment. This would mean that it was necessary, not only to carry on with the idea of numbers, that those numbers necessarily should have an empirical, physical and phenomenal significance in the orders of description of the formation of the universe. This raises a fundamental question of what really the *sāmkhya* principles that once were. Why did the Veda hold the numbers, just as it did to geometry, so close to it's fold?

Universal Principles

Today, after 5000 or more years after the formulation of the *Ṛgveda* contents, a question that would arise in the modern mind would be that what possible ways these Vedic theories as espoused here, would benefit the present times. Is there anything in it, as expounded here, more important than the glimpses of mere elements of history? Are we not satisfied and content with the ritualistic and religious significance of the Veda along with the sublime nature of the Vedic *śabda*, as it existed today? After all no one would accept the Vedic contents brought forward here as pure science of any nomenclature. None would possibly find it religiously invigorating and refreshing. None would find it directly strengthening the prevalent Vedanta thoughts. None would find it contributing to the *bhaktiprasthāna*. None would directly find a God named and signified. Then what exactly it did to help man, his mind and his environment as on today? How did it strengthen his basic existence, if at all? The answer would not be brief and simple. We have drifted much away from the Vedic ambiance and realities. In a way, we have drifted away from that Truth, truthfulness and have got accustomed to a different set of realities. The Vedic theories never shied away from realities, but only informed us about the inexplicable nature of many, including the nature of our existence, the manifestation of the universe and the ultimate realisation of the Supreme Divinity. The Veda did not advise us to do this or follow this path. It did not ask us to believe in this or that God and accrue the attendant benefits. On the other hand it did not intimidate us in any way. It stated absolute and unassailable truths. For this, it told how the universe got manifested, progressed and brought forward its striking similarities to our own existence, its relevancy for all times, which in other words brought out a set of timeless values.

Due to its non-pontificating and non-pretentious and yet authoritative styles, its constant habit of equating the objects, events and phenomena of the earth duly scaled up to a universal level, its very ability to directly dictate or stipulate values beneficial to man would be found difficult to redeem. Much would depend on the reader and his attitudes. As stated earlier there were no arguments mounted in the *Ṛgveda* to which the reader could attach himself and proceed further. In most of the reading, he has to recognise some such principles, all by himself. He would have no preceptor who would declare that these and these are the Vedic teachings. The fact that the *Ṛgveda* demands a high level of contemplation and commitments from the reader makes it altogether a difficult subject, but with endless possibilities.

A significant method adopted by the Vedic sages, while describing the cosmic events connected with creation and in the elaboration of the "*brahmatatva*", was that the imagery used were drawn from this earth and from the surroundings of man. As a part of this programme, the objects animate, inanimate and the phenomena visible and clear to man was selected along with the universal principles of *Agni* and that universal intellect and dalliance, as capable components of description. Appropriate events and earthly existences were compared with the cosmic events and a set of scaled up equivalences were proclaimed. It was the realisation that such descriptions and a language would not be enough to effectively communicate, that brought in the geometry and a system of *yajñas* to carry things forward. It could be surmised that when the Vedic hymns manifested in the form of odes to a divinity and as a huge set of descriptions of the creation of the universe, it somehow hid several universal discrete principles that could be gleaned out of the same descriptions. Today it could be considered as important to come up with such universal principles as well, along with the kind of narrations that this book provided or still better by using other methods of interpretation. However, such principles might not surface as clearly as was observed to happen in the case of *gāyatri*. Every verse or even a hymn might not provide an individual and distinct principle as such. In a way, as far as the *Ṛgveda* is concerned, it was the *parokṣavāda* that we were hearing all the while, that was worthwhile listening to.

When the objects and phenomena of this earth were found liberally used in the descriptions, when those things were found reflected into the description of the process of creation and into the "*brahmatatva*", the same should be expected to reflect back into the universe, including our earth and its inhabitants, as a corresponding set of principles applicable to man and his earth. There have to be a trans-commutation and reciprocity ever relevant. The text should have to manifest as the source of many important principles of earthly existence as well. This indicated an immense scope for a fresh and sustainable approach to the interpretation of the Veda on new lines and to come up with such principles and theories that would benefit the future mankind. For, as we all say the Veda is a repository of timeless principles of creation and existence. It is an account of eternal Truth from which we could draw at will.

The Veda gave a primordial status to *śabda*, which we realised in the universal scale as the fundamental cosmic vibrations of divine origin. This *śabda* was assigned the capability to create things, all afresh. So it was found, on this earth among all the living things and man in particular. Anything uttered remained with a potential to create and get multiplied through the living objects and get transmitted to unimaginable distances with or without modifications. It was stated that in the case of the *ādisṛṣṭi*, these sounds first manifested as the divine prayers and praises. Prayers and praises based on " *vāk*", meaningful words uttered. But prayers and praises addressed to whom? Primarily to oneself, before to anyone else. These prayers and *vāk*, therefore, invigorated oneself, before it mattered to anyone else and that was the reason for its getting allocated a primary status and a capability to create. Initially, it was oneself being an infinitesimal and primordial part of a whole and an element of the future universe, that this divine prayers got addressed to the self. In a similar manner, it would be with the hope of a direct communion with a Supreme God, that man would utter, by his being in front of a temple and a deity or not, those words of prayers which were primarily addressed to himself. He was seeking a direct communion and access to a Supreme Divinity; he as an infinitesimal part of the whole. He was seeking redemption and progress to a more well refined state. Thus a significant Vedic dictum and a universal principle of prayers emanated from the *Ṛgveda*, i.e, of prayers that would be conducted in a divine presence.

The well declared interactive nature of creation could be termed as the most significant source of all the principles that could be gleaned from the Vedic texts. It was the very base for the well established belief of the inevitable destiny that followed all, as a sequence of eventualities with which India is most familiar. While detailing the extent of this interactive nature, strong levels of bond and its gradually diminishing scales were sketched out. Let us now assume that a particular chain of events originated and moved. Alternately, let us imagine that a particular sentiment was expressed to the surroundings. Both would have its own repercussions and gradual dilution and indeed several branching offs. From those states and from those seed matters new events or ideas could get born and the process could get repeated to the surroundings. However, it would be found that the Veda discounted its ability to cause any change to totally unrelated and distant events and thoughts, in spite of the presence of that widely prevalent interactive forces. In short, the Veda discouraged superstitions, while still mooted the idea of eventualities. In spite of an all pervasive interactive nature being acknowledged and strongly put forward, there was very realistic assessment of its strengths and prevalence. A Supreme divinity would not think of shuffling the universe at will, interfere in its composition or redefine it as He liked.

The Veda declared the existence of several systems as an essential feature of a stable and calm universe, which in other words also meant that there indeed existed an absolute necessity for a well defined structure in everything. That applied to one and all, commencing from our own self, through our surroundings, society and to wider circles of a collective existence. It suggested that the lack of structure will result in the collapse of a system. The Veda only presented a well structured universe, though with multiple components and streams of individual nature, qualities and dimensions, which applied to the very structure of the divine nature as well.

The Veda had its own set of standards for the realisation of this universe. It did not declare the visible, the audible and those that fitted into the means of human perception as unreal. At the same time, it seemed to suggest that in all such perceivable objects and phenomena, there existed an element of the intangible. It did not suggest any non-existence but only existence with this touch of intangibility in each and everything. Perhaps it differentiated reality from truth and seemed to suggest that truth would be that expressive component of reality, susceptible to the means of human realisation. The reality would be the sum total of the *vyakta* and the *avyakta*. It was upon the first manifestation of Truth, that the universe could ever take shape. It was the physical beginning of all.

Conclusion

The principles that were found formulated and presented in the Veda might have been under discussion for a very long time in the Vedic period, as vaguely indicated by suggestive terms that appeared in some of the hymns given here. The boundless extent of their imagination spread over several subjects, coming from and instituted by many sages (in spite of the statement of *apauruṣeyatva*) might have produced slightly varying accounts and approaches of the same subject. But here we have seen that they were comfortable with mutually complementary theories and ensured that those received their equal attentions. They not only acknowledged such accounts but went into direct reference to those and accorded it a covalent status, while bringing out their own thoughts on the subject under consideration. We could imagine that one of the first acts of the *yajña* culture was to prepare a visual stage truly representative of those original *yajña* of the universe. Whatever geometry, description and dramatic content that went into this might have taken in other aspirations at a later period or could have run concurrently. Expositions of the nature of the Supreme Divinity might have not only been necessary, these rituals could have been efforts for a direct communion with God. As we know it now, the *yajña* was a ritual that commenced before sunrise, that which defined the cardinal directions, that which executed specific geometrical configurations on the ground and that which followed a routine of rituals with great faith. So be it, but there could have been much more to it then and even now, for the one who aspired for more.

From the Vedic accounts it was deduced that the route of realisation of truth and the meanings of the very Veda could only be in terms of the *pañcendriya* i.e, by a system of understanding through the statements in terms of *dṛśya-śrāvya-sparśa-ghrāṇa-rasana* faculties. In short, that way realising the effects. The most fundamental of cause was described as *śabda* and the vibrations that would create and propagate. That way the whole of the *Ṛgveda* came as a description of cause and the effect in association with divine manifestations. It was this *śabda* that moved to all points of creation or suddenly appeared as a precursor in appropriate levels. The cause and effect manifested as "*manasā vācā karmaṇā*" and in that order. It appears that from the Vedic period itself it was believed that the *śabda* is everything. The words that proclaimed this, i.e., the Veda itself was accorded a primordial status and a capacity to create benevolence around, both in terms of *vāk* and *śabda*. In view of a wide acceptability for this, seen to have come from the Vedic period itself, it could be surmised that it was sufficiently convinced and proved during those times.

We have considerable difficulty in truly understanding the nature of everything of those times. Thus in spite of accosting the word *yajña* from the beginning of the *Ṛgveda* we are almost unable to understand its status in any measure more than the way it is seen conducted today. The *yajña* of those times could be taken as both subjective and objective. With a primordial status allotted to the *śabda* as cause and to the *yajña* as the first act of creation, those were re-enacted in the *yajña* conducted by the sages along with the *śabda* of chanting the Vedas. A shroud of supra-mental and non-differentiating consciousness enveloped these acts to the extent of subjectivity merging into the objectivity; cause and effect manifesting in unison. While it is very improbable that the Vedic *śabda* was taken as the *śabda* that appeared in the creation of the universe, the re-enactment of the basic process of creation by the *yajña* along with the *śabda* might have been given a very high status in the order of rituals and prayers. It almost amounted to be the description of Truth and Divine nature and performing a *yajña* becoming a direct access to Truth and Divine powers.

Though the *Ṛgveda* came to us from a very distant past from a people who were labeled as primitive, these Vedic *śabda* of universal wisdom and meaningful expressions bewildered us considerably. That too when we find that in spite of knowing that all matters about the origin of the universe could only be termed as inexplicable, they ventured to describe about it and declare that it was possible to make a thousand statements of scientific coherence. The desire for bringing out the nature of the Supreme Divinity must have been strongly felt. That unfathomable nature of the universe then got repeated in a text kept in the same fashion with the same interactive content and shining styles. That universal consciousness repeated as a conscious divinity that pervaded all through the text. For the present, let us hope that we could one day get back into that universal tolerance that the Veda proclaimed. Let that shining consciousness above and around us guide us for ever. The truthful and fearless expressions of the Veda, whether as science or as universal principles or as personal realisations or as the sublime *śabda* that would resonate around us, would always be a unique experience unmatched by anything that manifested on this Earth. For deriving appropriate values as times pass by, for admiring the forces of nature, for the glimpses of a Supreme Divinity, let us visit the Veda again and again. ⋆⋆⋆

Glossary

Aditi - a divinity.

Agni - fire; the god of fire.

Aṅgiras - referring to the sage of this name.

Aryama - a divinity.

Aśvin - a pair of divinities.

Atharvaveda - one of the four Vedas.

ādhibhautikta -metaphysical.

ādisṛṣṭi - the first of creations.

akṣa - eye; axis.

amṛt - that which gives immortality.

āṅgika - by way of symbols as part of playacts.

ananta - endless.

aṅgulaṃ - a finger width;(30mm).

annabhāva - the food principle.

antarikṣa - the atmosphere, sky.

apauruṣeya - not coming from men.

avyakta - apparent, not visible.

Bhaga - beautiful; a divinity.

Bhāvavṛttaṃ - cosmogony.

Bṛhaspati - God who defined the extents of the universe.

Brahma - God Supreme.

bījabhāva - the seed principle.

bījasatta - the essence of the seed principle.

brāhmaṇa - literature on rituals.

brahmāṇḍa - universe as the cosmic egg.

chandas - the metrics of a verse.

citi - the altar.

Dīrghatamas - a renowned vedic sage.

dhātu - an elementary constituent in Sanskrit language.

dhūLībhasma - fine and filtered Ash.

gāyatrīmantra - the *gāyatri* that is recited.

gāyatri - the traditional prayer with 24 syllables.

garuḍa - the divine bird often referred as *Suparṇa*.

Hiraṇyastūpa - a vedic sage and poet.

hasta - 24 *aṅgulas*.

havirdhāna - a hall in the *mahāvedi*.

hiraṇyagarbha - the golden egg of divine origin.

Indrāvaruṇa - the combination of *Indra* and *varuṇa*.

Indra - God of commencement of creation.

icchāśakti - the will of the mind.

indrata - a bright point of origin or a singularity.

Jātavedas - for *Agni*; the properties manifested.

jagat - the lively moving universe.

kṣatra - dominion, supremacy.

kalpa - a fabulous period of time.

karmendriya - the five activities by hand, leg, larynx, reproductive organ and excretory organs.

Mārtāṇḍa - the cosmic egg.

Mitrāvaruṇa - the combination of *Mitra* and *varuṇa*.

Mitra - a divinity.

māntrikata -magical nature.

mayobhuva - wonderful space- the heaven/sky.

nābhi - the navel; the hub of a wheel.

nemi - the rim of a wheel.

nirukta - the compendium of *dhātu* and phonemes.

Pūṣan - God who purified, as if winnowed.

Praśnopaniṣat - one of the principal *Upaniṣad*.

Prajāpati - the lord of everything manifested.

Prakṛti -the primordial form till the end.

paṇḍit - scholar.

pañcabhūta - earth, water, air, fire and sky.

pañcendriya - the five senses.

pada - here, a term; also stage, step etc..

prācīnaśāla - the eastern hall in the Vedic altar space.

prapañca - the universe.

prathama - the first.

praugam - a trapezium or forepart of carriage harness.

puruṣaṃ -120 *aṅgula*.

Rudra - a divinity often identified with *śiva*.

Ṛgvedasaṃhita - the text of *Ṛgveda*.

Ṛgveda - the most ancient of the four Vedas.

rāśīcakra - a full circle of the zodiac.

rāśi - 1/12th of the zodiac.

rāja - a king; but also bestowing and giving birth.

rathacakra - a circular altar with spokes like a wheel.

ṣoḍaśakalā - the 16 principles of cognition.

ṣoḍaśakala - 16 part realisation.

Sāma - referring to *Sāmaveda*.

Śakti - divine and creative power.

Sarasvati - the river *Sarasvati*.

Satya - the Truth.

Sat - primordial True state.

Savita - God of a shining intellect.

Soma - a divine transparency that covered all.

Suparṇa - a divine falcon that became the universe.

sūkta - hymn.

sadas - a hall at the west end of the *mahāvedi*.

sṛṣṭi - creation.

sthiti - the state of existing.

śūnyata - total emptiness.

śabda - sound, speech; primordial vibrations.

śruti - intelligent hearsay.

tattva - principles.

triṣṭubh - fraction of 2/3 and 4 X 11.

turīyāvastha - the fourth state of the mind.

uttaravedi - the altar at the east end of the *mahāvedi*.

Vācaspati - the Lord of words.

Vāyu - God of wind.

Vanaspati - the god of the forest and plenty-ness.

Varuṇa - the god of waveform propagation.

Viśvakarma - the Creator.

vācika - by words spoken as part of playacts.

vāk - the word uttered.

vaidikayajña - the *yajña* performed by mankind.

vedi - the platform for performance.

viśvacakṣus - the eye of the universe; the epicenter.

viśvatomukha - the face from which creation started.

visarjanenā - by excretion.

vyāhṛti - the cicular stages of the atmosphere (sky).

vyakta - manifest, visible and evident.

yājñika - the performer of *yājña*.

yūpa - a wooden pillar at the east of *mahāvedi*.

yajamānapatni - wife of the performer of *yajña*.

Index